World War I

Debating Historical Issues in the Media of the Time

The Antebellum Era: Primary Documents on Events from 1820 to 1860
David A. Copeland

The Revolutionary Era: Primary Documents on Events from 1776 to 1800
Carol Sue Humphrey

The Reconstruction Era: Primary Documents on Events from 1865 to 1877
Donna L. Dickerson

The Progressive Era: Primary Documents on Events from 1890 to 1914
Elizabeth V. Burt

The Civil War: Primary Documents on Events from 1860 to 1865
Ford Risley

The Early Republic: Primary Documents on Events from 1799 to 1820
Patricia Dooley

World War I

Primary Documents on Events from 1914 to 1919

Ross F. Collins

Debating Historical Issues in the Media of the Time
David A. Copeland, Series Editor

Greenwood Press
Westport Connecticut • London

Library of Congress Cataloging-in-Publication Data
Collins, Ross F.
World War I : primary documents on events from 1914 to 1919 / Ross F. Collins.
p. cm. – (Debating historical issues in the media of the time)
Includes bibliographical references and index.
ISBN 978-0-313-32082-8 (alk. paper)
1. World War, 1914-1918. 2. History, Modern—20th century. I. Title. II. Title: World War One. III. Title: World War 1.
D521.C587 2008
940.3–dc22 2007032456

British Library Cataloguing in Publication Data is available.

Library of Congress Catalog Card Number: 2007032456

ISBN: 978-0-313-32082-8
ISSN: 1542-8079

First published in 2008

Greenwood Press, 88 Post Road West, Westport, CT 06881
An imprint of Greenwood Publishing Group, Inc.
www.greenwood.com

Printed in the United States of America

The paper used in this book complies with the Permanent Paper Standard issued by the National Information Standards Organization (Z39.48-1984).

10 9 8 7 6 5 4 3 2 1

Contents

Series Foreword

As the eighteenth century was giving way to the nineteenth, a wise Boston judge said in the January 1, 1799, issue of the *Columbian Centinel*, "Give to any set men the command of the press, and you give them the command of the country, for you give them the command of public opinion, which commands everything." One month later, Thomas Jefferson wrote to James Madison with a similar insight. "We are sensible," Jefferson said of the efforts it would take to put their party—the Republicans—in power, "The engine is the press."

Both writers were correct in their assessment of the role the press would play in American life in the years ahead. The press was already helping to shape the opinions and direction of America. It had been doing so for decades, but its influence would erupt following the Revolutionary War and continue into the 1920s and farther. From less than forty newspapers in 1783—each with circulations of around 500—the number of papers erupted in the United States. By 1860, newspaper circulation exceeded 1 million, and in 1898, Joseph Pulitzer's *World* alone had a daily circulation of 1.3 million. By the beginning of World War I, about 16,600 daily and weekly newspapers were published, and circulation figures passed 22.5 million copies per day with no slow down in circulation in sight. Magazines grew even more impressively. From around five at the end of the Revolution, journalism historian Frank Luther Mott counted 600 in 1860 and a phenomenal 3,300 by 1885. Some circulations surpassed 1 million, and the number of magazines continued to grow into the twentieth century.

The amazing growth of the press happened because the printed page of periodicals assumed a critical role in the United States. Newspapers and magazines became the place where Americans discussed and debated the issues that affected them. Newspapers, editors, and citizens took sides, and they used the press as the conduit for discussion. The *Debating the Issues* series offers a glimpse into how the press was used by Americans to shape and influence the major events and issues facing the nation during different periods of its development. Each volume is based on the documents, that is, the writings that appeared in the press of the time. Each volume presents articles, essays, and editorials that support opposing interests on the events and issues; and each provides readers with background and explanation of the events, issues, and, if possible, the people who wrote the articles that have been selected. Each volume also includes a chronology of events and a selected bibliography. The series is based on the Greenwood Press publication, *Debating the Issues in Colonial Newspapers*. Books in the *Debating the Issues* series cover the following periods: the Revolution and the young republic, the Federalist era, the antebellum period, the Civil War, Reconstruction, the progressive era, and World War I.

This volume on the World War I era focuses upon the issues that affected the nation from the period just before "the war to end all wars" through its conclusion. The newspapers of this period were not the chief source of debate about this conflict. Instead, magazines were where Americans debated the issues of whether the United States should enter the war, and they were where Americans debated whether Germany was provoked into the war or whether it was the aggressor. In this volume, both media are used to demonstrate the way the press helped to shape American opinion on the issues of relevance to this global conflict.

Chronology

1914 June 28: Austrian Archduke Franz Ferdinand assassinated in Sarajevo, Bosnia.

July 28: Austria-Hungary declares war on Serbia.

August 1: Germany declares war on Russia.

August 3: Germany declares war on France. France sets up the Bureau of Censorship.

August 4: Britain declares war on Germany.

August 4: Germany declares war on Belgium. Germany invades Belgium.

August 8–16: British army arrives in France.

August 24: German army enters France.

September: "I Want YOU!" recruiting illustration first published in the *London Opinion*.

September 2: In response to German Propaganda Bureau, Britain sets up a secret War Propaganda Bureau.

September 5–10: Schlieffen Plan leads to the First Battle of the Marne. German advance halted at Marne River.

October 29: Ottoman Empire (Turkey) joins Central Powers.

December: The Carnegie Endowment for International Peace begins study on the political and economic impact of the war.

1915 January: Women's Peace Party forms in Washington, D.C.

April: First gas attack of the war; Germans use chlorine gas at Ypres.

April 26: Italy joins the Entente Powers.

May 1: Advertisements from the German government appear in major American newspapers warning passengers not to travel on the *Lusitania.* Few pay attention.

May 7: *Lusitania* passenger liner sinks off Irish coast. United States nearly declares war on Germany, is dissuaded by Germany's promise to restrict its submarine warfare.

October 12: Edith Cavell, British nurse working in Belgium, is executed by the Germans as a spy.

1916 February 2: Britain introduces conscription, the last European belligerent power to do so.

May: 135,000 march on New York's Fifth Avenue in favor of greater U.S. preparedness for war.

July 4: War poet Alan Seeger dies on the French battlefields.

September 15: First use of British tanks in battle.

November 7: Woodrow Wilson faces Charles Evans Hughes for a second term as president. Vote is so close that election is in doubt for several days.

1917 January: The value of U.S. exports to Europe, mostly to the allies, reaches nearly four times its prewar level.

February 1: Germany announces its intention to resume unrestricted warfare.

March 15: A provisional democratic government overthrows the monarchy in Russia.

April 6: The United States declares war on Germany.

April 13: Committee on Public Information is established under George Creel.

May: U.S. Espionage Act makes treasonous speech illegal.

May 19: U.S. government announces the appointment of John J. Pershing as commander of the American Expeditionary Force.

June 25: First U.S. troops arrive in France.

July: Chancellor Bethmann Hollweg resigns; Germany effectively becomes a military dictatorship.

November 7: Bolshevist coup in Russia marks the beginning of more than 70 years of Communist rule.

1918 In this year fifty-eight African Americans are lynched, mostly in the South; 110,000 move north to Chicago between 1916–1918.

January 8: Wilson unveils his Fourteen Points as a basis for peace.

Spring: Epidemic of a new and spectacularly lethal "Flanders Fever" strikes the troops. It becomes the Spanish Flu epidemic that kills millions worldwide.

April 5: German immigrant Robert Prager from Illinois is murdered by pro-war mob.

May 16: U.S. Sedition Act further limits free speech.

September 12: American Expeditionary Force opens St. Mihiel offensive near Verdun, Pershing's first major battle. By September 16, the salient is under allied control.

November 9: German Kaiser Wilhelm II abdicates, flees to Holland. The last of the great European monarchies comes to an end.

November 11: On the eleventh hour of the eleventh day of the eleventh month the guns fall silent. World War I is over.

1919 First U.S. Income Tax code, part of the Revenue Act of 1918 (actually passed February 24, 1919), is passed by Congress to help finance the war, includes progressive income tax rate of up to 77 percent.

June 28: The Treaty of Versailles is signed in the Versailles Palace Hall of Mirrors.

Introduction: The American Press in World War I

American Journalism on the Eve of War

By 1900, the journalism of Western democracies had reached a pinnacle of power and influence. Nearly everyone could read, and most read a daily newspaper, perhaps two or three, as well as several magazines. Costs of periodicals had dropped to levels almost everyone could afford. Every political movement, every ethnic group, every cause published a periodical. People read them and responded to their appeals and crusades. There was, after all, no other real mass media; movies were still infants, radio was experimental, television was two decades away. Government leaders listened to the press and responded. Sometimes they were one in the same. Walter Lippmann of the *New Republic* played a key role in World War I armistice deliberations and his magazine was called the unofficial voice of the Wilson administration. Theodore Roosevelt, the era's most prominent politician, called magazine journalists "muckrakers" for their expositions of the seemy underside of capitalism—but he also wrote for those magazines to argue his cases and ridicule his opponents. In fact, many influential Americans—politicians, generals, university professors, and academics—wrote for newspapers or, perhaps more often, for magazines, as the nation wrestled with the challenges of industrialization. The mass media today is fractured, its influence split, its voices a vast cacophony. On the eve of the World War I, Americans and in fact all the warring countries had no doubt: the printed word held great power.

By 1914 that power had been channeled into two formats: newspapers and magazines. American newspapers, some 2,500 of them, had seen circulations soar as a penny press became accessible to nearly everyone. The excesses of sensationalist yellow journalism had waned into a form of printed journalism still prevalent today: restrained, objective writing striving to be fair, clearly separated from opinion pages. Signatures (or bylines) were rare, even on editorial pages. Advertising hyperbole had been reigned in by law and agreement among advertisers, while professional reporters aimed to file facts and description. By the eve of the war, a reader of most metropolitan daily journalism would expect to find sober news articles free of writer opinion along with some interpretive pieces featuring extended descriptions based on eyewitness observations. Opinion and debate were generally limited to editorial pages. The tenets of fact-based objective journalism—as established by Adolph Ochs in the *New York Times* beginning in 1896—had become de facto standard for all respectable American newspapers.

Nonetheless, the lively and polemical press that had been a familiar fixture of nineteenth-century America before the rise of industrial journalism had not been lost. In fact, it had developed into magazines, a medium that became before World War I the most significant public space for American debate and the first truly national mass media. During the decade and a half before 1914, nationally circulated magazines reduced prices to a dime, circulated in the hundreds of thousands, and attracted reporters intent on finding a national forum for debate and exposé of injustice and equality. By World War I muckraking was on the wane, but the voice of these periodicals in American life still resonated. It was this American mass medium that presented the great debates of the Great War by making no pretense of the kind of objective reporting that had become the standard for newspapers. Important periodicals such as the *New Republic*, the *Nation*, the *New York Times Current History*, *Current Opinion*, the *Masses*, and the *North American Review* offered debate from cover to cover, produced by the era's leading figures. Because they were circulated so widely across the nation, periodicals like these produced World War I's greatest polemicists and became the era's most widespread forum for public discourse.

The Press Faces the Great War

The outbreak of World War I in summer 1914 came as a shock no less to the participating nations themselves than to the onlookers such as the United States. No political leader could say exactly how it happened. A delicate house of cards supported by unstable secret treaties and shaken by risky political decisions cascaded into a general war no one could seem to avoid. This inescapable black hole of human misery dug through four and a half years of human history, its bleakest, bloodiest pages up to that date. It was directly the cause of the even blacker chapter of World War II, and indirectly to blame for most of the worldwide violence and misery that marked the rest of the century. At the dawn of another century, even the U.S. war in Iraq can be traced to decisions made by colonial powers following World

War I. An American simply cannot understand his or her country's role in the world without understanding its basis in the war of 1914–1918.

Even as war was declared on August 4, 1914, the world knew this was going to be the Great War long dreaded. American reporters leaped to the boats for Europe to cover the catastrophe. But covering this war would prove daunting. Not only did it eclipse in scope any human conflict in history, starting with a 420-mile front in the west, but military and civilian governments also did all they could to control and censor the reporters. In fear of the great influence of mass media in that era, European governments banned or controlled movements of reporters to the front and meticulously censored their reports. On August 5, Britain cut German cables to the United States, which guaranteed that journalists would have to cable their articles through British minders. This was the first in a series of events that helped to push America to see the war from the allies' point of view. Germany was left at a disadvantage in its attempts to sway American opinion, although Berlin's leaders, even the chancellor himself, regularly saw publication of their views in U.S. periodicals.

The American press initially responded to the war as the government advised, by declaring "strict neutrality." A *Literary Digest* survey of leading editors in the third month of war found 105 favored the allies, 20 favored the Central Powers, and 240 declared strict neutrality. At first this neutrality really was strict: the government blocked not only active aid to belligerent powers but also forbade extending credit or loans to governments who needed money to fight and to buy supplies from the United States. That scrupulous neutrality lasted as long as nearly everyone presumed the war would last—a few weeks. But by fall it became clear that swift victory had eluded the allies. The Western Front had congealed into a scar of trenches that more and more looked as breachable as the Great Wall. Additionally, prewar American trade had relied on strong European markets. Without that trade, an economy already barely climbing from recession could spiral back. American businesses saw huge market potential as warring nations poured their countries' treasure into the battlefields and the U.S. government soon relaxed the neutrality rules to allow the loans and credit necessary for overseas trade. Most of this trade was with the allies because a British naval blockade isolated Germany. William Jennings Bryan, a strict neutrality advocate who served as Wilson's secretary of state, protested (and resigned finally in June 1915). But the template had been struck; the ostensibly neutral United States would actually forge vital economic ties to the allied side.

More and more American publications slid from principled neutrality down the allied slope, but the defining incident was the May 7, 1915, sinking of the *Lusitania,* hit by a torpedo from a German submarine. More than

1,000 civilian passengers died, including more than 100 Americans. The Germans could make a good case in favor of their actions—the passenger liner secretly carried munitions for the allies—but nothing could sway many Americans from affirming that Germany had showed brutal disregard for human life in both their sinking of unarmed ships as well as its invasion of neutral Belgium. By the end of 1915 most American editors had fallen from neutrality to the allied side. Notable exceptions included newspapers owned by William Randolph Hearst, remaining strongly anti-British, as well as German-language publications, the socialist press, and the black press.

As the United States tilted more and more obviously toward the allied side, hawkish leaders found increasingly fertile ground for their arguments on preparedness. The American army and navy had atrophied to the point where they could hardly be expected to fight any kind of full-scale war, to say nothing of the enormous fight in Europe. American operations against Mexican rebels in 1916, during which 12,000 troops tried unsuccessfully to capture Pancho Villa, helped to convince German observers that the United States army was inept and wouldn't be a concern even if the Americans eventually did declare war on them. Well-known leaders such as General Leonard Wood and Theodore Roosevelt wrote to argue that the United States must change and must grow its army and navy to be prepared for a dangerous world. The preparedness issue—fueled by implicit fear and hatred of Germany—reached a frenzy in spring 1916 to the point that 135,000 people marched down New York's Fifth Avenue in support. Pacifists, meanwhile, wrote in support of neutrality noting that it was exactly this kind of thinking that got the major powers into war in the first place. The debate played to a nationwide audience in the important public affairs magazines of the era and included articles by the country's most prominent figures.

It was, of course, a debate that ended with America's entry into the war on April 6, 1917. Advocates for preparedness had won but the country still faced a long road to war. It would be more than a year before any American troops saw significant action in France, and U.S. munitions manufacturers never did supply enough ordnance beyond simple rifles and cartridges in a war mostly fought with machine guns and artillery. Other debates that came to an end with the beginning of U.S. participation included placing blame for war, the virtues of neutrality and pacifism, the truth of atrocity stories, the qualities of German culture, the need for negotiated peace, and, most troubling, the virtues of free speech and civil rights. President Woodrow Wilson had long withheld his support of preparedness and going to war. His critics excoriated his supposedly irresolute behavior. But Wilson worried about war's implications on a salad-bowl democracy of recent immigrants, many of them from Germany or anti-British Ireland. The United States was not only fractured on ethnic lines but also on racial and social lines. Antiwar socialist workers' groups enjoyed strong support at high levels of society. African Americans and women were less inclined to acquiesce to the country's pernicious racism and sexism. Wilson worried that war would substitute force for reason, slogans for arguments, and, as he told *New York World* editor Frank J. Cobb, "conformity would be the only virtue."[1]

Not everyone agreed that the war could kindle a social eruption along cultural and racial fault lines. War advocates like Wood and Roosevelt believed conscription and training could actually bring the country together, to "yank the hyphens" out of "hyphenated Americans," such as German-Americans or Irish-Americans. Liberals and progressives including Walter Lippmann and John Dewey supported the war in hopes it would promote values of health and social welfare, resolve labor unrest, engender good habits of citizenship, and rekindle moral and economic virtue. They would be disappointed.

The War Declaration: Discussion Over

Despite the debates, everyone knew that war meant temporarily suspending some civil liberties. "The first casualty when war comes is truth," famously noted California Senator Hiram Johnson. Speaking of American press control tactics during World War I, he was not entirely correct. It wasn't so much that government propagandists and the press lied. It was that they controlled and mostly eliminated the voice of those who opposed the war in any way. Like the bar brawler who shouts "discussion's over!" before throwing the first punch, in the fevered days leading up to war the government joined American mobs in brutally silencing opponents whether they be pacifists, socialists, or German sympathizers. Some who tried to continue the debate barely escaped with their lives. At the end of March 1917 the newly organized Emergency Peace Federation employed retired Stanford University president David Starr Jordan to speak in major East Coast cities. On April 1, a mob in Baltimore stormed the building where Jordan was speaking, and he barely escaped when peace supporters briefly stopped the patriotic zealots by singing the Star Spangled Banner.[2]

Federal and state authorities moved slowly if at all against this harassment—clearly illegal in most cases—of dissidents. But soon the legality of silencing and punishing anyone who even vaguely spoke against the war would become less clear. Two weeks after the war declaration, the government began to erect a three-tiered structure of press control. The first tier encouraged voluntary compliance. Most publications were only too happy to acquiesce, reflecting a historical trend of journalists and their readers to offer strong initial support to their country taking up arms. For those few publications and their sponsoring groups that did not rally to this call, the second tier relied on new laws that could force compliance and punish deviance. The final tier copied France and Britain by encouraging general homefront support for war through government-created propaganda bureaus such as the Committee on Public Information.

In democracies such as France this opinion-control operation morphed into a sweeping censorship office that read every line of copy produced in the entire country. The United States had no such inclination. Instead, the Wilson administration relied on industrious private citizens to ensure patriotic support. People were encouraged to inform authorities of any suspicious behavior. Vigilante violence was tolerated and private spying and tips led to searches and arrests without warrant.

For the "disloyal press" in particular, laws allowed the post office to put publications out of business by denying them mailing privileges. The definition of disloyal became so vague after the May 16, 1918 Sedition Act, which targeted "disloyal, profane, scurrilous or divisive language," that an exceedingly conscientious postmaster, Albert Burleson, pounced on scores of publications. In a few cases Wilson himself intervened, notably quashing the suspension of the prestigious liberal *Nation* magazine. Ever-energetic, if sometimes injudicious, Roosevelt joined the frenzy by calling for suspension of the anti-British Hearst press and execution of anyone found to be disloyal. But the publications that suffered most, German-language and socialist, were minor and of relatively small circulation. Hearst's publications, in fact, escaped punishment.

Editors and civil libertarians expressed concern over this control, although cautiously, given the political climate. They noted that not only was this pervasive net of control subverting citizens' First Amendment rights, but also that propaganda and repression would encourage mob intolerance and individual lawlessness. When the war came to an end with the armistice of November 11, 1918, the suppression of dissent did not. In fact it rose to a fever pitch fed by fear of "Reds" (Bolshevik Communists) bleeding from Russia to violently overthrow Western democracy. That radical American workers' such as the International Workers of the World (IWW) were sympathetic to the anticapitalist appeal of Bolshevism was undoubtedly true. But the "Wobblies," as they were nicknamed, were a small voice and a feeble threat. Still, a series of bombings and bomb scares in 1919 led to ferocious government crackdown of any dissidents. Attorney General A. Mitchell Palmer asked an eager 24-year-old named J. Edgar Hoover to head the new General Intelligence Division to suss out suspicious radicals. Hoover collected 20,000 cards describing presumably disloyal individuals.

Many of those targeted were immigrants because they were easier to bring to trial and deport. Much of the press, including the *New York Times,* supported Palmer's "resolute will and alacrity" after January 2, 1920, when he launched coordinated raids on radical organizations around the country: 33 cities, 22 states, 4,000 people arrested.[3]

These police-state tactics proved to be a low point of the Red Scare era. As the frenzy faded, those convicted were freed, mail privileges were restored to dissident publications, and the country's lawmakers began to consider the true meaning of the First Amendment and civil liberties. But no one in authority apologized. Throughout succeeding years world democracies failed, dictators rose, and the reforms of society so anticipated by progressives failed. The Great War's morning after proved to be numbing disillusion for Americans who put such hope in what was supposed to be a fight for the beacon of hope for humanity. By the 1930s a majority of Americans agreed with a Congressional committee that blamed greedy industrialists and special interests for a war that cost more than 100,000 American lives. The Wilsonian idealism of America as hope for the world, a vision of a new world order, and the hope of moral virtue of a New World redeeming a tired, corrupt Old World proved to be straws in the wind of a bleak globe consumed by despair and evil. To persuade Americans to try again in a new great war was going to be a tough sell for Franklin Delano Roosevelt. But just as a sneak attack on the *Lusitania* galvanized support for World War I, another naval attack clinched the argument in favor of World War II. On December 8, 1941, the day after FDR's "day of infamy" at Pearl Harbor, the United States joined a second world war.

Selection of articles from the vast archive of publications produced during this era was based on reference to the most prominent nationally circulated periodicals whose editors favored publication of extensive debates on important war-related issues. Some of the opinions were reprinted from other newspapers and other sources. Also included are publications of relatively small circulation but influential readership and edited by prominent leaders, such as the *Masses* (Max Eastman) and the *Crisis* (W.E.B. DuBois). Other publications, such as *National Geographic* and *Popular Science,* are included for distinctive perspectives on wartime issues. Some publications consulted (*Cosmopolitan* and *Bookman,* for example) were not used because they contained few articles debating wartime issues.

In matters of style, the author has preserved spellings as published in the original periodicals. Serbia in 1914 was spelled Servia, for instance, and some magazines even spelled such familiar words as today, to-day. The older spellings should be easily understandable to modern readers, and help to give authority to the original texts. Obvious typographical errors have been corrected.

Publications Containing Articles Excerpted for This Volume

Annals of the American Academy of Political and Social Science
Atlantic Monthly
Chicago Defender
Crisis
Current Opinion
Delineator
Independent
Masses
Nation
National Geographic
New Republic
New York Times Current History
North American Review
Popular Science
San Francisco Chronicle
Scribner's
World's Work

NOTES

1. Francine Curro Cary, *The Influence of War on Walter Lippmann 1914–1944* (Madison: State Historical Society of Wisconsin, 1967), 38–39.

2. David M. Kennedy, *Over Here: The First World War and American Society* (Oxford: Oxford University Press, 1980), 14–15.

3. Robert H. Zieger, *America's Great War: World War I and the American Experience* (Lanham, Md.: Rowman and Littlefield, 2000), 201.

Chapter 1

Who Started It? The Allies

World War I has emerged as the greatest example of a war begun for both simple and complex reasons. The simple reason was the trigger event, the assassination by Gavrilo Princip in Sarajevo of Archduke Franz Ferdinand, heir to the Austro-Hungarian throne, and his wife, Sophie. As the archduke was visiting one of his country's more recalcitrant recent acquisitions, an assassin (perhaps encouraged by separatists) jumped on the open car's running board and fired with the newly invented automatic pistol perfected by John Browning, an American. Its use was a sample of what was to be a war dominated by lethal new technology. The assassination occurred on June 28, 1914.

The press took notice of the assassination, but no one considered it a precursor to a world war. Thirty-seven days later vast armies were on the march. What happened during those days kept historians busy throughout the rest of the century, publishing a weight of thousands of books and articles. It was of no less interest while the war was being fought. The debate over who started World War I began only weeks after the war declarations, even before stalemate settled into the Western Front during the fall. The United States, officially neutral, enjoyed a press debate more wide ranging and nuanced than that of the European belligerents because the powers at war censored their journalism so that little debate over war guilt could be considered. In Europe, while the war was on, there was no doubt: to blame was the enemy, whoever that happened to be.

But in America, a country declared to be aloof from the fighting, who was the enemy? While American sentiment tended to favor the Entente powers—the allies of Britain, France, and Russia (and Italy after May 1915)—journalists were at first not at all convinced that they could be held blameless for the conflict. While it was true that Germany's attack on a neutral country could easily cast blame on that nation, the complex background to the war nuanced the simple answer. Research after the war continued to consider this thread of argument. A mountain of diplomatic documents held in secret in czarist Russia, in particular, but also in all belligerent nations were eventually made public. They presented a remarkable web of treaties that snared countries into making promises for which they would pay terrifying costs. The treaty web that formed the Entente helped to explain the reasons why these powers could actually be blamed for war.

The Entente Cordiale of Britain and France crystallized into a formal treaty in 1904. It stated that if one partner were attacked, others would go to its aid. Curiously, this treaty belied centuries of historic warfare between the two countries separated only by the English Channel. In fact, these countries had almost gone to war only a few years before over colonial disagreements such as the "Fashoda Crisis" of 1898. On the other hand, Britain had maintained a longstanding friendly relationship with Germany, an important trading partner. But a German threat was growing after its several self-governing states united in 1871 under the domination of Prussia. It had begun a ship-building plan to challenge British supremacy of the seas, an arms race of *Dreadnaught* class battleships. An alliance with this growing power might have been helpful for Britain, but negotiations ended in failure. Germany remained hostile to Britain's handling of the Boer War in South Africa (1899–1902). Without Germany's support, Britain turned to another growing power, Japan, for its alliance, and to its erstwhile enemy, France.

France had been diplomatically isolated since the Franco-Prussian War of 1870–1871. Britain, the world's foremost sea power and overlord of the world's most far-reaching colonial empire, could be a useful friend regardless of a few centuries' unpleasantness. Thus, growing German power and its challenge to French colonial interests could be balanced.

France and Britain did find common ground in their forms of government. Both had evolved into true democracies, still uncommon in Europe. On the other hand, a French alliance with Russia seemed improbable. Czarist Russia was Europe's most repressive monarchy, and one of Europe's least stable. A 1905 revolution there had been repressed successfully, but at a bloody cost, and seething resentment raged through successive waves of suicide bombings, assassinations, robbery, and terror perpetrated by powerful revolutionary opponents. Lenin and Stalin may have been living in exile (Lenin in Switzerland and Stalin in New York), but their spirit threatened an increasingly corrupt and curiously clueless monarchy.

France, on the other hand, had reached a zenith of success both culturally and financially. Paris had become the world's cultural capital. Its press was Europe's freest, its politics most democratic. Rich financiers invested their wealth around the world—including Russia, a country that had secretly funded Parisian financial publications to promote Russian bond sales. That France's moneyed elite had invested in Russia served as part of the reason the French government sought a treaty with the czar. Additionally, Germany remained France's implacable enemy as long as it refused to give back territory annexed after the 1871 war, never mind that Alsace and Lorraine were as much German by cultural heritage as French. A Franco-Russian alliance could squeeze Germany in a geographic vise from west and east and, in case of war, give France a formidable second front. The Triple Entente (Britain, France, and Russia) became the fateful alliance that was to bind the allies into a world war.

Could this alliance, made to counter jealousies and rivalries of a growing German challenge, be blamed for war? Certainly in the interwar period—between World War I and II—many journalists and historians concluded that blame could indeed be cast that way. The "total bankruptcy" of the secret treaties, it was contended, dragged participants into a war they didn't want. Even David Lloyd George, British prime minister from 1916–1922, wrote in his 1933 *War Memoirs* that "nations slithered over the brink into the boiling cauldrons of war."

But the United States had been far removed during all this diplomatic wheeling and dealing. It joined the war on the allies' side after almost three years of carnage. Could it also have been partially to blame? It could, some writers contended, because its growing economic power also threatened Germany, and its obvious unofficial support of the allies in munitions and loans made it a death merchant allowing the war to continue. Some even blamed Belgium for unwisely opposing German troops while allowing French soldiers to enter the country.

Recent scholarship after a century of careful perusal of documents and carefully reasoned debate has still not given us a definite answer to the question of war guilt. Some of the following debates, which took place without the benefit of historical hindsight, still make good arguments today.

Britain Blamed for War

Count Julius Andrassy, Hungarian Deputy and Former Minister: "The Mistakes of the Allies"

German authorities early in the war often criticized British propaganda for misrepresenting Germany and its ally, Austria-Hungary, both in its own press and the press of neutral nations. Germany was less able to promote its version of events because it could not directly reach the United

States after Britain severed its overseas cable the day after the war declaration. While certainly true that Britain embarked on a comprehensive campaign to discredit Germany after the war began, the evidence that it did so before the war started, as suggested here, is less certain. British newspapers did reflect concern over the growing German colonial power and challenge to London's naval supremacy, which may have resulted in a more negative view of Germany before the war. Nonetheless, we have no reliable survey evidence to show this.

New York Times Current History, April–September 1916

In England, through word and pen and picture, the great mass of the people had been forced into the delusion that Germany wanted a war with England, that Germany wanted to swallow up England. Germany would appear on English soil some day with its armies and destroy everything.

Consequently it is the biggest kind of a political lie when the English statesmen continue to assert that England was forced to take up arms in order to protect Belgium. Oh, no! the constant and long-continued open and secret incitation of hatred against Germany in England was the only thing that made it possible for the English Government to take a hand in the war, not to protect Belgium, but to destroy Germany's dreaded and annoying competition. Or does any sensible man really believe that the year-long anti-German agitation and, I might say, cultivation of the specter of invasion, was, or could have been, unknown to the English Government? Impossible, for the gentlemen of the English Government surely know how to read, and they are very shrewd.

J. A. Baer, Milwaukee, Wisconsin, Letter to the Editor: "Justice to Germany"

German military leaders long realized that in case of war, they must attack France from the north to avoid its string of fortifications, and attack quickly, before French forces had time to discover the intended path, and before their Russian allies had time to close the vise from the east. The Schlieffen Plan, worked out by the late Alfred von Schlieffen, faced the awkward question of Belgian neutrality. Germany hoped Belgium would permit a march-through, after a generous promise of compensation. It did not, forcing Germany to readjust fatally its meticulous timetable for reaching the French border.

Nation, September 3, 1914

Sir: Doubtless many readers of the Nation will vigorously dissent from your editorial, "England and War," of August 13, in which you assert that

Germany is responsible for this war: for it seems too plain for argument that England, and not Germany, is the proximate cause of the present war, as she has been many times in the past.

Your further contention that Germany has violated the Neutrality act has no merit, because England forced Germany into the breach by obstructing German attack on the northern coast of France. Germany was perfectly fair in the matter with Belgium, for she notified her of the intention, and promised her compensation for all damage done.

It seems to the writer that it is only fair that the Nation print an unbiased and unprejudiced article upon the cause of the present war, showing the exact stand taken by each contending country.

France Blamed for War

Count Johann von Bernstorff, German Ambassador to the United States: "Germany and the Great War"

Count von Bernstorff as German ambassador in Washington, D.C., was called on to provide the pro-German case after direct communication from Germany became difficult without its cable through Britain. As American anti-German sentiment built throughout the months of 1915–1916, however, von Bernstorff increasingly found himself isolated. He was even accused of abetting a German spy plot in the United States (this was apparently true). His argument that Belgium was pro-France is undoubtedly correct, but at the time he, like the generals, were not privy to the tactics planned by their adversaries. In fact French General Joseph Joffre did not intend to invade through Belgium, but based on "Plan 17" intended to march straight east through Lorraine and Ardennes. Initially successful, French troops had to be pulled back as the Schlieffen Plan brought the enemy within 50 miles of Paris.

***Independent*, September 7, 1914**

The violation of Belgian neutrality is an action which is universally regretted in Germany. But it was considered an absolute military strategical necessity. If Germany had entered France by the routes of Metz and Strasbourg, the French army would have entered Belgium and fallen on our right flank. We had absolutely reliable information that this intention existed in the French army. We were absolutely sure that Belgium would not be able to defend her neutrality against France, and would probably not even be willing to do so, as her fortresses had all been built against

Germany and not against France. Furthermore, on the first day of the war French motor cars with French officers passed thru Belgium to reconnoiter in Germany without being stopt by Belgian authorities. Equally French aeroplanes flew over Belgium without being stopt and bombarded German cities. Our information about the French army was furthermore corroborated by the fact that English generals visited Brussels in the spring at the time when the coalition was preparing for war against us. The governments of the coalition cannot suppose that we do not know that during the visit of King George to Paris the military negotiations were going on between England, France and Russia for the purpose of a joint attack against Germany.

Russia Blamed for War

Theobald von Bethmann Hollweg: "Germany's Appeal to America"

Theobald von Bethmann Hollweg, as chancellor of Germany through the first three years of war, became the restraining voice for a country that was falling more and more into a military dictatorship. Here he reflects the viewpoint absolutely believed without question in Germany: that their country had to go to war to avoid facing destruction by semicivilized Russian "hordes." Germany's contention that Russian mobilization was the cause of the war has been carefully considered by postwar historians, many of whom have found that argument to be somewhat credible. Russian authorities knew Germany would consider mobilization to be equivalent to a declaration of war. Germany had said as much. But this era's tactics had been devised based on machine-age munitions technology bringing immense firepower onto an adversary. Survival depended on one thing: to bring your firepower to bear on an enemy before he could do it to you. That meant speed was paramount. As Russian civilian leaders contemplated the consequences of mobilization, its generals beat a frenzy of impatience as each hour put them in more and more danger. Finally the generals had their way, and one thing indeed became certain: Russian mobilization meant war.

***Independent,* August 24, 1914**

The war is a life and death struggle between Germany and the Muscovite races of Russia, and was due to the recent royal murders at Serajevo.

Theobald von Bethmann Hollweg became Germany's most familiar civilian face during World War I. As chancellor he struggled to defend his country's policies in opinions written for American media while struggling at home to maintain civilian power over a country increasingly sliding into military dictatorship. He lost both struggles and in 1917 resigned. Courtesy of Library of Congress.

We warned Russia against kindling this world war. She demanded the humiliation of Austria, and while the German Emperor continued his work in the cause of peace and the Czar was telegraphing words of friendship to him, Russia was preparing for war against Germany.

Highly civilized France, bound by her unnatural alliance with Russia, was compelled to prepare by strength of arms for an attack on its flank on the Franco-Belgian frontier in case we proceeded against the French frontier works. England, bound to France by obligations disowned long ago, stood in the way of a German attack on the northern coast of France.

Necessity forced us to violate the neutrality of Belgium, but we had promised emphatically to compensate that country for all damage inflicted.

Now England avails herself of the long awaited opportunity to commence war for the destruction of commercially prosperous Germany. We enter into that war with our trust in God. Our eternal race has risen in the fight for liberty, as it did in 1813.

It is with a heavy heart that we see England ranged among our opponents.

Notwithstanding the blood relationship and close relationship in spiritual and cultural work between the two countries, England has placed herself on the side of Russia, whose instability and whose barbaric insolence have helped this war, the origin of which was murder, and the purpose of which was the humiliation and suppression of the German race by Russian pan-Slavism.

We expect that the sense of justice of the American people will enable them to comprehend our situation. We invite their opinion as to the one-sided English representations, and ask them to examine our point of view in an unprejudiced way.

The sympathy of the American nation will then lie with German culture and civilization, fighting against a half Asiatic and slightly cultured barbarism.

Richard von Kuhlmann: "von Kuhlmann's Reichstag Address. German Foreign Secretary's Summary of War Situation and the Storm It Raised"

The secret treaties that bound Britain to support Russia in case of war were not known in 1914, but, as Richard von Kuhlmann noted, they were pretty clear by 1918. That Russia would not have gone to war without allied support is likely true, but that Russian mobilization guaranteed war is still a matter of argument. By 1918 most everyone in the United States believed as matter of course that Germany fought for domination of Europe. Postwar research seemed to discredit this view. But another generation of research leaves us less certain.

New York Times Current History, April–September 1918

I believe that one can say, without fear of contradiction, as the result of revelations, that the deeper we go into the causes of this war the clearer it becomes that the power which planned and desired the war was Russia; that

France played the next worst role as instigator, and that England's policy has very dark pages to show.

England's attitude in the days before the outbreak of the war was bound to strengthen Russia's desire for war. Of this there are proofs enough in the documents already published.

On the other hand, Germany did not for an instant believe that this war could lead to the domination of Europe, much less to the domination of the world. On the contrary, the German policy before the war showed good prospects of being able satisfactorily to realize its essential aims, namely, the settlement of affairs in the East and Colonial problems by peaceful negotiation.

Belgium Blamed for War

Roland G. Usher: "Was Belgium Neutral?"

Belgian irregular troops fought a resistance action that infuriated German officers and resulted in civilian executions and other atrocities. While no invading troops behaved impeccably in this war, German army actions against Belgian civilians were embroidered by the allies to provide justification for the war against a brutal conqueror, along with the claim to save the honor of "poor little Belgium." It is clearly true that had Belgium not resisted, the allies would not have had influential propaganda that helped to persuade the United States to join the war. On the other hand, had Belgium opened its gates to German troops, France, which only barely held off the invasion as it was, might have lost the war within weeks. In that sense, perhaps Belgium was indeed to blame for a war that lasted more than four years.

New Republic, November 28, 1914

Whatever the diplomatic facts may be, whatever the technicalities of alliances and treaties eventually prove to have been, Belgium was clearly an ally of France as England was. The Belgian army and its dispositions, the Belgian forts on the German frontier, were prepared with the advice, at least, of English and French generals. Plans for the cooperation of the three armies were undoubtedly made. Let us not quibble over the question whether this was not an infringement of the neutrality. The Belgians knew—let us say it once more—that the neutrality of Belgium was a fiction because Belgium was not neutral ground.

The United States Blamed for War

George Louis Beer: "America's International Responsibilities"

The argument that the allies can be blamed for the war by bottling up German expansion has been debated for decades. Usually to blame is Britain, perhaps France, less so the United States. It was, however, clear that America was on its way to becoming the force to be reckoned with in world trade. Militarily, however, the United States Army was of derisory strength in 1914, a fact that Republican leaders such as Theodore Roosevelt decried. While perhaps plausible that German leaders feared future challenge by the United States, there seems to be little evidence it was a concern in Berlin before 1914.

Annals of the American Academy of Political and Social Science, July 1916

In that the United States resolutely refused to become involved in any European matters and, furthermore, in that, because of its patent unwillingness to use more than moral suasion, it left to others the protection of its policies in the Far East, we cannot escape a degree of negative responsibility for the existing world-war. An examination of recent international history and of the fundamental aim of German world politics will make this nexus apparent.

There is a disconcerting vagueness about Germany's ambitious plans, but the general underlying thought is unmistakable. When the German statesmen, economists, and publicists tried to pierce the veil of the future and to picture the world toward the end of this century, they saw three great political aggregates—the American, the British, and the Russian—outranging in cultural influence and potential strength all other states of western civilization and dwarfing a Germany whose political growth under existing territorial arrangements could apparently not compete with theirs. Hence the insistent striving for a repartition of the world in conformity both with Germany's actual military strength and with some hypothetical future need for more land for her growing population as well as for new markets and fresh sources of supply for her expanding industries. There was no question either of any real need or of any actual handicap under existing conditions. As these plans for expansion could be realized only at the expense of the British Empire or of the Monroe Doctrine, the enemy of enemies in German eyes appeared to be the so-called "Anglo-Saxon block." The Anglo-Saxon, says Paul Rohrbach in his widely-read book Der Deutsche Gedanke in der Welt, "have spread over such vast expanses that they seem to be on the point of assuming the cultural control of the world, thanks to their large numbers, their resources and their inborn strength."

Roland G. Usher: "America as a Cause of War"

Colonial expansion in the late nineteenth century was justified, among other things, by arguing that colonies could provide a market for manufactures of the mother country. Germany most likely found this argument compelling as it confronted Britain and France more than once on European colonial expansion policy. This almost led to war in 1905 and 1911. Germany arrived late in the grab-fest for colonial power, but nevertheless established an African presence. (Which it lost after the war. This turned out to be fortunate for Germany, because decades later it did not face costly and violent decolonization issues.) Trade with the United States also was important, although not nearly as important as the British–United States connection. The following argument suggests that Britain would be more likely to oppose rather than ally itself with the United States. Anglo-American tiffs over trade on the high seas strained relations between the two English-speaking nations before 1917.

***New Republic*, February 20, 1915**

It is rather startling to contemplate the possibility that the United States may have been the indirect cause of the present European war, that the reaction of America upon Europe may be in more than a figurative sense at the bottom of the economic difficulties that are themselves the fundamental factors which European nations are seeking to solve. . . .

The expanding market for European produce is gone. The undeveloped territory able to absorb European population, capital, and manufactured goods to an unlimited extent has disappeared, never to return. The European monopoly of the American market due to our own inability to manufacture has also passed. Instead of a customer eager to buy, the European nations now find a stalwart competitor, quite able to undersell them in their own markets, and whose competition is each year more dangerous than the year before. Instead of selling to the United States any surplus that they can produce, the European nations find themselves confronted annually with a larger volume of American produce in their own markets. Where they could once almost ask their own price, they must now rigidly reduce their profits in order to sell their output.

Have we not here at least one cause of the scramble for colonies in expanding markets which began about 1890 when the economic independence of the United States was becoming clear? Does not the rapidity with which the United States has developed since that time explain to some extent the imperative need of expanding markets which the European nations feel? A new solution of their problem had to be found, and was a difficult to discover as the economic relationship between the United States and Europe had been extraordinary and unprecedented.

All Allies Blamed for War

Philipp Scheidemann, Chairman, German Socialist Party, and Ex-Vice President of the Reichstag: "Germany's Peace Conditions. What the Socialists Desire"

German socialism was among the strongest in prewar Europe. Its presumption was that in case of war European socialists would unite in a general strike and make war impossible. The speaker here reflects the reality that the real motivating force at the turn of the last century was not socialism, but patriotic nationalism.

***New York Times Current History*, April–September 1916**

If, at the beginning of the war, millions of us rallied enthusiastically to our country's call, we did not do so with the intention of imposing the will of Germany on the world—as our enemies have so often falsely accused us of doing. No, we rallied around the flag in order to prevent the independence, the unity and the national position of the German Nation from being destroyed by an immense hostile coalition. A peaceful and reasonable nation such as the German may, in moments of great excitement, be dominated by a feeling of indignation, but it does not revel in thoughts of vengeance and extermination. It seeks to acquire the position in the world to which it is entitled next to the other nations, but not above them.

Gentlemen, I have spoken candidly. I have been able to say openly that we desire peace, because the German Nation is sufficiently strong, and because it is resolved to continue the fight in defense of home and country should its enemies not wish for peace.

Oswald Garrison Villard: "Germany Embattled: An American Interpretation"

Oswald Garrison Villard, during the war years, became one of America's most prominent liberal editors (he was the son of publisher Henry Villard and the grandson of abolitionist William Lloyd Garrison). Villard was publisher of the influential liberal magazine Nation *as well as the* New York Evening Post. *As a pacifist, Villard tried to reflect the complexity of casting blame for the war, in this case explaining the prevalent view in Germany. It is true that the colonial affairs of Britain and France strained their credibility as moralist protectors of small nations, but at this time surely most ethnocentric Britons believed that Belgium was a quite different case from its colonies.*

Scribner's, December 1914

That some Germans realize that her moral position would be far stronger to-day had she left Belgium untouched is deducible not merely from the chancellor's confession that she had violated a law of nations; it is admitted frankly by a few, like Professor Paul Natorp of the University of Marburg. Yet even he has convinced himself, like all Germany, that the French would have marched in with the consent of England and of Belgium itself if the Germans had not; they are the more certain of this now that the Germans have found the telltale papers in Brussels showing that the British were plotting with the Belgians what they should do if Belgium were invaded. That French troops and officers were actually crossing the boundaries when the Germans were, and that some were already in Liege, Namur, and Antwerp, is believed from one corner of Germany to another.

But even if this were to be disproved, the Germans as a whole are behind the chancellor in his belief that to invade Belgium was justified by that direst necessity that knows no law. It was the only way to protect their own unfortified Belgian frontier. Why could not the Belgians have realized this and spared themselves all that they have suffered by letting the Germans march quietly through? The Kaiser's troops would have disturbed or injured no man; they would have made good any injury done and paid handsomely as they went. For the rest of the world to cry out against what happened as a result of Belgian folly, in the manner that it has, passeth understanding from their point of view. For England to protest seems to Germany the height of hypocrisy. England standing for the rights of small nations—the same England that wiped out the Boer republics; that consented shamefully to Russia's crushing out of Persia; that connived at France's swallowing of Morocco when the ink on the treaty of Algeciras guaranteeing Moroccan integrity was scarcely dry! Merely to state the case against "perfidious Albion" is to prove its shamelessness.

Hence the Germans have convinced themselves that England's seizing on Belgian neutrality as a reason for war was but the hollowest of shams. Everything that is now disclosed but proves in Berlin a long-planned conspiracy to ruin Germany because of her success in the world. It is envy that is at the bottom of it all, a wicked, criminal envy because German ships are filling the seas and German commerce is growing by leaps and bounds and her merchants are capturing the marts of trade hitherto the private property of John Bull. It is all so clear and plain that Germany could not understand why the rest of the world could not see it, too.

Questions

1. Why would Europeans believe that the invasion and occupation of an African nation such as South Africa or Morocco was different from the invasion and occupation of another European country, such as Belgium?
2. Germany was a mostly Lutheran and Roman Catholic nation before 1914 while Russia was mostly Russian Orthodox. How does this reflect the German fear of invasion from Russian "hordes"?
3. Why would Belgium not acquiesce to allowing Germany to march through its country on its way to attacking France, considering that Germany promised to compensate Belgium for any damage caused?
4. If mobilization, that is, preparing troops for war, is not the same as actually attacking another country, how could Germany argue that Russian mobilization was a *casus belli* (reason to go to war)?

Chapter 2

Who Started It? Germany

As the months turned to years, more and more Americans tipped toward the allied viewpoint, blaming World War I on Germany. German propaganda could not reach the United States as easily as British propaganda, and, of course, had to be translated for the majority of Americans. Moreover, Germany was not able to mount a clever propaganda campaign with the same force as the extensive British operation. German leaders still worked within a monarchy and they did not have the kind of powerful press found in the democratic nations of Britain and France. Furthermore, the German press did not have the same close ties between its journalists and politicians. In England, on the other hand, influential publishers became important politicians. And in France, journalism actually brought Georges Clemenceau to the prime minister's position. German leaders did not know how to compete for the ears of journalists, and through them, public opinion.

Even if Berlin had been able to mount a strong public relations campaign, its efforts might have failed. Germany's military decisions succeeded in alienating neutral countries, particularly the United States, more thoroughly than anything the allies did. Getting off on the wrong foot in the propaganda war, Germany invaded Belgium when that country refused to open its roads to advancing German troops. German Chancellor Bethmann Hollweg, in a final interview with the British ambassador aiming to keep Britain out of the war, famously called Britain's guarantee of Belgian neutrality a "scrap of paper." That ill-considered remark was passed around the allies throughout the war as proof of German perfidy. Shocking stories about German atrocities as troops marched through the low countries fueled wild exaggeration that became a central pro-ally argument no civilized American could ignore. Subsequent events only solidified American presumption that Germany started the war.

Because the allies won, that presumption was written into the Treaty of Versailles. The famous Article 231 of the 1919 peace treaty declared that Germany was solely responsible for the war. It read:

> The Allied and Associated Governments affirm and Germany accepts the responsibility of Germany and her allies for causing all the loss and damage to which the Allied and Associated Governments and their nationals have been subjected as a consequence of the war imposed upon them by the aggression of Germany and her allies.

Germany vigorously, stridently, violently contested what it believed was a gross overstatement considering Russia's bellicose mobilization, the secret web of allied treaties, and German losses of 1.7 million soldiers, plus another 1.2 million from its ally Austria-Hungary and 325,000 from Turkey. In a response similar to that of Russia when Berlin presented the draconian Treaty of Brest-Litovsk, Germany refused to sign until threatened with renewed war. The Versailles treaty reflected German blame throughout by demanding war reparations unreasonable given the postwar state of the German economy along with its loss of all colonies and the former French provinces of Alsace and Lorraine. But it was nearly impossible, in an atmosphere of frenzied allied hatred of anything German, to do much less, despite Wilson's argument for treatment less harsh. Allied propaganda could perhaps be partly blamed for the white-hot public opinion that tied the hands of the Big Four leaders at the peace table. But only partly. After all, it was Germany that had invaded Belgium, brutalized civilians in occupied nations, torpedoed passenger liners, and proposed pacts with Mexico. Additionally, the Kaiser's spiky mustache made it easy for cartoonists to demonize his rule over the "militarized country." Germany could adduce counterarguments for all this (except perhaps the Kaiser's mustache), but nuance over the war's responsibility was not popular in 1919.

Reconsideration of war guilt became more popular in the interwar decades. As new democracies fell to totalitarianism it was clear that the war to end all wars had ended nothing, but had begun a lot of things, most of them bad. Historians began to spread war guilt so widely that everyone and no one became responsible for World War I. In any case, one thing was certain: Article 231 infamously gave extremists something on which to fasten their rhetoric, the shame of the blame. Indeed, Hitler found fertile political soil in exploiting the treaty's casting of blame.

A generation after the end of World War II historians reexamined the war guilt question. New documents made public in the early 1960s led development of the Fischer school to return to the original 1918 argument. German historian Fritz Fischer determined that Germany did indeed perceive itself to be subject to a containment policy perpetrated by its enemies, the response to which could only be war. The assassination of Archduke Franz Ferdinand merely offered a pretext. Powerful evidence for this conclusion cannot be entirely discredited, and the Fischer school still has its adherents. More recent scholarship has argued, however, that Germany did not start the war on purpose. Its diplomats simply reflected the approach of the time, taking risks but expecting results to be limited. Berlin did not expect its saber-rattling support of Austria-Hungary to lead to general war. Diplomatic brinksmanship had reached the edge before, in 1905 and 1911, but had not tipped over it. This time, apparently, the brinksmen lost their footing.

Other recent historians are not convinced. More recently a country thought to have played a minor role, Austria-Hungary, has been pulled back into the spotlight. Would that creaky old polycultural nation have gone to war against Serbia without German support, knowing full well Russia would come to the small country's aid? Decades of scholarship presumed not. More recent scholarship isn't so certain. Had Berlin not given Vienna the famous carte blanche to go to war, Austria might have gone ahead anyway to maintain credibility as a major power. What is more, it was Vienna that blocked London's attempt to set up an emergency peace conference during the summer of 1914.

Still, most contemporary historians conclude that Germany must be held substantially accountable for starting World War I. Germany pursued an aggressive stance; its diplomats could hardly have missed the obvious conclusion that war would be a likely response. If war it must be, then, the German government reflected its domination by military leaders in starting it immediately and quickly, before its enemies had a chance to twist the vise. It has been suggested that Berlin did not expect Britain to break its neutrality, as the precise commitments of the secret treaties were unknown to them. Indeed Germany did plead with Britain to remain neutral. But London had repeatedly voiced its ringing support for the integrity of neutral Belgium. Germany's need to march through that country, as specified by Schlieffen years earlier, could not have left German leaders with much hope of London's neutrality.

Germany Blamed for War

C.D.M.: "What America Thinks of War"

Probably few Americans understood, or even knew about, Germany's fear of Russian mobilization in 1914, and so saw the war as an aggressive German attack on the Western Front. Ignorance of Eastern European political affairs during this period could be blamed partly on American newspapers and magazines. Few had correspondents in Eastern Europe; nearly every major newspaper had correspondents in Paris and London. And cable censorship in London from the beginning colored reports to emphasize allied viewpoints. German arguments got through piecemeal, and late, after public opinion had already been formed.

***World's Work*, September 1914**

At the outbreak of the great war in August, 1914, I made it my business to ramble about the streets of New York among the crowds watching the newspaper bulletins, at cafes, on streetcars, talking with everyone I came across. the current of popular feeling was not difficult to trace. Denunciation of the Kaiser was in most cases a sure passport to the approval of the little knot of listeners who gather to every argument. From the Battery to the Bronx, everywhere I found a definite anti-German sentiment. Not against the German people, of course, who are bound to us by close ties of blood and commerce; but against the Kaiser and the whole armor-plated superstructure of German militarism which seems to have cudgeled into war a people flourishing in the arts of peace, a people whose genius is for literature and art and commerce, the kindest-hearted people in the world. Sympathy with the Germans there exists in abundance, and horror at the task which their troops are called upon to perform. But approval of the German war office? No!

John Jay Chapman: "The Bright Side of the War"

This excerpt clearly shows four years of British propaganda casting Germany as uncivilized barbarians. Such an attitude stretched credibility; centuries of high achievement in German science, art, music, philosophy, and literature had heavily influenced Western thought. Britain, for centuries often an ally and seldom an enemy of Germany, certainly knew this, but war seemed to demand temporary amnesia.

***Atlantic Monthly*, January 1918**

The invasion of Belgium gave the world a shock like the slipping of the earth's crust. It was an earthquake which had been silently maturing for centuries; and when it came it shook the globe to the centre. Every one knew, when he felt that oscillation, that the future of humanity was at stake.

The declaration by the Germans that their will was law rang with a note of defiance toward Creation: it was an attack upon every man. Moreover, it was blasphemy. It rent the inner veil in the breast of many a man who knew little of Germany, and little of religion. Not the sage only, but the man in the street, had a vision: a spasm ran through him. He was frightened, to be sure; but he was more awed than terrified, for he felt within himself that the powers of the universe were rising to meet a crisis.

Those powers soon made themselves felt. the great crash of evil was followed by a counter-crash of sanctity and heroism—of faith in every form. The regeneration of the world did not wait for the end of the war, but began at once. France became, within a fortnight, the image of Joan of Arc. Unsuspected heroes and heroines flocked to the scene of conflict from distant lands. The sign of innocent suffering aroused in onlookers a pity which turned in many cases into sublime passion, and which in every case increased the intellect, generosity, courage, and unselfishness of those who felt it.

The world-war began thus suddenly with the satanic announcement that might makes right—as clear a statement of the proposition as ever was made—followed by a spontaneous roar of denial from peoples in whom the instinct of self-preservation rose to meet the challenge. It was the metaphysical element—the claim of the Germans—rather than their brute power, that awakened the antagonism of the world. Man's nature vibrated to its roots against their idea. That idea is Self-Will. The instinctive piety of man abhors it. The mythology of every race condemns it. Self-will is, and has always been, the quintessence of Evil.

The struggle between good and evil which is generally invisible and can be apprehended only by instinct, has been dramatized by the war, and the whole world has become the stage of a miracle play. Humanity enacts its great allegory. The size and expense of it are appalling, but the substance of it is familiar, and the vividness of it casts into the shade very thing heretofore seen upon the earth.

Richard Dobson: "Lest We Forget: Who's Responsible for the World's Greatest War"

Who threw the first punch? Who first stepped over the line? Common experience based on school-day skirmishes tends to pin blame on whoever hit first. The comments here apply this rhetoric to the beginning of World War I. But while Germany may have invaded first, it merely reflected universal military belief of the time (and still common today) that the best defense is a good offense. A 1914 European division (normally 14,000 soldiers) benefited from machine age technology that could concentrate immense firepower on an enemy: 120,000 rounds of small-arms fire, and 1,000 shells, per minute. To survive this firestorm the reasonable response was avoid it altogether, by attacking first. Germany declared war on Russia August 1, on France August 3, and on Belgium August 4. After that, the old battle custom of polite pause to allow the enemy to take to take the first shot could result in annihilation. Modern warfare was to force a thorough rethinking of what constituted a "fair fight," although the world wouldn't really admit that until World War II.

New York Times Current History, April–September 1916

Yet on this same day, Saturday, Aug. 1, Russia assured England that she would on no account commence hostilities if the German army did not cross the frontier, and France also declared that her army should be kept six miles from her frontier so as to prevent collision. This was the situation de facto when very early on Sunday morning, Aug. 2, 1914, the German troops invaded Luxemburg, a small independent State, which had been guaranteed by all the powers the same neutrality as Belgium. The die was cast and the great war begun.

Intercourse between Germany and Great Britain continued for two days, but the crisis was reached in a heated interview between the German Chancellor with Sir Edward Goschen, the British Ambassador at Berlin, over the word "neutrality" and the phrase "scrap of paper," which was followed by Germany's refusal to withdraw her troops from Belgium, by Belgium's appeal to England for aid under the treaty, and then by the declaration of war between Germany and Great Britain.

Editorial, *Le Temps, Paris:* "Was the War Forced on Germany? A Terse French Reply"

Germany did indeed plan its "eastern objective," stopping Russia, before wheeling its troops toward France. This was most likely the only reasonable way to counter an obvious allied plan to squeeze Germany in its geographical vise. It would not be implemented, however, until after the war declaration, so was not a cause of war as much as a tactical move. The complexity of what mobilization meant to Russia and to Germany, however, still is a key question in tracing the war's beginning. Some historians contend that Russian mobilization did not mean war, but it also seems understandable given fearsome armaments and military assumptions of 1914, that it would require Zen-like nerve to stay the course of peace after a hostile nation began steamrolling 4,423,000 soldiers toward the borders.

New York Times Current History, October 1916–February 1917

The central argument of the Chancellor is the Russian mobilization. He would have had Russia refrain from mobilizing, in spite of the Austrian mobilization, in spite of the declaration of war against Serbia, in spite of the military preparations of Germany indicated by all the Consuls from July 26 onward. He would have wished that the occupation of Belgrade should not be considered an act of war, but a simple guarantee. This would have meant that, England and France remaining neutral, the conflict would have been "localized," that is to say, it would have allowed Germany to attain its eastern objective at once, and to turn then against its western objective. Thus, by the force of circumstances, the confession is included in the public prosecutor's own address to the court.

Editorial: "The Real Crime against Germany"

Appealing to Americans who were proud of their democracy was the argument that it was not the German people per se, but a militarist monarchy that launched a war against the their will. Evidence in Germany, however, showed the German person-on-the-street supported the war as zealously as those in every other belligerent nation in 1914. In fact the Kaiser was less enthusiastic about seeing his country go to war than were many of his subjects.

Nation, August 13, 1914

We have received protests from a number of German sympathizers against the attitude adopted by the Nation in fixing the responsibility for the war in Europe mainly upon the Kaiser. We are assured that this is a holy war into which Germany has been forced against her will; that she is the only bulwark between the rising tide of Slavism and the endangered civilization of Western Europe, and, therefore, that enlightened sentiment the world over should side with her as against the aggressions of the Powers like England and France, whose real motives are jealousy and envy of the wonderful commercial growth of the Kaiser's empire.

The Nation has always entertained and expressed the highest admiration for the German people, but never for the Germany of the Kaiser. We have never believed that a people of essentially noble quality should be subject to the will of an autocratic king or emperor, however enlightened he may be, or however ardent a guardian of peace during a long period of years. Never have we upheld the Germany of the mailed fist, of the autocracy of militarism; against its excesses, its encroachments upon civil rights, its assertion that it constitutes a sacrosanct caste superior to any other, we have protested in season and out of season.

Editorial: "Germany Appeals to America"

The excerpt here offers evidence for those who contend that it was not so much British propaganda that persuaded the United States to join the war, but German political and strategic decisions that Americans could not accept. That began with the invasion of neutral Belgium on August 3, 1914. Plausible arguments from Germany that the Belgians would have allowed French troops to march through on their way to Germany, that Belgium would be well compensated for damage, and that Berlin held no ill will against Brussels but simply had to cross if Germany were to pursue an effective strategy, did not register to most Americans. Emotional slogans such as "violation of neutrality," "atrocities," and "scrap of paper" appealed more readily to a people who often declared themselves more moral and free from the machinations of the Old World.

Nation, October 15, 1914

What our German friends in their eagerness to have the towering moral influence of the United States on their side, do not realize is that the judgment of this country was based upon a calm consideration of the facts leading up to the war, and upon the invasion of Belgium as set forth by the Germans themselves. American good opinion was forfeited when the Kaiser rejected Sir Edward Grey's two distinct offers to assure peace, when the "scrap of paper" incident occurred, and the Chancellor admitted the flagrant violation of the law of nations. This judgment cannot be swayed by the thrilling uprising of the German nation, its readiness to sacrifice its best, or its wonderful unanimous belief in the justice of its cause. These things do not affect the moral issues at all, any more than does the fact that the British, who have connived at the wiping out of the nationality of Persia and Morocco and destroyed the Boer republics, are in an inconsistent role in going to war for the independence of small countries. The Frankfurter Zeitung in a recent issue, declares that America will come to Germany's aid as soon as the statements of returning American travelers are published and German newspapers cross the seas. A bitter disappointment is before all Germans who hope for this. Indeed, we fear that the end of it all will be their early retreat to the position taken by the Berlin Tageszeitung, as reported last week in these words: "We, however, do not need to regard the public opinion of the world. In the last instance, the German people, united with the Emperor, are alone competent to decide the correctness of Germany's course.

Austria-Hungary Blamed for War

Editorial: "Germany's Appeal to America"

Decades of World War I research discounted the patent observation that it was Austria-Hungary's ultimatum to Serbia that caused the war.

Not that the ultimatum was not the trigger, but the reason this local conflict could lead to general conflagration, the argument goes, must be sought in economics, diplomacy, and perceived threat. But recent scholarship returning to the beginning has found the aggressive behavior of a decrepit empire probably can be counted as a significant, if not sole, cause for the war.

Independent, August 24, 1914

Russia did not begin the war. It was begun by Germany's ally Austria against a small Slav nation, Servia. It is incredible that it had not Germany's consent. "We warned Russia," Says the Chancellor [Bethmann Hollweg] "against kindling this world's war." But it was not Russia that kindled it, but Austria. Doubtless Germany did warn Russia not to help Servia, but to let little Servia be gobbled up. That is, Germany stood behind Austria in the grab. Russia stept in to defend her feeble sister; and Austria knew, and Germany knew, and all the world knew that it was to be expected. And so the great war began, not Russia's war, but that of Austria, and her backer who had made it possible previously to absorb Bosnia.

The Chancellor says that the purpose of Russia was "the humiliation and suppression of the German race by the Russian pan-Slavism." There is no evidence that Russia desired any such thing and the world does not believe it. Russia does object to Austrian and German seizure of small Slav countries, but she does not try to seize German territory. Nor did Germany need at all to fear Russian aggression. . . .

In this war it is impossible to give the approval asked for to our good and powerful friend Germany. We regret that she is in the wrong, and are profoundly sorry that she has brought on herself the condemnation of the world.

Serbia Blamed for the War

Paul Darmstaedter, Gottingen, Germany, Letter to the Editor: "The German Point of View"

Serbia's rejection of Austria-Hungary's ultimatum was the immediate cause of World War I, certainly, just as Gavrilo Princip's assassination of Archduke Franz Ferdinand was the immediate cause of the ultimatum. But to argue that one man or a minor Balkan nation can be solely to blame for a world war is to miss a larger picture of tangling alliances, military necessity, and national pride. No rational person on June 29, 1914, who read about the assassination assumed it would lead to general war a few weeks later. It was Woodrow Wilson who proposed a new international order to assure that such minor events would never again produce such terrible consequences. The first of his famous Fourteen Points called for "open covenants of peace, openly arrived at, after which there shall be no private international understandings of any kind but diplomacy shall proceed always frankly and in the public view."

Nation, November 26, 1914

Sir: As a subscriber to the Nation for many years, I beg you to insert some lines in your paper, not to gain the sympathy for our cause, but to state the justice of our standpoint. I have entirely missed in your journal, and also in other American papers, an impartial discussion of the causes of the present war; I find a good deal of wrong information, based on the infamous lies of the English press, and, of course, false conclusions drawn from false premises. Allow me simply to state some facts which were obvious some months ago, and which are now quite forgotten.

The present war originated in the Servian conflict: Austria could not longer tolerate the dangerous agitation in her southern provinces, and Russia found it necessary to protect that kingdom of criminals by force of arms. The mobilization of the Russian army was the signal for the general war, a fact that cannot be denied. But the Servian question was only the occasion that led to the war; the real causes, and, of course, the real responsibilities for the war must be found in the policy of the different states in the last years. You cannot deny that Germany and Austria have constantly worked for the preservation of peace, even at the cost of their own interests. Germany did not profit by the South African war, nor by the Russo-Japanese war, to settle her controversies with England and Russia; Austria kept peace in the time of the Balkan wars and sacrificed great interests to the cause of the European peace. Germany renounced Morocco for the preservation of peace. The German and the Austrian Governments have done all for that cause; they have never had any aggressive tendencies against other nations.

[response]

Editorial: "'British Lies' and American Sentiment"

Neither communication of falsehoods from England nor suppression of truths form Germany has had any appreciable influence upon the formation of American opinion. The war is now in the second half of its fourth month, and we have yet to see, among all the voluminous statements of the German case, the exposure of a single "British lie" which had any part in determining the sentiment of the American people.

What did determine that sentiment it is easy enough to recognize. One has only to turn to what was said in representative American papers at the very beginning; what was said before there was any talk of atrocities and before the German cable was cut. . . . Right or wrong, these judgments—as to the responsibility for the immediate bringing of the war, and as to the nature of the international crime involved in the invasion of Belgium—were based upon the broadest and most patent considerations, and not in the least upon "British lies"; right or wrong, these same judgments were arrived at simultaneously by almost the whole American press; and right or wrong, no technical pleas concerning the exact date of mobilization, or other unessential details, can possibly break them down. Nothing that the champions of Germany have brought forward lessens by a feather's weight the force of the two fundamental facts—her undeviating insistence on Austria's pound of flesh, which made peace impossible, and her violation of Belgium, which made England's participation in the war inevitable.

That the case is not so simple when the more remote—if you please, the deeper—causes of the war are examined, we do not deny. To determine the rightfulness or unrightfulness, the wisdom or the folly, of the policies of the various nations in the course of the last ten, or twenty, or forty years, is an undertaking which will tax the powers of the future historian.

Questions

1. Why would Americans, who believed in democracy, such as that of the United States, presume that German citizens were opposed to the war?
2. Could Germany's case that it could not defend itself without passing through Belgium make a reasonable argument today for countries wishing to invade other nations?
3. Is the country that "fires the first shot" always to blame for starting a war? Can a moral case be made for preemptory attacks on another nation?
4. Mobilization means calling a country's troops to prepare and deploy for war. Would we consider the argument that such action provokes, and not prevents, an eventual war legitimate today?
5. Despite the value of free speech in democracies, Britain was able to control and censor all journalism coming from Germany and bound for the United States, and so influenced Americans on the war. But does a government in a democracy have the ethical right to control a neutral nation's access to foreign news?

Chapter 3

Who Started It? Society

In one of the most influential books published shortly before the war, Norman Angell's *The Great Illusion* (1910) claimed that a general European war could not be possible. He argued a war could give a nation no commercial advantage; large capitalists and financiers who had forged interlocking commitments throughout the world would have too much to lose. The huge success of "Norman Angellism" sprinted the book to sales of more than two million, but his theory was not unopposed. Socialists argued that not only were capitalists in favor of war, they could profit by selling munitions and provisions to both sides, and so would encourage a war declaration. Preventing the catastrophe was up to the international proletariat. Masses of workers would simply drop their tools and declare a general strike, making war impossible.

Both prewar predictions, of course, turned out to be wishful thinking. Nationalism, that is, identification with one's country and its call to patriotism, proved to be far more powerful a force in 1914 than socialism or even capitalism. In France the state kept a secret list of socialists, radicals, and others thought likely to oppose the nation's call to arms. These purported troublemakers would be liable to arrest should war come. But when war came, none was arrested. There was no need; many had already volunteered to serve, and those who did not, supported the war. France exemplified the experience of all belligerent nations, including the United States after the war declaration on April 6, 1917.

Perhaps this seamless support for war can be considered a contributing cause for war. If the Great War had not received so much public support, would it have lasted so long, or even started? Historians who consider blame for the war more widespread than simply politics observe that politicians and populace both marched into the conflict under a series of mistaken assumptions that made war more palatable. Most obvious was that the war would

British reporter and pacifist author Norman Angell became famous for The Great Illusion *(1910), his book-length argument that war would ruin European economies. He was unable to prevent war, but did receive a Nobel Peace Prize in 1933 for his work. Courtesy of Library of Congress.*

be short. "Troops home by Christmas," was the presumption in Britain and France, maybe sooner. Some evidence could be found for this myth based on the previous major war fought in Europe. The Franco-Prussian war of 1870–1871 lasted just five months. Of course, this war had been fought more than 40 years prior to World War I. War technology at the apex of the machine age had become more thoroughly murderous. And the French, who lost the Franco-Prussian war, had become more militarily competent. Lord Kitchener, Britain's war secretary, spoke as one of the rare voices in power who declared that the boys wouldn't be home by Christmas, or anytime soon. But few believed him.

The tremendous firepower of modern armies seemed formidable on paper, but had never been tested in general war. True, the hideous

Russo-Japanese war of 1905 (losses: 210,000 people) could have given western leaders an inkling of what they would be facing. People weren't paying attention. Uniforms bore the gay colors of soldiers who fought a hundred years before in wars that (sometimes) offered a field of opportunity for glory and honor. Cavalry charges were readied to inspire the troops to break through the enemy's lines. Indeed, a war could offer a purification of the spirit, a noble sacrifice to remind the soldier and those at home of essential human virtue obscured by decades of decadent prosperity. Conscripts and volunteers poured to the mustering stations arm-in-arm with comrades and girlfriends, laughing, flowers in their buttonholes.

Of all the illusions that could be blamed for the enthusiasm in which Europe swarmed to the battlefields, the denial of modern war's reality was most pernicious. Millions of British, French, German, and Russian men drove toward each other carrying the sentiments of élan and the tactics of speed, huge human freight trains bearing down on each other on the same track. The result was no less explosive. Artillery barrages beat down from above as anonymous as a driving sleet of steel; the majority of soldiers died never seeing their attacker. Waves of attacking troops melted away under machine gun fire like butter in a hot pan. And what of noble sacrifice? About 400,000 men made that sacrifice in the first months of war. Only strict censorship in all fighting nations hid the truth from the home front. Governments feared that if the shocking toll were known, civilians would no longer support the war. But the truth crept in as nearly everyone lost a husband, a brother, a parent, or a friend. War was no longer a sporting challenge. But by then it was too late to stop.

Arguments that a militaristic society caused war became particularly popular in prewar America. The United States had no military power to speak of, not by world-class standards. The nation had not been militarily threatened since the Civil War. A strong thread of American pacifism reached through a variety of groups, religious, socialist, and immigrant—that last group formed of people who emigrated to avoid forced military service and frequent fighting in their home countries. The United States had no draft. It had no airplanes, no tanks, and few field guns or machine guns. Was this a good or bad thing? Good, claimed the pacifists: it was just this type of militarism, particularly in Germany, that led to the war.

The peace treaty of 1919 attempted to address warmongering militarism, particularly in Germany. Presumption that highly sophisticated German military schools and advanced armament works contributed to the war encouraged the victorious powers to strictly limit Germany's army and armament industry. It didn't work. The argument that World War I happened because Germany was built as a militaristic state gained credibility as yet another war loomed. On September 1, 1939, no one remained in doubt as to which country was to blame for the war.

General Discontent Blamed for War

Byron W. Holt: "The Prevention of the Fundamental Cause of War—Discontent"

The influence of progressive interpretations of historical events reached a zenith at the turn of the last century, 1900. It would be hardly surprising to see such a view applied to finding the underlying cause of World War I, to point to the clash between the wealthy and powerful and the poor and working class. Some historians do believe Germany became warlike in response to European powers attempting to stifle its expansion. It is more difficult to point to internal political conflict as a direct cause of war. In fact, those at the bottom of the privilege scale flocked as patriotically to the front as those of the governing classes.

***Popular Science*, January–June 1915**

It is because the economic foundations of most so-called civilized governments of to-day are unsound and rotten that our political structures are breaking down. That is why we have the present great war—a war centered in Europe but reaching to the remotest corners of the earth. It is because there are special privileges and special privilege takers and givers in Europe that millions of her bravest and best men are now killing each other. The share of the "grafters"—the land, tariff, patent and other special privilege grafters—became so large that production could no longer be profitably continued. The producers were in rebellion. They were voting for socialism and for other isms inimical to the ruling powers in the monopoly and military-ridden countries of Europe. Rents, debts and taxes became unbearably high; that is why, in my opinion, there is now, in Europe, the greatest and most hellish war of all time.

The crowned heads of Europe, and particularly of Germany and Austria, saw economic and political disaster ahead. Their only hope of continuing in power lay through warfare and the capturing of surrounding territory on which tribute could be levied. In no other way could wholesale repudiation of debts be much longer avoided.

Discontent, widespread, political discontent, and anarchy, are the forerunners of strife and wars, just as surely as happiness and contentment are the harbingers of peace and good-will.

Leaders Blamed for War

Editorial: "War and Public Opinion"

The author's contention that a militaristic German culture combined with political blunders could be blamed for war has in recent years seen renewed historical interest. Germany was indeed built on strong militaristic foundations. The country's first chancellor, Otto von Bismarck, who manipulated his country's foreign policy against powerful threats with the calculation of Bobby Fischer at a chessboard, resigned in 1890 following clashes with a headstrong (if lesser skilled) new king, 29-year-old Wilhelm II. Foreign policy blunders following Bismarck's departure helped to create the alliances that threatened Germany—particularly between Russia and France.

***Popular Science*, July–December 1914**

When public opinion in regard to war is as subject to emotional control, the way of wisdom is to avoid war and the conditions leading to war, even to the extent of holding that there never is a good war or a bad peace. The only gleam of hope in the present situation is that public sentiment in this country is against war and against the nations which, rightly or wrongly, are supposed to be the aggressors, and that each nation is anxious to disclaim responsibility for the existing chaos. In its inception the war was an affair of militarists and diplomatists, and Germany was unfortunate in combining these two classes in the same clique. All would have been different if there had been a Bismarck to whom the military machine was subordinated; there might have been war between Russia and Germany, but there would have been no European war. Conditions were better in Great Britain, and diplomacy tried to prevent war, but when war came then diplomacy had involved the people in its tricks.

Charles A'Court Repington: "The Direction of the War"

Repington became one of Britain's most important wartime journalists, known chiefly for exposing a scandal involving the manufacture of defective shells. Writing for the London Times, *he was able to bring his long military experience and extensive contacts to his sometimes caustic but insightful articles. His astute explanation of why German military and civilian leaders ought to be blamed for the war is extraordinarily prescient, given that information about German general staff meetings did not become available to scholars until the 1960s. His distaste of the preemptive war reflected general Western sensibilities at this time; also considered immoral were attacks on civilians, either on the sea or from the air. Subsequent experience of the horrors of World War II, followed by an evil plethora of terrorism and genocide throughout decades of world-wide strife, have considerably blunted today's sensibilities over what should be considered immoral war-making.*

Atlantic Monthly, August 1918

Opinions concerning the origin of the war and the responsibility attaching to various personages in various states for the outbreak of hostilities vary a good deal. My view is that the general staffs of the Central powers deliberately determined on what they called a preventive war, in order to forestall the moment when Russia's impending military reorganization was likely, if not certain, to prevent the accomplishment of those ambitious projects on which nearly all Germans of the ruling caste had set their hearts.

This view will, I think, be shared by those few who followed closely the game of military beggar-my-neighbor which was played in the war offices of Continental Europe in the years just preceding the fateful August of 1914. Military bill followed military bill in rapid succession. Germany, by her last effort in this sense before the war, had beaten everything that France could do; whereupon Russia, arriving late on the scene, outdid Germany by military projects so vast in their scope, and so far-reaching in their effects, had they been given time to mature, that the German General Staff held that it could not allow this event to happen, and determined upon a preventive war at some date in the neighborhood of January, 1913, when the nature of the Russian reforms became fully known. A pretext was soon found in the Austrian Archduke's murder at Serajevo; and from that moment until all Europe was aflame the Germans steadily blocked all practicable avenues to peace.

A preventive war is the most immoral of acts and the most detestable of political crimes. To drench the world in blood because something may happen which has not happened, is both criminal and foolish; and so it was always considered by Bismarck, who left on record his abhorrence of a preventive war. When a power is in a position, or feels that it may be in a position, of military inferiority in relation to rivals, it can set its diplomacy at work; and there are many chances that some turn of fortune's wheel will bring about a change in the general situation. The friendships and enmities of states are not permanent, but evanescent. In our time we have seen the most kaleidoscopic changes in international relations, and history is full of them. Do not the episodes of this war suggest that, if Germany had left well alone, she would have accomplished more by peaceful intercourse than she has gained in arms? Is it not probably that her bugbear, Russia, would have been soon transformed into a democratic state, from which no military aggression was to be feared? Has the preventive war been worth while? who can affirm it? It is a question only whether it was most criminal or most foolish.

Armaments Blamed for War

Charles Edward Jefferson, D.D.: "The Nemesis of Armaments"

Whether to consider the prewar European armaments race as a principal cause of the war became a question of major debate in the United States before 1917. The question was particularly pertinent as groups squared off for debate on whether America itself, which in 1914 was lightly armed and not committed to large-scale arms development, ought to follow Europe's lead to prepare for a dangerous new era.

***Independent,* August 17, 1914**

"Armaments are a form of national insurance." The doctrine has been promulgated thruout the world. The insurance comes high, but we must have it. A man insures his house; a nation must insure itself. Compare the annual cost of an army and navy with the aggregate wealth of a country, and any one can see that military and naval expenses are a mere bagatelle.

Six nations of Europe went into this scheme of insurance. Within the last thirty years they have paid in premiums six billion, five hundred and ninety-two millions of dollars, and now they find they are not insured at all.

Some fool in southeastern Europe threw a lighted match, and instantly all Europe was in flames. Why? The whole house had been saturated with kerosene.

Military and naval budgets are not insurance, they are kerosene. Their function is to render a nation inflammable. Europe had been so repeatedly drenched with kerosene that one match was sufficient to start an instantaneous and continent-wide conflagration: Russians, Germans, Frenchmen, Englishmen all heard at once the roar of the blazing rafters above their heads. The house is burning, and now other billions of dollars must be expended in putting out a fire which was made possible by the very means which were devised to prevent it.

Fate Blamed for War

Hermann Keyserling: "A Philosopher's View of the War"

War has been a scourge of all human history, defining countries and creating monarchies while desecrating humanity. Are human beings, then, instinctively drawn to killing each other? Is war truly inevitable? Woodrow Wilson, a philosophical idealist whose view of a better future stood on strong principles of religion and ethics, intrinsically believed that it was not. World War I was to become "the war to end all wars," a mandate accepted by both the troops on the battlefield and the proponents at home. Wilson hoped a League of Nations could enforce this ideal. It failed. The hope of so many proved to be another great illusion, as the war to end all wars turned out instead to be the mother of wars throughout the rest of the century, even beyond.

***Atlantic Monthly*, February 1916**

All great wars are truly fated. It is of little importance what immediate set of causes occasioned them. Had Germany's conscious intentions been never so kind and her official morale never so exemplary, the mere fact of her gas-like expansion within a world packed with aggressive traditions, whose equilibrium depended on opposition instead of collaboration, would sooner or later have caused conflict; which in turn would inevitably have expanded into a world-war, because in this age of universal interdependence any serious shock to one larger part of the whole must needs upset the whole. Germany's ambitions were no more than the premium movers of this catastrophe than were Bonaparte's dreams of world power the first cause of that of a century ago.

It is certainly true, that Napoleon always maintained that his was not a premeditated career; it is surely as true, that the Germans never strove consciously to set the world on fire; both were driven to act as they did by circumstances over which they had no command. Again, in both cases the revolutions would have happened, in some form or other, if the immediate causes we perceive had not been acting; the ancient regime would have fallen, in all Western Europe, without the Corsican's sword; the European equilibrium of yesterday would have upset without the pressure brought to bear from within by German armaments, because both events were due in any case as inevitable stages in evolution.

Professor G.T.W. Patrick, University of Iowa: "The Psychology of War"

Modern writers have often assumed that the popularity of competitive sports can be explained because humanity is instinctively warlike, and sports as a sort of stylized battle can act as a temporary substitute. World War I certainly broke into a Western world primed with violent attitudes: the cult of the duel as a defense of honor had seen popular acceptance all over Europe, despite official discouragement. A principle of courage and aggressive, "manly" fights encouraged many to perceive war as a purification and renewal rather than evil. The baleful anonymity of death on this war's trenches and battlefields tempered this kind of spirit in most Western nations, as the duel lost its luster and the ideal of a purifying war became obscene cant.

Popular Science, July–December 1915

Ever since the war began, sociologists, economists, philosophers and political theorists have tried their hands at explaining the causes of the war and with small success. Its roots must be sought in psychology and anthropology.

To those acquainted with the psychology of play and sport, war is more easily understood. The high tension of the modern work-a-day life must be periodically relieved by a return to primitive forms of behavior, as in football, baseball, hunting, fishing, horseracing, the circus, the arena, the cock-fight, and the prize-fight, and the countless forms of outing. Man must once again use his arms, his legs, his larger muscles, his lower brain centers. He must live again in the open, by the camp-fire, by the stream, in the forest. He must kill something, be it fish or bird or deer, as his ancestors did in times remote. Thereafter come peace and harmony and he is ready once more to return to the life of the intellect and will, to the life of "efficiency."

Periodically, however, man seems to need a deeper plunge into the primeval and this is war. War has always been the release of nations from the tension of progress. Man is a fighting animal; at first from necessity, afterwards from habit. In former centuries when the contrast between peace and war was not so great, it was undertaken with more ease and less apology, almost as a matter of course. Life was less intense then and the reaction of war less extreme. Now in the face of an advanced public sentiment, of peace societies and arbitration hoards, the tension has to become very great, the potential very high before the spark is truck and, when this happens, we have the ludicrous spectacle of the warring nations apologizing and explaining to an astonished world.

War, therefore, seems to act as a kind of kartharsis. The warring nation is purified by war and thereafter with a spirit chastened and purged enters again upon the upward way to attain still greater heights of progress.

Capitalism Blamed for War

A British Officer: "Radical's Progress"

Antiwar warnings to Americans from the war's witnesses in the trenches often sprinkled through the country's as-yet uncensored press. But these horrific descriptions could not upset prowar Americans who believed Germany had offended the United States in particular, and the civilized world in general, and must be stopped no matter what the cost. The presumption that capitalist greed caused the war was most common in America's Midwest, at this time a center of socialist ferment based on agrarian immigrants often treated unfairly by eastern industrialists. North Dakota's rural activists supported their home-grown Non-Partisan League, so strong during this era that it ran the state government and spread its antiwar attitude throughout the region. Most historians are convinced, however, that capitalist greed cannot be held responsible for the war. Industrialists were opposed to a conflict that disrupted the growth of international trade, even if some of them eventually profited.

***Atlantic Monthly*, February 1916**

The narrative which follows is made up of letters written by an officer of the British merchant marine to an American friend in close sympathy with the creed they formulate. These letters cover a correspondence of many years, the earlier dating from the South African War, where the writer distinguished himself by his courage in action, and some of the later from the Dardanelles campaign, which found him serving as chief officer of one of his Britannic Majesty's transports. The order in which the letters are printed has been designed by the person who received and arranged them to throw into relief the writers' Progressive views toward Socialism; but no liberties have been taken with the text. to an individualist, it is interesting to note that the degree of tense social control now exerted by the state in Great Britain may drive a Socialist into the kind of revolt usually associated with individualistic doctrine. We may add that the writer has been known to the editor of the Atlantic for many years through much correspondence and many talks. We can vouch for the genuineness of the letters.

—The Editors.

How would any one of your American jingoes like to be twenty-seven years old with both eyes shot out and both wrists shattered by shrapnel? The man I mean was a young Scot. I helped him up the gangway. He stood six feet three—a beautiful specimen of physical manhood. After a day aboard he suffered terrible torture from the heat of the weather and of the ship, and also from the swarms of flies attracted by the smell of blood. He could not lie on a cot, so we had to fence off a corner in the 'tween decks, carpet it with pillows and mattresses, and let him grope round in his agony. On the spots were the blood had soaked through his eye- and wrist-bandages the flies clustered in black clots. He moaned night and day and was scarcely conscious. He was totally blind, and even the sense of touch was denied him, because his wrists were so shattered that they would have to be amputated.

Another man—a Lancashire Fusilier—was shot in the intestines. His torture was frightful. He raved like an animal and died in agony.

The majority of the wounded men were unconscious, and died so.

One evening I buried twenty-seven of the best my country ever produced, all Scots fusiliers. The words, "We therefore commit his body to the deep" are graven on my very soul. It is at this part of the service that the body is slid overboard. For full an hour after this first burial, the thought of these countrymen of mine being sewn up in blankets and dumped overboard like so many bundles of rubbish—I had a terrible craving to get at the throats of the capitalists and jingoes who are responsible for it all. Submarine commanders cannot be blamed for sinking Lusitania. They are simply doing their jobs and obeying orders. Those who issue such orders cannot be got at; at least, not yet.

Day after day these burials went on. Later I refused to attend them. The finish came when one body stuck to the stretcher by reason of the blood having oozed through the wrappings and congealed. The body had to be pried adrift before it would slide of its own weight into the sea.

I cannot tell you any more just yet. I sicken as I write.

The stupidity of it all!—the wrong men doing the fighting and bearing all the suffering. Kindly-hearted fathers killing other kindly-hearted fathers at the behest of—whom? One cases to wonder if mothers in the future will ask why they should go through nine months of labor and then rear children—for this. I should like to have had a few thousands of American mothers on the quay at Alexandria every time we discharged our freight of managed humanity. Or, better still, those in your country who are clamoring for war: let them volunteer to come over as stretcher-bearers only.

Colonialism Blamed for War

Editorial, W.E.B. Du Bois: "World War and the Color Line"

W.E.B. Du Bois, one of the country's most influential early civil rights leaders, edited the Crisis *for 25 years, a publication sponsored by the National*

Association for the Advancement of Colored People (NAACP). His caustic and angry commentary reflected what he saw as a despicable irony that Woodrow Wilson was claiming world moral leadership of the United States while doing nothing to combat vicious racism and lynchings at home. Du Bois came to see that oppression of non-white races was not simply an American question, but a worldwide concern, as colonial powers were themselves racist at base in their occupation of mostly "dark-skinned" nations. After the war he sailed to France to observe the treaty process as the NAACP representative.

Crisis, November 1914

The present war in Europe is one of the great disasters due to race and color prejudice and it but foreshadows greater disasters in the future.

It is not merely national jealousy, or the so-called "race" rivalry of Slav, Teuton and Latin, that is the larger cause of this war. It is rather the wild quest for Imperial expansion among color races between Germany, England and France primarily, and Belgium, Italy, Russia and Austria-Hungary in lesser degree. Germany long since found herself shut out from acquiring colonies. She looked toward South America, but the "Monroe Doctrine" stood in her way. She started for Africa and by bulldozing methods secured one good colony, one desert and two swamps. Her last efforts looked toward North Africa and Asia-Minor. Finally, she evidently decided at the first opportunity to seize English or French colonies and to this end feverishly expanded her navy, kept her army at the highest point of efficiency and has been for twenty years the bully of Europe with a chip on her shoulder and defiance in her mouth.

The colonies which England and France own and Germany covets are largely in tropical and semi-tropical lands and inhabited by black, brown and yellow peoples. In such colonies there is a chance to confiscate land, work the natives at low wages, and make large profits and open wide markets for cheap European manufactures. . . .

As colored Americans, then, and as Americans who fear race prejudice as the greatest of war-makers, our sympathies in the awful conflict should be with France and England; not that they have conquered race prejudice, but they have at least begun to realize its cost and evil, while Germany exalts it.

Questions

1. European rivalry for colonial control of many African nations before World War I has been blamed as a cause of the war. How could this

form the basis of W.E.B. Du Bois's argument that the underlying cause of World War I was Western racism?

2. Ethical standards of war have changed in the decades since World War I ended. Today nations including the United States have engaged in what Repington would call a preventative war, and have accepted high civilian casualties. Why do today's dangers seem to obligate democratic nations to adopt different ethical standards from those common at the last century's turn, around 1900?
3. Is it possible, as many hoped at the end of World War I, to find a way to end all wars in the world? Or at least a way to avoid another world war? How?
4. Corporations generally oppose war because it disrupts trade and often costs money in taxes, lower demand for many manufactured products, and fewer affluent buyers willing to indulge in luxuries during a time of sacrifice. But not all businesses suffer from war. Besides armaments dealers, which businesses might benefit?

Chapter 4

The Atrocities of War

One key to understanding why neutral, isolationist America turned against Germany in World War I is the atrocity stories. These tales of shocking treatment perpetrated by German soldiers against innocent civilians mixed fact, exaggeration, and pure fiction into a toxic brew of propaganda certain to outrage even the most stern supporter of strict neutrality. If an American were unsure whether to believe British and French claims that the enemy truly was behaving in a beastly manner, then he had only to listen to those who saw and told their stories. Most story-tellers were Belgian refugees. About 15 percent of Belgium's 7.5 million people fled advancing German troops in August 1914. They supplied eager allied debriefers with a litany of reports documenting the German executions of civilians and deliberate destruction; some specific instances of brutality were truly inhuman. Stories most repeated among the allies and neutrals came from witnesses who said German troops rounded up babies and cut off their hands. Sometimes whole nurseries would be filled with handless babies. A second common and lurid atrocity story told of not only the usual rapes but also of German soldiers chopping off women's breasts. A British woman actually was able to produce a farewell letter from her sister in Belgium who had experienced this horrific act—a letter later proven to be a forgery. A third common story asserted that Belgian priests had been tied to their church bells as human clappers. But the most offensive story of all involved soap and tallow; Germans were purportedly shipping the dead from the battlefields to rendering plants.

All four common stories were found after the war to be fabrications. Common sense might have indicated that some could not be possible. A nursery of handless babies? How would they possibly survive more than a few minutes without extensive surgery? In 1928 Arthur Ponsonby published an influential book, *Falsehood in War-Time,* which debunked most of the atrocity stories. People realized they had been duped into supporting a war built on lies. Noted a December 6, 1926, editorial in the Richmond, Virginia, *Times-Dispatch*, "These frank admissions of wholesale lying on the part of trusted governments in the last war will not soon be forgotten." Even during the war the Committee on Public Information, set up by the U.S. government to promote the war, was hesitant about transmitting extreme atrocity stories that could fan anti-German anger with possibly dangerous consequences against German-Americans at home. Decades of historians followed Ponsonby's lead in presuming all the atrocity stories were made up.

But were they? Recent historiography has taken a new look at atrocities supposedly well documented during the war, and has found that those who swore the stories were true may have been credible, at least sometimes, and in some places. That doesn't mean that Germany alone need shoulder blame. During World War I no invading army behaved perfectly when faced with hostile civilians threatening resistance by sniper and booby trap. While Germans did not mutilate babies and women, victimize priests, or render human beings into fat, they did in fact execute 5,500 Belgians during the first two months of occupation, did engage in collective executions, and did deliberately burn buildings. However, the Russians did no better, and accounts of mutilations perpetrated by the Russian army are so credible that they likely did occur. Stories of babies impaled on bayonets, of attackers raping and blinding their victims, and of summary executions flowed from the eastern fronts as well as battlefields in the Balkans. Truth of terrible mutilations from those fronts melded with some brutal incidents in the north to paint Germany with one bloody brush.

France and Britain escaped charges of atrocities. But that may not have been based on their perceived abundance of morality. These allies occupied very little enemy territory and thus had few opportunities to perpetrate such unfortunate incidents.

Atrocity charges moved beyond specific actions by soldiers in the field and into strategic decisions made by generals or even civilian politicians. Germany did bomb civilian Paris. It did execute a British nurse as a spy. But were these truly atrocities? The spy was named Edith Cavell and she worked in Belgium as a nurse when war broke out. She perceived it to be her patriotic necessity to refuse evacuation to England and stayed in Belgium and tend to her duties. Those duties included not only nursing, but also helping to arrange escapes for allied prisoners of war caught in the German occupation. This, as everyone knew, was action subject to trial and execution in all belligerent nations. Germany duly tried Cavell, and duly executed her, not anticipating the fuel it would offer to allied propagandists. Protests from Berlin that Cavell knew what she was doing, was fairly tried, and clearly was a spy subject to execution in any wartime nation could not overcome the allied stories of "poor Edith Cavell," the helpless woman who served to appease the brutal blood lust of a heartless conqueror. The story was told that as she was being led to execution, she fainted, and the vile Germans shot her right there on the ground. Except that they didn't. No matter; a major part of the atrocity story industry was the ability to grow fiction from a kernel of truth.

Did allied countries execute women as spies? Certainly. Two years later France executed exotic dancer Mata Hari who was accused of being a double agent. While Cavell was undoubtedly guilty, Hari's guilt was less certain. Even today historians believe she may have been innocent and unfortunately fell into the frenzied swirl of wartime intrigue and intolerance. When thousands are killed every day on the battlefields, life becomes cheap and the bar of evidence for guilt drops. But Germany was not able to exploit Hari's death for its propaganda. During war, spies, after all, are executed.

During the interwar period, disillusioned Americans blamed the false propaganda of World War I for stirring up irrational frenzy in support of a war that America shouldn't have fought. This disillusionment led to personal and public affirmations that "we're not going to be fooled again." In 1933 Adolph Hitler rose to power in Germany. New atrocities stories flowed from Europe. As in the Aesop's fable of the boy who cried wolf, Americans were slow to believe. This time the stories proved to be only too tragically true.

Outrage over Atrocities

Anonymous: "The Chant of the German Sword"

Realization that armies could target civilians shocked decent-minded Americans in 1914. Armies fought only other armed soldiers, critics contended. Soldiers reacted to hapless civilians with kindly respect. Germany's 1914 fear of surreptitious reprisals in Belgium produced a bloody response that may indeed have been an overreaction, but Berlin defended its rationale, pointing out the danger of civilian snipers and terrorists. Also defended was Germany's rationale for torpedoing civilian liners such as the Lusitania. Berlin argued that the ship was carrying munitions for Britain, so blame fell not on Germany but on a cynical British government. The shelling of Paris in 1918 was less defensible, but the pattern was set; civilians were no longer off limits. Despite the stories, few of the estimated 10 million people killed in World War I were noncombatants.

***New York Times Current History*, October 1915–March 1916**

It is no duty of mine to be either just or compassionate; it suffices that I am sanctified by my exalted mission, and that I blind the eyes of my enemies with such streams of tears as shall make the proudest of them cringe in terror under the vault of heaven.

I have slaughtered the old and the sorrowing; I have struck off the breasts of women; and I have run through the bodies of children who gazed at me with the eyes of the wounded lion.

Day after day I ride aloft on the shadowy horse in the valley of Cypresses, and as I ride I draw forth the life blood from every enemy's son that dares dispute my path.

It is meet and right that I should cry aloud my pride, for am I not the flaming messenger of the Lord Almighty?

Germany is so far above and beyond all the other nations that all the rest of earth, be they who they may, should feel themselves well done by when they are allowed to fight with the dogs for the crumbs that fall from her table.

When Germany the divine is happy, then the rest of the world basks in smiles; but when Germany suffers, God in person is rent with anguish, and, wrathful and avenging, He turns all the waters into rivers of blood.

Vernon Kellogg: "At Von Bissing's Headquarters"

The more extreme atrocity stories of baby and female mutilation were shocking. But more restrained U.S. journalists did not wish to promulgate what was to many educated Americans clearly absurd. In a journalistic era when facts mattered, the press sometimes did try to ascertain the truth. Undoubtedly the description here could be well authenticated. It could perhaps be argued that Germans in World War I (and again in World War II) were the first to deliberately target civilians. But allied bombing of Dresden and Hiroshima toward the end of World War II affirmed a modern standard that any living thing, elderly, woman, child, infant, or dog, was from now on a legitimate target of war.

***Atlantic Monthly*, October 1917**

However, a pacifist, or a neutral, is hardly to be made into an adherent of a war against any people on the basis of being ever so convinced of the stupidity of that people's form of government, or because of an ego-maniacal overestimate, on the part of this people, of its form of Kultur. And it was something more than any conviction of this kind that turned our group of American neutrals in German-occupied Belgium and North France into a shocked, then bitter, and finally blazing band of men wishing to slay or be slain, if necessary, to prevent the repetition anywhere of the things they had to see done in those tortured lands.

The Germans entered Belgium in August and September, 1914; we began to come in November. Hence we saw none of the "atrocities" of the invasion—we saw only the results of them. Among these results, as seen by use, were, I hasten to say, no women without breasts or children without hands. But there were women without husbands and sons and daughters, and children without mothers and fathers. There were families without homes, farms without cattle or horses or houses, towns without town halls and churches and most of the other buildings, and even some without any buildings at all, and a few without many citizens. But there were cemeteries with scores and hundreds of new graves—not of soldiers; and little toddling children who came up eagerly to you, saying, Mon père est mort; ma mère est morte." They were distinguished from some of their playmates by this, you see!

Anonymous: "Austrian Atrocities in Serbia: A Policy of Extermination"

Postwar research cast doubt on the more extreme claims of torture in Belgium, but harrowing stories from southern Europe can not be discounted. The account here presages the horror that became commonplace in Nazi-occupied countries two decades later. Reference to Cerberus, the mythical Greek beast that guarded the gates of the underworld, must have made a vivid image to the educated of a generation steeped in classical literature, just as perhaps today's readers would identify with the repulsive monsters of the movie series "Alien".

New York Times Current History, October 1917–March 1918

In the Autumn of 1917 Dr. Tresic Pavicic, a Jugo-Slav Deputy, delivered a speech in the Vienna Parliament giving the most revolting details of the atrocities committed against Serbians. It publication in the Austro-Hungarian press was forbidden, but a portion of it got into a Croatian paper, and from this it was translated and forwarded to England by Reuter's Agency, with endorsement as to its authenticity. . . .

The fate of those shut up at Mostar, Doboj, and Arad was much more terrible, said Dr. Pavicic, who then proceeded to give the narratives of two survivors—one a publicist and the other a Deputy—as follows:

Story of Two Survivors

At Mostar we were thrown into underground cells with robbers, brigands, and gypsies. There, on the foul soil, we were supposed to move, sleep, and eat. In this den the most terrible man was the jailer, Gaspar Scholier. Armed with a hooked baton of iron, which he called "Kronprinz," he visited his captives all too often, to strike them recklessly with his "Kronprinz" on the head and shoulders. I do not repeat the bestial curses, the satanic shouts of this monster. Only with money could one calm for a moment the fury of this Cerberus.

Among these unfortunates was Rinda Radulovitch, editor of the Nation, (Narod) and the Orthodox priest Tichy, who died at Arad, in Hungary, as a result of all the tortures inflicted upon him by this ferocious beast, who literally tore his flesh from him with his iron baton. He would come among his victims at night and choose fresh subjects for torture. Those who wished to prolong this existence had to hold up their hands and show how many banknotes they were ready to pay. Hundreds died.

At Doboj things were still worse. Along with Serbian and Montenegrin prisoners came crowds of civilians, old men, women, and children, driven from home—forced to travel in open cattle trucks. Hunger was found to be the simplest and cheapest means of sending these people to another world. Women with four or five children were given a soldier's loaf to last them five days. Often a mother would be already dead when her little one shook her to wake her to ask for bread. At first from fifteen to twenty of these persons died daily, but later there died on one day alone ninety-two. Trustworthy approximate figures show that more than 8,000 innocent victims met their death in this place.

Defense of Atrocities

Editorial: "Dum-Dum Bullets and Human Nature"

Hollow-point or soft-point bullets have excited controversy since their development by the British in India at the end of the nineteenth century. These bullets expand on impact, compounding damage to surrounding organs and tissues. Proponents have argued that not only do they protect a defender with enhanced "stopping power," they are less likely to pass through a body and injure innocent bystanders. Nevertheless, they were declared illegal in warfare by the rules of the 1899 Hague Convention (a series of meetings that regulated the rules of warfare).

Independent, October 12, 1914

Already there have been hurled back and forth across the frontiers of Europe accusations that each of the participants in the Great War is using dum-dum bullets. This is nothing new. The same thing has happened in every war since the dum-dum was invented.

It were well not to take these charges and counter charges too seriously. They sound too much like the bitter accusations that fly about wherever boys indulge in the mimic warfare that makes up so much of their play. The cry of "You're another" is seldom convincing.

It were well also not to believe implicitly the charges of sporadic cruelty and pillage that are rife, especially against the Germans. We hear more of those made against them because we get more news of all kinds from the Allies than from the other side. . . .

War is brutal business. It would be matter for wonder if in great armies, made up of mere men, war did not brutalize many and cause them to revert to habits of barbarism. No general indictment should be framed against any nation in the Great War because of the individual acts of cruelty and bestiality of individual men.

The sack of Louvain and the bombardment of the Cathedral at Rheims stand on a different footing. These were deliberate, official acts not of individuals but of the German Army. For them the German nation must answer to the world. But news of sporadic outrages should be accepted with reserve, interpreted in the light of the inherent cruelty of war, ascribed not to the deliberate barbarity of a nation, but to the pitiable weakness of individual human nature.

Oliver Madox Hueffer: "The Savage Civilian"

After the declaration of war, those in Europe who clung to a shred of reason when considering the enemy were shouted into silence. Woodrow Wilson feared the same thing would happen in the United States. Although it could not be helped, the Committee on Public Information did try to control the most sensational stories likely to whip an angry and fearful wartime population into a possibly dangerous frenzy. Those in America who continued to voice mild protests that the "Huns" may possibly be human beings found themselves not only shunned and humiliated but, if their opinion could be perceived as treason, fined and jailed.

***Nation,* December 3, 1914**

I was at a dinner-party in London a few weeks ago and very tactlessly put forward some mild expression of my belief that the Germans were very probably human beings after all, and that the stories of their atrocities might be exaggerated. Nobody hit me, but I happened to meet next day in Lower Sloane Street the lady next to whom I had been sitting, an acquaintance of some years. She crossed the road to tell me that if I was a traitor to my country I might have the decency to keep it to myself.

Now, it is a curious fact that just as the Dutch husband of the war-like lady agreed with me that the British had not committed atrocities in South Africa, so a man at the English dinner-table who was a soldier at the front entirely agreed that the Germans made a very decent foe, all things considered, and that their "atrocities" were, if not altogether invented, very much exaggerated. I have not dined with any German ladies since the war broke out, but I have very little doubt that, if any German suggested that the English, the Russians, the French, or the Belgians were not blood-stained murderers, plunders, and ravishers, he would be promptly taken to task as was I myself.

Gottlieb von Jagow, German Secretary of State of Foreign Affairs: "Are Americans Fair to Germany?"

Aerial attacks by biplane on civilian targets occasioned protests on both sides, but in World War I did little damage compared to their devastating effects during World War II. The German long-range bombing of Paris in 1918 did cause several score of civilian deaths, shot from a remarkable large-caliber gun that was brought forward by rail. It propelled a shell nearly into space—a real wonder of German war engineering. German protest that Britain's naval blockade also punished innocent civilians certainly is true. German food shortages during the 1917 "turnip winter" are correctly blamed for the death of thousands. But Americans did not see the consequences of such a slowly effective "atrocity" as they did the immediate effects of shells and torpedoes.

New York Times Current History, April–September 1916

When our Zeppelins attack London, which is a fortified city defended with cannon, full of soldiers and prepared as far as it can be to resist attack of land or air, the American papers teem with the most vitriolic articles about the "Huns." When the airmen of the Allies attack absolutely unprotected German towns and villages without one cannon or one soldier in them and kill old men, women, and children, your papers are either silent or else they give a carefully expurgated account, without bitter criticism therein, and, much more significant, the letters which appear in the American newspapers, signed by readers of the papers, exhibit (in the main) only horror at our legitimate aerial warfare and none at the entirely unjustifiable conduct of our opponents.

Also by prohibiting absolutely the importation of fodder necessary to enable our cows to furnish milk of a good quality Great Britain is warring on the little children of Germany, and when philanthropic people in the United States, who wish to help the children, desire to ship milk for their use, Great Britain interposes its sea veto. Our children are fully as dear to us as the children of Americans are to them. What do the press and the people of the United States really think of a warfare directed against little children?

J. Mandery, Rochester, N.Y., Letter to the Editor: "In Defense of the Kaiser"

Section II, Article 10 of the Hague Convention on war signed in 1910 clearly stated, "It is especially forbidden to employ poison or poisoned weapons." But that article was one of many violated during the Great War, as expediency had no bounds against a barbarian enemy presumed to be evil incarnate. Who was first to roll out the chlorine gas really didn't matter (although Germany is given the credit, on the Ypres battlefield, in 1915), as all armies soon found poison gas to be just one more tool available when necessary. Article 23 of the Hague Convention stated that it was also forbidden "to employ arms, projectiles, or material calculated to cause unnecessary suffering." It is hard to say that the horrific wounds left by shells were any more humane than those left by the more controversial poison gas or dum-dum bullets.

North American Review, July 1915

Sir—May I be permitted to make a few remarks on the article about the Kaiser by Allan McLane Hamilton, M.D., LL.D., in your June number?

He says on page 875, "He it is who receives such promptings, suggestions, and orders from God that lead him to make ridiculous proclamations and to direct his army to violate all the rules of civilized warfare."

I understood that when the "contract" regarding Belgium was broken, self-defense and necessity were given as the cause. I have not read anywhere that the Kaiser stated he was guided by "such promptings." And I have not seen any "ridiculous proclamations" purporting to be verified by the Kaiser.

There are citizens of the United States who break contracts without the excuse of self-defense or necessity. . . .

I doubt if the methods of German warfare, examined in the light of history and the facts of warfare by the English, for instance, are at all extraordinary. As far as using poisonous gas is concerned, I understand that French introduced poisonous gas, but were merely not so successful in its use. It would seem that in this particular instance the Emperor was slightly justified in his self-conceit. And just the other evening I saw an advertisement in the American Machinist which told of the superior quality of the ammunition it advertised over that of other ammunition of the same kind, and, if I am not greatly mistaken, the superiority consisted of merely in its greater effectiveness. Is not that considered the most important thing in ammunition of all kinds? When men begin to make war, are they inclined to use the less effective methods of killing their enemies, especially if the same method was introduced, though less effectively, by their enemies?

Just because you are different from me does not prove that you are insane, or vice versa, does it?

William Lyon Phelps, Professor of English Literature, Yale University: "War"

While the vast majority in all belligerent states flocked enthusiastically, even light-heartedly, to support each government's call to war, not everyone was fooled about what they would encounter. Lord Kitchener in Britain warned that the war would be arduous. A few editors in the south of France, far from the battlefields, called the war "an abominable nightmare, a catastrophe." That attitude was shared by many Americans in 1914. But by 1917 the grim realities of war had been overtaken by the patriotic fervor that prescribed duty in opposing what had become the "Hunnish hordes."

***North American Review*, November 1914**

It is absurd to deny that there have been cruel outrages in Belgium and France; just as absurd as it would be to suppose that there will be no outrages in Germany if the allied forces occupy that country. It is equally absurd to express surprise or horror at these events. They are a necessary part of the horror of war, and invariably follow it. War means murder and destruction on the largest possible scale. There is nothing beautiful about it; nothing fine; nothing admirable; nothing noble. Why lift up the hands in amazed protest when bombs are dropped on cities and women slaughtered by soldiers? These things are a natural part of war. Is there any torture for a woman worse than the murder of her son? If both parties in this conflict rejoice when they murder a particularly large number of young men, why should any one be astonished or grieved at the murder of old men, children, or women?

War means that so-called civilized nations have relapsed into barbarism, and that formerly rational and peaceful citizens have become frenzied demons. Does any one suppose, when a million armed men bent on murder and destruction occupy a country they are endeavoring to destroy, that courtesy, gentleness, consideration, are the words to describe their conduct? War is now what it always has been, not a courteous joint debate, but hell on earth.

Oswald Garrison Villard: "Germany Embattled: An American Interpretation"

American culture is inclined to support the underdog. This may have contributed to easy acceptance of British propaganda, which painted the agony of "poor little Belgium." Evidence is strong, however, that the atrocities perpetrated by German troops did not stem from basic animosity for anything Belgian, but from sabotage and threats carried out against them by the Belgians. Certainly some German response surpassed the boundaries of decent behavior, even during wartime; Germany cannot be let off the hook for helping to define twentieth-century brutality. No matter how much apologists tried to explain it away, most Americans just could not swallow Germany's occupation of a small neutral nation that decided to take a stand against the world's greatest military power.

***Scribner's*, December 1914**

Nothing to Germans could be worse than these slanders save what they themselves tell of the Belgians, of furies in skirts putting out with cork-screws the eyes of helpless German wounded and pouring boiling water upon them; of uniformed citizens shooting out of cellars and from attic windows, and rising treacherously, as in Louvain, when led by priests and professors. Nothing surprises them more than that any one should look upon the burning of Louvain as else than a just punishment for acts directly contrary to the laws of war. When their own villages have been shot to pieces and burned by Russians without its creating an outcry in America, they cannot see why the burning of Belgian villages, the natural result of shelling troops out of them, should seem anything else than an ordinary incident of war, the hell that is war that they, under their Prussian generals, propose to make so terrible a hell by legitimate severity that their enemies will soon submit.

The fact that the Belgians lied to all the world about Liege, and similar misrepresentations, the Germans are ready of bear with as part of the game. But not the calumnies of their troops, as if they were Bulgarians or Serbs or Greek marauders. That is the last straw, and the head-lines, "Wir Barbaren," "Wir Unmenschen," now appearing in the German press over records of British and French prisoners' appreciation of their kindly treatment testify to the hurt inflicted. And so we have the German professor spurning their British decorations and academic honors, and the terrible prospect that between these two Teuton nations, which ought to be the best of friends, there will exist at the end of the war, whatever the outcome, a bitterness and a hatred beside which the latent hostility of French and Germans since 1870 will seem mere childish irritation. The Germans simply cannot understand when they hear that Englishmen of German names are changing them because, as in one recorded case, they say that the Germans have been carrying on war "contrary to every dictate of humanity."

Charles Frederick Carter: "Atrocities in War"

Charles Frederick Carter reminded Americans that so much of the beastly behavior pinned on Germany could also be pinned on some of the country's own troops during the Civil War, and after, during the Indian Wars. Civil War general William T. Sherman's "March to the Sea" terrorized defenseless civilians in Georgia and South Carolina, a strategy expressly designed to bring about collapse on the home front—just as the German bombing of Paris was designed to hasten the disintegration of French morale. When battles become "total war," demanding participation of civilian forces as well as soldiers, those at home also become possible targets.

World's Work, November 1914

An important point to be borne in mind is that what is readily part and parcel of warfare is denounced as abuse and atrocity. Sherman never coined the aphorism so frequently attributed to him, though he did his honest best to make war fit his alleged definition. What he did say was, "war is cruelty; and you cannot refine it." Napier said, "War is hellish work." Both understated the fact.

Massacre of Non-Combatants "Legitimate"

For example, the Germans were within their rights in destroying Louvain and massacring its male inhabitants if the latter fired upon German soldiers, as the latter allege. The Hague Regulations, so often paraded as the loftiest expression of the world's awakened conscience, sanctions the course of the Germans, always assuming that their contention is correct. And as all the competent witnesses for the Belgians are dead, the Germans clearly have the best of the argument.

Anonymous, "The World War"

Editors of the country's most prominent African American press, such as W.E.B. Du Bois and Robert S. Abbott, repeatedly reminded Americans that outrage for atrocity ought to begin at home. Lynchings of black Americans, predominantly in the South, occasionally drifted to major northern cities, and reached a zenith of hundreds a year during the first third of the century. The perpetrators, no less than home-grown terrorists, were seldom punished because rampant racism presumed that "colored folk" were likely guilty of whatever crime they were or were not supposed to have committed and were not worth the trouble to defend. These true atrocities against African Americans contributed to their mass exodus from the South to northern cities during and after World War I.

Crisis, November 1914

But the Independent [newspaper] acknowledges our guilt:

"That this is a barbarous country in spots is undeniable when we learn that in 1913 as many as 79 colored men and women were killed by mobs, lynched without trial. The crimes charged against them were various, some serious, others trivial. Some of the victims were doubtless innocent. the figures prove a shocking degree of barbarism to exist with us; and the only relief we find is that there is a pretty steady decrease in the number. In 1892 there were 155 lynched, and 154 the next year. At this rate of decrease we may be quite civilized 20 years from now. There have been only 22 lynchings in the first six months of the present year."

And the Boston Traveler and Evening Herald, adds:

"Here is a record of atrocities for which we venture to say no parallel can be found in any of the 'barbarous' nations now at war, and compared with which the atrocities charged against the German soldiers would appear for the most part as trifling indiscretions incident to the heat of war.

"Before we throw any more stones at the Germans, let us be sure we are not living in a glass house. If war is what Sherman said it was, it is natural to expect a few human devils in an army of three or four millions of men engaged in deadly conflict; but who would expect to find mobs of human devils at work in times of peace at the very feet of Liberty Enlightening the World?"

Cavell Execution Defended

Franklin Edgerton, Philadelphia, Letter to the Editor: "The Case of Miss Cavell"

One reason neutral sentiment weakened over the German execution of Edith Cavell was probably because she was a female caregiver. She was easily portrayed by British propaganda as an unwitting innocent caught in the callous grip of the foul occupier. France's later execution of Mata Hari, also a woman, did not see much protest. After all, Hari was an exotic dancer, or in many people's minds, a prostitute, whose life was not as valuable as that of the purportedly wholesome nurse Cavell.

Nation, November 11, 1915

Living in a place under German control, she was secretly recruiting troops for Germany's enemies. Her acts were acts of direct and conscious participation, on the anti-German side, in a war which could be no means be said to be ended. And these acts were being conducted by underground methods within the German lines.

When spies of a hostile army are caught, they are usually executed at once, without regard to sex. This may be a barbarous practice, but all the present belligerent nations, as well as all other civilized and Christian nations, regard it as a just and necessary one. Miss Cavell's act was, perhaps, not technically espionage, but, to my uninitiated mind, her activities seem to have been even more dangerous, to the Government against whom they were directed, than those of most spies. If, then, it is not barbarous to execute spies after a military trial, I cannot see why it was barbarous to execute Miss Cavell after a military trial—granted that the "offense" in both cases is legally recognized, which appears to be an undisputed fact.

Dr. Alfred F. M. Zimmermann, German Under Secretary for Foreign Affairs, "A Defense of the Execution"

Berlin's defense of the Cavell execution was probably justified under generally accepted practices of dealing with wartime spies. In fact, some in Germany probably considered it generous that she was not executed immediately without trial. But German leaders, as bovine as they repeatedly proved to be on the propaganda front, blundered the case until it became a cause célèbre for those who hoped to depict their enemies as "murdering monsters." Arthur Zimmermann was to prove his breathtaking insensitivity to American public opinion again in early 1917, when he admitted to writing the telegram that suggested a German-Mexican alliance against the United States.

New York Times Current History, October 1915–March 1916

I have before me the court's verdict in the Cavell case, and can assure you that it was gone into with the utmost thoroughness, and was investigated and cleared up to the smallest details. The result was so convincing, and the circumstances were so clear, that no war court in the world could have given any other verdict, for it was not concerned with a single emotional deed of one person, but a well-though-out plot, with many far-reaching ramifications, which for nine months succeeded in doing valuable service to our enemies to the great detriment of our armies. Countless Belgian, French, and English soldiers are again fighting in the ranks of the Allies who owe their escape to the activities of the band now found guilty, whose head was the Cavell woman. Only the utmost sternness could do away with such activities under the very nose of our authorities, and a Government which in such case does not resort to the sternest measures sins against its most elementary duties toward the safety of its own army.

All those convicted were thoroughly aware of the nature of their acts. The court particularly weighed this point with care, letting off several of the accused because they were in doubt as to whether they knew that their actions were punishable. Those condemned knew what they were doing, for numerous public proclamations had pointed out the fact that aiding enemies' armies was punishable with death.

Cavell Execution Decried

Editorial: "The Case of Miss Cavell"

The Cavell case was drawn into the world's press partially because German occupiers most likely hoped they would not have to act, and so moved slowly. They knew for some time that Cavell was hiding allied soldiers and helping them escape to unoccupied Holland. They warned that anyone harboring fugitive soldiers would be shot as a spy. Cavell obviously knew she was one of those for whom the warning was issued, and associates who helped her run the escape network urged her to flee. But presumably out of a martyr's sense of exception, she continued until authorities were forced to shut off her pipeline. Cavell's determination to stay at her post in patriotic duty to her country perhaps excited inspiration as soldiers too remained in their positions facing certain death.

Nation, November 11, 1915

Our correspondent [Franklin Edgerton] places the case of Miss Cavell throughout on a par with that of a spy, whereas the essential reason both for the interposition of our Minister and for the world's indignation at the brutal disregard of that interposition lay in the fact that she was not a spy. Had she been a spy, it may be presumed that the military authorities would have seen no reason for rushing her execution in the dead of night a few hours after her sentence had been pronounced and without informing our representative that she had been sentenced.

Another point well deserves attention at the hands of those who find fault with the fierce condemnation passed upon Germany by neutral countries for this act, when no such outcry has been raised over executions of spies in England or France. These fault-finders seem to forget that nobody inquired whether in the course of fifteen months of war Germany has not executed an untold number of spies—and whether among these there was not a woman—and that it was not until she committed this barbarous act against a woman who was not a spy that she was made to suffer the reprobation of the world. If Germany wishes to receive no harsher censure than her enemies, let those who govern her policy draw the line of deliberate and ferocious inhumanity somewhere near the point where the other nations of the world draw it.

—Ed. The Nation

James M. Beck, Late Assistant Attorney General of the United States: "The Case of Edith Cavell"

Western opinion regarding women before the war sat squarely on the side of what today would be called sexist discrimination. Women were perceived as fragile innocents, mothers, and caregivers. They were generally not allowed to vote and they were expected to remain at home. But the demands of World War I cleared the factories as the draft called more and more males to the front. Someone had to do the work, and women volunteered. They faced repeated harassment and prejudice from male colleagues, many of whom likely believed that the "gentler sex" could not possibly be guilty of doing work that could be of harm to the German army.

New York Times Current History, October 1914–March 1915

One can to some extent understand the Berserker fury which caused a von Bissing to say in effect to this gentle-faced English nurse, "You are in our way. You menace our security. You must die, as countless thousands have already died, to secure the results of our seizure of Belgium"; but can we understand or in any way palliate the attempt to hide the stains of blood on that prison floor of Brussels with a cobweb of self-evident falsehoods?

These stains can never be washed out to the eye of imagination. . . .

Let our nation begin with the case of Edith Cavell, and demand of Germany the dismissal of the officers who flouted, deceived, and mocked the representative of the United States. that concerns our honor as a nation.

And you, women of America? Will you not honor the memory of this martyr of your sex, who for all time will be mourned as was the noblest Greek maiden, Antigone, who also gave her life that her brother might have thee rites of sepulture? Will you not carry on in her name and for her memory those sacred ministrations of mercy which were her lifework?

Make her cause—the cause of mercy—your own!

Questions

1. Given today's attitudes toward women and their role in society, would Americans react with as much outrage at the execution of Edith Cavell as they did in 1915?
2. Are executions of civilians ever justified in occupied nations during war?
3. Military leaders argue that in total war, civilians are legitimate targets. While in 1914 this was still a controversial issue, today it is beyond debate that the U.S. military has caused hundreds of thousands of civilian casualties over the course of the century. Why do arguments made against this in 1914 seem to be disregarded today?
4. Were the atrocities committed by the invading armies in Europe truly equivalent to the lynchings of black Americans in the United States? How were they alike and how were they different?
5. Given the widespread horror of World War I battle deaths, why did the comparatively limited civilian atrocity stories seem to serve as much more effective propaganda for the allies?

Chapter 5

War and the American Economy

To a nation convinced of its moral and political superiority over Europe, the economic benefits brought by war could be an embarrassment. Winners and losers in war can be found not only among those fighting in the battlefields but also among those fighting in the marketplace. One of the winners in this case clearly was going to be the United States.

The country had been wracked with prolonged debate about the role of capital and labor in an industrializing America: the huge and perhaps dangerous concentrations of private wealth and power, the exploitation of labor, particularly among large immigrant populations, the oppression of minorities, and the country's role in the world as a newly emerging economic power. The war would not do much to address many of these problems, despite fond hopes of progressives like Walter Lippmann. But it certainly would address one question: the role of an American economy in a world at war. In fact, the United States would end up reaping huge economic benefit from the war—a historic shift in world power and influence from the Old World to the New. Is it morally defensible to enrich one's self on someone else's wicked war? That was the troubling question.

Whatever the answer was, and the press reflected vigorous disagreement, the reality was that American businesses were going to benefit one way or another. Initially the Wilson administration resisted Americans doing business with belligerents. Wilson's general distrust of big business and financiers stemmed from his representing Democrats, the party at the time in opposition to corporate interests. His detractors in the Republican Party, particularly Senator Henry Cabot Lodge, Theodore Roosevelt, and Charles Evans Hughes (who opposed him in a close 1916 reelection campaign) were backed by America's largest capitalists. In August 1914 the government declared that neutrality meant no association with any fighting nation, regardless of whether they were trading partners before. That meant no loans or credits to even the country's most important European trading partner, Britain. Perhaps this fastidious interpretation pleased socialist secretary of state William Jennings Bryan. Perhaps it would have been acceptable had the war really been as short as people thought it would be. But war continued into the fall with no signs of an end and a lot of signs of stalemate. America's businesses looked at their ledgers and found that trade restrictions were starting to have dire consequences. Wilson's administration already had been trying to deal with an economic downturn; could it weather a possible worse depression caused by adherence to its own purist principles? After a few months the government relented as the pressure to resume trade from both sides of the Atlantic became irresistible. But it was not the same agreement as before the war. In theory the neutral United States could trade with any power offering an attractive deal. In reality the British blockade of the Central Powers made that impossible. British navy vessels dominated the north Atlantic, stopping and searching merchant vessels carrying supplies bound for Germany. A list of contraband goods subject to confiscation grew to include just about anything worth trading. Angry protests from Washington contending that the allies had no right to disrupt trading of neutral nations fell on deaf ears. But Britain did compensate Americans for seized goods.

Germany, on the other hand, began to see that the consequences of the increasingly effective blockade would (1) slowly starve the country of resources, even food, and (2) more and more buoy the enemy with loans and credits, provisions, and even munitions. The German surface navy had not reached a level that could successfully challenge Britain. Its undersea navy might. The problem with expanding the German submarine, or "U-Boat" (*Unterseeboot*) campaign centered around difficulty of commanders to identify and warn civilian ships. International law demanded that an enemy warn a merchant ship of impending torpedo attack and allow passengers to flee in lifeboats before the vessel was sunk. To do this, however, would not only risk response from possibly armed ships but also give a captain time to radio nearby navy vessels, which could reach the site and disable the submarine with depth charges. Moreover, many ostensible passenger liners carried a secret manifest of munitions. Whether it was ethical for a ship carrying civilian passengers, including women and children, to ship weapons bound for allied soldiers is a question no one during World War I seemed interested in asking (beyond a few anti-British editors and German-language newspapers). But nearly everyone voiced outrage at German submarines attacking American ships bound for Britain. It was one thing to confiscate merchandise, quite another to kill citizens of a neutral country.

The issue nearly plunged the United States into war in 1915. On May 7, a German submarine attacked the *Lusitania* off the Irish coast. Surprising even

William Jennings Bryan's (right-wing) progressive politics led him to run unsuccessfully for president, but finally join a presidential administration as Woodrow Wilson's secretary of state in 1913. He clung to his belief that the United States should remain strictly neutral, even as Americans moved toward sympathy with the allies, and finally resigned after Wilson's strong protest in response to Germany's sinking of the Lusitania. *Courtesy of Library of Congress.*

the U-Boat commander, the ship exploded and sank in minutes, drowning more than 1,000 passengers and crew, including 123 American civilians. Among the civilians lost was Alfred G. Vanderbilt, heir to one of America's great industrial fortunes. Wilson's angry response to Germany demanded that Berlin restrict its policy of submarines targeting merchant ships. Those opposed to the president thought that his response was not enough and that war ought to be declared. Wilson responded by saying that there was such a thing as being "too proud to fight." Germany did indeed back down, but probably not in response to the U.S. ultimatum. Germany in 1915 had not built enough submarines to launch a truly effective unrestricted campaign. In 1917 Germany would revert to its former policy of submarine warfare, and the United States would declare war. The specific act, then, which drew America into war was based on economic considerations.

War is a tremendous financial burden to any nation. The immense cost of World Wars I and II shattered European economies, fomented revolution, and in the ensuing economic shambles, shifted the mantle of premier world power to the United States. A nation in debt to the Old World throughout the nineteenth century, America for the first time became a creditor nation. By 1915 its economy boomed based on the huge demand for goods to fight the European war. The credit American industry had extended to Britain and France spiraled to levels that made U.S. bankers nervous; by 1917 it had reached $2 billion. What if the allies lost the war and couldn't pay their debts? It was suggested by American socialists that the United States declared war on Germany for precisely this reason, a war not for civilization and democracy, but for capitalism and greed. While historians tend to discount this as a major reason, the obvious financial structure under the country's war declaration served to perpetuate the economic good times that paradoxically benefited America during World War I.

Prosperous, yes, but still the United States had to find a way to pay for its huge commitment to fight in the Great War. Who should pay? Congress opened the country's treasury. To fill that treasury would require both taxes and loans. Which to rely on most was a political question. Liberals and socialists believed taxes should fund the operation; taxes on wealth and taxes on industry. Wisconsin progressive Senator Robert La Follette declared that if the country were to initiate conscription of men, it also should initiate conscription of wealth, the rich capitalists paying for a war that benefited them. Opponents argued the opposite, saying more payers of the newly constitutional income tax ought to do their bit in an everyman's war. Treasury Secretary William McAdoo (an industrialist and Wilson's son-in-law) preferred relying on loans. He believed wealthy Americans would pour contributions into a series of Liberty Loan bonds backed by the U.S. government at a rate of 4 percent. This could not only be an investment for the rich but could also be something any American could buy—and ought to. A huge propaganda campaign assured success of the bond issues as a major way to fund America's participation in the Great War. The war cost the United States more than $22.6 billion, nearly $276 billion in today's dollars.[1]

War and Capitalism: The Evils

Allan L. Benson, Candidate of the Socialist Party for President of the United States: "Socialism vs. Militarism"

Wealth in America at the turn of the last century was concentrated into a small oligarch of incredibly powerful tycoons. Theodore Roosevelt, among others, aimed to break the "trusts," particularly those of J. P. Morgan (railroads) and J. D. Rockefeller (oil). Other progressive activists worked to root out political corruption and labor exploitation. By 1914 both had seen some success, but socialist claims that American businesses abused labor and wielded great political power still could not be discounted. Whether they also favored war is less certain. War is a disruption of trade that most capitalist forces oppose. It is true that World War I benefited American industry with lucrative contracts and loans. Morgan in particular maintained close financial ties with Britain. But while economic considerations certainly can't be ignored, many historians contend that the United States entered the war for reasons other than simple greed.

Independent, October 30, 1916

We challenge the statement of President Wilson that militarism is not here because, notwithstanding our great military appropriations, there is no desire in America to attack others. We know the people of America are peaceful. We know the peoples of Europe were peaceful. But we also know the European war is of economic origin; we know there were capitalists in Europe who preferred war to the sacrifice of what they regarded as their interests, and we believe there are great capitalists in America who would prefer war to the sacrifice of their interests.

Socialists also charge that all of President Wilson's legislation was incapable of ending the industrial depression until the European war dumped so many billions of gold into the country that business had to revive; that such "prosperity" as we now have, while it means hundreds of millions to the capitalist class, means only more work for the workers for wages that, however "high," are only as high as the cost of living; that the average railway profit of $4100 a mile went to 607630 stockholders who represent but six-tenths of one per cent of the population; that the profits of other corporations are similarly absorbed; that the increase, since 1913, of $41,000,000 in the national wealth still leaves the workers upon farms and in factories with no prospect for the morrow but more work for a bare living and that what this nation needs is not a great foreign trade, but such economic arrangements as shall enable productive workers to consumer the full value of their own products.

Courtenay De Kalb: "The Formula for Peace"

Economic preoccupations certainly can help explain America's wars during its first hundred years. A basis of the American Revolution was an economic dispute, as was the War of 1812. The U.S. Civil War pitted two dramatically different views of the American economy against each other. Even the brief Spanish-American war displayed capitalist overtones. But historical research argues that these wars can't be reduced to a simple question of money, that the passions of those who fought and sacrificed could only be sustained by ideals of freedom, liberty, and patriotism. Similarly the Great War motivated its supporters for more than mere money. Even those who themselves were from the moneyed classes died in great numbers. In Britain they actually died in greater percentages than those from the working classes.

Atlantic Monthly, December 1917

It may strike some minds as paradoxical to affirm that war is an economic phenomenon, yet the great majority of all the wars of history and particularly of modern history have been nothing less than attempts to adjust a continuously unfavorable trade-balance by resort to arms. Surely the great gathering of the nations in battle array, that now astounds and awes the human race, can by no possibility be regarded in any other light than that of a transference of the war of trade from the country-house to the field of Mars. Our minds are likely to be tricked into false reasoning by the boasts of democracy and the thunders of autocracy, for the solution of the great problem of civilization does not lie in more forms of government—neither in democracies nor in empires. It is far deeper than these; it might be said that, considered as a means of supplying human needs, it is not definitely related to either. It is not the way in which we are governed that determines whether or not we will get on with our neighbors peaceably; it is what we use our government to accomplish for us as nations that determines the matter.

Adolph von Harnack, Professor of Theology and General Director of the Royal Library, Berlin: "Professor Harnack Scorns American Ideals"

Berlin repeatedly complained that in supplying the allies America was not at all neutral. Some American socialists agreed, and the considerable anti-British faction in the United States, particularly Irish-Americans, deplored the government's acquiescence to doing business with Britain. But money talked and it was wartime trade that by 1915 pulled the country out of recession an into an economic boom. Wilson was an Anglophile himself who probably did indeed have less interest in things German, but so did many Americans on the east coast of Scots-Irish (Northern Ireland) descent.

New York Times Current History, April–September 1917

The hostility of the United States against us is reducible to the inconvenience which was caused to America by German economical efficiency. A second reason is that America feared to lose the enormous capital she had invested in the Entente from the beginning, in the firm belief that the latter would be victorious. Now America is witnessing the chances of victory gradually disappearing, and rushes to save what is possible.

America conducted silent war against us long before the declaration of war, and never was particular in choosing her means. Wilson and many Americans with him have undergone an ugly development from an honest democratic republicanism to a bedizened empiricism. In addition. Wilson distinguishes himself by amazing ignorance about Germany. He is an intellectual moralist, but without any depth whatsoever.

Anonymous: "The Strain of War"

The war cost all the allies a total of $125.7 billion and the Central Powers a total of $60.6 billion. Germany spent the most ($37.7 billion) with Britain a close second ($35.3 billion).[2] These enormous sums turned prosperous Europe from creditor to debtor, to the benefit of the United States. Britain would never regain its position as premier power just as France would never regain its cultural hegemony. Austria-Hungary shrank from major power to minor. Russia became a Communist pariah. As for Germany, economic ruin fed evil undercurrents that had existed for centuries in Europe, exploding into the racist hatred of Nazi dictatorship. After five centuries Europe had lost its position as the center of world power, finance, and culture.

Nation, August 12, 1915

Statements of Finance Ministers in various of the belligerent countries were given out last week. As to them all, there is an unavoidable suspicion of "bluff." The facts are not covered up. There need be no question of the sincerity with which it is affirmed that the nations will cheerfully bear even more back-breaking loads. But in what M. Ribot tells us of French finances, Mr. Asquith of English, the Minister of Finance in Petrograd of Russian, and Herr Helfferich of German, it is impossible not to feel that there is something deeper than the words used. The sums of money dealt with are of such magnitude that they become meaningless to the mind. England has floated a loan of $3,000,000,000, but this will last only till next Christmas—hardly so long, in fact! Germany has soon to go to her people for another two billions or so. This war has long since left off thinking in hundred millions. Treasure, supplies, human life—all are subject to exhaustion at a gigantic rate. Guerre d'usure, the French call the trench-fighting. But what is being used up is not only soldiers: it is the ultimate resources of the nations at war.

Attempts to hide this truth are vain. Statesmen may seek to paint color of rose. The press may be drilled to a parrot-like optimism. Even the people who suffer may be moved by patriotic feeling to say that the hurt is nothing. But the ghastly wounds which have been inflicted upon the national life are visible under the bandages. And they are becoming more gangrenous every week. All the shifts, all the recourses, all the saving and the skilled organizing–yes, and all the heroic endurance–cannot prevent the eye of common-sense from perceiving that a perfectly enormous wastage of blood and wealth is draining the vitality of the belligerents.

Simon N. Patten, PhD, Wharton School of Finance and Commerce, University of Pennsylvania: "The Financial Menace to America of the European War"

Predicting political and social change is notoriously difficult, but most people realized a reckoning would come following the Great War. Reckoning not only in economic terms but also in labor unrest, political paybacks, and a swamp of dislocated peoples and countries set free by powers no longer in existence. This was particularly the case in the Middle East, for centuries dominated by Ottoman Turkey. After Turkey's political disintegration, the Arabian peninsula and surrounding peoples found themselves in a vacuum of power. Allied victors tried, but no one could put the broken pieces into any kind of stable Humpty-Dumpty. The world still is dealing with the consequences.

Annals of the American Academy of Political and Social Science, July 1915

It is not the treaty of peace that settles the burden of the war, but the financial adjustment following the crisis which the war creates. The French did not pay the indemnity at the close of the Franco-Prussian War. The ownership of the world's resources was settled by the crisis of 1873 with its destruction of values. The great losses were those of Germany and America and they were thus the real payers of the war expenses.

It should be remembered that at present America is getting nothing but paper credits for the enormous export of food and arms. Imports have fallen off and little gold is imported. The financial crash at the close of the war alone will determine the value of this paper. How much will the farmers gain from selling their wheat for an advance of fifty cents a bushel if at the close of the war their land falls 20 per cent in value? If two billion dollars' worth of securities are returned in exchange for food and war material while the crisis lowers all our stocks and bonds by 20 percent, we have not only given the food and arms to Europe for nothing but have also paid a bonus. We figure out great profits today, but they are after all only paper promises. Tomorrow the reckoning will come and then the holders of securities will bear the burden. Happy will be the man who has kept gold in his own pocket and has let his confiding neighbor have the glittering gains the stock market offers.

W. S. Rossiter: "War and Debt"

The huge cost of the war left the victorious allies determined to make their enemies pay. The only enemy that could was Germany. Based on the Treaty of Versailles, which determined that Germany was solely responsible for the war (Germany itself had no voice in the preparation of the treaty), Berlin was required to pay 6.6 billion British pounds ($1.5 billion, $16.1 billion in today's dollars) in war reparations, the last payment coming in 1966. The country's refusal, or inability, to pay reparations provoked the French to invade and occupy the industrial Ruhr Valley in 1923, although that did nothing but upset the German economy and spread anger throughout the country. In the end, Germany paid little toward the large figure after a worldwide depression hobbled the vibrant Weimar Republic's economy of the late 1920s.

Atlantic Monthly, May 1916

There remains but one factor likely to exert an effective influence in the future against war. It is a new factor and possibly it may prove to be important. War has become too scientific. The romance and the appeal to instinct have both been eliminated. It takes long to wipe out the age-old conception of war—with its beating drums, clash of arms, marching hosts, and survival of the strongest. Yet this conception related to a past age. When it is once realized that war has become a mere operation of innumerable machines upon the earth and in the clouds against unseen foes; that it is an affair of burrowing in the earth to escape explosion and strangulation, and that it means ultimate destruction without reference to physical strength, instinct may revolt, and men are likely to refuse to become merely the victims of a science.

Finally, as the indebtedness of the warring powers becomes greater, the more hopeless may become the possibility of payment. The mere burden of interest, indeed, under easily developed conditions, might prove a source of actual revolution. There are, in fact, grave possibilities, for it is clear that an indebtedness of over $50,000,000,000 cannot be materially increased without becoming a menace. This war may leave Europe lean, hungry, and desperate, with industrial life interrupted or destroyed, and millions of armed men unemployed. Across the ocean lie the United States, with national wealth of nearly $200,000,000,000, which has been actually increased by the disasters of Europe.

The attempt of a desperate man to take by force is not unusual. Might not such an attempt be made by desperate nations, even in the twentieth century?

William A. Wood: "Who Pays for the Cost of War?"

William A. Wood presents the common-sense view of war's cost, and certainly World War I broke the dynamism of Europe as it bequeathed the responsibility of world power, eventually world superpower, to the United States. But war also sometimes breaks the burden of outdated tradition and inefficient operation in a manner impossible to do during peacetime. The disastrous German occupation of France during World War II allowed a new French government to eliminate a discredited and often corrupt press and begin with a clean slate. Japan's and Germany's heavy material losses during that same war gave both countries the opportunity to start again from scratch to produce two of the world's strongest economies.

***New York Times Current History,* April–September 1917**

A nation at war is keeping a ledger, and as the balance is on the debit side, redoubled efforts are necessary to restore the equilibrium. No juggling with figures can offset this inexorable law of nature. No human reasoning can compensate nature for the consumption of her resources; nothing but human labor can compensate her. Her bounties contain no values until they are carved out by specific and productive human energy; and when these values are once created in the form of wealth, they fall under the law of metabolism. If man hastens the breaking-up process by recklessness or by war, he must pay for it in continued expenditure of effort, he must pay the cost. When a man borrows anything from nature he may use it or not, as he wills; but in any instance what he borrows must be returned to her reservoirs.

War quickly destroys what man produces, but the cost is paid for, not in money, but by labor augmented many times over as a price paid for the follies of men. Constructive labor yields permanent results; war uproots them. Battleships are not paid for by Governments, but by subjects of a nation. A thousand men on a warship produces nothing; the same men in action destroy both ship and enemy. The payment of taxes comes out of human labor; the payment of interest on loans is a double burden, falling on those who now live and labor, and striking hard against those who are later to become creators of the nation's wealth. We are still paying pensions on a war that ended 102 years ago. Wars are paid for in human sacrifice—in human lives; but they are also paid for in sacrifice that eats up the products of man's labor; and when these visible things are shot to pieces, an increase of human energy alone can replace them.

War and Capitalism: The Benefits

Edward S. Mead, PhD, Wharton School of Finance and Commerce, University of Pennsylvania: "The Situation of the United States at the Close of the War as a Question of National Defense"

The hatred that so effectively fed the frenzy of World War I abated in post-war America like a passing tsunami. By the 1920s, Germany had become an important trading partner. U.S. financial institutions made loans to Germany to allow them to buy more, and to pay back reparations, but after the 1929 crash of the U.S. stock market, banks worried about default, and called in loans. In Germany, this made it impossible to continue to pay reparations for World War I and in 1931, Berlin suspended payments. As unemployment soared and social unrest split Germany's fractious political parties, the message of a small extremist group called the National Socialists (Nazis) found sympathetic ears among powerful publishers like Alfred Hugenberg, who spread their views to disastrous effect.

***Annals of the American Academy of Political and Social Science*, July 1915**

The financial situation of the United States at the close and as a result of the European war can be forecasted with a fair degree of accuracy, and the result of the forecast can be regarded with a degree of satisfaction. Indeed it is difficult to understand the basis of the forebodings expressed in many quarters that the interests of the United States will be in any way injured in the process of world readjustment which must follow the conflict. The probable results of the war upon our principal competitors have been set forth in the various papers read at this and previous sessions with substantial unanimity of opinion. We know that European nations will be burdened with enormous debts, with resulting heavy taxation which must increase the overhead charges of industry. We know that the loss in their working population and especially in their directing and executive population, has already been severe and continues to increase. We have no reason to expect that the war will settle anything except the endurance of the fighters, so that the crushing burdens of armament will continue to be borne.

We can reasonably expect, moreover, that the conflict, when it finally dies, will leave a legacy of hatred, of jealousy and suspicion, among the warring powers which will, for many years, interfere with the extension and cultivation of friendly commercial relations. That the United States is certain to profit from this situation is evident. While no fighter lovers the neutral bystander, at any rate he does not hate him. The American manufacturer will have in future an easier time in competition with his foreign rivals in the markets of their enemies. No matter if the temporary war trade dies with the war, the connections formed can be turned to profitable account in advancing the interests of American export trade.

William C. Redfield, Secretary of Commerce, Washington, D.C.: "America's International Trade as Affected by the European War"

Progressivists in early twentieth-century America believed that the efficiency of science and progress could become a force of positive change in society. Many such as Herbert Croly, editor of the New Republic, *moved from neutrality to support the war in hope that the fundamental change forced by the dictates of total war could form the basis of social improvements. World War I did indeed force substantial change in American society, but to the disappointment of many on the liberal side, most of those changes proved temporary.*

Annals of the American Academy of Political and Social Science, July 1915

It seems clear to me that if we do our part we shall change our place among the great competitors. The world is never the economic gainer in the last analysis by war. The losses must be absorbed and we must do our share of absorbing, but in the process of absorption places relative to one another may be exchanged. No one, I think, would be surprised to find the United States second in the world's competition, if the war shall long continue, be astonished to find her first. It depends, of course, not merely on what is destructively done yonder but on what is constructively done here.

If we are willing to lay aside passion and prejudice and partisanship, to look at things with an international instead of a parochial viewpoint, to realize that effectiveness is patriotism and that inefficiency is unpatriotic; if we are ready to give up inertia and take a step forward out of ourselves to the help of others; if we remember that commerce is mutual exchange to mutual benefit and not a species of industrial war; if we can learn the lesson that the well-paid workman is the cheapest producer and that science must be applied to industry if we are to win; if these things can be done I see no reason why, with our resources and intelligence and organization, we may not become the first among the world's great trading nations. We shall have to give up a good deal if we are to reach that goal. We must abandon mutual distrust and pull together. We must not think that gain made in any way that greed may dictate is a thing that the conscience and spirit of America will permit. We must remember that in industry a social wrong makes no economic right and that factories cannot be so operated as to injure our fellow creatures for our own personal gain. The men and the women in the mill and the children kept out of the mill must have their chance. We shall not gain by grinding, but by growing.

Charles Frederick Carter: "The Effect of the War on the United States"

The United States had spent most of the nineteenth century as a supplier of raw materials to Europe and a buyer of finished products. This was already changing as the country's rapid industrialization powered new factories capable of huge output. The country's sweeping Great Plains could feed a world at war; farming seemed prosperous for a change. Before the war, wheat could seldom command a dollar a bushel but by 1915 it reached $1.25 with no limit to demand. More than 10 million new acres of wheat were planted and the price per bushel rose until it reached an unheard of $2.20. Farmers' euphoria, however, was tempered by rising costs of inflation. Federal agriculture policy failed to placate the agricultural belt, most of which voted against Wilson's Democratic party in 1918. It was the Republicans who eventually saw to it that Wilson's vision for a League of Nations was defeated in Congress.

World's Work, September 1914

The belligerents had been spending upward of a billion dollars a year in preparation for war, which was the best possible way to make war inevitable. This vast expenditure served no useful purpose, but, together with the earning capacity of four million men withdrawn from useful labor to serve in the armies, was as utterly lost as if it had been sunk in the depths of the ocean. Besides this, financiers had just completed the task of raising considerably more than a billion dollars to foot the bill for the wars in the Balkans, added to which England was still paying interest on a debt of more than a billion dollars incurred in the Boer War. The economic convalescence of the nations must be slow, because they were financially anemic before the war began.

Still there is a streak of silver, even in this sombre cloud. The warring millions will have to be fed and clothed somehow. At whatever sacrifice, they will have to raise money with which to buy the necessaries of life, and to a large extent they will have to buy from us. they must find some means of getting provisions across the sea, if they have to send a whole fleet of battleships to convoy each freighter. Also, the rest of the world must turn to us now for the manufactured goods formerly purchased from the warring nations.

Theodore H. Price: "Do Wars Really Cost Anything? The Fallacy of 'Economic Waste' Refuted by All Modern History—The Constructive Benefits of War in Increasing Production, Reducing Extravagance, and Strengthening Credit—An Explanation of the Surprising Rebound of Business since the European Conflict Began"

The irony of World War I—perhaps of all wars—is that it did not cause universal economic ruin. Even in the principal belligerent nations—Britain, France and Germany—some suppliers of essential warstuffs became rich as governments awarded hasty contracts with insufficient oversight. Indeed, the Great Depression of 1929 really did not end until World War II ramped demand. Producing goods for the express purpose of destroying them, or destroying other goods so they can be remade, seems to perversely meet a central demand that makes capitalism work.

World's Work, **March 1915**

Business is undoubtedly improving. Week by week, mills are reopening. Bank clearings are increasing. Exports are phenomenal. Investment securities are finding a market, and even cotton is advancing in price despite an unconsumed supply that is the largest in the world's history.

What does it mean? From Aristotle to Mill and since, all economists have taught that war is waste, yet the greatest war in history seems to be quickening the wheels of industry and intensifying the activity of commerce. . . .

In August, it was predicted and believed that the war would be brought to an end ere this by the complete bankruptcy of the Powers involved, but lo! their borrowing power is undiminished and the supply of credit at their disposal is larger than ever. Looking back on the history of the world for the last hundred years, we find the same sequence in the commercial and financial record. The first effect of war is panic caused by the impact of the shock. Thereafter, within a comparatively short period, capital becomes abundant, business revives, speculation is quickened, and a period of financial activity follows that generally becomes a veritable boom before peace can be discerned and continues for several years thereafter.

War and Capitalism: The Challenges

L. P. Jacks: "Loyalty Once More"

It seemed almost possible in the 1920s that economic cooperation would bring the world together in peace. The Great Depression, beginning in 1929, destroyed that illusion. Although World War I had made the United States the world's dominant economy, actions in America can be blamed for the European depression that fed fuel to old hatreds and jealousy. Without American loans Germany could not repay reparations. Britain and France relied on reparations to pay their own debt to U.S. creditors. A high tariff designed to protect American businesses smashed world trade, which dropped by two thirds as global industrial production fell by more than a third. Cooperation among nations could not be sustained in a world of distrust and fear.

Atlantic Monthly, February 1918

There is a disposition in many quarters to treat the economic problem on a national basis, or, at least, on a group basis. But I am convinced that a strict consideration of its nature will reveal it as a world-problem which can only be solved internationally. The United States possesses peculiar advantages which may seem to give exemption from the extreme form of the peril, but it may well be doubted if these, great as they are, would make America a real exception to the rest of the world. So far as the other belligerents are concerned, the case is quite clear. They will be confronted with economic conditions which they cannot meet without each other's aid. They must choose, as I have said, between cooperation and ruin. The task is so great they nothing short of a combined international effort can accomplish it. "Goodwill or downfall" must be the motto of them all.

And not only must loyal cooperation be the law among the nations in their totality. It must be equally the law among the various groups, classes, parties, and individuals in each of the nations concerned. In the immensely difficult conditions that await us after the war we shall find a new application for the lesson we have learned during the war—the lesson of working and enduring together, the weak not shrinking from their share, the strong willingly accepting more than falls to them on a counting of heads. Sacrifice and effort will be demanded all round, and that on a scale yet greater than that to which the war has accustomed us.

Everything depends on the response. If by one means or another capital and labor can be brought to an accommodation, if classes can be induced to sink their jealousies and suspicions. and if we can all make up our minds to pull together, then we shall assuredly pull through and pull through triumphantly. We shall then look back on this war as having taught us the lesson that brought us at last to our senses; and good will come out of evil. But if the old misunderstandings still flourish, if our industrial life is to repeat the old process of wasting its best energies on internal strife, I see nothing but confusion and defeat in store for industrial civilization. In all these matters we have come to the parting of the ways. We must either change our temper and our methods, or we must perish.

Editorial: "The Week"

Court decisions related to the creation of a federal income tax interpreted the U.S. Constitution in a way that made such a tax impractical. The Sixteenth Amendment was designed to make a federal income tax possible; in 1913 Wyoming became the thirty-sixth and final state needed to ratify the amendment. The tax was set at one percent on a personal income of $3,000 or less (more than $36,000 in today's dollars), and a surtax of six percent on those making more than $500,000. The Revenue Act of 1918 raised that to a progressive tax rate up to 77 percent. Postwar Republican administrations in the 1920s reduced the income tax, but it never dropped to prewar levels.

***Nation*, July 6, 1916**

That militarism cannot be run on the cheap is shown by the bill to provide fresh revenues. The problem was to raise something like $500,000,000 a year in new taxes, and the Ways and Means Committee of the House proposes to do it in ways which have been fully indicated in advance. The income tax is to be doubled. There is to be an inheritance tax, in addition, of course, to State inheritance taxes. Manufacturers of munitions of war are to pay a heavy tax on their gross profits. All the new imposts, in fact, are upon accumulated wealth. This was abundantly predicted. Congress has had its appetite whetted by previous taxes of that kind, and is ready to go on with the process indefinitely. It is now certain that every large new Federal expenditure will be met in this fashion. If we are to spend $500,000,000 more a year for ships and guns, we shall know hereafter in whose pockets the money is to be found. There is already an outcry against the new taxes, but as it comes largely from those who have been clamoring for armament without end, it is impossible to have much sympathy for it in their case.

Editorial: "The Senate and the War Taxes"

The 1918 Revenue Act relied on a variety of taxes to fund the war, including estate taxes, excise taxes, tax on excess profits, and personal income taxes. Treasury Secretary William McAdoo also believed in the importance of Liberty Loan programs, declaring that if a person can't lend his government $1.25 a week at 4 percent, he doesn't deserve to be a citizen. Loan programs financed two thirds of American participation in the war.

Nation, June 14, 1917

Both Congress and the people have been gradually getting away from the influence of captivating phrases. The argument for "conscription of incomes as well as conscription of men," the denunciation of people who do not have to shoulder rifles yet who object to having their private means commandeered, has been employed as if the well-to-do were objecting to any increase in the income tax. This is not in the least the situation. The Government's right, as part of its war power, to call to an unlimited extent on private wealth if the emergency requires it, is quite beyond dispute. But so is its right to call on every citizen, young or old, to join the army. The real question to be decided in either case is how far that power ought at a given time to be invoked, and this must be settled in the light of the economic interests of the country, and therefore of the Government itself.

Anonymous: Advertisement

Publications did their bit to raise money for the war by offering free space to federal propaganda organizations such as the Committee on Public Information. Most heavily promoted were Liberty Loans, because they were voluntary, unlike the income tax. The higher 1918 tax rates as specified in this advertisement would mean that someone who earned about $12,000 or less in today's dollars would still not have to pay an income tax.

Independent, January 26, 1918

Warning!
This year YOU must pay an Income Tax.

Don't feel that the new income tax does not apply to you—you may be pretty sure it does.

Single persons with incomes of $83.33 or more a month ($1,000.00 or more a year) and married persons with incomes of $166.66 or more a month ($2,000.00 or more a year) must file a statement of this income with the Government. It is the only income above $1000 and $2000 which is taxed.

This statement must be filed on a form which the Internal Revenue Representative in your community has. To locate him, ask your employer, the Postmaster, or any Banker.

Get the necessary form at once. Your statement must be filed before March first and you must not neglect it—for two reasons:

First: it is your patriotic duty in helping to win the war.

Second: there are severe penalties to be visited upon you if you do.

This announcement is published by the INDEPENDENT to help the Government collect these taxes—and thus aid in winning the war.

Questions

1. Does a neutral nation in wartime have the ethical responsibility to forbid trade, loans, and credits to any warring nation, even if it hurts the neutral nation's economy?
2. If a nation at war establishes conscription as a way to raise troops, is it also reasonable to raise money for the war by appropriating profits of industry?
3. Which seems more fair as a means to pay for war: income taxes or bonds (i.e., loans to the government)?
4. Should a country's richest class assume the largest financial burden for financing a war?

Notes

1. "Encyclopedia of the First World War," www.spartacus.schoolnet.co.uk/FWW.htm.

2. Ibid.

Chapter 6

Arms Sales to the Allies

On the eve of war, world financial markets stopped: stock markets suspended trading, merchants suspended shipping, and workers lay down their tools to prepare for a new responsibility, soldiering. U.S. finance industries were not at war, but the effect of closure in Europe swept west to threaten a collapse of the New York Stock Exchange, as traders panicked by the uncertainty of a world war flooded the floor with orders to sell. On July 31, 1914, Wall Street closed trading. It would not fully reopen until April 1915.

The export and import of goods to the United States from Europe stopped. Denied opportunities to sell to three of their biggest trading partners—Britain, France, and Germany—American suppliers in succeeding weeks found themselves in serious cash flow trouble. To rekindle the trade that was of central importance to the American economy, the Wilson administration would have to reconsider its ban on loans and credits to warring nations. In fact, the question addressed only credit to allied nations. Britain had been America's most important European trading partner before the war, and that country's blockade of merchant ships to Germany made it practically impossible for American businesses to trade with the Central Powers.

Secretary of state William Jennings Bryan strongly opposed credit to the allies. Strict neutrality, he maintained, meant no credit. But without credit the allies could not fill their huge shopping list of wartime needs. Particularly important was food to feed armies of millions, iron and steel to feed the munitions industry, and munitions themselves to feed the guns on the battlefields. Most of the debate over European trade policies in many American minds did not include the ethics of extending credit to warring nations. Few could subscribe to the purist view of Bryan, who considered credit to the allies a violation of strict neutrality. (A socialist-leaning progressive, Bryan resigned as secretary of state in June 1915. He was replaced by a more pliable Robert Lansing.) In the fall of 1914 Washington eased trade restrictions. The U.S. economy began to recover from the shock of the guns of autumn as exports increased dramatically to fill the needs of Britain and France. By November 1914 exports had surpassed those of any prewar month that year. By May 1916 the United States was sending goods to Europe totaling nearly $475 million, compared with about $162 million in prewar May 1914. Revenue climbed to more than $613 million in January 1917, the eve of America's entry into the war.[1]

How much of this trade increase represented war materiel to the allies? The majority. In fact, in 1914 the United States exported about $189 million in munitions and related material such as chemicals, iron, and steel. By 1916 it totaled almost $1.2 billion. By 1915 orders for steel swamped U.S. steel works. New blast furnaces opened, 74 of them in 6 months, exports increased four-fold, and machinery exports more than doubled in a year. Clearly, German protests were accurate: the United States was supplying the allies with the supplies that allowed them to continue the war. In fact, industries and financiers such as Bethlehem Steel, du Pont, and J. P. Morgan were so enriching themselves as men murdered each other that they were given the name "merchants of death," coined in an influential book by that name published in 1934.

This was the basis of the debate, as it has been so many times since in the United States. Can the country claim a moral high ground while profiting by supplying war materiel to nations at war? The question took center stage in the debate between those who believed for religious and moral reasons that their country should not sell arms and related material. Others agreed, not on those grounds, but on the grounds that the agreements between powerful armaments industries and governments corrupts international discourse and leads to more warmongering. Those opposing this view argue that armaments are necessary for defense, and that without American competition other countries will fill the gap.

Disillusionment that World War I apparently settled nothing led Americans in the 1920s and 1930s to encourage investigations of institutions presumed to have inveigled the public into fighting. The international banking and armament industries in particular were targeted. Senator Gerald P. Nye, a former newspaper editor in favor of reform who had made a reputation battling corruption, became chair of a congressional commission the mission of which was to investigate the profits of banking and munitions industries during the war. The North Dakota senator's committee investigation of the "merchants of death" concluded with a report that blamed the big arms business for pushing Americans over the edge into the deadly cauldron of World War I's battlefields. The commission's findings included this indictment:

> The committee finds also that there is a very considerable threat to the peace and civic progress of other nations in the success of the munitions makers and of their agents in corrupting the officials of any one nation and thereby selling to that one nation an armament out of proportion to its previous armaments. Whether such extraordinary sales are procured through bribery or through other forms of salesmanship, the effect of such sales is to produce fear, hostility, and greater munitions orders on the part of neighboring countries, culminating in economic strain and collapse or war.

The report fueled a backlash against U.S. participation in war and isolationist sentiment that led to neutrality laws in 1935 and 1937. It was, however, a report strongly put in question, in fact generally discredited, by more recent historical research. While a web of financial power did bind members of the Wilson administration, such as treasury secretary McAdoo, to America's business interests, and did bind the country as a whole to the fortunes of the allies, the country was propelled into war by a nearly universal belief that Germany had become a murderous rogue that must be stopped to save Western civilization.

ARMS SALES: YES

Anonymous: "Would an Embargo on Arms Involve Us in War?"

It is hard to see how a decision in 1915 to stop supplying war materiel to the allies would threaten the United States with war, as indicated here. Germany not only was in favor of such an embargo, it was also complaining bitterly that the supposedly neutral United States was in fact not neutral at all. But many Americans in 1915 worried that America was so unprepared for war that it could not defend itself against an attack by powerful European states. Those could indeed argue that to displease heavily armed nations would be unwise. The U.S. Army had already shown in its clumsy pursuit of Mexican revolutionary Pancho Villa that it probably could not be counted on to withstand a serious invasion.

Current Opinion, August 1915

According to Professor Ellery Stowell of Columbia University, we have no right, during the progress of hostilities, to modify our neutrality regulations in any way such as to materially affect the interest of either belligerent, "unless such modification is necessary to protect our interests or to provide for the national security." To interfere now with the shipments of arms for any other reason "would be an unfriendly act toward the Allies, who would have us absolutely at their mercy should they wish to retaliate." The *Chicago Evening Post* does not believe that Germany dares to ask us to establish such an embargo, because such a request would constitute a precedent and would debar her from selling arms in the future to warring nations—a thing she has always done, and which she wishes to be free to continue to do. *The South Bend Tribune* can see but one outcome to such interference: "We would be drawn into the war as certainly as the British fleet sails the seas." *The Springfield Republican* thinks that the agitation for an embargo has had very little effect except to drive a disordered mind into an attempt at murder. "If the United States should unhappily become involved in war with Japan," it asks, "would it be to our interest to be cut off from purchasing munitions in Europe?"

Editorial: "What Ought We to Do?"

The viewpoint that "if we don't do it, someone else will" has echoed through a century of debate over U.S. arms sales. The author's opinion here reflects the efficiency of capitalist specialization, which dictates that each country do what it does best and rely on imports for articles that other countries can do better. A century of experience has shown, however, that capitalistic rules don't always apply to arms sales: many countries that buy from worldwide suppliers also spend large percentages of their own wealth on weapons.

***Independent,* April 26, 1915**

The sale of munitions of war by neutral nations is one of the evil practices which the custom of nations still permits because international law is in a state of incomplete development comparable with that of private law in the tenth century. But the moral aspect of the case is not the only one to be considered. The practical results of an international agreement preventing such sales by neutrals to belligerents must be taken into consideration as well.

If no nation, in the time when war comes upon it, may buy arms in another country, each nation of the world would doubtless set up vast storehouses of rifles and cannon, shot and shell, and erect its own manufactories for every kind of war material. In time of peace every nation would thus arm to the teeth. The race for armament would become madder than ever; and no nation, however small, would dare to be left behind. All the evils and dangers that the making of arms and munitions now brings with it—pressure toward war, increase of armies and navies, corruption of government servants—might be vastly increased.

Editorial: "Selling Death"

American debate over arms sales extended a larger debate before the war about the role of the United States in a new century. The initial presumptions that almost no one questioned emphasized the purity of the New World; its morals; its political power untainted by the centuries of the animosity, betrayal and deceit of the Old World. How should America use its store of ethical credibility? Should it maintain its position as the world's most powerful neutral nation, or should it become a strong military state and climb into the world's miserable business? It took a second world war to reach a definitive answer: the United States would come down on the side of military might.

Independent, September 6, 1915

The argument that the exportation of munitions to the Allies should be stopped may be reduced to the following propositions:

1. It makes our country a workshop of death.
2. It is for profits, not patriotism.
3. It compromises us in the eyes of humanity.
4. It makes us an ally of the Allies.
5. It fosters an industry whose interest will be to extend militarism in the United States.
6. It theoretically enables a small state to buy arms when attacked, but practically this right is of little value, as the small state is likely to be completely invested by its greater and more warlike antagonist.

The official justification by the Secretary of State of the exportation of arms can be epitomized as follows:

1. It is the accepted rule of international law, which no nation should break.
2. It is and has been the universal practice of nations—Germany and Austria included.
3. It is unneutral in that it would deprive England of her superiority on sea and not Germany of her superiority on land.
4. It enables the United States to keep a small military establishment in time of peace.
5. It enables all nations to go without storing up vast reservoirs of military supplies.
6. It thus tends to the peaceful method of settling international disputes.

This is the issue. Which are right, the preachers or the statesman? For our part, we believe that each one of the six points made by either side is well taken. Then it comes to a question of which is the most right. . . .

Selling death is an undoubted evil. Refusing to sell death, when the alternative is what it is, is likely to result in even greater evil.

Is not the statesman the better moralist?

Charles Noble Gregory, LL.D., Washington, D.C.: "The Sale of Munitions of War by Neutrals to Belligerents"

The Krupp family's 200-year-old heavy industrial factories in Essen, Germany, have been at the center of the arms trade controversy since they began building cannons in the 1840s. By the turn of the century it was the world's largest industrial manufacturer, and half of its output was devoted to armaments. Krupp's inventive ordnance during World War I included some of the largest field guns ever seen, propelling projectiles higher than any human object had ever reached. It served as a lynchpin of German military might during both world wars, supplying arms to worldwide fighting forces unimpeded by questions of ethics or law. After World War II, however, Alfred Krupp was sentenced to 12 years for employing slave labor. At the start of the twenty-first century, Krupp had merged with a competitor to form ThyssenKrupp AG. Its Web site lists a huge variety of industrial products. A search for artillery turns up nothing.

Annals of the American Academy of Political and Social Science, July 1915

With respect to the rights of our citizens as neutrals to sell munitions of war to any belligerent power, it is submitted:

1. That these rights are in no way denied by the rules of international law.
2. That these rights are not forbidden by any municipal statute or ordinance except as to vessels of war and, in certain limited cases, as to our neighboring American republics, when the latter are involved in civil strife.
3. That such rights have been constantly exercised in this country since the beginning of its history and in like manner have been habitually exercised by the manufacturers of the most enlightened commercial nations of the world, not only in remote times, but during all recent wars.
4. That such rights were fully recognized and reserved by the conventions of the Second Hague Conference in 1907.

5. That the maintenance of such rights is wise and necessary as their abolishment would force upon all nations a policy of the highest military and naval preparedness, which policy is one of vast economic loss and deeply hostile, instead of favorable, to peace.
6. That the fact that certain belligerents are prevented by the forces of the other from taking advantage of our markets does not make sales to those who have such access a breach of neutrality.
7. That the powers which most severely attack this right have greatly profited by habitually exercising it in all recent wars and, under parallel circumstances, where the market was accessible to but one of the belligerents, have continued these sales to the other.

Horace White: "Selling Arms to the Allies"

Horace White makes an argument similar to that made in subsequent wars, that war was necessary for ultimate peace, and that during war no amount of armament production can be too great. His pessimistic conclusion reflected a familiar view in the prewar United States that the war might not solve anything. The 1919 Treaty of Versailles, which fell short in addressing worldwide tensions, so disappointed some journalists that they could only reiterate their fear that it would take another world war to solve dilemmas occasioned by the first one. The eruption of World War II in 1939 came as a melancholy affirmation of these pessimistic predictions.

North American Review, July 1915

The belief of the great majority of people of the United States is that Germany began the war without sufficient cause, and that when she invaded Belgium she made herself the outlaw of the nations—a country whom no agreements can bind.

Closely connected with this thought is the conviction that no limit can ever be put to the world's expenditure for armaments while one incorrigible outlaw is at large. Even in time of peace the cost of armies and navies goes on increasing, and this is logical. If ever a nation may declare war at its own whim it may reasonably estimate beforehand the cost of it and provide for it accordingly. There is no reason why it should pause short of the last dollar in its treasury, and the last male inhabitant capable of carrying a gun. The costs of armaments will go on increasing until the entire net earnings of the human race are absorbed in death dealing instruments or until a supreme tribunal shall be established to decide international disputes and to enforce its decisions. It is the opinion of most Americans that the most incorrigible and dangerous outlaw and armed maniac now existing is Germany and that the first and indispensable step toward a restriction of armaments and a quiet world is to throttle and disarm her, and that no price is too great to pay for such a consummation. Any result of the present war which falls short of this will be the preliminary to a new armament and another war on a wider scale than the present one, since the United States will make preparations for the next one and most probably take part in it.

Arms Sales: No

Anonymous: "Our Country as 'a Workshop of Death'"

Opposition to arms sales came primarily from religious leaders, socialists, pacifists, and German immigrants. Arguments reflected the basis of each of these groups; those of religion argued morality, as reflected here. The warning of a powerful lobby of arms dealers threatening democratic foundations has seen its echo throughout the century, most famously in President Dwight Eisenhower's 1961 farewell speech. It was this former World War II general who warned, "In the councils of government, we must guard against the acquisition of unwarranted influence, whether sought or unsought, by the military-industrial complex."

Current Opinion, August 1915

Our country is fast "becoming a workshop of death."

This is the way a pamphlet begins which has been issued in protest against the trade in munitions. It is signed by the Rev. Dr. Charles F. Aked, formerly of England, now of San Francisco, and the Rev. Dr. Walter Rauschenbusch, of Rochester Theological Seminary. Our government, so runs their joint argument, has power to forbid the exportation of arms. If the nation is silent, it consents to what is done. With us it is no question of self-defense, but merely a question of cash. We in this country have taken high ground on war questions. "If this war proves to be the bloody angle at which the road turns from ages of warfare to an age of peace, history for centuries to come will study the part played by different nations on this Calvary of humanity. Is America, then, to stand in the sigh of posterity with a bag in its hands?" Stress is laid upon the after-effects of building up large plants for the production of war materials. "They will create an

American war party. When the foreign market fails, they will turn to the home market and we shall feel their influence in the demand for American militarism." The sale of arms by neutrals is not to the advantage of small and peaceful nations. It was Great Britain, not the Boer republics, for instance, that profited by such sales. Our government prohibited the exportation of arms to Mexico, and there has been no explanation why that action would not be a just precedent in dealing with the one-sided war-trade with Europe. "Our trade in arms is bad because it is inhuman; it is also bad because it is so plainly and tremendously one-sided that our whole neutrality is tilted to a dangerous angle and needs the prop of labored arguments. However our theories may run, the fact is that we are to-day part of the economic and military system of Great Britain and her allies."

Edmund von Mach, Cambridge, Massachusetts: "An Argument against the Exportation of Arms"

Progressive Americans such as John Dewey and Walter Lippmann favored increased regulation of American business. They hoped the demands of war would encourage the government to impose more control over American industry. And indeed Washington learned from England and France that to maximize efficient output the state could control industry through consortiums. Railroads were put under government control and industry was coordinated through the War Industries Board. But it required more than two years of war for the European allies to develop truly powerful ways to centralize war production. In the United States the war ended before these experiments of greater government participation in private industry could be completed. To the disappointment of progressives, Republican administrations after the war dismantled wartime boards and controls.

***Annals of the American Academy of Political and Social Science*, July 1915**

1. What is morally wrong for the government is morally wrong also for each individual citizen.
2. When a large number of individual citizens persist in the commission of acts which run counter to the moral obligations of their government, the government has the right and the duty to take steps to prevent such acts.

3. It is contrary to the spirit of American institutions and the ideals of the American people, for the government to disclaim responsibility for the continued and open acts of a large number of their citizens.
4. American dealings with other nations must be bona fide and according to the sprit, and not only the letter, of any compact or understanding.
5. It is not unneutral for America to "blaze a new way," or to regulate the conduct of her citizens by laws, proclamations or otherwise, even during the progress of a war.

This last assertion has been severely attacked by the advocates of an unlimited trade in death-dealing arms. They have argued that the Allies would be justified in considering the laying of an embargo on the export of arms to be an unneutral act. The Allies could not claim this, because they themselves have forced several—if not all of the neutral states of Europe—to declare embargoes of various kinds against Germany and Austria since the war began.

The case in favor of stopping the traffic in munitions of war, therefore, may be summarized as follows:

1. The government of the United States cannot, either legally or morally, export arms to either of the belligerents.
2. The export of arms by the citizens of the United States has grown to such large proportions that it is known to all.
3. The government of the United States cannot advance the excuse that it is not morally responsible for the acts of its citizens.
4. The president and secretary of state have publicly declared, and asked for votes on the strength of their declaration, that the government has the right "to blaze a new way" and that it is not restrained from giving expression in law to the moral sense of right and wrong of the American people.
5. It is, therefore, the right and consequently the duty of the American government to have legislation enacted which will make it legally wrong for individual citizens to commit acts, the moral wrong of which nobody can deny.

Questions

1. If a neutral nation sells munitions to a country at war, must that nation accept partial responsibility for prolonging that war?

2. Should munitions manufacturers, and others who profit from arms sales, be required to pay high taxes or fees for the privilege of trading with nations at war?
3. Critics of the Wilson administration contended that the government joined the war to protect loans that America's large banks and financiers had made to Britain and France. Is this a legitimate reason to join a war considering that if the allies defaulted on loans to Americans, hardship and job loss in the United States would result?

Note

1. Charles Gilbert, *American Financing of World War I* (Westport, Conn.: Greenwood Press, 1970), 34.

Chapter 7

Preparedness

In many ways World War I reflected the Western values widely accepted at the turn of the last century, around 1900. Because some of these related to the virtues of military service, many Americans who supported allied goals also admired German military culture for its supposed organizational efficiency and the "vigor" of its martial traditions. Leaders such as Theodore Roosevelt believed good military training could make a man stronger, more clear thinking, perhaps more noble, certainly less criminal. As for the "hyphenated Americans," that is, recent immigrants (particularly German speaking), a dose of conscription was thought to encourage a patriotic change from presumably corrupt Old World traditions to the superiority of New World values. Roosevelt also criticized Irish-Americans for insisting the United States remain neutral. In fact the former president himself believed Woodrow Wilson should have drawn a harder line against German war tactics. Compulsory military service could "yank the hyphen" out of these supposedly unpatriotic immigrant Americans.

The value of human diversity, which had become a U.S. model at the end of the twentieth century, would have been little understood at the beginning. The nation's minorities, including Native Americans, African Americans, and immigrant populations, were encouraged to adopt the English language and Western names and customs. But immigrant and minority populations formed a huge patchwork resistant to assimilation at a time when the only mass medium was published material, the only national medium general-circulation magazines, and the only school districts locally controlled. Military service could offer a way to quickly assimilate immigrants. As George Creel, director of the wartime Committee on Public Information, argued, universal military training would "jumble the boys of America altogether," and that could crumble the old lines of class and origin.

Wilson agreed with Roosevelt on very little, but also distrusted hyphenated Americans. He saw the hyphen as a metaphor for a knife poised to sabotage the nation. But he was not convinced compulsory military service was the answer. The United States had not fought a major war since the end of the Civil War (1861–1865). Its armies and navies were small, its air force nonexistent, its artillery nearly so. But this befit a deeply isolationist country protected by two oceans without obvious threat beyond the recent Mexican annoyance. Additionally, many Americans had recently immigrated from central and eastern Europe just to avoid forced military service that disrupted their lives for repeated escapades perpetrated by arrogant monarchs. How would they respond to American conscription? Would violence be likely? It had happened before, in 1863, when a call for a new draft in New York City turned into a riot that left scores dead. Irish-Americans had led the way in those riots. As a group they were not happy with a likely U.S. alliance with Britain, the centuries-old occupier of Eire. Moreover, forced military service twinned with the concept of preparedness produced European states armed and ready to fight at the drop of an ultimatum. Wasn't it preparedness, argued Wilson, that led the Old World into such desperate straits in the first place? Why would the United States want to emulate tactics proven so disastrous?

The question of preparedness took on central importance both on the street and in the philosophical parlors. In May 1916 on New York's Fifth Avenue, 135,000 marched in support of preparedness. General Leonard Wood harangued crowds with his criticism of Wilson's go-slow approach to building military strength and instituting conscription. Wood set up a training camp to offer, for a fee, martial-minded businessmen an opportunity to receive the salubrious effects of military training on weekends. Most of those who attended these camps came from the same class that most strongly supported preparedness—the eastern upper classes. They believed that conscription could also knit the American class divide that fueled socialist groups before the war.

Wilson's tempered approach to preparing the country for possible war became the main plank of his 1916 reelection campaign. "He kept us out of war," bragged Democratic supporters. That might have been exactly why some of Wilson's detractors would vote against him. They long ago were fed up with German U-Boat campaigns, spying, and attempts to sabotage domestic shipping to Britain, projects that were sometimes hatched from the very top of the German embassy in Washington. But a majority of Americans still opted for neutrality, tattered as it might be. Wilson beat Charles Evans Hughes, former New York governor and U.S. Supreme Court justice, in the century's closest election. Wilson was returned to power but even he knew that by the end of that year he could no longer keep the United States out of the war. The linchpin on which the precarious peace depended, Berlin's promise to restrict their submarine warfare, was going to fall apart, and Wilson knew it.

By the dawn of a new year, preparedness proponents were winning their case. Wilson had already made some moves to add more weight to the U.S. Army and Navy. His administration realized that surely the United States was on its way to war. He and Secretary of War Newton Baker argued over and over that a draft was unnecessary, even un-American, accepting another antidemocratic principle that had given Europe such woe. Then, shortly before the country declared war on April 6, 1917, Wilson suddenly changed his mind. In May the Selective Service system was launched.

It seems that the Wilson administration opted for compulsory service based on a brief of the experience in Britain. Unlike the continental powers, Britain did not impose a draft until 1916. Two years before, at the war's outbreak, a call to the colors produced an army of recruits from all walks of society: educated, those with trade skills, and general laborers. With no controls on enlistment, the men who signed up simply threw down their tools in industries vital to the war effort. Shortages and industrial dislocation left the country scrambling to run a wartime economy, but there was more to it than that. In the years before the draft England's best educated proved themselves to be among those most keen on military service. These men from the upper classes died in numbers so shocking that it literally left the realm with a shortage of leadership that crippled the nation for a generation.

The U.S. government realized it could not allow the same kind of inefficiency and waste to hamstring its own war effort. Control of enlistment would allow the government to call on men who could be spared from running the country's vital industries, while still collecting together an efficient force for the battlefields. This meant educated men and skilled workers would be carefully evaluated before being allowed to board the ships at Hoboken, New Jersey, the port of embarkation for most of the doughboys. Great enthusiasm to enlist from the college men was dampened, authorities pointing out that patriotic service did not always mean fighting in France. But most of the men who were turned away from service in the battlefields showed great disappointment as government arguments for alternative service fell far short of convincing to the young educated men convinced the Hun was threatening to destroy Western civilization.

Roosevelt was one of those most enthusiastic about throwing some college boys at the German lines. Although he was now nearly 60, he thought it a bully idea to regroup a regiment similar to the Rough Riders that made him so famous during the Spanish-American war. Officers and most men in this volunteer troop would be drawn from the prestigious East Coast universities. The thought of an aging Roosevelt shipping off to France and tramping about causing a sensation in the press, but little effect in combat, encouraged Wilson to propose that no volunteers would be allowed in the new national army: conscripts only. Congress eventually awarded Wilson the opportunity to say no to Roosevelt, and Wilson wasted little time in doing so.

The Selective Service arrangement implemented in June cleverly allowed the government to suggest it was not simply implementing an old-style draft. In fact, Wilson declared it was not a draft at all, merely a selection of candidates from a pool of every patriotic man who clearly would volunteer, that is, nearly everybody. Selective Service boards were set up among local folk to avoid the stigma of young men pressed into military service by a board of military officers from Washington. Those detractors who worried that a general call for volunteers would require motivation by sensational and dangerous propaganda were relieved to learn that a more orderly process was planned. But patriotic enthusiasm spilled through sober rationalism as enthusiastic government officials permitted a festival atmosphere on registration day. In any case, an almost universal enthusiasm for war that Europe had experienced two and one-half years before played a repeat in the United States. The difference was that in August 1914 no one new how violent and murderous the war would be. By spring 1917 a flow of eyewitness descriptions and photos showcased the ghastly lot of the Great War's trenchmen. Yet few stopped to reconsider, possibly because they believed the dash and vigor of American doughboys would surpass the tired caution of European soldiers. But the recruits who considered themselves lucky enough to be selected for service in France found that dash and vigor did not shield them from machine gun and mortar.

Virtues of Being Prepared for War

John J. MacCracken, PhD, LL.D., President, Lafayette College: "The Basis of a Durable Peace"

As citizens of a traditionally neutral power, some Americans during World War I looked to other historic neutrals for guidance. Switzerland is perhaps the most famous neutral state. It declared its neutrality in World War I (and would do so again in World War II), and at the same time prepared for possible invasion. Unlike the United States, however, which made extensive trade agreements with the allies, Switzerland also remained economically neutral. In 1920 Geneva became the home of the League of Nations.

Annals of the American Academy of Political and Social Science, July 1916

I take the opposite view of preparedness from that of Professor Patten. I do not believe that "consciously to prepare drags our social life down to the level of a border town" unless that means the level of such border towns as Geneva or The Hague. Nor that "the present war is a good illustration of how preparedness adds fuel to passions and makes conflict inevitable." Neither do I agree with Professor Patten as to the disastrous effects of some form of universal military training, which would be no more burdensome than the Swiss system, would not only make for preservation of peace within our borders, but would make for democracy by uniting all Americans in at least one common interest, and would supply a certain obvious defect in the moral training now furnished by our public school system. On the other side, I am ready to go farther than Professor Patten probably would by willing to go, in favoring a revision of the doctrine of sovereignty and the yielding of the right to make war to an international tribunal or a league to enforce peace.

Edward S. Mead, PhD, Wharton School of Finance and Commerce, University of Pennsylvania: "The Situation of the United States at the Close of the War as a Question of National Defense"

Military historians often consider the "cult of the offensive" as another cause for war. Today we might use the old saying, the best defense is a good offense. The war's generals universally believed that the speed and verve of patriotic and enthusiastic soldiers could save the day. The victors would be those whose troops could muster the most vigor. A confident, fearless charge might have served in Napoleon's time, but already by the U.S. Civil War it was becoming clear that modern weapons could easily outfight élan. No one learned and generals brought the same tactics to World War I: waves of men on the open fields running toward their target, which they seldom reached. As Charles De Gaulle, who was wounded in World War I, observed, "not all the courage in the world could withstand this fire." [1]

Annals of the American Academy of Political and Social Science, July 1915

No one ever attacks in war. Japan did not attack Russia in 1904. The South did not attack the North during the Civil War. Germany did not attack Belgium and France. Attacking is bad form. The thing to do is to defend, always remembering the military maxim that the best defense is a strong, sudden, unforeseen attack. So we will assume that the United States would never attack anyone, no matter what the provocation, no matter how vital the interests involved. We should, however, defend ourselves if attacked, and at present we are by no means prepared even to protect our shores from invasion, much less to carry the war to our foes.

It is time that the American people—the richest, and at the same time, the most excitable and sensitive people in the world—should realize that they are living in a world of force and should make their preparations accordingly; that they should draw from the Scriptures not merely the mild doctrines of peace, non-resistance and submission to wrong, but should remember that the same Scriptures contain the warning, peculiarly applicable to the United States at the present time, "When a strong man armed keepeth his palace, his goods are in peace, but when a stronger than he shall come upon him, he taketh from him the armor in which he trusted, and divideth the spoil."

Henry D. Estabrook, New York, "Bewaredness"

Many advocates of preparedness constructed a common-sense argument based on personal experience: you wouldn't leave your home unless you know police and fire fighters were protecting you, so why should military preparedness against foreign aggression be any different? The small, low-cost army maintained by the country before World War I did respond to internal skirmishes such as the "Indian Wars," Spanish-American War, and, in 1916, Mexican incursion. But Americans who looked toward the immense armies fighting in Europe took little comfort in the country's modest force. Unsaid was exactly how a foreign invader would cross the seas to invade the United States at a time before long-range aircraft and missiles.

Annals of the American Academy of Political and Social Science, July 1916

Specifically, and as a national issue, preparedness means a military equipment adequate to the defense of this government against possible foreign aggression, and to give sanction to the just demands of our government upon all those who would otherwise disregard them. It is amazing to me that any genuine American should oppose a program looking to this end. Why should our government maintain sheriffs, policemen, a constabulary, and a militia to enforce its demands upon its own citizens, but with fatuous imbecility take it out in scolding and making faces at a foreign enemy? The placid assumption of the pacifists, so called, that perparedness necessarily means war with somebody, or that those who are in favor of it are less concerned than themselves in preserving the peace, is on a par with that assumption once made by Mr. Bryan that all those who were in favor of an honest dollar and opposed to the free coinage of silver at sixteen to one were enemies of the common people to be crucified on a cross of gold.

Editorial: "'Preparedness' for What?"

The tradition of neutrality and isolation from Europe's supposed corruption drove American politics throughout much of the nineteenth century. But by the twentieth century the growing economic power of the vast democracy made such sentiments old-fashioned in the eyes of those who anticipated America's greater role in international politics. The country's response to the Great War became the central event over which this debate would be conducted. Those who opposed traditional isolationism as childish for a country that had "grown up" and was ready for worldwide power won the day as America finally entered the war. But the isolationists had only lost one battle. The sentiment again took a lead after the disillusionment of the Treaty of Versailles. Congress did not ratify the treaty, did not join the League of Nations, and permitted the country to drift backward into isolationist legislation. Only with World War II did Washington realize that isolationism and neutrality were no longer possible for a country that was becoming the world's greatest power.

New Republic, June 26, 1915

If the American people are to be mentally and morally prepared for peace and war they must substitute a positive for a negative responsibility in foreign affairs. Their geographical isolation, like their rigorous constitutionalism, was an advantage during youth, but it accustomed Americans to a provincial and indifferent attitude toward the problem of world politics. It prevented them from thinking internationally and from seeking to adjust their own national interests and ideals to those of other countries. The war has done away with the isolation; it has done away in part with the indifferentism; but it has not done away with the provinciality and the consequent inexperience. Instead of thinking and acting as a self-contained democracy whose virtue depended upon it isolation, the American people must think and act as a democracy whose future depends upon its ability to play its part and assume its responsibility in a society of democratic nations.

Editorial: "Women and Preparedness"

Most countries join wars at least partly based on fears, but it was harder to make the case that the United States was facing a threat. After all, it is bordered east and west by two huge oceans. Canada was friendly and Mexico was militarily weak. This editorial does not specify how what happened in Europe could happen in the United States, but the challenge does evoke the fear that something might.

Delineator, February 1916

Do not prepare for war, say we women folk. Yet war exists!

Think about it! Don't lay your newspapers down with a sigh, saying "Nothing but war news! I'm sick of it!" Think about it! Consider that all your old world-standards have been destroyed; that you and every other newspaper-reader in America to-day owe it to your country, to your hearthstone, to build new standards, new ways of living, in the face of a bloody and stupendous fact. War does exist!

Then ask yourself if you are so willing to believe that what has happened to West Russia, to Poland, to Belgium, to France, to Galicia, can not happen to America, that you will continue to say: "We shall not arm ourselves."

Editorial: "When Peace Comes, What?"

William Jennings Bryan ran, unsuccessfully, three times for president on a Democratic ticket, the final time in 1908. In 1912 he supported Wilson's candidacy; the victorious new president acknowledged Bryan's support by naming him secretary of state. Bryan proved to be an absolute pacifist, beyond Wilson in his opposition to tangling the United States in the war. He resigned in 1915, and his antipreparedness call to strict neutrality waned in influence as the country tipped toward war. After the war, Bryan, a conservative Christian, challenged Clarence Darrow in the famous 1925 Scopes trial pitting Biblical creationism against the theory of evolution. The trial further shattered Bryan's credibility. He died just five days after the trial's close.

North American Review, April 1917

We are all, despite Mr. Bryan, coming to realize the necessity of being well prepared for war before war comes upon us, so as to meet its initial onset with complete readiness. So we should recognize the necessity of being fully prepared for peace before it comes back to the world, so that the moment it comes we shall be ready for its problems and its opportunities.

We are now pretty generally convinced that universal service is the only rational and effective method of securing military preparedness, at any rate in harmony with democratic principles. We ought equally to realize the necessity of universal co-ordination of industries and complete co-operation between the Government and private enterprise, as the only rational and effective method of securing the industrial and commercial efficiency which will enable us successfully to defend ourselves and to improve our opportunities in the era of restored peace which will presently come to the world.

Theodore Roosevelt: "Criticism of the President's Message"

Time and again from 1914 to 1917 Wilson resisted his antagonists who tried to push the administration to a prowar stance. Theodore Roosevelt was most prominent of those critics. The charismatic—or histrionic, depending on one's viewpoint—former president wanted to see a big army and wanted to see it now. Wilson moved as slowly as the country's geographical insulation from Europe's threat allowed. He did support a modest build-up beginning in 1915. This disappointed the antipreparedness voices who thought he had sold out, and the propreparedness side, who thought he had done too little. But this temporizing middle ground effectively helped to draw enough support to win Wilson reelection in 1916.

Theodore Roosevelt (removing hat) greets newspaper reporters, c. 1910. As the country's most famous American of the era, the former president's criticism of Wilson's policies enjoyed extensive coverage. Roosevelt was himself a prolific writer, regularly offering his opinion pieces to a variety of publications. Courtesy of Library of Congress.

New York Times Current History, October 1915–March 1916

In his present message President Wilson advocates as necessary certain propositions for putting this country in a state of preparedness to defend itself against foreign aggression. In his message one year ago he said such propositions were hysterical and improper. I am glad that he has changed his mind, but I am sorry that he has not taken the trouble to study the subject so as to make his proposals reasonably adequate to the country's need. His proposed enlargement of the regular army is utterly inadequate. With certain of his statements it is almost impossible to deal, simply because it seems incredible that their apparent and obvious meaning can be their real meaning.

For example, he says: "We will not maintain a standing army except for uses which are necessary in time of peace as in time of war; and we shall always see to it that our military peace establishment is no larger than is actually and continually needed for the uses of days in which no enemies move against us." What that means I have no idea, and I am certain that no one else has any idea, including the President himself. "What "necessary use" have our forts and our coast guards "in time of peace?" How is our field artillery "continuously needed for the uses of days in which no enemies move against us?" I ask these questions seriously. I defy any man to give me a serious answer which shall not show that the statements are absurdities. . . .

He has met a policy of blood and iron with a policy of milk and water. Indecision, and the treatment of conversation as a substitute for action, and, above all, the making of threats which are not carried into effect, but a premium upon exactly the form of anarchy and conspiracy of which the President complains. Nine-tenths of wisdom consists in being wise in time.

Editorial

The argument that a lack of preparedness cost the United States in previous conflicts attracted promilitary forces, but was not convincing to skeptics. Other wars, or threats of war, were so different from World War I that comparisons seemed overdrawn. In both the War of 1812 and lesser disputes, the United States confronted the British in matters of trade and foreign policy. To expect the United States during this time to engage in an arms race against the world's foremost military power would seem to have been not only expensive and futile, but also provocative. U.S. forces easily drove Spain out of its colonies; it seems no amount of preparedness could have ensured a less bloody guerrilla war in the Philippines following the U.S. invasion.

New Republic, December 19, 1914

In an interesting letter published in another column of this issue, Mr. Robert Herrick states as the first and presumably the most important lesson of the present war that the "one sure way to precipitate war is to prepare for it." The inference from this assertion is that the best way to avoid war is not to prepare for it. American history does not encourage us to accept this inference. The United States was absurdly unprepared for war in 1812, but its unpreparedness did not prevent it from going to war with a light heart. It was relatively still more unprepared when President Cleveland challenged England in 1896, but every one who remembers the public sentiment of that time knows that the overwhelming inferiority of effective naval force would not have prevented this country from fighting. We were saved from war by the forbearance of England, not by the pacifism of unpreparedness. Finally, we went to war with Spain about two years later without having made any previous preparation, and consequently a great many thousand American lives were unnecessarily sacrificed. Nations do not avoid war by preparing for war, but neither do they avoid war by being unprepared for war.

Arthur W. Page, Editorial: "The Press on Preparedness"

The majority of American newspapers before the country's entry into war reflected a majority of Americans in leaning toward the allied viewpoint. British propaganda hoped to sow that fertile ground by encouraging the neutral United States to become less neutral and more warlike, with the presumption that sooner or later the country would actually join the war. And when it did, it would undoubtedly choose the side of the allies. Historians dispute the power of this propaganda, but Britain's censorship office can be credited with controlling much of the war news that flowed from Europe to the United States.

World's Work, November 1915

Of the 261 representative newspaper editors whose views have been obtained, only 6 showed any doubt of a need for stronger national defense. . . .

Many reasons are advanced to explain just why preparedness is essential. The Wichita (Kan.) Beacon points to "the astounding lesson of German system and efficiency," and the Binghamton (N.Y.) Press bluntly adds: "We have been nearly drawn into war with a nation fighting to the limit of its strength. Within ten years we may be confronted by that nation at the height of its power." the Philadelphia North American declares that "there has never been in history, we think, a more striking example of temerity than has been furnished by the United States during the last half year in formulating demands which at any tine may involve it in war, while neglecting the most elementary precautions to enforce its high-sounding words or even to resist further aggression." The Philadelphia Record observes that "the present war teaches that war may happen in a week. It teaches the enormous advantage of preparation in men and munitions to meet an onset."

Drawbacks of Being Prepared for War

Robert Herrick, Chicago, Letter to the Editor: "Mr. Herrick on Armament"

The dreadnought was the first of a new class of battleships built in Britain beginning in 1905. The most formidable floating armada in history, each supported 10 12-inch guns, 24 3-inch guns, 5 torpedo tubes, and armor plating nearly a foot thick. Its steam turbines reached nearly 25,000 horsepower. Fearing their own navies had become obsolete, Britain's rivals, particularly Germany, launched their own dreadnought-building campaigns. The competition became the century's first arms race, shorthand for expensive competition of the preparedness doctrine. In 1914 Britain had 19 dreadnoughts and Germany had 13.

New Republic, December 19, 1914

Sir: The Naval Auxiliary League, a self-consulted organization "boosting" from Washington for a larger navy, has recently opened an office in Chicago, presumably to further its propaganda in the Middle West by taking advantage of the present European war fever. This is but one of numerous indications that the people of the Untied States are being subjected to a systematic campaign in favor of armament. The press, so far as I see it, seems to be entering with enthusiasm on this "cause," propagating fears, creating hypothetical enemies ready to destroy us, urging America to imitate Europe in its delusive methods of "preparation." This increasing agitation is of course one of the evil results of the European insanity that must be expected; it is also a vivid illustration of modern methods of creating hysteria in a democratic state. For the war spirit, whether caused by an illusive fear or an instinct for aggression, is as much a form of hysteria as any pathological state, and Americans unfortunately are only too prone to suffer from attacks of this sort of hysteria.

Without entering into arguments advanced for increasing our army and navy, I wish to state three propositions that the present war has proved so far as it has proved anything: first, the one sure way to precipitate war is to prepare for it, a truth that psychologists have long been aware of. Europe prepared for war intensively for two generations—it was only a question of time when it got war. If we want war with Japan we are doing our best to bring it about, and have been especially since the anti-Japanese agitation, expressed in certain timorous legislation in California. Second, armaments, no matter how up-to-date, are always out of date unless immediately employed, and give their possessors merely a paper advantage over an imaginary foe. As Mr. Wells urged on his countrymen before the outbreak of the war, "dreadnoughting" is both an expensive and delusive game, while intelligence, technical skill, and invention are perpetually changing the terms of warfare. Third, a final decision—to use the current military phrase—is the one result modern war does not produce. War has apparently degenerated from tactics through massed force to the decision by physical exhaustion—its logical conclusion. To speak any longer of the "arbitrament of arms" is as silly as to speak of a trial by combat or other medieval fantasy.

Senator John Sharp Williams: "The Ties that Bind: Our Natural Sympathy with English Traditions, the French Republic, and the Russian Outburst for Liberty"

The cost of preparing for a war that may or may not come evolved into a debate centered as much on questions of class and geography as on defense. Already in early 1916 the Wilson administration had moved toward a modest increase in military expenditures, asking for $300 million. Progressives in Congress hoped to use this request to adjust the newly constitutional income tax to hit harder on high-income Americans. These were the same forces who generally opposed preparedness, and hoped the wealthy in the east who worried about German invasion would worry less when they discovered how much military build-up would take directly from their own accounts.

***National Geographic*, March 1917**

A man who comes upon my place and goes through a pathway that is not a public highway, or who incidentally destroys some property that is growing, I can forgive; but one who comes up to me and tells me that he is going to do it whenever he pleases, because he is stronger than I am, is a man whom I cannot forgive.

Germany thought she was stronger than we; and she is right just now. These ready nations assume a great deal in connection with the unready nations. We two branches of the English-speaking race—across the sea and here—have always been unready for war, thank God, and shall remain so, because we think it is better to call out the full power of the people when the emergency comes than it is to keep them weighted down for 20 years in order to do one year's fighting. As a rule, people do one year's fighting out of each 20 years of their actual existence. We have done less, of course.

Alexander Dana Noyes, Financial Editor of the *New York Evening Post:* "'Preparedness,' Military and Economic"

World War I was a war fueled by emotions but fought by technology, a combination that proved to be horrifyingly deadly. Historians describe the initial exuberance for war as extending to all countries—including the United States in 1917, after two and a half years of ugly slaughter had long torn away any illusion of noble sacrifice. And yet, Americans still believed the New World was morally superior to the old, and that this somehow meant Americans also would be more efficient on the battlefield. High casualty rates showed otherwise. Why the Great War was such a war of emotions in America is hard to explain. To be sure, most war is accompanied by emotional outburst and patriotic zeal, but in America before 1917 little reasonable evidence could be adduced for any serious threat from Germany or any other belligerent. The power of propaganda to whip up anger and fear, while not measurable in these presurvey days, might be at least partially to blame.

Scribner's, June 1916

For the sudden vogue of the "military preparedness" propaganda, there seem, in the view of the ordinary calm observer, to be several different causes. One, and undoubtedly the most convincing, is the belief that for actual defensive purposes, our land forces are not such as to admit either of immediate effective resistance or of rapid expansion into an armament which would be effective. This consideration, to be sure, is of itself no more true to-day than it was ten years ago, or a quarter of a century ago. Particular incidents of the European war, however, have instilled into the minds of many people the further idea that things may happen in this world of ours whose occurrence we supposed, as recently as the middle of 1914, to be wholly inconceivable. This could not fail to be a powerful secondary influence in the "preparedness" discussion.

Yet no one can have missed the third influence: the presence in the United States (and elsewhere throughout the world) of an emotional hysteria, engendered in very infectious form by the controversies of the war. It has not been easy for any individual to keep himself in hand, so to speak, during this clash of strong emotions—which, as a matter of fact, could not possibly be avoided, even in the everyday conversation of the office, the club, or the dining-table. Coming on top of the actual events of the present war, this violence of feeling, and the inevitable resultant extravagance of inference, have rendered peculiarly difficult the sane and sober discussion of problems of national defense.

Washington Gladden: "A Plea for Pacifism: Will America Yield to the Armament Madness?"

Throughout the conflict pessimistic minds maintained that World War I was only the beginning and that even more horrible wars based on invidious diplomacy backed by ever more deadly armament would become the plague of the century. Wilson borrowed this pessimism, turned it around, and announced that his administration's goal in joining the Great War would be to establish a new world order based on his Fourteen Points. This would become a war to end all wars. Even the men in the trenches believed they were making war for immortal peace. Germany asked for an armistice based on the Fourteen Points. The staggering disillusion of the interwar world, when it became clear that millions seemed to have died for nothing, can even be read on the faces of the soldiers who in 1939 marched into another war that fulfilled the previous decades' bleakest predictions. Few celebrated the beginning of World War II as people had celebrated the beginning of World War I.

Nation, August 3, 1916

The policy of preparedness may be advocated by honest men, but it has a way of working out its own results. Armaments mean war, and sooner or later they bring war. Of course, they are for self-defense. All the belligerents on the continent of Europe are fighting on the defensive. Ask them! Now that is the logic of preparedness. No matter what you intend by it, that is what it means; you never can make it mean anything else. The kindling of suspicions and fears always will go hand in hand with the work of building the armament.

One fact we may as well face. If we are going to have war indefinitely, it will not be the same kind of war, it will wax worse and worse continually. Experience makes that plain. This war is immeasurably worse, more fierce, more relentless, more inhuman than any war in history. And the next war, for which we are urged to get ourselves in a state of preparedness, will be as much more diabolical than this, as this is more devilish than any which have preceded it. Thousands of minds, furnished with all the resources of Kultur, will be constantly at work inventing new machinery for mangling men; new methods of inflicting torture; new appliances for erasing the beauty of the earth and ruining its fairest monuments, for making its loveliest lands uninhabitable.

Thomas P. Gore, United States Senator from Oklahoma: "America's World Influence"

Senator Thomas P. Gore was one of America's most distinctive politicians. The first blind senator elected to Congress, he was called the "blind orator" for his excellent speaking and debating ability. As a Populist he ran unsuccessfully for Congress, but in 1907, running as a Democrat, he was elected senator from Oklahoma. Gore supported the Wilson administration until the administration's decision to join the war. He opposed wartime policies including conscription, deficit financing, government controls over industry, and the League of Nations. He was defeated for reelection in 1920, again elected in 1931, and served until 1937. Gore was father of Tennessee Senator Albert Gore, and grandfather of Vice President Al Gore.

Annals of the American Academy of Political and Social Science, July 1916

I heard a senator assert the other day that unpreparedness is the pathway that leads to war. Of course, the senator reasoned well. Who will be so bold as to deny that unpreparedness for war begets war? Was it not the unpreparedness of Germany that precipitated her into this holocaust of blood and fire? Was it not unpreparedness on the part of Russia and on the part of France that broke their peace and dragged them into this carnival of slaughter? Was it not unpreparedness on the part of Austria, Italy and Great Britain that plunged them headlong into this whirlpool of blood, this whirlwind of flame? Who will deny that unpreparedness caused this war? Who will deny that preparedness would have prevented this war? Is not this the logic of militarism?

Did it ever occur to you that every nation on the globe which has prepared for war has got what it prepared for? Did it ever occur to you that the United States, the only great nation under the sun which is unprepared for war, is the only great nation which is today enjoying peace and its infinite blessings? Does this suggest the relationship of cause and effect?

Whatever may be done by our government to further naval and military preparation, whatever may be essential in the way of further naval and military preparation, the United States should continue in the future as in the past to rely chiefly upon moral rather than upon military force, and to dedicate itself to the principles of humanity and to the idea and ideals of peace, arbitration and international justice.

S. N. Patten, PhD, University of Pennsylvania: "The Basis of National Security"

S. N. Patten makes an unusual connection between a sort of "cult of the offensive" argument in favor of preemptive attacks on threats, while maintaining that preparedness should be limited. In truth, the United States did end up following a similar formula. Its preparedness was comparatively low when it declared war in April 1917, despite the fact that the National Defense Act of June 1916 had expanded the army from 90,000 to 175,000, and established the Reserve Officers Training Corps (ROTC). Other legislation expanded navy shipbuilding. But to take the offensive on the huge scale of World War I required more than a year of preparation. The first significant U.S. contribution on the battlefields did not take place before summer 1918.

Annals of the American Academy of Political and Social Science, July 1916

The difference between a pacifist and an emotional patriot is not in the fact of defense but in the bases on which it should rest. Two of these bases are sound even in most advanced nations: first, the best defense is an instinctive defense based on our primary reactions and not on premeditated plans. The prepared nations will get into trouble oftener, do more bluffing and suffer more in the end than they who act only when they see some wrong is committed. Be sure there is some clearly defined cause and then act quickly at any cost until the end is attained. The action of the North in our Civil War is a good example of the virtues and failures of instinctive defense. No one would deny that this action was wiser and more democratic than would have been any amount of conscious military preparation. But something is involved in instinctive defense which most people overlook when the principle is applied to national affairs. No preconceived restraints, no traditional policy, no antique notion of law or right should check the alertness or vigor of effective national protection. Any real danger must be instantaneously guarded against not merely by negative measures but by positive attack.

Anonymous Letter to the Editor

Progressivism in twentieth-century America included proposals to reform American education. Many argued that the traditional approach, which emphasized formal lecture and memorization of classics-based subjects, should be modified to include material of more practical nature and informal activities in which students could learn by doing. Interest in practical subjects led to legislation passed in 1917, the year the country entered the war, to provide funds for vocational education. Educators such as John Dewey had argued for change years before the Great War began, but more emphasis on practical learning certainly would fit well into the country's wartime needs.

***Delineator*, June 1915**

I am the mother of four beautiful boys, the oldest fourteen. In my veins is the blood of seven Revolutionary soldiers. I am sure I am not a coward, and would respond if called upon to serve my country. The question is: How best to serve it?

I believe that all future time will be influenced by what we do now. Also, I believe if we increase our army and navy we will be tempted to use them. The man who is ready for a fight will surely find that fight sooner or later. But the man who refuses to fight rarely has any trouble in that direction. No, we don't want defenses of that sort.

The picture of "England's Women Training for Home Defense" in the April Delineator makes a shudder run over me. Women were made to give life, not to take it. The picture of the boys and girls in the February Delineator brings the tears. Little innocents—training for what? And not because I am not patriotic, for I never see the flag unfurled without a thrill of love and patriotism.

I believe thoroughly in any training that develops the boys and girls physically, mentally, and morally, that they may be a greater asset to the nation and at the same time get the most out of life for themselves.

Now, is there no way in which this vast amount of money that is spent for armies and navies can be used to educate the world in ways of peace? We, with our big, beautiful country, surely can take the lead and see such an example that peace will be so attractive, our country so great and the brotherhood of man so strong, that other nations will follow. What a movement with which to be connected! Would it be possible for another nation to march through our land and kill and destroy if we did not wish to fight?

Don C. Seitz, Manager, *New York World:* "Moral Influences in a Durable Peace"

Michel de Montaigne, the great sixteenth-century French essayist, was from a wealthy Bordeaux family. Castles by the 1500s were obsolete for military defense, but Montaigne retreated to the family tower in 1571 as a metaphorical defense, calling it his "citadel." He isolated himself in the library there for almost a decade while composing his famous essays. These did not often address military matters, but Montaigne did observe, related to preparedness, that "A man may repose more confidence in a sword he holds in his hand than in a bullet he discharges out of a pistol, wherein there must be a concurrence of several circumstances to make it perform its office, the powder, the stone, and the wheel: if any of which fail it endangers your fortune. A man himself strikes much surer than the air can direct his blow."[2]

Annals of the American Academy of Political and Social Sciences, July 1917

It is history that the common people rarely make war. War begins either through oppressions or the obsessions of the great. The assailed, perforce, must fight. To save themselves to commit reprisals or to resist. We have been reluctant here to feel that such a step would become necessary and even now make a slow business of it. That preparedness may be needful because of the aggressiveness of others I cannot deny. To the argument that it is an insurance for peace I do emphatically dissent. Montaigne once observed that the walls of his castle on the mountain from which he took his title were in bad repair. Indeed, there was more breach visible than bastion. His neighbors were always reproaching him for permitting such dilapidatedness to prevail and pointing out the peril he underwent. The philosopher answered by saying he had noted that the strongest defenses had to stand the most assaults. During twenty years no hostile force had ever tackled the mountain, but his well-walled neighbors had to withstand many a fierce foray!

It is no time now to argue our own position. We have taken unexceptionable ground, even though departing wide from our ancient principles. World power means world responsibility, if we choose to make it so. The giant declines to remain longer supine. We do not greet the change eagerly. There is doubt in many an American mind as to the wisdom of so wide a purpose. Yet there could be no other justification save to aid the cause of universal democracy. If the task brings us to a world-state where rules can be made the servants of the people, the die will have been well cast. But there are perils beyond. We, too, may forge tools that will cut their owners. We may take on a lust for conquest that will bring evil in its train. We will surely fill the minds of men with the excitement and confusion of war and when it is over these minds will not adjust themselves to the humdrum of an industrious and quiet life, but will remain idle and distracted to the end of their days. This is one of the greatest evils growing out of such a conflict. The dead and wounded count much, but the mentally disabled count far more.

Oswald Garrison Villard, *New York Evening Post*: "Preparedness Is Militarism"

Oswald Garrison Villard was one of America's most prominent pacifists and progressive editors and writers during World War I. As grandson of abolitionist William Lloyd Garrison, Villard doggedly pursued idealistic causes regardless of the winds of American public opinion. It cost him and in 1918 he lost his New York Evening Post *because his antiwar sentiments had become so unpopular. Villard also supported rights of African Americans during one of the most violently racist periods in American history. He was a founder in 1909 of the National Association for the Advancement of Colored People (NAACP), supporting its famous leader and editor, W.E.B. Du Bois.*

***Annals of the American Academy of Political and Social Science*, July 1916**

It is a militarism which eats up such vast treasures in wood and iron and steel as to make ridiculous even in our unprepared country any campaign for the preservation of national resources. What will that avail if our defense bill next year is to be more than half a billion dollars?

Surely so intelligent a people as our own is not long thus to be deceived as to the significance of the new use of the old enslaving cries of patriotism, of national safety, of rallying about the flag. Nebraska and Michigan have just bid us believe that others will soon see how for us, too, the paths of military glory "lead but to the grave"—to the despair that wrings the hearts of Europe and of England for all who stop to think of the losses to the world from a war which could never have come but for the armies and navies built up for defensive purposes and the war-parties born of them, the real reason for which war no man knoweth. American sanity and intelligence will speedily see that the outcry for more soldiers and ships comes not from the masses of the people, but from the fortunate classes in life, and particularly from the very classes that have heretofore battened upon every special privilege. The coming of "preparedness" spells but a new phase of the old battle of democracy against privilege.

American sanity and intelligence and wisdom ought to see to it when the war excitement is over and news of preparedness is no longer featured in the press as once were the free-silver fallacy and the battles against the trusts and the railroads, that their government faces the other way. Indeed, for right-thinking people this is the time to let the time-serving and compromising administration in Washington know that they expect of it the highest "preparedness" in the form of a readiness to take the lead at the peace conference in proposing international disarmament or in calling a conference for this purpose simultaneously with the peace conference. As Mr. Lansing and Mr. Wilson rise to this opportunity, so will their final standing be at the bar of history.

John J. MacCracken, PhD, LL.D., President, Lafayette College: "The Basis of a Durable Peace"

In expressing his disagreement, John J. MacCracken presents several common criticisms of preparedness. The debate over the cost of keeping a large military during peacetime never has been settled. The United States after World War I damped down its military from more than two million to 204,000 by 1920. This was the last time the United States would choose to question a doctrine of preparedness. From fewer than 200,000 soldiers, by 1945 the Franklin D. Roosevelt administration had expanded the military to more than eight million to fight World War II. Subsequent wars required a return of the Selective Service; at its peak, nearly half a million troops fought in Vietnam. The commitment to preparation has cost the country many trillions of dollars. The 2004 Pentagon budget alone was $379.9 billion. In comparison, World War I cost the United States about $22.6 billion, or about $227 billion in today's dollars.

Annals of the American Academy of Political and Social Science, July 1916

I take the opposite view of preparedness from that of Professor Patten. I do not believe that "consciously to prepare drags our social life down to the level of a border town" unless that means the level of such border towns as Geneva or the Hague. Nor that "the present war is a good illustration of how preparedness adds fuel to passions and makes conflict inevitable." Neither do I agree with Professor Patten as to the disastrous effects of some form of universal military training, which would be no more burdensome than the Swiss system, would not only make for preservation of peace within our borders, but would make for democracy by uniting all Americans in at least one common interest, and would supply a certain obvious defect in the moral training now furnished by our public school system. On the other side, I am ready to go farther than Professor Patten probably would by willing to go, in favoring a revision of the doctrine of sovereignty and the yielding of the right to make war to an international tribunal or a league to enforce peace.

Arthur W. Page, Editorial: "Civilization vs. 'Kultur'"

Arthur W. Page presents a case historians have long debated: Germany prepared for war because it intended to go to war. The debate has not been settled, but it does seem clear that Europe before the war had prepared to an extraordinary scale, and that the guns backing their diplomacy encouraged brinkmanship. Expressions dating from World War I—the "mailed fist" of Austria to Serbia, Germany's "gunboat diplomacy" against British and French colonialism—suggest a warlike attitude backed by actual firepower.

World's Work, June 1915

The present war proves, as any practical man can see, that a nation that does not wish to be imposed on must have the ability to defend itself. The innocence of Belgium did not save her from Germany, nor has the innocence of China saved her from the impositions of Japan.

But the present war proves nearly as clearly that great armaments are likely to beget enemies even faster than they develop strength. Great armaments need not necessarily begat enemies, but if they encourage a people to believe in force alone, as they are very likely to do, they become a source of weakness rather than strength, for they raise up enough enemies to nullify all preparations. This is what has happened to Germany. No country could be better organized for war. Germany had the greatest army in the world. It was bigger than the French army, more powerful than the Russian army, superior to any other army. The rulers of Germany knew this and they seemed to believe also that their rights were as wide as their army was efficient.

Editorial, W.E.B. Du Bois: "Preparedness"

The influential African American editor repeatedly and correctly called the Wilson administration to task for its hypocrisy. If Wilson had any deplorable weakness, it was his obvious racism. He was a product of the South, raised in Virginia, Georgia, and South Carolina. As were many men of his age, he was convinced of the superiority of white Christian people.

Crisis, March 1916

Is there any "preparedness" for Christianity, for human culture, for peace or even for war, that is more pressing than the abolition of lynching in the United States? Alas! We have little hope of reaching the ears of the President. He is too busy yelling for the largest navy in the world.

Samuel T. Dutton, LL.D., New York: "United States and War"

Japan was an ally of Britain, and so became part of the allies during World War I. Before the war it had grown from an isolated society into a major, sometimes threatening, military power. Disagreement between Japan and the Theodore Roosevelt administration over Russian reparation payments and U.S. treatment of Japanese immigrants led to fear of Japanese interference in the U.S. occupation of the Philippines and possible war with Japan. A 1908 treaty soothed hard feelings. Japan joined the scramble for colonies by warring with Russia and China in 1895 and 1905. Victorious in both cases, by 1910 it controlled Korea and Taiwan. During the war Japan's naval forces occupied several German colonies in the Pacific.

Annals of the American Academy of Political and Social Sciences, July 1917

Another relation of America to the war is that of our relative unpreparedness. In the eyes of many this is to be deplored and some have thought it to be a national crime. I cannot agree with that point of view. If Great Britain and France had been prepared as Germany was it would have been difficult to say who caused war. France was only moderately prepared and did not wish the war. Russia wished to avoid it. The communications of Sir Edward Grey to the Central Powers during the few days preceding the war show conclusively that Great Britain earnestly sought to prevent the war. The preparedness of this country as compared with that of Germany was far below the requirements of the modern war. Ten years ago Colonel Roosevelt as President was clamoring for six battleships per annum. Some of us pacifists (the term pacifist was then in less disrepute than at present) thought that two were enough. We deprecated having our government act as though it were preparing to fight Japan. I now thank God that we built battleships only moderately. We have far less old junk on hand now and our friendship with Japan has been growing year by year in spite of Captain Hobson and the yellow press. Furthermore, ships built ten years ago would be of very little use now. Naval defense has been revolutionized by the present war and we do not know today what will be required two years hence or five years hence. We do know that we will have to build a different type of ship from those demanded two or three years ago. Of the three hundred war vessels listed in a recent journal many are out of date; like automobiles warships must be of 1917, 1918, and 1919.

Our army has been too small, everybody knew it, but in prosperous times it is hard to get enlisted men. I wish to say that while I believe there has been a lack of efficiency in the administration of the departments of war and navy, I am glad that we have thus far maintained the reputation of not fearing our neighbors and have not needed to heap up great armaments. Moreover, I believe that when this struggle has reached its logical conclusion we can then adapt a policy of greater moderation in expenditure for the enginery of war.

Questions

1. The United States today has clearly come down in favor of preparedness. Because its military is the world's most powerful, are political leaders, as some during World War I argued, more likely to use that power to start wars?
2. Critics of the dreadnaught-building campaign claimed this costly armaments race drained government money from other programs while doing nothing to preserve peace. How could participation in an arms race enhance the preservation of peace?
3. How was the concept of military preparedness related to American disputes between upper and lower classes during World War I?
4. In a democracy that guarantees personal freedom to individuals, when is it fair—if ever—for a government to require military service?

Notes

1. "Unjustly Accused: Marshal Ferdinand Foch and the French 'Cult of the Offensive,'" First World War.com. http://www. firstworldwar.com/features/foch.htm.

2. Michel de Montaigne, "Of War-Horses or Destriers," Great Books Index. http://books.mirror.org/gb.montaigne.html.

Chapter 8

U.S. Foreign Policy in the World War I Era

In August 1914 Woodrow Wilson was just a year and a half into his first term as president, following one of the most significant elections in U.S. history. The new century had greeted an America facing tremendous social, cultural, and political change. Massive industrial growth had turned a generally agrarian country into a great power of the machine age. Huge fortunes floated tycoons of immense wealth and power while average Americans worked long hours at low pay in dangerous conditions. Racial hatred had reached a zenith not seen since days of slavery, with hundreds of blacks lynched every year. A large immigrant population sent children to work, lived in squalid tenements, and more and more often supported the socialist press.

Socialism during this period reached the highest mainstream audience in America that it would ever see. In 1912 one of Wilson's credible opponents for president was Socialist Party candidate Eugene V. Debs, who campaigned against the power of capitalism. In 1916 he won election to the House of Representatives from Indiana, but the 1918 war hysteria brought him to jail for a vaguely antiwar comment that was part of a longer speech. (He was pardoned without apology three years later by the Harding administration.) In the plains states, farmers representing strong immigrant populations struck against eastern financial interests by establishing a home-grown socialist party, the Non-Partisan League. The league was particularly influential during World War I, complaining that prowar forces merely shilled for capitalists who demanded war to protect their financial interest in an allied victory.

The role of the changing nation so split political parties that Republicans tore off to form a new party, the Progressives or "Bull-Moose" Party. This split might have been inconsequential to national politics if not for its leader, Theodore Roosevelt, the most well-known and controversial political figure of the era. Roosevelt had served as president starting in 1901, when as former vice president he filled out assassinated President William McKinley's term. He was reelected in 1904. Roosevelt used his prodigious intellectual energy and personal persuasiveness to battle what he called the "trusts," the immense power of large industrialists. His progressive polices led to new laws regulating railroads, hazardous food and medicine, and greater stewardship of natural resources.

Roosevelt's foreign policy reflected his belief that the United States was ready to play a more important role in world affairs, and to do that needed a larger military backing. His campaign to "speak softly and carry a big stick" reflected personal commitments to living what he called the "strenuous life" of cowboying, big game hunting, adventuring, and fearing nothing. In character it seemed he could not be more different from the introspective Wilson who, a reporter complained, had a cold-fish handshake. But Wilson proved to be a man of extraordinarily strong vision and commitment to principle.

Republicans did not necessarily support some of the progressive policies of its charismatic leader. When Roosevelt declared his intention not to run for a third term as president, he named his secretary of war, William Howard Taft, as his replacement. But after Roosevelt returned from a big-game hunting expedition in Africa, he discovered that Taft's more conservative policies had split the Republican Party. Supporters persuaded him to run again under a third party, the Progressives. But Roosevelt's strong showing at the polls, along with a million votes cast for socialist candidate Debs, split the vote to carry a Democrat to the White House.

Like Roosevelt, Wilson's strength was forged by childhood challenges. Roosevelt was asthmatic and sickly and from childhood, obliged to wear thick glasses; Wilson was dyslexic. Wilson overcame his affliction to establish himself as a young intellectual star, a popular Princeton University professor who spoke of America's class injustice and the excessive power of big business. Publications in popular magazines gave him national fame, and he became president of Princeton in 1902. His strong progressivist work as newly elected governor of New Jersey swept him to Washington on a wave of reformist sentiment.

Wilson aimed to further his domestic policies without an inkling that his presidency would be dominated by foreign affairs and, what is more, that his decisions would become critical to the destiny of the entire globe. When war was declared in August 1914, he immediately sided with the country's traditional policy of neutrality. Fearing the country's festering divisions of class and immigrant origin, he warned on August 19,

> I venture, therefore, my fellow countrymen, to speak a solemn word of warning to you against that deepest, most subtle, most essential breach

> of neutrality which may spring out of partisanship, out of passionately taking sides. The United States must be neutral in fact, as well as in name, during these days that are to try men's souls. We must be impartial in thought, as well as action, must put a curb upon our sentiments, as well as upon every transaction that might be construed as a preference of one party to the struggle before another.

Wilson worked for the next two and a half years to end the war by providing neutral negotiating opportunities to the belligerents. He sent his aide, Colonel Edward House, to Europe in hopes he could bring warring nations to compromise. As late as the end of 1916, Wilson again proposed a "peace without victory," but by then warring nations had raised the death toll's stake in victory to such a level that no compromise could be possible.

Meanwhile Wilson refused to be drawn into the war that hawks like Roosevelt had demanded as early as 1914. His opponents had plenty of ammunition; Germany's invasion of Belgium, its atrocities (real and made-up), and its submarine campaign against merchant shipping were more than enough reason for those who wanted war. In fact, Washington nearly declared war in May 1915 following the sinking of the passenger liner *Lusitania* on which 128 Americans lost their lives. Germany protested that the liner was carrying munitions and was thus a legitimate target. Additionally, the German government had warned American civilians against sailing on the *Lusitania* while it was still in New York Harbor. Newspaper advertisements and notes to passengers publicly called the Cunard-owned liner a candidate for a torpedo. But in an oblivious response that resembled the cartoon character's famous "What, Me Worry?" grin, most Americans sailed anyway. Alfred Vanderbilt, a tycoon's son, crumpled and threw away the telegraph message he had received that warned: "Have it on definite authority the *Lusitania* is to be torpedoed. You had better cancel passage immediately." He died when the ship exploded and in minutes, sank.

Responding to Wilson's ultimatum demanding Berlin restrict its submarine warfare, Berlin promised to suspend attacks on merchant shipping. While his critics called him a coward for not going to war, Wilson declared that America was "too proud to fight." Democrats were able to parley Wilson's recalcitrance into its 1916 campaign slogan: "He kept us out of war." Opposing Wilson was a compromise candidate, respected U.S. Supreme Court Justice Charles Evans Hughes, who was expected to heal the fissure of the party between progressives and conservatives. Unfortunately, Hughes prevaricated on most issues, earning the nickname "Charles Evasive Hughes." He lost to Wilson—but barely. In fact, historians have noted that had only 4,000 Californians voted for Hughes, he, and not Wilson, would have led the country through its most trying period since the Civil War.

Wilson by this time had concluded that he could no longer keep the United States out of war. Intelligence clearly indicated that Germany intended to suspend its promise to restrict its U-Boat campaign, and it was this issue that had brought the two nations to the brink 18 months prior. Still, when Germany announced its intention early in 1917, Wilson still did not immediately ask for a war declaration. He asked Congress instead for the right to arm merchant ships. Was this the last step before war? Berlin's unwise skullduggery made it so. German foreign secretary Alfred Zimmermann secretly telegrammed Mexico City to propose an alliance against the United States. Presumed benefit to Mexico would be recovery of territory lost in 1848. Germany also hoped that, despite its alliance with Britain and France, Japan would assist, given its formerly acrimonious relations with the United States during Theodore Roosevelt's administration. The proposal was not perhaps quite as absurd as it appeared. German observers of the U.S. military's clumsy pursuit of Pancho Villa had convinced Berlin that American troops were not much of a threat. Additionally, by 1917, Germany had suffered the United States victualing its enemies for nearly three years. Germany seemed to have nothing to lose but the propaganda battle. In America, proponents of preparedness had warned of possible invasion by Germany. It seemed far-fetched—until now. When Washington made the Zimmermann telegram public (it had been intercepted by Britain and turned over to Wilson), the country rose in indignation. How could it possibly be true? At this moment it might have been wise for Zimmermann to retreat into sage denial. Instead he freely admitted sending the message, one of the more obvious examples of Germany's ever witless public relations during this war.

On April 2, 1917, Wilson asked Congress to declare war on Germany. He concluded:

> There are, it may be, many months of fiery trial and sacrifice ahead of us. It is a fearful thing to lead this great peaceful people into war, into the most terrible and disastrous of all wars, civilization itself seeming to be in the balance. But the right is more precious than peace, and we shall fight for the things which we have always carried nearest our hearts—for democracy, for the right of those who submit to authority to have a voice in their own governments, for the rights and liberties of small nations, for a universal dominion of right by such a concert of free peoples as shall bring peace and safety to all nations and make the world itself at last free. To such a task we can dedicate our lives and our fortunes, everything that we are and everything that we have, with the pride of those who know that the day has come when America is privileged to spend her blood and her might for the principles that gave her birth and happiness and the peace which she has treasured. God helping her, she can do no other.[1]

A few implacable pacifists tried to block the declaration, but were swept away by an almost unanimous declaration. The American age of neutrality was over.

Misguided Foreign Policy

Theodore Roosevelt: "Utopia or Hell"

Despite his warmongering reputation during World War I, Roosevelt had impressive credentials as a peacemaker. As president, he negotiated a "Gentleman's Agreement" with Japan that sidestepped a possible U.S. war with that country over immigration issues. He persuaded Germany to avoid war over a colonial dispute with France over Morocco (the Algeciras Conference of 1906). His work as mediator to end the Russo-Japanese war won him the Nobel Peace Prize in 1906, the first American to be so honored.

Independent, **January 4, 1915**

Elaborate technical arguments have been made to justify this timid and selfish abandonment of duty, this timid and selfish failure to work for the world peace of righteousness, by President Wilson and Secretary Bryan. No sincere believer in disinterested and self-sacrificing work for peace can justify it; and work for peace will never be worth much unless accompanied by courage, effort and self-sacrifice. Yet those very apostles of pacifism who, when they can do so with safety, scream loudest for peace, have made themselves objects of contemptuous derision by keeping silence in this crisis, or even by praising Mr. Wilson and Mr. Bryan for having thus abandoned the cause of peace. They are supported by the men who insist that all that we are concerned with is ourselves escaping even the smallest risk that might follow upon the performance of duty to any one except ourselves. This last is not a very exalted plea. It is, however, defensible. But if as a nation we intend to act in accordance with it, we must never promise to do anything for any one else.

The technical arguments as to the Hague conventions not requiring us to act will at once be brushed aside by any man who honestly and in good faith faces the situation. Either the Hague conventions meant something or else they meant nothing. If in the event of their violation none of the signatory powers were even to protest, then of course they meant nothing; and it was an act of unspeakable silliness to enter into them. If, on the other hand, they meant anything whatsoever, it was the duty of the United States as the most powerful, or at least the richest and most populous neutral nation, to take action for upholding them when their violation brought such appalling disaster to Belgium. There is no escape from this alternative.

Walter Lippmann: "United States and International Relations"

Lippmann is considered one of the twentieth century's greatest journalists. He began his career in magazines, edited the New York World *from 1929 until its demise in 1931, and wrote a syndicated column until 1967. During that time he also won two Pulitzer prizes and published nearly two dozen books. Lippmann's unquestionable influence on Woodrow Wilson can be traced through many of his ideals that influenced the president's Fourteen Points. Lippmann was a progressive who supported the war hoping it would lead to a better America. But he became one of the most prominent and influential of Americans disillusioned as the interwar period proved that World War I solved little.*

Annals of the American Academy of Political and Social Science, July 1916

Surely, no one will dare to come before you urging us to a policy of armed isolation. For isolation is out of the question because it postulates an impossibility. It assumes that we can somehow or other ignore the fate of the British Empire; it assumes that somehow or other we are not concerned with the disintegration of sea power; it assumes that we can compete with British trade, the British marine, and the British navy without bringing disaster upon ourselves. Those who talk of isolation merely reveal their indifference. They simply refuse to face the stern realities which a change in world conditions has revealed to the imagination. We are in a time when the inadequacy of language is a cause of despair. For all that we care about hangs upon a vision of what sea power means, and upon the will to act upon that vision.

Anonymous: "The President and Foreign Affairs"

Throughout the nineteenth century American presidents were preoccupied with domestic issues, often at a very detailed level. As the federal government was much smaller than it is today, their job included such mundane decisions as hiring postmasters and sending out troops to quell local skirmishes. Presidents did not travel abroad. Woodrow Wilson had never been overseas before steaming to Paris in December 1918 to negotiate the Treaty of Versailles. He was the first American president to cross the Atlantic Ocean.

Nation, July 6, 1916

Will it in the future be necessary to each of our candidates for the Presidency some personal knowledge of other countries and experience abroad? The question seems fantastic, particularly when one recalls how few of our Presidents have really known anything of Europe before being called to the White House. But when one remembers that foreign affairs have loomed larger under President Wilson than domestic issues, and that either he or Mr. Hughes will have to deal with the momentous settlement of the European war besides the Mexican problem, it is perfectly evident—as, indeed, it was prior to the catastrophe abroad—that our Presidents must more and more concern themselves with foreign affairs. Particularly will this be so if we move toward a world court or take some other step towards internationalism.

The value of such a personal knowledge of other countries is so clearly illustrated in Mr. Wilson's case by his lack of it, one could almost wish for a requirement that no one be allowed to qualify as President without at least two years of residence abroad. Of course, Mr. Wilson is not an exception to the rule. The whole period of "shirt-sleeves diplomacy" we went through in the last year was based in large part upon ignorance of other people's aims and objects and methods of doing business. These we took pleasure in flouting in order to prove our superiority. But at every turn in his dealings with Europe, notably Germany, Mr. Wilson has been handicapped by ignorance of the points of view of other peoples.

Editorial: "The Autocrat of American Policy"

Despite the wide gulf between the views of Wilson and Roosevelt, both presidents sought an expansion of executive power at home and abroad. Both were highly persuasive speakers and prolific writers. Roosevelt's personal charisma and vigorous appearance could not be matched by the more reserved Wilson, who also couldn't match Roosevelt's "horse-trading" skill with Congress—tragically, as it turned out. Sometimes during Wilson's administration the president's principled aloofness led to prickly encounters with journalists, who could show particular skill at exasperating both civilian and military leaders. But generally the Wilson administration enjoyed uncritical press support for its wartime decisions.

North American Review, February 1917

The newspapers of January 9 reported that President Wilson, at his weekly conference the day before with the Washington correspondents, had severely scolded the American Press. It was by no means the first chastisement that the journalists of the United States had received from that quarter, nor is it likely to be the last. The President, it appeared, "was particularly annoyed at the reported statements that he intended another peace note." He regarded such statements as "capable of the most serious damage." He told the shrinking correspondents quite flatly that speculation in the Press about international affairs "had embarrassed the Government in the past and that unless it stopped the country might eventually be drawn into war."

We can recall nothing quite like this since the Lord Curzon of twenty-five years ago—he was then Mr. Curzon, and the Under-Secretary for Foreign Affairs, and an extremely omniscient young man with an over-powering Oxford manner—used to be represented in the London papers, and without any great exaggeration, as opening his speeches with some such shattering pronouncement at this: "Unless there is absolute silence on the Front Opposition Bench, I can no longer be responsible for the Peace of Europe." Unless absolute silence is henceforth maintained by the American Press on all matters of international politics, and editors and correspondents and publicists cease their intrusive speculations on questions that are no concern of theirs and that the President alone is competent to discuss, Mr. Wilson, it appears, can no longer be responsible for the Peace of the United States.

Such a claim, such a warning, such an admonition, invites to thought. It is but the latest of many incidents that reveal the extraordinary conditions under which the foreign policy of the country is conducted. They are conditions that are thoroughly and dangerously undemocratic. They combine a concentration of power in the hands of one man and a secrecy in the exercise of it such as, we believe, can be paralleled nowhere else on earth.

Count E. Reventlow, from the *Illustrirte Zeitung*: "The Neutrals in This War"

The United States vigorously protested Britain's high-handed tactics as its Atlantic blockade grew bolder and effectively isolated Germany from neutral trade. British navy ships stopped merchant vessels, boarded and confiscated an ever-growing list of "contraband" destined for Germany through other neutral countries, particularly Scandinavia (London compensated merchants for confiscated goods). Britain blacklisted American merchants thought to be particular offenders. The United States protested that Britain had no right to do this, but nothing changed. Germany made a credible argument that submarine warfare was its only recourse against a blockade designed to starve the country. When U-Boat 20 torpedoed the liner Lusitania *in May 1915, however, Americans complained that boarding and confiscation was one thing, but murdering American civilians was quite another. German indications of regret were hardly credible since the government celebrated the sinking, even forging a commemorative medal.*

New York Times Current History, October 1914–March 1915

The United States has put up with all England's violations of sea rights and all maltreatment of neutral commerce, although these were quite unprecedented. On the other side, the United States has ignored the fact that the German Government, at the beginning of the war, expressly declared that it would be ready to ratify all hitherto unratified agreements concerning maritime rights, in order to secure the rights of neutrals and neutral commerce in this war. But when Germany, through just necessity to defend herself against England's starvation war, launched her U-boat war against English commerce, after giving loyal notice of the fact, the United States assumed an attitude of bitterness against us. As already said, it is to be hoped that the spirit of equity and impartiality will gain the upper hand in Washington. Germany knows that she is defending her rights, and from the beginning of the war has been sincerely ready to care for and safeguard the rights of neutrals.

From the beginning of the war the United States was in a position to unite with the maritime neutral States and to enter into an agreement with them to defend neutral shipping and neutral rights trampled under foot by England. Norway, Sweden, Denmark, and Holland would have been grateful to America for this, and together they would have formed a powerful group which even Great Britain would have had to respect. For Great Britain is commercially dependent on the United States. But nothing whatever came of this, because of America's leaning toward our enemies, so that the minor maritime States of Europe have had to put up with severe treatment at England's hands. The English Government said to them: We regret if you suffer, but it is better that you should suffer than that Great Britain should suffer.

While the United States further reaps great advantages from the war, and will have wrested from Great Britain her commercial and financial supremacy to a great degree after the war, while North America will stand free and unexhausted after the war, with a mightily swollen check-book, the maritime neutrals of Europe have seen leaner days than ever before. Add to this, that Great Britain presses more hardly on each of them, to induce it to surrender its neutrality. Holland and Denmark would be the most useful to the Britons, and therefore the firm stand of these States up to the present is the more worthy of recognition.

G. Lowes Dickinson: "Democratic Control of Foreign Policy"

The scandal of the "secret treaties" became to Americans a prime example of the difference between the corrupt Old World and the virtuous New World. Historians throughout the interwar period scoured the treaties that were made public in an attempt to pin blame for the war. A conclusion was that everyone was to blame based on these interlocking obligations made in foreign offices without consulting parliaments. Later historiography has cast some doubt on this secret diplomacy as a principal reason for war, but the idea of closed-door meetings and agreements was so offensive to Wilson that he made its elimination Point One of his Fourteen Points: "Open covenants of peace openly arrived at, with no secret international agreements in the future."

Atlantic Monthly, August 1916

On November 23, 1912, there appeared in the London Times a remarkable article, from which the following is an extract:

> "Who then makes war? The answer is to be found in the chancelleries of Europe, among the men who have too long played with human lives as pawns in a game of chess, who have become so enmeshed in formulae and the jargon of diplomacy that they have ceased to be conscious of the poignant realities with which they trifle. . . ."

Presently, under the stress of war, this truth became too intolerable to be credible. People cannot fight unless they believe that they are fighting for a great cause; and so, in fact, they always manage to believe it. None the less, these voices at the outset of the war were the true ones. It is a diplomats' war. None of the peoples wanted it, and none of them would have stood for it, if in some way they could have been jointly consulted in the light of full knowledge of the fact. But they were not consulted, either jointly or severally, no more in the countries called democratic than in the autocracies. If they had been, there would have been no war. Hence the movement for the democratic control of foreign policy.

That movement, I believe, is essentially sound. The existing situation, in democratic countries, is on the face of it preposterous. On questions of domestic policy, in such countries, the people are constantly consulted. An insurance bill, a shop-hours bill, an education bill, a land bill, are canvassed eagerly and passionately in Parliament and the country. the whole press is set in motion; public meetings are held, deputations are arranged, ministries rise and fall. But where hundreds of millions of money and hundreds of thousands of lives are concerned, where the very existence of the country is at stake; where the decision to be taken involves not an extra tax, or a tentative experiment in social legislation, easily to be recalled or modified if it does not succeed, but the immediate summoning of the whole manhood of the country to kill and be killed in ways of unimaginable horror; when, in short, that very thing to the fostering and development of which every act of man, private and public, is rightly and exclusively directed; when life itself is to be destroyed wholesale, that decision, the most terrible any nation can be called upon to take, is precipitated by the fiat of half a dozen men, working in the dark, without discussion, without criticism, without a "by your leave" or "with your leave"; and those who are to sacrifice, in pursuance of it, everything which hitherto they have created and cherished, have no other choice than to accept the decision and pay the intolerable price. Surely only a god should have such power over men! And we give it to an emperor or a secretary of state.

That, in brief, is the general case for democratic control of foreign affairs. And to any one who believes at all in the root principle of democracy, the control by men of their own lives and their own affairs, it must seem a strong one. there are, however, real difficulties felt in accepting it even among men otherwise democratically minded.

Robert J. Lansing, United States Secretary of State: "Our Foreign Policy in This War"

Robert J. Lansing, an expert in international affairs, became secretary of state after William Jennings Bryan resigned in protest of Wilson's wavering neutrality following the sinking of the Lusitania. *Lansing urged caution against those foes of his administration who would have declared war immediately. Less than a year later that same passion would also infect Americans.*

***New York Times Current History*, April–September 1916**

The peoples and Governments at war are blinded by passion; their opinions are unavoidably biased; their conduct frequently influenced by hysterical impulses which approach to madness. Patience and forbearance are essential to a neutral in dealing with such nations. Acts, which, under normal conditions, would be most offensive, must be considered calmly and without temper.

August Schvan, Stockholm, Sweden: "Six Essentials to Permanent Peace"

Nationalism, the fairly modern idea that a person belongs to a particular nation with its own culture and history, fueled the patriotism that antagonized old empires before World War I. Threats to the Ottoman and Austria-Hungarian empires encouraged wars and violent resistance, as nationalist separatism confronted central control. World War I, in the larger sense, can be blamed on burgeoning nationalism, from Germany to Italy to the Balkan states. Leaders responsible for the Treaty of Versailles hoped to control destabilizing nationalist sentiment through Wilson's Fourteen Points, which emphasized self-determination, and supra-national control of foreign affairs. But the world was not ready to surrender the supremacy of nation-states to international control, as advocated here. It still is not.

Annals of the American Academy of Political and Social Science, July 1915

This conquest of the globe by knowledge, by science, or whatever we choose to call it, brings with it the foundations for permanent peace and disarmament, provided we draw all the consequences which it implies. The most important is that the national governments no longer should be allowed to retain any functions of sovereignty outside the borders of their respective nations. The time has come when national governments should occupy the same positions as our municipalities. They should simply become administrative boards over such wide areas as the needs of nationality demand.

Then public international law will become as superfluous as it is fictitious. It can be replaced by a code of international behavior so simple, so definite and so concise, as to be the intellectual inheritance of all men and women in every clime while that fiction which is commonly supposed to regulate the most momentous intercourse between the nations is known only by a few hundred professors of whom no two agree to the exact meaning of the different stipulations of the international law.

In order to establish this code and thereby secure permanent peace, I would suggest that the coming Peace Congress should eliminate the functions of political government from the field of international relations. Though somewhat hidden from the public, this process has already begun. We are today all aware that practically no idea, no discovery, no invention can for any length of time remain purely a national possession. But how many of you realize that there already exist nearly one hundred and fifty international public unions like the postal union, the sugar commission, the institute of agriculture and other similar institutions where national sovereignty is more or less yielding to cosmopolitan experts.

In order to eliminate political influences from international intercourse, in order to do away with that secret diplomacy which has deluged the annals of mankind with oceans of blood, we have but to proceed further on that road. National sovereignty must at all times and in all circumstances stop at the national borders. The state must cease to be an entity opposed to other states. to reach this goal the general acceptance of six cardinal principles should form the basis of the coming peace treaty.

The six are: the principles of nationality; of universal free trade; of a world citizenship; of a planetary jurisdiction; of an oceanic police; and of a standardization of the national police forces.

Astute Foreign Policy

Editorial: "Mr. Roosevelt and Peace"

The Hague, capital of the Netherlands, has become host city for several international conventions that have considered the rules for the conduct of war and settlement of international disputes. The first was held in 1899, at the suggestion of Russian Czar Nicholas II; about two dozen countries participated. A second conference was held in 1907 at the suggestion of Roosevelt; 44 nations took part. The Laws of War ratified at that convention clearly address neutral nations. Articles one and two state:

The territory of neutral Powers is inviolable.

Belligerents are forbidden to move troops or convoys of either munitions of war or supplies across the territory of a neutral Power.

***Independent,* January 4, 1915**

Mr. Roosevelt Finds Mr. Wilson and Mr. Bryan derelict in their duty for not enforcing the Hague Conventions, which are being violated with impunity by some of the belligerents in the present war. . . . Does this mean that if Mr. Roosevelt were President now, he would, for instance, have used the army and navy of the United States to compel Germany to evacuate Belgium, England to cease strewing the high seas with mines, and Japan to make reparation for violating China's neutrality? We have ourselves urged that even at this late date Mr. Wilson should protest in broad terms against all violations of international law by whomsoever committed and give notice that the United States intends to bring them up for judicial consideration at the close of the war. But to go beyond that and have the United States enter the European conflagration in order to punish international promise breakers is like burning the house down to roast the pig.

George Harvey, Editorial: "The German Attitude"

Wilson enjoyed great respect as a peacemaker, the only mediator believed morally fit to find a course between seething hatred of the warring powers. He built his reputation by refusing to join the war despite repeated provocations, even temporizing by asking only for power to arm merchant ships as Germany in early 1917 renewed its commitment to unrestricted submarine warfare. He reiterated his country's special status as an "associate power" even after joining the war. After the war the president spent months in Paris away from the White House hoping to negotiate reasonable terms for a lasting peace. Despite his prestige, however, he failed to quell the emotional need of the broken and exhausted allies for retribution and revenge. That planted the dragon's teeth of Greek mythology that spouted into a new world war a generation later.

***North American Review*, October 1915**

Surely it is going too far to say, as Mr. Roosevelt says, that "for thirteen months the United States has played an ignoble part among the nations." Methods may prove to have been mistaken and futile, but there is nothing "ignoble" in the exercise of tolerance towards a distracted neighbor who hitherto has been our friend. Nor is there anything unworthy in striving through appeals to reason instead of by dire threatenings for a clear understanding which should make for peace between great peoples. It is not true, moreover, that "the President has been given ample time to act rightly, and he has either not acted at all or has acted wrongly." On the contrary, he has made unmistakably plain, to Germany and to the world, the grounds upon which America bases her irrefragable rights as a neutral nation, and the strength of his position in each instance has been enhanced, not impaired, by the dispassionateness and friendliness of his presentation.

Questions

1. Roosevelt and Wilson differed on many matters of American policy. In what areas did they agree?
2. Why did "secret treaties" become such an important issue during and after the war?
3. Was Germany justified in its explanation for its attacks on neutral merchant shipping? Why or why not?

4. Passion and patriotism often overcome rational conversation when a country chooses to join a war. Why?
5. American presidents generally have had little foreign affairs experience before becoming president. Should this be considered an important qualification for the person in the White House?

Note

1. "Primary Documents: U.S. Declaration of War with Germany, April 2, 1917." First World War.Com. http://www.firstworldwar.com/source/usawardeclaration.htm.

Chapter 9

German Culture

The tremendous history of German contribution to world culture could hardly be underestimated even after Germany became the purported enemy of humanity. It could be demonized, however. Allied propagandists collected Germany's achievements under the umbrella of the German word *kultur*, an epithet for all that was deemed evil in German society. The implication here was that while many centuries of German achievement could not be denied, the growth of Prussian militarism to dominate Germany after 1871 had perverted German ideas to a fiendish end.

In was true that Prussia, with its capital in Berlin, grew to dominate Germany's loose confederation of separate states before the 1871 unification. Otto von Bismarck as Prussian prime minister worked to engineer a single German state dominated by Berlin. He goaded both Austria and France into war against the Prussian army, and defeated both in a matter of weeks and months. As antagonist Austria found itself isolated from Prussia's ambitions. Napoleon III of France found that his country had unintentionally provided a crystallizing force that pulled south Germany into a unification agreement that was ironically struck at the Versailles palace near Paris. Germany's victory terms included reparations and the surrender of French Alsace and parts of Lorraine. This proved to be an annexation troubling to Berlin. The territories had see-sawed between Germany and France throughout the centuries, but by this time most living there resented a return to German control (50,000 moved to France after the annexation). France even more resented the loss of these eastern provinces. *La révanche* (revenge) for the loss of Alsace-Lorraine fed French resentment for decades and, some historians argue, can be partly blamed for French enthusiasm to join World War I.

Bismarck's triumphant unification of a country bound together by culture and language but separated into small states created a new European power, formidable and aggressive. Its cultural influence now was matched by its worldwide economic and political force. Under Kaiser Wilhelm I, former Prussian king, a parliament could wield limited control over domestic policy. But the crown kept control over foreign policy, and could not be abolished. What is more, the Kaiser appointed the prime minister, who through the crown controlled the military. And based on Prussian standards, to control the military was, in effect, to control the state.

While many European countries conscripted large armies to fight frequent wars, only Germany could truly be called a militaristic society during this period. Prussia brought to the rest of the new country its system of conscription combined with a professional aristocracy of officers who were trained at prestigious military schools. These men played roles not only in the military operations of Germany, but also in its government, a bureaucratic cadre dedicated to protecting the highly conservative aims of the military, and opposed to a society increasingly turning to socialism. In fact, the 1912 parliamentary elections returned 112 socialist deputies. Chancellor Theobald von Bethmann Hollweg found himself in an almost impossible situation dealing with a powerful military, an autocratic Kaiser, and a socialist parliament. The military always dominated German politics, however, and by the end of the war Germany had become a de facto dictatorship.

Historians sometimes hold spirited "what-if" debates, one of which is "what if Bismarck had remained chancellor?" Bismarck relied on military solutions as a way to realize his life goal, German unification. He realized, of course, that wars leave hard feelings, and so after 1871 he tried to protect German ambitions through diplomacy. Most importantly, he knew France would remain a threat, and so negotiated his way out of the geographic squeeze between France and Russia by turning a more amiable eye east. The Reinsurance Treaty of 1887 assured that Russia and Germany would remain neutral in case one went to war with a third power. An alliance with Austria-Hungary promised either would aid the other in case of attack by Russia.

The Reinsurance Treaty lasted only three years, until Czar Nicholas II did not pursue its renewal. And here is the key point of the "what-if" question: Bismarck, finally fed up with the meddling of the new Kaiser Wilhelm II, resigned. Russia subsequently joined France, which was then at diplomatic loose ends and looking for an ally. Unlikely as it would appear given the dramatically different political systems, France and Russia forged just what Bismarck had feared, an alliance that squeezed Germany. Could Bismarck's diplomatic skill have derailed this agreement? Furthermore, Kaiser Wilhelm's dreams of Germany dominating Europe in power and influence led to his aggressive posture in the world political arena at the turn of the century. At his back was the world's greatest army, based on universal draft, highly trained officer corps, and close relationship with the crown and the government. The Kaiser joined conservative forces in Berlin based on military and economic might to challenge the power of Europe's great colonial powers, particularly Britain and France. Britain's century-old dominance of the seas could be challenged by German naval construction, resulting in the dreadnaught battleship arms race before the war. Colonial policies could be challenged by ship.

Most readily available for challenge was France's intention to create a protectorate in Morocco, with Britain's blessing, but disregarding Germany's economic interests. Bernard von Bülow, the Kaiser's anointed successor to Bismarck, proposed that Wilhelm II personally represent German interests in Morocco by dropping by during a Mediterranean cruise. The Kaiser did so, with hesitation, declaring German sympathies for Moroccan independence as a challenge to France and British influence. German demands for an international conference on Moroccan matters led to an agreement in Algeciras, a Spanish city, in 1906, but the agreement did not advance Germany's plan to hamper French influence in Morocco. On the other hand, Germany's aggressive stand did scare Britain and France into a closer relationship already established through the Entente Cordiale of 1904. In 1911 Germany tried again, this time relying on its navy. The German gunboat *Panther* steamed to Agadir, a Moroccan port, as an obvious threat to French expansion in Morocco. The Germans then demanded concessions in the French Congo as compensation. The 1911 settlement of this "second Moroccan crisis," a small chunk of the Congo to German colonial interests, gave France free reign in Morocco. War had been averted a second time. But Germany's aggressive determination to thrust itself into a major role on Europe's colonial stage, and the threat to back up its claims with proven military skill, solidified the alliance among the nations of the Triple Entente: France, Britain, and Russia.

By the eve of World War I, Germany, a latecomer to colonialism, had managed to secure several minor colonies in Africa and the Pacific, all of which it lost after the war. Germany acquired a reputation for colonial brutality, particularly after conflicts in 1904 between German settlers and native people in German Southwest Africa (Namibia) resulted in Berlin dispatching troops to a war that killed about 1,700 Germans and at least 25,000 native Herero. A growing international reputation for German cruelty and bellicose diplomacy based on military might created the universal allied belief during the war that a certain *kultur*, the result of nefarious Prussian ideals, had driven the entire German people into conflict with civilized Western values. Historiography has see-sawed in its interpretation of German militaristic culture as a cause of war. Nonetheless, it seems certainly true that by the first years of the 1900s German foreign policy was controlled primarily by an aggressive military structure that was autocratic in nature and pervasive in society. That structure was encouraged by an often pugnacious Kaiser and abetted by the country's civilian leaders. They agreed the force of this new European power must be grown within a preexisting diplomatic structure in Europe, a structure the Germans feared would marginalize their influence. It was the fearful potential of its military that encouraged other powers to try to contain a Germany intent on expanding its influence. Bismarck's shrewd diplomacy may or may not have been able to navigate these hazards. Yet in using the military as a tool to build a united country, the "Iron Chancellor," as he was sometimes called, seemed to show that German success could be gained through just such belligerent means.

German Culture: Good, Misguided

Rudolf Eucken: "Rudolf Eucken on the Tasks of German Idealism"

Germany in the eighteenth and nineteenth century produced some of history's most important philosophers. Immanuel Kant, Georg Hegel, Arthur Schopenhauer, and Johann Fichte considered the philosophy of idealism (philosophy based on the idea or image) while others considered philosophy of materialism (philosophy based on existence and observable events).

New York Times Current History, October 1915–March 1916

Report of a speech by the famous Jena Professor of Philosophy in the Urania, Berlin's popular science institute, printed in the North German Gazette of Nov. 26.

How different is German idealism! It aspires to create in man a new life of freedom and cordiality as the upper story of an edifice based on the purely material life. This new world of the spirit, of mental labor, of freedom, and of intellectuality, by no means consists in fleeing from the world, but is victorious and heroic enough no longer to fear the opposition of the world. Through this, the world becomes the workshop of the spirit and the consciousness of this gives one the joy of life, as one feels himself to be a part of the great organization of humanity and can co-operate as an active spirit in the work of elevating and shaping the world.

Professor Eucken showed that this genuine German sentiment—the idealistic philosophers are the real interpreters of the German character—is able to solve the greatest problems of the present time.

The nineteenth century has shown us the great significance of the visible world and a great change in ideas already had begun to take effect when the war began. Nevertheless, idealism would again have its great task to fulfill. Eucken disputed the opinion that idealism, with its cheerful faith in the human character, had been shipwrecked. Of course, many of our fanciful beliefs had been shattered.

Kuno Francke: "The True Germany"

Germany was a johnny-come-lately to the Gilded Age race to acquire colonies. France, Britain, Portugal, and Spain as Europe's original colonial powers had been dividing the world since 1500. By 1900 Spain and Portugal lagged, but France and Britain busily set to work slicing up territory in Africa and the Far East. Italy, Belgium, Japan, and the United States joined to a minor extent, along with Germany, subscribing to the view that a major power could be defined by its colonial empire. Colonies were in their essence an opportunity for one militarily advanced nation to dominate another, politically and economically, in an attempt to enrich the mother country. Those who supported colonialism pointed out that the occupying power brought advanced technology and infrastructure that improved the lot of the locals. Some locals disagreed, forcing colonial powers to fight repeated rebellions, often with results both tragic and bloody. It was Europe's disputes over their colonial empires that nearly led to general war in 1905 and 1911, and left bitterness between Germany and the allies that contributed to the Great War.

Atlantic Monthly, November 1915

How is it possible that a people animated by such a spirit, a people which for a century has assiduously and devotedly labored to produce types of human personality as noble and enlightened as any people ever has brought forth—how is it possible that such a people should suddenly appear to large numbers of intelligent observers as an enemy of mankind, as a menace to the security and peace of the world? Much of the hostile criticism of Imperial Germany, of its alleged sinister raving for world-dominion, or its atrocious conduct of the war, is outright slander and willful distortion. It is indeed a grim mockery to have the tentative and circumscribed efforts made by Germany during the past twenty-five years for colonial expansion denounced by the enemies of Germany as dangerous and intolerable aggression, when one remembers that during these same years England throttled the independence of the South African republics, established a protectorate over Egypt, partitioned Persia—together with Russia—into "spheres of influence," encouraged France to build up an immense colonial empire in Cochin China, Madagascar, Tunis, and Morocco, allowed Italy to conquer Tripoli, and helped Japan to tighten her grip upon China. As to the manner of the German conduct of war, here also a huge mass of extraordinary exaggerations and a vast amount of anonymous aspersions have been indulged in. For the rest, these accusations find their explanation in the fact that Germany thus far has in the main been able to ward off the enemy from her own soil and to transfer the deadly work of destruction into the enemy's country.

And yet, there is a residuum of truth in the assertion that Germany during the last generation has overreached herself. So far as this is the case, she bears her part of the guilt of having conjured up the present world calamity. In saying this, I am not thinking of Germany's consistent policy of formidable armament. For I fail to see how Germany could have afforded not to prepare for war, so long as she found herself surrounded by neighbors every one of them anxious to curb her rising power. What I am thinking of is a spirit of superciliousness which, as a very natural concomitant of a century of extraordinary achievement, has development, especially during the last twenty-five years, in the ruling classes of Germany.

The manifestations of this spirit have been many and varied. In German domestic conditions, it has led to the growth of a capitalistic class as snobbish and overbearing as it is resourceful and intelligent, counteracting by its uncompromising Herrenmoral the good effect of the wise and provident social legislation inaugurated by Bismarck. It has led to excesses of military rule and to assertions of autocratic power which have embittered German party politics and have driven large numbers of Liberal voters into the Socialist ranks, as the only party consistently and unswervingly upholding Parliamentary rights. In Germany's foreign relations, it has led to a policy which was meant to be firm but had an appearance of arrogance and aggressiveness and easily aroused suspicion. Suspicion of Germany led to her isolation. And her isolation has finally brought on the war.

Anonymous, Letter to the Editor: "The People and the Kaiser"

The German-speaking peoples of middle and eastern Europe spread over a variety of countries. Ethnic Germans before World War I lived not only in Germany but also in Austria, Switzerland, Poland, Hungary, Romania, Russia, and throughout the world, including the United States. Germany has been, throughout most of history, one people living in many countries; Bismarck's dream to unify the German nation did not even consider German-speaking Switzerland and Austria. Moreover, before the war Germans had become avid travelers, particularly enjoying the resorts in the south of France. To people who disdained "German imperialism," German tourists themselves nevertheless were well regarded as informal diplomats from their country. A French newspaper in 1914 even published a story of a French soldier captured by the Germans but treated kindly because a German officer recognized him as the son of a French resort owner he had known before the war.

Nation, November 12, 1914

Sir: The writer is another of the thousands of Americans who are glad to acknowledge a deep debt of gratitude to the noble German people. It was his privilege to spend a year and a half in study and travel among them, and many were the kindnesses received while there; and to this day he loves to speak in terms of sincere admiration of the fine character of these people as he learned to know it. Their naturalness and simple-hearted kindness cannot be forgotten. And now, in these frightful days, when "misery like a flood" is inundating that great nation, nothing but sympathy, deep and compassionate, goes out toward them. Perhaps the profoundest depth of sympathy is reached when one reflects that such a people hold their fortunes and their lives subject to the word of a single "war lord," who was once reported as saying to his troops: "If I command you to shoot your father, it is your duty to obey." And when we further reflect that Germany is not only in possession of the mightiest army the world ever saw, but that she is also the greatest nation of scholars in the whole world, to such an extent that in the great majority of subjects the foremost authority is likely to be a German, our sympathy deepens at the thought that one man can send them forth to slaughter.

Professor Ferdinand Jakob Schmidt, University of Berlin: "A Holy Legacy of the Fallen Heroes"

German aggressiveness and historical documentation have convinced many historians that the German foreign ministry clearly did not have the most docile of intentions, as described here. But foreign policy was secret business before the war. Treaties were private. And the German military caste that dominated foreign policy decisions tended to shut out journalists and academics in allied countries who perhaps knew at least a little more about the true course of their government's diplomacy.

New York Times Current History, October 1915–March 1916

This article appeared in the Illustrirte Zeitung of Nov. 18, 1915.

Who among us Germans was not a friend of peace, deceiving himself in the belief that we were strong enough always to down the demons of war?

So far as we were concerned, there was no need for peace associations and peace congresses in order to convince the world that nothing was further from the thoughts of the German Nation than the desire to crush the liberty of other nations. What we wanted was to make a determined effort to reach the position due us among nations, by means of the economic and spiritual progress of our national powers, thus fulfilling our historical destiny in the service of mankind.

Yet a remarkable thing came to pass: it was peace that brought upon us the most fearful of wars! Not the strength of our arms but the superiority of our peaceful labor brought on this war of nations.

So the blind powers of destruction were let loose and we experienced their gigantic might more terribly than ever before, as the war of nations raged around us. All was menaced; our life, our freedom, our honor. But the power of our enemies did not overcome us and the iron scales of world destiny included to our side. Not for us, but for our hate-filled opponents, were those annihilating "mene tekel" words—"weighed and found wanting"—written in letters of flame on the walls.

Their men have fallen. But we have achieved this victory only at the cost of a huge sacrifice demanded from us by cruel fate. Whose head is not torn in his bosom at the thought of all the splendid men who have died for the Fatherland?

These men have left to us a splendid legacy for which they gave up their lives. What is our inheritance from these fallen heroes? None other but the duty to devote ourselves to the great cause of crowning our national German unity.

James Norman Hall: "Out of Flanders"

Soldiers on both sides returning from the trenches repeatedly complained about civilians who clung to ridiculous ideas about battlefield experiences. In particular, French soldiers were offended over the journalism that turned their adversaries into cowards while the French poilus *(doughboys) laughed at bullets. Perhaps the frenzy of hatred seething from the home front in all nations can be blamed on pervasive propaganda less likely to reach the battlefields.*

Atlantic Monthly, October 1916

Three of us sat on the firing bench
Watching the clouds sail by—
Watching the gray dawn blowing up
Like smoke across the sky.
And I thought, as I listened to London Joe
Tell of his leave in town,

That's good vers libre with a Cockney twang;
I'll remember, and write it down. . . .

One night at the Red Lion,
I was talkin' about the time
Nobby Clark got 'it out in front of our barbed wire.
Remember 'ow we did n't find 'im till mornin',
An' the stretcher-bearers brought 'im in;
Broad daylight it was,
An' not a German firin' a shot
Till we got 'im back in the trench?
Well, they was fifteen or twenty in the pub,
An' not one of 'em was glad old Fritzie acted w'ite!
Wouldn't that give you the camel's 'ump?
They'd sooner 'ad Nobby an' the stretcher-bearers killed,
If only the 'Uns, as they call 'em,
'Ad played dirty an' fired w'ile they was bringin' 'im in.

Another time I was a-tellin' 'em
'Ow we shout back an' forth acrost the trenches
W'en the lines is close together,
An' we gets fed up with pluggin' at each other.
An' I told 'em 'bout the place
This side o' Messines, w'ere we was only twenty yards apart,
An' 'ow they chucked us over some o' their black bread,
Arter we'd thrown 'em a 'arf dozen tins o' bully.
Some of 'em did n't believe me an' some did.
But sour? S'y! "Ere! They was ready to kill me
Fer tryin' to make out that Fritzie's a 'human bein''!

It's a funny thing. The farther you gets from the trenches
The more 'ate you finds;
An' by the time you gets to Lunnon—
Blimy! They could bite the 'eads offen nails
If they was made in Germany.
I reckon they're just as cheerful an' lovin'-like in Berlin.

German Culture: Evil, Destructive

George P. Mains, Harrisburg, Pennsylvania, Letter to the Editor: "Victory Must Be Absolute"

World War I became for the allies no less than a moral crusade against evil incarnate in the person of the Kaiser and his imperial government. In the journalism from 1914 to 1918 it is possible to discover a progression that heaps more and more responsibility onto the troops to save the entire western world from the depths of destruction and despair. Perhaps government propaganda can be credited. But recent historians have suggested that the development of this moral crusade came just as much from people talking to other people in everyday life. As the horrific death toll could not be hidden, those who died could not be allowed to die in vain, and so an idealized immensity of their sacrifice comforted grieving survivors.

***North American Review*, November 1918**

It is not un-Christian to say that Germany merits merciless and incessant hammering until she is utterly beaten down. She is an impenitent sinner. She brings forth no honest fruits meet for repentance. Until she does this, neither God nor man can forgive her. She stands justly arraigned at the bar of civilization as the supreme criminal of history. She has paraded her infamous and immeasurable depravity by enacting upon the largest scale all the notorious arts of deception, of cruelty, of incendiarism, of rape and of murder. She has turned the world of trade into a chaos. She has desolated the fairest of lands. The winds of the world are laden with the wails of widows and of orphans, made such by her cruelties. In pursuit of her murderous ambitions she has mangled, crippled, and made blind the virile young manhood of a whole generation. The present Germany merits no consideration from civilization. I do not say that she should be utterly destroyed. But her intolerable arrogance, her wicked duplicity, her insane obsession of superiority over all the rest of mankind, her inhumanity to man, her brutal and frightful policies of dominion, her beastly and conceited stupidity—these all ought to be relentlessly scourged out of her.

Her wanton, barbarous, and still menacing wickedness has already cost civilization too much to permit any halfway or compromising measures in the final settlement of this war. Germany unwhipped is as dangerous to civilization as would be a mad dog let loose upon a picnic ground.

Louis H. Gray: "Prussian Frightfulness and the Savage Mind"

Prussia before 1914 represented the largest of German states, claiming parts of modern Russia, Poland, and Lithuania. It also represented the world's most rigidly militaristic culture, its troops most highly disciplined and led by generals from the aristocracy. Berlin was its capital and Konisberg (now Kaliningrad, Russia; Immanuel Kant taught at the Konisberg university) its second city. After World War I Prussia was shorn of territory to create a "Polish Corridor" to the sea, separating East Prussia from the rest of the state. World War II began when Hitler invaded Poland to reclaim this lost territory. In 1947 the occupying allies abolished the legal state of Prussia.

Scribner's, March 1918

Prussian "frightfulness," in plain words, is a revelation of fear; the Prussian is a bully, and, like all bullies, he is at heart an arrant coward. He began the war, in the last analysis, simply because he was a coward. He feared Russia, he feared Britain, he feared that he might not speedily gain the economic supremacy which he was slowly acquiring; so obsessed was he by fear that he feared his own people. Fear is the subjective factor in the psychology of "frightfulness," just as arrogance is its objective manifestation.

But why should the Prussian be so peculiarly a slave to fear? Germans are not cowards, save those that are under the Prussian yoke. Here, perhaps, lies the key to the entire riddle.

When an Arab historian begins his record of his native town, he should, by strict rule, start with some account of the creation of the world. We need not go back quite so far, but we must catch a glimpse of the way in which Prussia was subdued, and see who were the peoples who once dwelt there, and who were the peoples who subdued them.

The conquerors were Germans or Teutons (the names are synonymous), a noble race in origin, but corrupted in Germany, as we shall see, by the worst that dying Rome could give. The conquered were Prussians, a primitive Balto-Slavic people, barbarians in the technical sense of the term. The fruit of the union of conquering German and conquered Prussian is still called Prussian; and thus we must constantly distinguish, in the light of history and ethnology, between the true German, who is an honorable man, now found chiefly in Scandinavia and England, and the debased German in Germany; just as we must not confuse the true Prussian—a Balto-Slav by race—with the modern hybrid Germano-Balt who has usurped his name.

C. Journelle: "Prussian Manners"

The Hohenzollern family rose in the 1400s to rule Prussia. The most well-known Kaiser (king) in the centuries before German unification was Frederick II "the Great." This so-called enlightened despot, who ruled in the mid-1700s, helped to shape the government based on military values, and worked to extend and enhance a strong army. The last Hohenzollern, Kaiser Wilhelm II, abdicated and fled to Holland in 1918.

Atlantic Monthly, May 1918

All the brutality, perfidy, and savagery manifested by Germany from day to day is not to be explained by any philosophic theory, or as a systematic policy. Temperament is an essential part of it. Moreover, there must be a special lack of the moral sense, an inherent deficiency of the sentiments of justice, honor, and charity. There must be an hereditary perversity. Intellectual perversion by the sophisms of a Fichte or a Haeckel would not have sufficed to make Huns, or to change men to wolves. Grafter upon a sound trunk, the Pangermanist heresy would never have sprouted. Never would Germany—leaders and flocks—have been able to sink so deep into her violent self-worship, her terrorism, and her unmitigated brigandage in war, if she had not glided into it by degrees through weakness of conscience and latent criminality. In reality, behind a false cloak of philosophy and policy, one can detect in her nothing more than revolting organs of the carnivora, retarded in their human development.

Editorial: "The Cup of Bitterness"

This editorial is, alas, all too prescient, as World War I did not extirpate a centuries-old military culture from recrudescence to launch another world war. While who was to blame for World War I is still a matter of spirited debate, nobody asks who started World War II. Prussian generals commanded many of Hitler's troops. They came from the same aristocratic Junker class established in the 1500s. An attempt during the Weimar Republic to reduce the power of this aristocratic class was blocked by German president Paul von Hindenburg—himself a Junker.

Nation, May 20, 1915

What element of excess there may be in the resentment at the Lusitania horror, what allowance must be made for error or exaggeration in the now thrice-told tale of German atrocities in Belgium, is little to the purpose. The main fact is that a great nation, a nation only a short time ago second to none in the honor and esteem of the world, stands now branded with a mark of infamy such as in our time has not been stamped upon the face of any people. To no man, however untouched with any feeling of Germany's greatness or any remembrance of what is high and noble in her people and her history, can such a spectacle be other than melancholy and depressing. To those who have personal associations with Germany, to those who have been accustomed to look upon her as in many ways an example and an inspiration, the thought of the tragic change in her standing before the nations is inexpressibly painful—so painful that one feels almost driven to discover some solace, to think of some possible good which may spring from this bitter evil.

If the war shall result in the defeat of Germany, we have all hoped that, terrible as would be the cost in human lives, in agony, in destitution, the world might yet find compensation for the sacrifice in one great and inestimable gain—the extirpation of Prussian militarism, the regeneration of Germany as a humane and liberal nation. But to no one who looked realities in the face could it seem a certainty that such would be the actual result. The possibility has stood before us that, defeated though she might be in arms, she might nurse a sullen and determined spirit of revenge, and proceed to reconstitute her strength in the spirit of the militarist imperialism under whose spell she has lain for a generation and more. By force alone this spirit cannot be exorcised; deliverance must come through a change of heart in the whole body of the nation. To this change of heart the defeat of her arms is indeed an essential prerequisite; but it is doubtful whether this would suffice. And it is because the moral humiliation to which Germany is now being subjected may prove to be the one thing needful to drive the lesson home, that we feel the shame of to-day may be the prelude to the regeneration of to-morrow.

Bertrand Russell: "The Future of Anglo-German Rivalry"

Bertrand Russell was the epoch's most important philosopher, who doubled as a pacifist and frequent contributor to the media's opinion pages. He was in fact jailed briefly in Britain in 1918 for his opposition to the war. His assertion that Germany hated Britain probably could be supported by extensive evidence—every belligerent nation hated all its enemies with fearsome passion—but the record does not indicate a historical animosity. Germany and Britain had usually been on reasonably good terms, certainly during this era. True, Britain feared German aggressive rivalry in its attempts to outbuild warships and its complaints about Britain's behavior in Africa, but these might not have been worth warring over. In fact, part of the reason Germany did so detest Britain during this period was because many Germans believed London should have remained neutral in a continental war, just as it had done before from its "splendid isolation" on the far side of the English Channel.

Atlantic Monthly, July 1915

If the Germans are to be believed, their only implacable and unappeasable enmity in the war is against England.

Toward France they express a kind of brutal, contemptuous liking. As providing opportunities for military glory in 1870 and again last August, France has deserved well of the Fatherland. Toward Russia they have the tolerance of merely momentary hostility, with the consciousness that the grounds of quarrel are finite and capable of adjustment. But toward England they express a hatred which nothing can satisfy except the utter destruction of England's power. Portugal, Spain, Holland, were once great maritime and colonial empires, but they are fallen from their high estate; so England is to fall, if Germany in its present mood is to have its way.

This attitude is not confined to journalists or the thoughtless multitude; it is to be found equally in the deliberate writings of learned men. Very instructive from this point of view is an article by the historian Eduard Meyer, in the Italian periodical Scientia, on England's war against Germany and the problems of the future. The erudite professor, following Mommsen, considers Germany as the analogue of Rome and England as the analogue of Carthage. He hardly hopes for a decisive victory now, but looks forward to a succession of conflicts like the Punic Wars, ending, we are to suppose, in an equally final triumph. "Especially in America," he says, but also in Europe, above all in the neutral countries, there are not a few well-meaning people who believe that this tremendous war will be the last for a long time to come, that a new era of peaceful development and of harmonious international peace will follow. I regard these views as a utopian dream. Their realization could be hoped for only in case we should succeed in really casting England to the ground, breaking her maritime dominion, and thereby conquering the freedom of the seas, and at the same time in so controlling our other enemies that they would lose for ever the desire to attack us again."

John Dewey: "On Understanding the Mind of Germany"

John Dewey's philosophy demonstrated the concept of pragmatism—emphasizing optimism, action, and change by human effort. This approach reflected the spirit many Americans of the early twentieth century believed defined the United States, and became particularly influential as "typically American" philosophy. A logical companion philosophy in ethics describes consequentialism, holding that what is most important is the ends, not the means. Dewey suggested it was this idea that drove the German invasion of Belgium.

***Atlantic Monthly*, February 1916**

In times of peace it is possible to idealize war. Imagination, left to its own devices, forgets the disagreeable and dwells upon the glory. In times of war, suffering, misery, the agonies of destruction, are too immediate and urgent to permit this course save to the hopelessly callous or the hopelessly romantic. Hence idealization is transferred to the cause for which the war is fought. Even the most righteous of wars involves many illusions of this sort; the less justifiable the war, the more surely do the emotions develop ideas and beliefs which may disguise the lack of justification. The vehement conviction of each warring nation of the absolute righteousness of its own cause is the whistling of children in the awful unexpectedness of a graveyard. But it is this only superficially. In its depths it represents the labor of desire to procure a moral justification which will arm action. Only the most placid or the most trivial of existences is endurable without some belief in its own moral necessity. How can the horrors of war be borne without conviction of moral justification?

Each nation naturally expresses its own moral grounds in the terms which its history has made familiar and congenial. The formulae chosen are appealing and convincing to other nations—say neutral nations—in the degree in which they are uttered in a familiar and understandable tongue. The average American understands the moral defense of Great Britain readily. It is couched in the terms which we should naturally employ in our own justification. So far as distance permits us to judge, France has been the least clamorous of all the nations at war; but her justifications, also, are uttered in a language which we understand, even if it be not so naturalized among us as the moral speech of England. But it is noteworthy that Americans—except German-Americans—who sympathize with Germany do not explain and justify her cause in the language which the Germans by preference employ. The former assign reasons of expediency and practical political necessity—not the broad sweeping moral reasons which the latter put forth.

The case of the invasion of Belgium is signally in point. American apologists sought for technical and legal justifications—the origin of the treaty in a Prussian, not an Imperial, guaranty, and so forth. They ignored the pleas of the justification by a superior national mission, by the doctrine that the day of the small nationality is past since it obstructs the required organization of humanity. The true Germans ignored the legal technicalities of their American apologists. The only point upon which the two agreed was that of the right conferred by military necessity. And this proffering of the doctrine of necessity was to most Americans a sign that the interests as well as the sympathies of their compatriots had become Germanized. In a most literal sense the mind of Germany is foreign to us; it is not to be understood without an effort.

Anonymous: "The World War, Causes and Effects"

As official publication for the newly created National Association for the Advancement of Colored People (NAACP, founded 1909), Crisis *repeatedly found racial irony in policies of the Wilson administration and racial motivation in the practices of other belligerent nations. The belief that white European races were superior to others may have been presumed throughout Germany, but that belief was hardly exclusive to that country. In suggesting German uniqueness,* Crisis *presaged the rise of Nazism and its truly virulent concept of a "master race."*

Crisis, December 1914

Dr. Jacques Loeb in the New Review analyzes with deep insight the "racial" problem underneath the present war.

"The present generation of Germans has been raised in the creed of the superior character of their 'race' and civilization and it is a fact that even the most enlightened Germans are not free from such ideas. Is it a wonder that when the government made it plausible to them that this superior race, this superior civilization, nay their homes, were threatened by the barbarian Russian hordes, all degrees of freedom of will were wiped out of the inhabitants of Germany except the one, namely, to blindly obey the command of the military leaders who were to save the threatened civilization and homes?"

German Militarism: The Virtues

Oswald Garrison Villard: "Militarism and Democracy in Germany"

Oswald Garrison Villard, a pacifist, undoubtedly reflected common German wisdom during World War I. Despite that, it was more popular among allied propagandists to separate the feelings of the "real Germans" from the wicked ways of their "imperialist" leaders. This could be done because Germany was not a true democracy. But allied propaganda did not reflect the actual situation in Germany. In truth, writers who actually traveled to Germany reported generally universal support for the government's wartime policies. While it certainly was fact that without the Prussian army Bismarck could not have unified the country, it was harder to extol Prussian martial virtue during the Napoleonic years. Napoleon's French army easily defeated Prussia in 1806, and Napoleon was finally conquered in 1815 by a combined force dominated by Britain.

Scribner's, February 1915

Ninety-three German savants who pledged their honor and reputation to the truth of their statements have recently declared that German militarism is one and indivisible with German culture. "Without it," they said, "our culture would long since have been wiped off the earth." From many other German sources come denials that Germany's militarism is a menace to the peace of Europe or to anybody else. It is defended, moreover, not only as a cultural but as a democratic institution. Germans are to-day thanking God for their militarism, on the ground that but for it Napoleon would never have been humbled and the German Empire would never have come to pass; that to its extent and thoroughness alone Germany owes her safety at this hour, when she is beset by the troops of nearly half the world, but has thus far carried on the war almost entirely on other people's soil.

Maurice Révai, Former Hungarian Deputy: "The Virtues of Militarism"

Germany's previous war was the Franco-Prussian war of 1871, which had forged the country itself. Berlin had, however, fought what could have been called a war in its colony of southwest Africa, modern Namibia, in 1904. It is hard to believe it would have been less belligerent than other colonial powers, but as late-comers to the colonial carve-up of Africa and the Far East, it had fewer opportunities to demonstrate its militarism in colonial combat.

***New York Times Current History*, April–September 1916**

Every impartial observer had had to take into account of the fact that the German Army is not a flock of sheep setting out under the order of a prince, but a people in arms, conscious that it is fighting for all that is most sacred in the world—Fatherland, freedom, and family.

But German militarism is, moreover, a guarantee of peace. Despite her formidable army, Germany had had no war for forty-three years, while during the same period her present enemies have carried on wars—and wars of conquest—in every part of the world. German militarism is just as old as the German Empire, and since it came into existence it has left every one alone, has attacked no one, but has kept the peace. However paradoxical it may seem, the military system based upon compulsory and universal service is better fitted to safeguard peace than any other. Some Englishmen have recognized this thoroughly. General Hamilton in a book published in 1910 said that the English Liberal Cabinet had rejected compulsory service, preferring a professional army, because it is only with such an army, and not with a national army, that wars of conquest in remote countries can be undertaken and foreign policy made to conform to the imperialist traditions and aims of Great Britain.

German Militarism: The Drawbacks

Anonymous: "How Prussianism Warps Men and Women, by the American Wife of a Titled German"

Most countries in Europe before 1914 (Britain being an exception) had conscription laws in force. France had recently extended its military service requirement from two years to three. That Germany required its young men to serve in the army was not unusual. The author of this piece argued that in the German model, however, the discipline of the army pervaded civilian life. Painting an entire civilian population with certain peculiar traits is a temptation fraught with chauvinist risk. Yet some historians argue that Adolph Hitler's Nazi regimentation worked particularly well in the 1930s because a temperament dating back to Frederick the Great had instilled an appreciation for military efficiency.

Independent, December 14, 1914

Conscription has been glibly advocated at times in England and even in the United States; let us see what it means in private life and trace some of its influence upon the everyday habits of a people.

In Germany, compulsory army service means a period of time spent in abject subordination to a new series of commands, on top of fourteen years of life past in subordination to parents, the pastor and the schoolmaster. Thus army service catches a man and puts him in a yoke again just in the years when a reaction might lead him away from restraint and toward liberty. Universal service means, furthermore, the subjection of the vast multitude of men to the few; to commands which it is not permissible even to question; to the instinct of obedience to inexorable authority, together with the concomitant idea that strict punishment does and should follow disobedience.

Obedience is made to appear respectable; disobedience, reprehensible.

Taken together with the old influences that still flow from the Prussian spirit of absolutism, this training explains how it has come to pass that Germans are so habituated to what many be described as alertness to infractions of every kind of prescribed regulation. Enter an empty doorway marked "Exit" or stroll over a bridge on the left hand pathway, and all the natives will stare at you or take pains to jostle you, so alive and resentful is every one to the fact that you are overlooking a rule. Leave a door open inside a railway coach, and the chance is that an indignant witness will tell you the regulations prohibit doors being left ajar, or he will report you to the conductor. Their zeal for obeying, and for seeing that everybody else obeys, would be phenomenal, I think, were it not to be accounted for by the fact of the military discipline the whole population undergoes or is infected by, after having been subjected to a previous course of discipline in the home, the school, the church and by the all pervading police.

Dr. Alfred F. M. Zimmermann, German Under Secretary for Foreign Affairs: "How about British Militarism?"

English attempts to control Irish independence movements clearly slipped into excesses of brutality. Zimmermann, of later telegram fame, wrote this shortly after the Easter Uprising of April 1916, an effort of Irish separatists to capitalize on London's preoccupation with the war. The ill-advised rebellion was crushed by British troops, who executed its incautious leader, Roger Casement, on his return from seeking arms in Germany—an obviously treasonable offense during wartime. Germany did not come to the aid of the doomed rebels, as Casement had hoped.

***New York Times Current History*, April–September 1916**

Ever since the beginning of the war our enemies have been shouting about Prussian militarism. Now the reign of terror in Ireland has shown the finest flower of British militarism. England has established conscription, which it professed to hate so bitterly as a German institution, but it did not take conscription to show to what lengths British militarism can go. Sir Edward Grey has dared to repeat again that England wishes to confer the blessings of freedom upon Europe. The bloodstained soil of Ireland shows just what this freedom means. The same British militarism has ground beneath its iron heels the helpless people of India.

The same riotish militarism has wielded its cruel sway in Egypt and the same militarism killed the helpless women and children of the Boers in South Africa.

This is what British freedom means. For British militarism has not changed. It is the same today as it was a century and a half ago, when it hired the Indians in America to massacre England's helpless colonists because they tried to throw off the yoke.

Questions

1. Some historians contend that the seeds of World War I were planted in the 1870–1871 war between Prussia and France. How could this war be blamed for a world war nearly a half century later?

2. Would Bismarck have been able to avoid German blunders that helped lead to World War I? What different choices might he have made?
3. How did Prussian militarism lead to World War I, and even World War II, according to some historians?
4. What are the possible benefits, and possible risks, of a militaristic society, as critics called Germany during this period?

Chapter 10

Traitors and Immigrants

A dramatic irony of America during World War I was the difference between the intensely idealistic rhetoric of Wilson's war to save democracy and the reality of the greatest assault on civil rights in United States history. The sweeping denial of rights and sometimes brutal treatment of minorities reached a zenith, not only in the more familiar areas of African American rights—more than 100 lynchings—but also in the areas of rights against large immigrant and political groups. Laws of 1918 punished scores of socialists, particularly those publishing well-known political weeklies, even for the mildest of criticisms against the government. Speakers both public and private who vaguely questioned American conduct in the war were reported to the authorities, arrested, fined, jailed, and sometimes lucky to escape murder. A few didn't. Immigrants, those "hyphenated Americans" as Theodore Roosevelt, Leonard Wood, Henry Cabot Lodge, and other war hawks called them, were treated as if they had few rights as human beings, say nothing of rights as American residents, often even American citizens. Second- and third-generation immigrants who may have had no connection to the Old Country beyond a last name were held suspect. In a well-known case of excess, Robert Prager, a German immigrant living in Illinois, was murdered by a mob in April 1918. Mennonites, as pacifists, were particularly targeted because by their religion they refused to utter patriotic comments. Finding pretexts to throw these antiwar Americans of German ancestry into jail under the Espionage Act victimized thousands. In fact, in 2006 a group of University of Montana law students organized the Montana Sedition Project, an effort to clear the names of 64 people, mostly immigrants, convicted under Montana's wartime sedition act. One of them, Ben Kahn, a Polish immigrant, was jailed for almost three years for saying during breakfast at a hotel that the wartime food restrictions were "a big joke."

In the most famous image of one of America's most important photographers, Alfred Stieglitz's "The Steerage" (1907) dramatizes the stark class division between America's new immigrants and upper classes. Woodrow Wilson feared the country's pervasive class antagonism might erupt into violence should the country join the war. Courtesy of Library of Congress.

Among immigrant groups most often targeted were those of German ancestry—even if they did not emigrate from Germany. In fact, many immigrants moved from German-speaking Russia to escape czarist oppression. Others came from the variety of German-speaking regions bound by religion, but not necessarily politics. In fact, a huge number of German immigrants had been settling in America since colonial times. Those who established themselves in Pennsylvania held onto their culture and customs through two centuries. These Germans, of course, were longtime American citizens, no more "German" than a United States citizen whose ancestors arrived on the Mayflower would consider herself "English" today. First- and second-generation Germans in 1910 totaled more than 8 million, of a population of 92 million, the country's largest immigrant group. Nevertheless, anything German became suspect. Teaching German language was banned in schools. German-language newspapers, the most important non-English publications in the United States by circulation and number, were forced to provide English translations to authorities, were harassed, banned, and hounded out of business. Despite repeated, almost pathetic, declarations of loyalty, German-language newspapers were seen by some to be inherently traitorous. Promises of loyalty were rejected as pretense. The publisher of one of the country's most important German-language dailies, the *Westliche Post* of St. Louis, said he would even publish in English if he could keep his Associated Press contract.

Nevertheless, this savage persecution did not match that suffered by African Americans. After all, immigrants usually suffered mere fines, imprisonment, and at worst, deportation. African Americans were murdered by lynch mobs who never feared the smallest possibility of judicial restraint. Racism marbled America from top to bottom, one of the country's lingering tragedies. But German-Americans were white. They had been long welcomed as among the country's most promising immigrants: hard workers, easily assimilated into American values, many from a nation that long had been a U.S. friend and ally. That the country would suddenly turn on these hapless Americans, particularly those whose religion determined their pacifism, seems a bizarre anomaly.

Part of the explanation lies in the belief of many in influential positions that in the American melting pot was dangerous, that those who did not readily give up their heritage to serve American ideals could become possible troublemakers, even traitors. Those ideals became closely aligned with the positions of mostly East Coast anglophiles. Wilson was himself of English heritage and appreciated English ideals. He and others particularly questioned the loyalty of German-Americans and other immigrants who could not accept a shift from neutrality toward the goals of Britain. In addition to Germans, Irish-Americans could not accept the position that England, the centuries-old oppressor of their home nation, could hold any sort of moral high ground in the war.

Support of American assimilation during this period spread expectations beyond mere proof of immigrant loyalty. This also was a period in which Native Americans were expected to embrace the white man's values even forbidden to speak native languages. One way to invite the many American minority groups representing other languages and cultures to come together as one, it was argued, would be through military service. Roosevelt's famous comment that a draft would "yank the hyphen" out of hyphenated Americans could be debated—until the United States declared war in April 1917. After that, conscription became a fact. Undoubtedly most military leaders feverishly worked to gather a reasonably trained fighting force of millions and cared less about whatever assimilation military service would or would not create in America. But the 4,355,000 men mobilized in World War I did indeed offer at least one way toward a great American leveling of culture during the twentieth century.

Another path toward assimilation might have been the hounding of those who persisted in clinging to heritage from the Old Country, most particularly Germany. Most Germans responded by complying. German newspapers folded, German heritage organizations disbanded, German political groups ceased to exist. More difficult were church groups traditionally holding services in German and German parochial schools. These were bullied out of commission by legislation and harassment. The Smith-Towner Act of 1918, supported by the National Education Association and American Federation of Teachers, provided for educational measures including "Americanization of immigrants" by forcing states to enact legislation requiring instruction in English, at the threat of federal funding cuts. A half dozen zealous states actually prohibited German foreign language instruction through primary school.

After 1920 the wartime emotional frenzy began to fade, and German-Americans again became more welcome in American society. While superpatriot reaction against immigrants obviously crossed any reasonable line of U.S. security concerns, a few Germans had indeed seemed to threaten the nation. The German embassy during the neutral period did encourage several attempts to sabotage U.S. shipping to the allies. A few militant pro-German leaders such as George Sylvester Viereck broadcast his German sympathies (in both world wars), but it seemed to be mostly the working-class folk, and not leaders such as Viereck, who suffered most—perhaps because they were uneducated, without connections, and therefore easier targets. German ethnic heritage might have revived, but for the advent of Nazism. In the 1930s, to celebrate German heritage was hardly a thing of pride. By the second half of the century German-Americans had been generally assimilated. Today they constitute no political or social force in American society beyond jovial polka bands.

Immigrants as Potential Traitors

Honoré Willsie, Editorial: "Be Born Again America!"

Among the provisions of the Smith-Towner Act, passed shortly after the war ended, were strong initiatives designed to reform the checkerboard of local school boards. Under a new federal department of education, emphasis was given to literacy programs as well as programs designed "to teach immigrants ten years of age and over to speak and read the English language and to understand and appreciate the spirit and purpose of the American government and the duties of citizenship in a free country."

Delineator, April 1918

When the Great War began in 1914 Herman Bauer obeyed the President's injunction as to neutrality, with apparent cheerfulness. But after America entered the war the cheerfulness gave way to a curious air of repression. One day, last Winter, sitting at the Elks Club, he suddenly rose and shouted:

"To hell with England! I'm glad the Lusitania went down! America is a nation of fools. We need Germany over here to give us sense—Germany's the greatest nation—"

Friends hushed him, but Secret Service men took him in tow and he was bound over to keep the peace. And this he does, but he is a broken man, his citizenship tainted, his family looked on with suspicion.

A curious and unhappy episode—one calculated to disturb all thinking Americans. Yet it is the thinking Americans who undoubtedly are largely to blame for the state of mind of Herman Bauer.

We have taken our great experiment in democracy with stupid complacency. If we thought about the matter at all, we believed that the mere passage through Ellis Island of an immigrant made a sound American of man, woman or child.

What fools we have been! The mere word democracy implies a thoughtfulness and an intelligence willed toward that philosophy of government. The great bulk of immigrants to-day came to America, not as did the founders of the nation, for political and spiritual freedom, but to make money. Somehow these immigrants must be trained into democracy so that it becomes a part of their brain fiber and not a mere veneering as with Herman Bauer.

This training belongs to the public schools. The schools were a failure as far as Herman Bauer was concerned. Children of foreigners will not breathe democracy in with the common air. From the time they enter at six until they leave school at fourteen or eighteen or twenty-two, they must be taught the essential principles that make the mankind attuned to democracy.

This and this only will save America from the alien. Thus and thus only will America experience a rebirth, sloughing off the grafting of Teutonic, of Slavic, of South European ideas which have been tainting its thought for a generation, and become that stern, clean, just democracy that was conceived when our forefathers knelt by Plymouth Rock and entrusted themselves—and us—to the Almighty.

Wayne Mac Veagh: "The Impassible Chasm"

American frenzy against the generation of Germans who immigrated at the end of the nineteenth century reached far beyond the facts of the Germans' true loyalty. Many Germans fled to the United States precisely to avoid conscription and a militaristic society under Prussian domination.

North American Review, July 1915

The first consideration which caused me pain was that so many of our fellow-citizens of German birth or descent have ignored the fact that there is an impassable chasm between the status of a citizen of our beloved Republic and that of a subject of the German Emperor. I took it for granted that those Germans who came here in these later years came with the same spirit of devotion to human liberty as those I had known in my early life, and that they came not at all to play the double part of availing themselves of the privileges of American citizenship while really championing the cause of a military monarchy, all of whose aims and methods of government were absolutely hostile to those of the country whose protection they sought. . . .

No matter where a man is born or how he is reared, when he comes to manhood he instinctively prefers to be a citizen or a subject. Our fathers preferred, and we ourselves and our children all prefer, to be free citizens, but we do not for that reason deny to anybody else the privilege of preferring to be the obedient subject of a Kaiser and a Military Caste. We only ask them in all fairness to themselves and to us to make their choice—to be loyal either to the fundamental principles of our Government or those of the government of the Kaiser, and to believe that they cannot be half loyal to the one and half loyal to the other. They must be wholly American, or wholly German, and if they really prefer the German system of government, they should return thither and enjoy it; but if they propose to continue to live here, then they must be loyal to the American system, and there is no possibility for them of mistaking what that system is.

M. A. De Wolfe Howe: "The Non-Combatant's Manual of Arms"

To ennoble righteous wrath as separate from venal anger has challenged humanity since antiquity. Aristotle's well-known comment requested what M. A. De Wolfe Howe seems also to wish for: a tempered anger. "Anybody can become angry, that is easy; but to be angry with the right person, and to the right degree, and at the right time, and for the right purpose, and in the right way, that is not within everybody's power, that is not easy." Wartime events proved such classical self-restraint to be difficult; Woodrow Wilson even found it necessary to speak against the excesses of a "mob spirit." But some historians have criticized his comments as tardy and half-hearted, particularly as he himself had previously questioned the patriotism of German immigrants.

Atlantic Monthly, October 1918

There are other German victories than those of arms—and their possibilities are legion. There is a deadly victory of the spirit. When American non-combatants are heard, for example, to complain that their government is too lenient to aliens of an enmity quite unproved, and to urge the severest courses toward them by asking in a tone of finality, "What would happen to an American in Germany under corresponding circumstances?" there is grave reason to fear that this victory of the spirit has been won. What would happen in Germany is precisely what should not happen in America, if our purposes in this war are what we know them to be; and the unconquered in spirit must be brave enough to say so.

Is the non-combatant, then, to go his ways in a mollifying mist of benevolence toward the foes of his country, leaving to its soldiers and sailors, whose business it is to slay and slay until the brute force of the enemy is subdued, this practice of the very negation of the gentler principle? A thousand times, no! While the soldier is killing a man, he must not stay his hand by loving him. He can love righteousness, and hate iniquity, with all his heart; and for the sake of establishing the one and overthrowing the other, he can, and must, perform deeds which at any other moment of his life would be impossible for him. But it is not the business of the non-combatant to slay. His good fortune is that he may make some discriminations in his hatreds. He may, and should, separate, in some measure, the personal from the universal, the petty from the immense. With all the intensity of which he is capable, let him hate, with a righteous, ennobling wrath, the evil thing which men of good-will on earth have joined themselves to destroy. Even while the bitter fight is on, we cannot tell ourselves too often what we know in our hearts, that when it is over we shall look back with less satisfaction on the smaller personal hatreds it has engendered, than on that large and truly righteous indignation which imparts strength to the fighting man.

Anonymous: "A German-American Menace?"

Of the belligerent German-Americans described below, perhaps the most prominent who organized pro-German propaganda in the neutral United

States was George Sylvester Viereck. Viereck, who had achieved some renown as a poet, tried to initiate German-American cultural ties in the years before the war. During the war he established The Fatherland *to promote German views and encourage U.S. neutrality, and assisted German propagandists. Despite his prominence—or perhaps because of it—he was able to avoid prosecution after the country entered the war, while continuing to publish.*

Nation, February 4, 1915

It would be difficult to take seriously the threat of some particularly belligerent German-Americans to organize for aggressive action "to break the power of England upon our Government, our public servants," if it were not that these fellow-citizens have been guilty of so many errors of taste as to warrant the fear that their judgment may once more be submerged by their emotions. "A great movement," we learn, "is under way to organize the German-American element and all German and Austro-Hungarian sympathizers" to balk " the attempt to deliver the United States into the keeping of England by the Tory element which controls the American press in New York and occupies seats in the Cabinet of President Wilson." This undertaking, it appears, has thrilled the "great mass of non-Anglican American citizens, bone and fibre," and opened many eyes to the horrible danger which threatens our country if this intolerable state of affairs continues. Indeed, the manifesto assures us that it is already too late to prevent the attempt, and that we are as "dependent upon England for our place and privilege in the world" as in 1812. This it is proposed to end in order to "assert and maintain our dignity as citizens of the United States."

Now, citizens of this country, whatever the land of their birth, have a perfect right to organize for any benevolent purpose that they approve. They can form societies, if they please, in order radically to alter our form of government or to induce it to change its foreign policy. If they are actuated by patriotic American motives, no one will object, however he may disagree with the aim. But when this organizing is plainly in the interest of a foreign Government, and would inevitably result in dividing all Americans into two camps over an issue foreign to this country, those who undertake it are playing with extremely dangerous fire. It will tend to inject hatred and bitterness into our treatment of questions relating to our foreign affairs, and the worst possible time for such a display of partisanship. If ever there was an hour when patriotic citizens should refrain from acts likely to embroil this Government at home or abroad, it is the present.

Our German-Americans, who are citizens, and not merely sojourners among us, were supposed when they took out their naturalization papers to have abandoned their allegiance to Germany, and to have sworn fealty to our institutions. Now many of them are acting as if they were never Americans at all, but merely Germans who live here for convenience. They are looking at this whole question, not from the American point of view, but the German.

Reinhold Niebuhr: "The Failure of German-Americanism"

Efforts by German propagandists in the United States came both from those who lived in America and those dispatched from Germany to counter British and French propaganda. But initial strong American support for U.S. neutrality waned after May 7, 1915. On that date the British passenger liner Lusitania, *steaming on its return voyage from New York, was sunk by a German submarine. Of the 1,201 people who died, 128 were Americans, some of them wealthy and prominent. Berlin protested that the passengers had been amply warned and that the ship was carrying munitions. But it could not overcome U.S. outrage that Germany would attack a passenger liner carrying women and children. By World War II attacks on civilians from all belligerents would kill hundreds of thousands.*

***Atlantic Monthly*, July 1916**

We see upon every hand that, where the German-American is hostile or indifferent to our ideals, he is, in some sense, false to his own. It is difficult to find an adequate reason for this peculiar situation in which German-Americanism is found. Perhaps it is due to the fact that German immigration was largely drawn from the peasant class of Germany, which is ignorant of, and unaffected by, the influences of the modern German university, which has had such a large part in molding contemporary German civilization. Perhaps it is caused by the fact that the German exodus to this causes German-Americans to remain true to customs and conceptions of the fatherland, causes them to perpetuate customs and ideals long since discarded in Germany itself.

Whatever may be the cause of the failure of German-Americanism, its failure is obvious. And this failure may be a contributory cause, not only of the lack of esteem in which German-Americanism is now held in this country, but also of the lack of understanding between Germany and this nation. This want of understanding may be only very indirectly responsible for the present ill feeling between the two countries. This seems rather to be due to more specific historical incidents. But the position of German-Americanism in this country would have been fortified against suspicions of disloyalty and a defense of the German cause would have been more convincing and effective had it been less indifferent to the ideals and principles of this nation and more true to its own.

Editorial, George Harvey: "The Hyphen Must Go"

After the Lusitania *incident—which nearly brought the United States to war—it became more clear that Britain was winning the propaganda battle and that Anglophiles were running the U.S. government. The many political and social groups that organized around the celebration of German language and culture found it increasingly difficult to operate. When the United States declared war in 1917, they could see that their cause was hopeless. Most disbanded as their members were pressured to renounce German culture and conform to a narrowing set of accepted American ideals. Speaking out even in a mild way against the government's policies could easily cost the freedom of a German-American. Churches, schools, hospitals, publishers, and other organizations built around the needs of German-Americans barely persevered through difficult times, despite the obvious fact that these mostly charitable organizations posed no threat to security.*

North American Review, March 1916

There is, however, something more required than the formal taking of the oath of allegiance; even though it should include a specific renunciation of every vestige of the dual citizenship which has been too largely held. The alien should in some way be endowed not merely with citizenship papers, but with an American mind, American sympathies, American ideals, and with so large a degree of American detachment from Europe that European affairs would no longer have more than academic interest for him. That is asking much, but it is not asking too much. If America is worth coming to, it is worth paying for; even the price of complete renunciation of the old country.

At present there are in the United States numerous leagues, associations, societies and what not, with hyphenated names and devoted largely to the work of keeping alive and potent in the hearts of their members an affection for the old country and an interest in its welfare sufficiently strong to control their political action; so that they will vote for or against this or that, not because they are Americans but because they are aliens, and not because of American interests and welfare but because of the interests and welfare of the old country. There ought to be some method of preventing such a spectacle as we have witnessed in this country for months past, of numerous bodies of citizens denouncing the President and Government of the United

States simply because they let their policy be directed solely by American interests and not by the interests of some foreign Power. American citizens must be Americans, pure and simple. The Hyphen must go.

Editorial: "The Opportunity of the German-Americans"

Prominent German-Americans, particularly publishers such as Bernard and Victor Ridder of the New Yorker Staats-Zeitung, *opposed Wilson in the 1916 presidential election. They believed Wilson and his administration had become so pro-British that any fair treatment of Germany would be impossible. Democrats seized on general German-American support of Charles Evans Hughes, the Republican candidate, to charge that the Republicans were the party of the German extremists in the United States. This strategy helped Wilson win one of the closest elections of the century.*

Nation, April 27, 1916

We have heard much in the years past about the German-Americans being the tie that bound the two countries together. Now let them prove it. Never again will such an opportunity come to them, for it is not merely the opportunity to keep the peace between the two nations, but perhaps to bring peace in Europe. For whatever the feelings of antagonism abroad, there is still no question that the President of the United States remains preeminently the man to initiate the peace negotiations at the proper time—which may be nearer at hand than most people realize. It is a remarkable opportunity for the German-Americans to redeem the terrible blunders made in their name by the Ridders, Viereck, von Skal, and many another, and to develop for once a bit of constructive statesmanship. Let them, as we urged last week, denounce the bomb plots and all the other conspiracies now seeing the light of day, by whomsoever committed; and then let them turn to the other side. An impassioned appeal to Berlin might give the very excuse the German Chancellor is waiting for to climb down gracefully. The German-Americans know, too, that the abandonment of the submarine war is not going to result in Germany's being starved out—at least their press has been repeatedly saying that Germany is invincible. They know that only 6 percent. of the British merchant fleet has been sunk; they know that with America's vast resources freely placed on the side of the Allies, victory for the Kaiser would be more impossible than ever.

Why should they hesitate to speak out, to act, and to act at once? They avow their loyalty and patriotism. Why not put that patriotism to the highest possible service?

Frank Perry Olds: "Disloyalty of the German-American Press"

The large German-language press in the United States fast realized its tenuous position and so responded by self-censoring and issuing vigorous statements of loyalty. But they still published in German. In a society that had become so anti-German it was renaming dachshund dogs "liberty pups" and banning Wagner's music, it was unlikely that anything could satisfy critics save a German publisher suspend his publication, burn down his plant, pulp his archives, and give what he had left to buy Liberty Bonds. This article is one of the most prominent of several harsh criticisms of the supposed duplicitous German newspapers. It was true that many German-language publishers held back their pens with sullen resentment.

Atlantic Monthly, July 1917

Newspapers printed in this country in the German language have said that they are loyal to the United States. Other editors have read their statements and believed them. Americans in general have been led to suppose that our pro-German press, once so emphatic in defense of Germany, is now supporting the United States in the prosecution of its war against the German Empire. But nothing could be further from the truth. The pro-German press of the country has merely revised its propaganda to fit its present needs.

Carefully avoiding anything which would lay them open to the charge of treason according to the letter of the law, German-American newspapers are daily violating its spirit by spreading a fabric of anti-government lies, anti-Ally calumnies, and anti-war agitations. It is their aim to bring defeat to the cause we have espoused by discrediting our motives, by preventing assistance to the Allies, and by causing discontent and opposition in our own country. Confidently expecting a German victory, they wish to hasten that desirable event by withholding our weight from the Allied offense.

In so brief a paper, it is impossible to do more than touch the main points of this new propaganda. That it exists is beyond question. The pro-German press has discovered a way to help Germany while keeping within the law. It is a new propaganda, apparently safe in showy cloak of lip-patriotism. The American people will do well, I believe, to give it their serious attention.

Since the beginning of the world war, the German press of the United States has consistently praised and defended every move of the Imperial German government. Every step of the American government in maintenance of its neutrality which did not redound to the credit and advantage of Germany, every step in resistance to German aggression, has been condemned. German-American newspapers went into paroxysms of joy over the sinking of the Lusitania, and their sharpest criticism of the Zimmermann note to Mexico was that it was "unwise." They deemed our neutrality "scurvy" and "one-sided." The German Emperor has been praised by them as mild, God-fearing, and faithful to the interests of his people; the President of the United States has been characterized as hypocritical, selfish, and unworthy of his high office. Count Zeppelin's services have been exaggerated; Admiral Dewey's services, in view of his defiance of Germany, have been minimized. Von Bernstorff has been called a true diplomat; Ambassador Gerard has been referred to as a "thing calling itself a diplomat." Before we entered the war, the German-American press existed, apparently, for the glorification of Germany and abuse of the United States. Then our war came.

When the President's message sounded through the halls of Congress, there were some men among us sanguine enough to hope for a complete change of heart in the German-American editorial bosom. Though we knew that German-Americans had steadfastly opposed a war between Germany and America, we thought that the actuality might convert them to a semblance of Americanism. It did not, but it made them more circumspect. They began to realize that opinions would no longer be viewed as "pro-German" or "un-American," but would be labeled "patriotic" or "treasonable." For obvious reasons, their first "patriotic" effusions were of undivided loyalty to the United States. Under cloak of that loyalty, they launched their new propaganda. . . .

Feeling in advance that war was inevitable, German editors had considered what to say as to its causes. On April 2, the Cleveland Waechter und Anzeiger thus presented its case:

> "Since Germany with her allies is rather sure of victory and of indemnification by the Allies, the only way in which the millions lent the Allies can be secured is by their modification into American bonds. To do that, of course, the American people must be brought to a state of war."

German-American editors agree that our war is really a last effort to save the money lent the Allies. We have financed the Allies and now we realize that Germany will win. We must convert Allied bonds into American bonds and prolong the war "in order to put off the day of peace, so that American business can adjust itself to the peace conditions as they will be after this most awful war is ended."

The real causes being thus disposed of, the "alleged" principles were discussed. the President had said that we were determined to overthrow Prussian imperialism to the end that democracy might be safe. Overlooking the main point, the Illinois Staats-Zeitung says, "We have just as much reason to continue the war for the dethronement of the Hohenzollerns as for that of the houses of Saxe-Coburg on the British and Belgian thrones, or against the Roumanian branch of the Hohenzollern family."

Edmond Defreyne: "Under Two Flags"

A "love it or leave it" mentality has accompanied most U.S. wars, at least at their beginning. It is an emotional call to patriotism by people who believe those who do not support their government in wartime must be accused of treason. Government-sponsored patriotism may be found in buildings and monuments. But from the personal standpoint it stems from an emotional demand for loyalty demonstrated through symbolic means, such as stylized ribbon magnets during the U.S. war in Iraq, or displays of flags during World War I. Desecration of the symbol—burning the flag, for example—in times of intense patriotism would be considered a treasonous act. Patriotism in this sense conflicts with the bedrock American value of free speech. As was often the case in World War I, free speech seldom prevails.

North American Review, October 1915

No Man can Serve Two Masters

Which flag is the flag of your country?
To which is your loyalty due?
No man can be true to two banners:
Come! Yellow? Or red, white, and blue?

Which Eagle? The one you adopted?
Or one that is spread on black cross?
Which motto? "E Pluribus Unum?"
Or "Gott mit uns?" Which wins the toss?

No honest blood runs through a siphon;
Allegiance is bound by one oath;
Two faiths can't be linked by a hyphen:
You're Yankee or Teuton—not both!

American are you, or German?
Free man, or autocracy's dupe?
Where stand you? By these States united:
Or "Fatherland," Kaiser, and Krupp?

Quit talking and writing rank treason
While under Old Glory you stand,
or break with us, fairly and squarely,
And GO!—with your heart in your hand.

—Edmond Defreyne, Unhyphenated American

Editorial: "The President's Indignant Arraignment of Disloyal Americans"

Wilson obviously reflected pro-British sentiments, but his concern about German conspiracies did have basis in fact. Germany was determined to undermine shipping to Britain in any way it could. That included skull-duggery, if necessary, and toward that end German agents made a number of attempts to disrupt and destroy American shipping toward Europe. Most of that accomplished little more than adding propaganda fuel to the allies' furnace. But one New Jersey dock explosion caused two deaths and a fair amount of damage. Incredibly, the leaders behind much of this sabotage were the actual German and Austria-Hungarian ambassadors themselves, Johann von Bernstorff and Constanin Dumba. Dumba was deported in 1915.

Current Opinion, January 1916

The purpose of the President in introducing this subject into his message to Congress was to ask for additional federal laws against the offenses indicated. A little while ago, he asserts, we would have thought such a disloyal course of action on the part of naturalized citizens incredible. "Because it was incredible we made no preparation for it. We would have been almost ashamed to prepare for it, as if we were suspicious of ourselves, our own comrades and neighbors! But the ugly and incredible thing has actually come about and we are without adequate Federal laws to deal with it." He urges the enactment of such laws at the earliest possible moment, for "such creatures of passion, disloyalty and anarchy must be crushed out. They are not many, but they are infinitely malignant, and the hand of our power should close over them at once." They have "poured the poison of disloyalty into the very arteries of our national life," and the gravest threats against our national peace and safety have not come from without but have been uttered within our own borders. The acts he specifies are: plots to destroy property, conspiracies against our neutrality and spying into the confidential transactions of the federal government. The heat with which the President speaks implies, so the N.Y. Evening Post thinks, that the government is in possession of a great deal more evidence of these dastardly offenses than the public has been aware of. The Springfield Republican, another paper close to Mr. Wilson, finds the intensity of his language "unexpected and perhaps surprising." The N.Y. Telegraph, a Tammany paper, thinks this passage of the address is one that will subject the President to the severest criticism as well as win for him the highest praise. It adds: "It is doubtful if any President since the foundation of constitutional government in this country has before singled out a particular group of citizens for such a castigation, and it is certain that the language of Mr. Wilson is unprecedented in its bitterness."

Immigrants as Potential Patriots

Anonymous: "The President's Words Denounced as 'Shameless' "

Wilson repeatedly castigated German-Americans for their supposed lukewarm patriotism and tendency to undermine American public opinion. After war was actually declared, German-Americans were caught in an impossible situation. They were expected to denounce their cultural heritage, and when some merely tried to lay low, they were denounced for inadequate patriotism. If others zealously rallied to the American flag, they were criticized for hypocrisy and for hiding their obvious disloyalty.

***Current Opinion*, January 1916**

From the German-American press, language is hurled back at the President in some few cases as vehement as his own. It is taken for granted that his references are to citizens of German, Irish and Austrian extraction, or, as Mr. Ridder puts it, to "those American citizens of foreign birth who have found repellent to their conception of American ideals the whole policy of the present Administration, from anglicizing American spellings to anglicizing American liberties." Mr. Ridder's paper characterizes the message thus: "A document more shameless than this is not recorded in the annals of American history." The German Herold, of New York City, is much more temperate and much more effective in its response. "We are absolutely sure," it asserts, "that President Wilson is mistaken in his assumption that foreign-born citizens are at the bottom of plots 'against the peace and dignity' of these United States" It proceeds to enumerate all the different plots that have come to public attention, naming each of the persons implicated and giving his nationality. It finds nineteen Germans, not one of whom has ever been naturalized, eight native Americans, and "perhaps just one naturalized citizen, and he not a German-American."

Editorial: "To German-Americans"

A propaganda technique of World War I, and used again in subsequent wars, tries to separate a country's people from its leaders. In emphasizing that an entire people cannot be bad, just badly led, those who are waging war can direct their hatred at a reasonable target and not demonize an entire population. In World War I the premise of this propaganda was incorrect; everyday Germans overwhelmingly supported their leaders. It is indeed popular to characterize the interwar fall of Germany to Hitler's leadership as Nazism, and not the real Germany. But Hitler rose to chancellor in a democratic election, despite his violent polemics. More recently, in the early twenty-first century, elections in Iran and among the Palestinian people empowered extremely conservative leadership with a long history of explicit violence.

***Independent*, February 19, 1917**

If the present issue were one between Germany and England we would expect you to sympathize with your Fatherland; if it were one between the United States and Germany we would expect you to support your adopted country, but with reluctance and perhaps misgiving. But do not look at it in that light. The present conflict is one that transcends nationality; it is a world-wide Civil War between the last strongholds of Feudalism and the rising tide of Democracy. There is no nation, considered as a nation, which Americans of every descent love more than Germany. We have had more quarrels with England, and even with France, than with Germany; our universities have drawn more inspiration from Germany than from any other land; we regard, and rightly regard, the German-American as one of the best elements of our citizenship. We hope that a liberal Germany may in the future become one of the most prosperous and powerful of the nations of the earth. The enemies of your adopted country are the military caste and the military machine that have ruined and disgraced your native country. Down with the Kaiser! Long live the German people!

Hermann S. Ficke, Dubuque, Iowa, Letter to the Editor: "The Loyalty of German-Americans"

Wilson's repeated pleas for tolerance and patience in his efforts to shorten the war and broker the peace should have been reflected in his treatment of minorities at home. They were not. In a Flag Day speech of June 14, 1917, he railed against German sympathizers seeking to sabotage the country's efforts while making "false professions of loyalty to its principles." Widespread circulation of Wilson's speech by the Creel committee for government propaganda assured that German-Americans would be looked on with suspicion for no other reason than a German-sounding name. They were not, however, actually rounded up into camps as Japanese-Americans were during World War II.

Nation, August 30, 1917

Sir: In the interest of a number of Americans of German descent, I wish to make a statement of the essential loyalty of the German-Americans of this vicinity. We have no interest in Prussian autocracy and no sympathy with Kaiserism. Our loyalty is alone for the democratic ideal as realized in the American Government. Fully half of the volunteers to the National Guard in the Middle West have been of German descent. We have read of riots against the draft, yet we have not seen any German names in the reports of the disorders. We have given freely to the Red Cross, yet we regret that no woman of German descent will be allowed to go as a nurse to Europe, while her brothers are accepted to fight and die for America. Is that fair?

We read in the leading periodicals that we should protest our loyalty, yet I have on my desk a letter from one of these periodicals refusing to print a statement of German-American loyalty. The leading comic weekly of our country has with rare humor pictured the German-American as Plot Deutscher, whose rotund body and feeble brain are active only in deeds of treason. With eminent fairness our daily papers place upon page one the report that the German-Americans plan to poison the corn salves, the porous plasters, and the apple pies of the nation, and two days later the refutation is put in an inconspicuous place on page ten. Business and professional men of German name are made to suffer a thousand petty ways, and they are told that they deserve and may get something worse.

This is cruelly unjust. The great mass of the Americans of German descent is with our Government in its defence of democracy. There is an old proverb, "You can catch more flies with molasses than with vinegar," and those who are feeding vinegar and vitriol to the German-Americans need not be surprised if they make themselves unpopular.

We are loyal; we are ready to make every sacrifice for the cause of democracy; we believe that no German name will ever be placed side by side with that of Benedict Arnold; and we demand fair play.

Professor Albert Bushnell Hart, Harvard University: "German-Americans and the United States"

German-Americans in the United States came from a variety of countries and for a variety of reasons. Many did not even emigrate from a German state; Germans from Russia heavily settled the Upper Midwest. Those who did come from Germany after the 1871 union often did so to escape militaristic Prussian society. Mennonite religious communities were almost by definition pacifist. Many immigrants opposed war for war's sake, and not because they agreed with German principles. But as the United States moved closer and closer to the allied viewpoint, to oppose war at all was to be a traitor, no matter what the reason.

***New York Times Current History*, October 1914–March 1915**

The alien German and the naturalized German have this in common, that they both came to the United States in order to better themselves. Nobody compelled them, nobody paid them. They made their own choice. If they ever accepted Professor Munsterberg's argument that Germany is much better governed; if the German education, social life, civil spirit, governmental efficiency really seemed to them so much higher than ours, then why in the name of the Temple of the Thousand Gods have they not all gone home long ago?

Every German who comes to this country as anything except a passing visitor thereby expresses his opinion that he does not like Germany enough to live there. If there is truth in one-tenth of the passionate adoration of all German methods, which has been so plentiful in the ultra-German-American press, we must make up our minds to lose several millions of our most esteemed fellow-citizens as soon as the war is over and the German steamers begin to run again.

(Miss) J. Mandery, Rochester, New York, Letter to the Editor: "From an Undaunted Champion of Germany"

This letter followed shortly after the sinking of the Lusitania *and the loss of more than 100 American civilians. Americans were so incensed that the arguments presented here, as reasonable as they might seem in today's light, could not overcome this age's emotional revulsion that a country at war might actually target noncombatants. American neutrality crumbled probably more from this incident than any other. It had already been primed with stories of German atrocities helpfully transmitted by British propagandists, the "scrap of paper" incident, and Germany's aggressive prewar posturing.*

***North American Review*, August 1915**

I am quite convinced that all German-Americans, including Americans of German descent, do put "America First." You cannot blame them, however, for resenting what seems to them the unjust discrimination against Germany expressed so forcefully and regardlessly in the American press.

You say, "We are not of those who would evade responsibility or avert criticism by shouting vaguely, 'Stand by the President'; that is a course befitting subjects, not citizens" (page 162). But (page 168) you speak of "the traitorous utterances of hyphenated editors who write as Germans." Does not that seem a bit inconsistent?

You intimate that Germany it was who "tore up 'the scrap of paper.'" The German minister said explicitly that he was referring to England's general attitude toward treaties when he used that expression. Did he not? I am sure that I read that somewhere. Some one separated the words from the context and stated that this was the self-confessed attitude of Germany.

You say that declaring a "war zone" was a "brazen violation of international law." Are we not very technical, suddenly, about our observance of international law? Did not the President advise Americans to leave Mexico when it became dangerous to remain there? Would it have been improper, then, to advise Americans to observe caution about venturing into the danger zone? I know a lady who sailed for England a day after the Lusitania. Her husband, an American, living in London, advised her to be certain to book her passage on an American ship. She arrived in England safely. Was that not slight enough caution to observe? . . .

Does anybody think that Belgium would have resisted Germany if it had not depended on England and France, if it had not, in fact, very likely had an understanding with these two nations? Why ignore all the data from various sources which seem to prove this? Oh, because we are pro-British.

Professor Hugo Muensterberg, Harvard University: "The Impeachment of German-Americans"

The purported efficiency of a German militaristic state has been admired from the country's inception, through the Nazi era, and perhaps even today. American military leaders during World War I did indeed find value in a German approach that could almost single-handedly hold out—nearly win, in fact—against a coalition of formidable foes from all sides. This efficiency was somewhat of a myth; historians have pointed to all kinds of waste in German bureaucracy during the war. It nevertheless maintained the best-trained military in the world.

New York Times Current History, October 1914–March 1915

The Germans felt this duty perhaps more than others from the European Continent just because their national ideals are so strongly contrasting with some Anglo-Saxon creeds. Had it been only the love for music and flowers, for Christmas trees and gardens, for folk songs and fairy tales, it would have been insignificant, and they might have sacrificed it with a clear conscience.

But endlessly more important impulses were at stake. Their whole devotion to the overindividual ends, their faith in the State as bearer of the ideals, their trust in thoroughness and discipline, in purity and loyalty, were involved. They had become almost unconscious of this contrast in the routine of everyday life. But the great struggle about the war has awakened the burning consciousness of the tremendous issue. They suddenly have felt with shame that they had not done enough to bring these German ideals into the American life and to arouse understanding for their eternal value. Now they suddenly knew that they would disgrace themselves as Americans if they were disloyal to their foremost American duty. They pledged to keep the fire of the German belief alive on their hearth forever.

Is our time unfit for this message of German idealism? Is American life not in need of this gospel of thoroughness and discipline? Is it really better for the American future if those impulses which speak the soul of Germany are eliminated in order that the Anglo-Saxon instincts alone keep control of the land?

George A. Plimpton and Kuno Francke: "Americans and German-Americans: Their Mutual Obligations"

The consequence of two world wars on German-American populations was indeed what Theodore Roosevelt had hoped: it "yanked out the hyphen." Today the German-American press, once the largest foreign-language press in the country, has been reduced to insignificance. Fewer than 20 still exist in all of North America, none of them dailies, in contrast to the 800 that existed early in the twentieth century. German-American cultural groups carry no political significance. German language programs in schools have been eclipsed by Spanish, which represents the new dominant minority. Nevertheless, the 2004 census showed that 43 million Americans identify themselves as being of German ancestry.

Independent, **February 26, 1917**

[Plimpton:] A war with the mother country of any of our fellow citizens should make the rest of us exceedingly charitable and liberal toward these fellow citizens in all our dealings. We should take especial care to guard ourselves from taking an attitude of suspicion toward them. We should always act on the assumption, stated in some of our German-American newspapers, "They are now American citizens, and they should be treated as American citizens" Of course, if any overt acts should be committed the offenders will be punished.

My feeling is, however, that in case of a war with Germany we should find that some of the very strongest upholders of our Government would be our

German-American citizens, whether naturalized or not. I cannot conceive of any German here wishing to see America worsted. There are many reasons why we should feel confident of the patriotism of our German population.

[Francke:] For obvious reasons, the great mass of German-Americans are fervently on the side of Germany in the European war. An alliance between this country and the enemies of Germany would therefore seem to them a crushing blow to their own most cherished feelings; it would make it extremely difficult for them to cooperate in the same friendly spirit as before with the political parties responsible for the alignment of this country on the side of Germany's opponents. Racial embitterment and resentment would poison public life in town, state, and Union. The very foundation of our national existence, freedom from racial rivalry and hatred, would be endangered. Knowing all this, the German-Americans should consider it their first duty to the country of their adoption to preserve it from the fatal effects of tribal strife by helping to stop its source: American participation in the European war.

QUESTIONS

1. What specific incidents encouraged neutral Americans to support Germany's enemies?
2. Why did Germany consider America "Anglophile?"
3. Why did supporters of the war believe that it was important to assimilate German-Americans during this period?

CHAPTER 11

Pacifism

Pacifism, the notion that all disagreements between humans should be solved by mediation, arbitration, or submission, has been part of Western philosophy since the Reformation. The Mennonites, a Christian sect particularly known for strict pacifism, was established in 1525 in Zurich. Its German-speaking adherents suffered through centuries of persecution for their unbending interpretation of the New Testament's denunciation of war. Many German-speaking Mennonites left their home countries rather than face conscription, particularly in Russia, and settled in the United States. America had no obligatory military service, common in Europe, and its reputation for religious and ethnic tolerance appealed to the deeply conservative Mennonites, many of whom settled in the Midwest.

Unfortunately, their steadfast pacifism was again put to the test during World War I. Mennonites were offensive to American mainstream opinion not only because they refused to support the war but also because they were German speaking and of German origin, so automatically suspect. The conscription that had forced Mennonites to flee Europe came to the United States on June 5, 1917, with the country's first draft registration since the Civil War. Mennonite conference leaders worked to obtain assurance from the government that those who chose pacifism on religious grounds would see their wishes respected. This included, at least for the more doctrinaire Mennonites, the wearing of uniforms, marching, carrying weapons, or, indeed, anything connected to the army. Some Mennonites also refused the possibility of alternative service, reasoning that even kitchen duty, medical work, or cleaning latrines was forbidden because they were not allowed to provide similar humanitarian aid to the enemy. Secretary of War Newton Baker assured these religious pacifists that they had nothing to fear, that their wishes would be respected, but that their men of service age should register anyway.

That was what he said. What he wrote in a confidential memo to the army camps made it obvious that conscientious objector status had not been clarified in Washington. Meanwhile, those espousing pacifism would be forced to train anyway in the hope that the melting pot of the army would persuade these men to abandon their pacifist beliefs. The concept was part of the larger goal many American leaders set for the army, to homogenize the nation by discouraging attitudes and behavior outside the mainstream. Should this fail, religious pacifists were to be segregated from other troops so that their disloyalty would not infect the rest of the men. Segregation of conscientious objectors inevitably led to abuse. Most of it consisted of name calling: branding the men as cowards, pro-Hun, or yellow. In a few cases the men were denied food, even beaten or tortured. Of the 2,000 Mennonite men drafted, 130 who declined service were convicted of disobeying orders and jailed. Sentences ranged from 10 to 30 years, mostly at the Fort Leavenworth, Kansas, military prison. Another two thirds accepted alternative service in construction or farm work. The rest remained isolated in army training camps.

Those Mennonites not qualified to serve did not escape harassment. Many Mennonite churches were painted yellow. Two were burned. But Mennonites were not the only religious pacifists targeted as the country slid from tolerance to war frenzy. Among those who clung to pacifism for political and philosophical reasons were some socialists and liberal progressives as well as some prominent African American leaders. The former presumed the war merely served as a tool of the wealthy who had made loans to allies and now feared default and so used the common folk to fight their capitalist war. The latter presumed the war was really a dispute over colonialism and most peoples oppressed by colonial powers were black Africans or a different minority culture. The most well known of several peace federations that sprang up after August 1914 was the American Union Against Militarism. Prominent liberals who combined to form the Union included Roger Baldwin, Oswald Garrison Villard, and Crystal Eastman, its first executive director. Eastman was sister of socialist publisher Max Eastman. The Greenwich Village feminist had become well known for her pacifism as well as her work in favor of birth control and "free love." Villard, born in Germany, was probably best known of the three, publisher of his father's *New York Evening Post* and owner of *The Nation.* This pacifist group worked against militarizing American society by opposing increased armament spending, expanded military training, and conscription. Baldwin replaced Eastman as director in 1916.

Baldwin's role as director became perilous as the group's pacifist platform was splintered by nearly universal wartime mania. The wide swath of civil liberties abuses both legal and informal encouraged Baldwin to seek a new role for the organization, one in defense of persecuted minorities who could not and would not support the war. Baldwin reinvented his organization as the

National Civil Liberties Bureau, working from New York to protect American rights of free speech and protest. Most risky, Baldwin adopted the cause of the International Workers of the World (IWW), the "Wobblies," who as radical socialists were hated for their declaration of conscientious objector status, and even more hated for their obvious refusal to support what they perceived as a capitalist government in a war for the money-lenders. In 1918 Baldwin tested the country's commitment to freedom by purposely violating the Selective Service Act, resulting in his arrest and trial, conviction and imprisonment. He was released in 1919 into the postwar "Red Scare" that targeted anyone suspected of being a Communist. Most zealous in his opposition to these perceived threats to American security was the young J. Edgar Hoover, leader of a new organization, the Federal Bureau of Investigation. Hoover immediately set about collecting data for files on suspected subversives such as Baldwin and Eastman. In 1920 the American Civil Liberties Bureau became the American Civil Liberties Union (ACLU) with Baldwin as president.

Ad hoc pacifist organizations such as the Emergency Peace Federation attempted to march and speak in favor of continued neutrality. Former Stanford University president David Starr Jordon perhaps unwisely agreed to stump the country for the group, but in Baltimore on April 1, 1917, he barely escaped an angry crowd of thousands who accused him of traitorous behavior. In Congress pacifists tried to delay the war declaration as long as they could, even though prowar lawmakers could count on a crushing majority in favor of fighting. Wilson was able to solidify support by portraying the war not as a battle against Germany, per se, but as a larger war against the forces of despotism, for a "world safe for democracy." Senator George Norris of Nebraska and Senator Robert La Follette of Wisconsin argued that it was more a war for a world safe for J. P. Morgan and other tycoons. Wilson joined most of the country in decrying these detractors, calling them "willful little men." Former president Theodore Roosevelt called for La Follette's hanging, declaring that the senator "has shown himself to be an unhung traitor." The country's voices of pacifism by 1917 had been thoroughly bullied into silence.

Pacifism: Cowardice and Misunderstanding

Philip Marshall Brown: "The Dangers of Pacifism"

Norman Angell, a former newspaper reporter in the United States and France, had become world famous by 1914 for The Great Illusion, *his argument that war was economically pointless. In a 1913 edition he asked,*

"Are we to continue to struggle, as so many good men struggled in the first dozen centuries of Christendom—spilling oceans of blood, wasting mountains of treasure—to achieve what is at bottom a logical absurdity, to accomplish something which, when accomplished, can avail us nothing, and which, if it could avail us anything, would condemn the nations of the world to never-ending bloodshed and the constant defeat of all those aims which men, in their sober hours, know to be alone worthy of sustained endeavor?" Angell wrote 41 books and was awarded the Nobel Peace Prize in 1933.

North American Review, July 1915

Pacifism is fostering the spirit of cowardice and a materialistic conception of life. It has stressed so vividly the horrors of war, has so effectively obscured the heroic, idealistic aspects of war, and insisted so strongly on the futility of war, that men are fast coming to believe that "peace at any price" is the best motto for a nation. It matters not what interests may be at stake, even independence itself; the great object of a foreign policy is to avoid war!

For the followers of Norman Angell everything is reduced to a matter of material calculation. Wars never pay, they say. A thousand men must not be "sacrificed" to protect a hundred fellow-countrymen in danger of torture and death at the hands of uncivilized ruffians. According to such a materialistic theory, a man of genius should resist the impulse to save a drowning child because his own life is of greater value to the community. The chivalrous, self-denying, generous spirit is not to be fostered when men of one's own blood appeal for help from abroad! The peoples of the Balkans should never "sacrifice" lives for the sake of their brothers under foreign domination!

Pacifism has inculcated such an exaggerated conception of the value of life as to treat it as something immortal, something which must be preserved; it is not something to be freely laid down in accordance with the precepts of Christianity!

Surely this is to lose sight almost completely of the spiritual values. In failing to glorify in the magnificent idealism of the soldiers of all the opposing armies now in combat who are joyfully giving their lives for something not themselves, who are inspired by a transcendent national ideal, pacifism is leading the rising generation to worship at a sordid, selfish shrine. It is fostering a spirit of cowardice of a peculiarly abhorrent kind.

Andre Cheradame: "Pacifism as an Auxiliary of Pangermanism"

Andre Cheradame argued against what later came to be called the politics of appeasement, that is, giving in to some demands of an adversary in hopes he will be satisfied. Most historians would challenge the idea that European powers appeased Germany before World War I. Before World War II was a different story. British Prime Minister Neville Chamberlain's famous agreement with Adolph Hitler in 1938 allowed German annexations in the hope of avoiding war. It did not. A comparable British action in 1914 would have been, perhaps, to allow Germany to march through Belgium, but this would have been impossible given the secret treaties that neither pacifists nor warmongers knew about at that time.

Atlantic Monthly, September 1918

The deep-seated cause of pacifism, generally speaking, is the very incomplete knowledge of external affairs—and, hence, of Germany—which unfortunately we are obliged to recognize in the countries now allied. The result of this ignorance is that those persons who are temperamentally inclined to idealism discuss war and peace through the medium of abstract principles and a priori theories, having no knowledge of definite facts, carefully scrutinized, to save them from errors. Thus they see foreign countries as they would fain have them and not as they are.

Now, it is from this category of minds, predisposed to theory, that the pacifists are recruited. Again, it is readily understood that, while they have very little familiarity with external material facts, they are even more ignorant of external immaterial facts—notably, the psychology of the German people. And each and every pacifist error has its definite basis in the ignorance. The acts of pacifist foreign policy from 1890–1914—the endless concessions made to Germany or Austria—were generally regarded in Great Britain, Russia, and France as wise and prudent and calculated to ensure peace; this estimate could proceed from nothing else than utter failure to comprehend Germany psychology.

Those persons in the Allied countries who believed and still believe that to make a concession to the Germans is the surest means of inducing them to respond with reciprocal concessions are absolutely mistaken. Prussianized Germany sees evidence of weakness in every voluntary concession, and is tempted thereby to demand more ere long. It is of vital importance that people in the Allied countries should become imbued with this fact, which is known to all those who have watched Germany closely. The Germans, by reason of an ages-old atavism which cannot be suddenly changed, respect nothing save material force guided by an intellectual force which knows them through and through.

Thus the only way to persuade Germany to preserve the peace is to constrain her to do so by forcible methods more powerful than her own and always ready to be set in motion.

Franklin H. Giddings, PhD, LL.D., Columbia University: "The Bases of a Just and Enduring Peace"

While some Christian sects such as the Mennonites opposed war in any context, others justified it in certain, specific situations. One well-known Christian philosopher who offered a justification for war was the thirteenth-century Catholic Saint Thomas Acquinas. His theory of a "just war," expanded by later philosophers, argued that it was the duty of a sovereign to defend his country against external enemies. External enemies of the United States during the Great War, as proposed by war advocates, were more ideological than physical, and few Americans truly feared actual invasion by German troops from across the sea.

Annals of the American Academy of Political and Social Sciences, July 1917

Happily the United States has dropped the fatuous belief that it could stand aside and, from safe isolation, watch the titanic struggle between liberty and despotism. In the moral order of the universe it is not permitted to a nation, any more than it is permitted to an individual, to be neutral upon the great fundamental issues of conduct. He who does not dare to stand for what in his inmost soul he believes to be right must surely die the second death of those who become the craven slaves to what they once held to be wrong. The United States will worthily play its part in the league of the democratic peoples to safeguard those political principles which the league of the thirteen original American states was the first power to proclaim. Pacifists, like the givers of indiscriminate alms, whom they mentally resemble, we may always have with us, but the American nation will not be a partner and accomplice of dynasty.

Grosclaude, French Publicist, Reprinted from *Le Figaro,* Paris: "If You Desire War, Embrace Pacifism"

The French, with British help, barely stopped Germany's advance in early September 1914, but certainly unpreparedness played little role in the allies' near defeat. The French had long planned for war, its "Plan 17" a template for quickly retaking Alsace and Lorraine and subduing the expected German invasion. French general Joseph Joffre miscalculated, however, not realizing until it was nearly too late that the main German army would invade from the north through Belgium. His remarkable sang-froid in the face of near disaster, along with exhausted German troops, set the front that was to change little over four years.

New York Times Current History, April–September 1916

Brother Americans, you whose sense of "struggle" has taught you the advantage of marching straight at a peril without turning away your face, look at us, meditate on our lot, and consider what that execrable, stupefying drug, pacifism, has made of our Europe.

The wisdom of the ages has declared, "Si vis pacem." ("If you desire peace, prepare for war.") Our wisdom of today tells you with the same certitude, "If you desire war, embrace pacifism." I offer that motto to your illustrious Roosevelt. It is with emotion that we see him urging upon you an active prudence. We are counting upon him to put before your eyes the lesson of our dreadful example. And, fallen into the ambuscade whither we were traitorously attracted, we raise out of the night the saving cry of the chevalier: "On guard, America! The enemy is upon you!"

Henry Rutgers Marshall: "The Pacifist at War"

Many former pacifists abandoned their principles to support Wilson in joining World War I. They did so not because they believed war to be a good thing, but because they believed Wilson's rhetoric that this war was different, noble, a final battle for a new world order that would sweep away the corruption and despotism of the past. It was "the war to end all wars." The enormous disenchantment during the 1920s and 1930s served as rejoinder to the bleak truth that this hideous war had apparently solved nothing.

Atlantic Monthly, May 1918

We have seized our opportunity to make another great step in advance, which would have been utterly impossible had we remained neutral. We, through our President, have enunciated an ideal of governmental aims, and governmental procedure, which never before has been brought clearly before the world; and we have been able to do this at a time, and in a manner, which have led all the great nations with whom we are in alliance to receive it with acclaim.

This last fact is, in itself, a great triumph in the cause the pacifist has at heart; for this approval of our President's words is certain to be made use of by statesmen in later generations to curb the aggressive tendencies of the jingoes among political leaders, whom we must expect to find from time to time in the future aiming to influence the legislative bodies of their day.

The rational pacifist thus enters this war because it looks towards the realization of his ideal. He cannot expect it to be the final war; but it may well be the last great war. In this sense, then, it is a war to prevent war.

And with all this in mind the pacifist, as an idealist, may well give, as many of them are now giving, all the strength that is in them to win this war; realizing that for the moment we must lay aside all thought of peace, devoting all our energies, without stint, to every action that looks to victory. Vast will be the treasure we shall sacrifice; bitter will be the suffering we shall incur in sympathetic cooperation with our allies. But we shall make the sacrifice with enthusiasm, and shall bear the burden of sorrow with courage, assured that in so doing we are helping to take a long step on the road to enduring peace.

We must win this war; and we shall win it.

Oscar S. Straus, Chairman, Public Service Commission, New York: "The Events That Presage a Durable Peace"

Absolute pacifists, mostly socialists or those basing their pacifism on religious belief, seldom changed their opinion as the United States tilted toward the allies. But progressive pacifists, the liberal thinkers who worked for social change before the war, were generally persuaded by German belligerence and Wilson's perspective that this was not a war for territory, but a war for ideals. Postwar realities shattered these illusions, leaving Americans more cynical.

***Annals of the American Academy of Political and Social Sciences*, July 1917**

Most of us, I think, have changed our views considerably since this war began. Many of our wise pacifists have developed into belligerent pacifists. I confess I belong to that school myself. Before this war began, the proposition presented itself in the glaring phrase, "Utopia or hell!" Can you blame us for choosing Utopia? We did not realize that we had to wade through the jaws of hell to reach Utopia. America is ready to march through hell to secure democratic freedom and the permanent peace of the world, founded upon law and justice.

Charles Edward Jefferson, D.D.: "The Nemesis of Armaments"

Andrew Carnegie, a Scottish immigrant who earned a fortune in Pittsburgh steel mills, is well known for his extensive philanthropy at the turn of the last century. He drew on assets of some $500 million based on the

1901 sale of his company to J. P. Morgan. Called "the richest man in the world," Carnegie spoke in favor of democracy, equality, and responsibilities of the wealthy to help society. His extensive philanthropy included establishment of the Carnegie Endowment for International Peace in 1910. World peace, he declared, was more important to him than any of his other projects.

***Independent,* August 17, 1914**

From the awful spectacle of Europe plunged into war two clashing conclusions are certain to be drawn.

The first and most obvious conclusion is that the pacifists are in a hole. They have been mistaken all along, and now their delusion is exposed. They have long been suspected of being visionaries and dreamers, but now the last doubt of it has vanished.

In the glare of the huge conflagration the peacemakers cut a sorry figure. A metropolitan newspaper editor scoffs at them as an "absurd group" on whom little sympathy need be wasted. He notes that they are not saying anything just at present and intimates that they should forever hold their peace. Such men—to quote one of our most distinguished fellow-citizens—are not only useless but mischievous.

The militarists, on the other hand, have been right from the beginning. All that they have said is true. Man is a fighting animal. Human nature cannot be changed. Nations have always fought, and therefore they always will fight. War soon or late is inevitable. The only sensible thing is to get ready for it.

The present predicament of the peace-workers is put graphically by a journal whose name the reader is left to guess. "It is in no gloating spirit that we call the attention of the Andrew Carnegies, the David Starr Jordans and other misguided peace enthusiasts to the vindication of the position of this journal which is furnished by this war array on the Danube. What has become of that army of bogies with which Mr. Carnegie, Dr. Jordan and others had peopled the imaginations of the unthinking? The roar of the guns in southeastern Europe has awakened those peace gentlemen from their foolish dream, and their phantom host of spooks has vanished into air."...

The peace workers are not so guileless, and ignorant, and impractical as they are painted. They know history, and they understand human nature, and they are acquainted with the laws of the world they are living in. They are familiar with every move that has been made in the last thirty years. The man who imagines that they are soft and green is dreaming. He is in the grip of a spook. What the peace-workers have said from the beginning is now being confirmed.

Pacifism: Patriotism, Wisdom

Washington Gladden: "A Plea for Pacifism: Will America Yield to the Armament Madness?"

Many Christians during World War I based their pacifism on biblical teachings, particularly those in the Bible's New Testament. The New Testament emphasized the importance of peace at least 14 times, including the apostle Paul's declaration "Live in peace: and the God of love and peace shall be with you" (2 Cor. 13:11). Other Christians, however, were able to find justification for war, particularly in the Old Testament.

Nation, August 3, 1916

I am a pacifist, if I understand that word, which is not in my dictionary. A pacifist, I suppose, is a peacemaker. And the teacher from whom I have learned what little I know about conduct once said "Blessed are the peacemakers, for they shall be called the children of God."

I sometimes hear the word "pacificist" spoken very reproachfully. There is a little more hiss in that word than there is in pacifist, and some people like to use words that have a good deal of hiss in them. But if pacificist is any stronger than pacifist, then I'm that. Perhaps a pacificist is not only a peacemaker, but a man who wants to make peacemakers. If that is what it means, I'm that. And if anybody says that it is silly to be a pacifist, I shall not quarrel with him. I have often, as St. Paul said, been counted a fool for Christ's sake, and I expect to be, as long as I live. And if anybody calls me a mollycoddle, my only answer is: "Very well; then I will try to be a fair-minded, just, honorable mollycoddle; I'll do my best to make it a name which everybody will respect. The name Christian was originally a word of contempt. It was flung at people because there was a hiss in it. And the day may come when the King shall say, 'Blessed are the mollycoddles, for they shall be called the children of God.'"

I am not, however, in favor of "peace at any price"—if I understand what that means. Peace is a good thing which I greatly desire for myself, and for my family, and for my city, and for my country, and for the whole world; but I don't want any good thing at any less than a fair price; I wish to pay for all the good I get all that it is worth. I want peace and I am ready to pay full market-price for it, which is justice and truth and trust and fair play and good-will and kindness and service: as a rule you can get it for that, and I don't believe you can get it for nay less—not the real thing, that you can live with and that will stay with you.

But of this I am equally sure: I don't want war at any price. That, indeed, is a costly luxury. It comes high in the market. You have to pay for it in carnage, slaughter, widowhood, orphanage, broken homes, crippled lives, desolated fields, ruined cities, and heaping measures of hatred and suspicion and fear. You can never get it on any other terms.

H. S. Canby, Yale University, Letter to the Editor: "We Who Once Were Pacifists"

After the United States joined the war, pacifism became identified with the political groups most likely to have espoused it: socialists and some labor groups. These people opposed the war as a "war of capitalism," but their position, merely considered ignorant, wrong-headed, or stupid in peacetime, became treasonous, seditious, and dangerous in wartime. One New York minister (Newell Dwight Hillis), urged forgiveness on the Germans "just as soon as they are all shot."

Nation, April 12, 1917

But what are we?—for the term Pacifist is being torn from us. Pacifist, in the current press, means coward. Pacifist means holding back from war in order to make more money. Pacifist means anarchist, dreamer, traitor to the state. Pacifism is a "poisonous heresy." What rubbish! What dangerous rubbish! Pacifism meant and means nothing of the sort. But if it is too late to complain of the abuse of a noble word, it is not too late to ask for a more honest description of the hundreds of thousands who think as I do—the one-time Pacifists. . . .

Invent a new term, then, for the myriads that call themselves Pacifists; or, if Pacifism is to be a reproach, apply it with discrimination. We will not be confused with the sentimentalists—the non-resistants, or half-resistants, who wish to sell goods to the Allies only and still keep clear of European responsibility. We cannot align ourselves with the reckless barbarians who care not what happens to-morrow so long as they fight to-day. We are a party, patriotic I know, self-sacrificing I hope, clearer thinking than some; a party of protest against prejudice and short-sightedness, rant and hysterical. We are against anti-nationalism and the sluggishness of a people not too cowardly to fight, but too comfortable to think; we are against dangerous jingoism that serves its own passions rather than the state.

Editorial: "Varieties of Pacifism"

Persistent opposition to joining the war, and to the preparedness campaign, tended to center in Midwest agrarian states. While immigrants to these areas included a strong percentage of ethnic Germans, opposition to war was based more on the suspicion that the same powerful industrial and financial concerns that had mistreated farmers now were clamoring for war to enrich big business. Widespread suspicion of preparedness supposed that munitions makers were secretly pushing for it. By 1917, however, most of these pacifists concluded that war was a certainty and so moved to support it.

Independent, March 19, 1917

Few things are more amusing than to stir up a real militarist or an excitable patriot with a few carefully mischosen words on pacifism and then stand back and watch the fireworks. All persons opposed to preparedness or an aggressive foreign policy are, you learn, the non-resistant poltroons who delight in being trampled on and would be "too proud to fight" if a foreign army should suddenly come boiling over the frontier headed directly for their wives and children (for further particulars see any outburst of our volcanic ex-President).

Now since we have the assurance of so many worthy gentlemen that this type of pacifist is what is ruining the nation, it is somewhat strange that we who count scores of ultra-pacifists among our friends and acquaintances have never met one of that sort. It is true that we once met a lady who opposed all foreign wars quite consistently, condemning the action of Belgium equally with that of Germany, but as she favors revolutions and is a militant suffragette with a sympathy for syndicalism, she can hardly be the type that the anti-pacifist has in mind. Indeed pacifist principles vary not in inverse but in direct ratio with personal courage and truculence. Hardly anybody is for peace at any price, but any particular war will be opposed for any of a number of reasons.

The United States is at the present moment facing a serious prospect of war with Germany. Many persons say that we should under no circumstances enter the present Great War. What are their reasons and their motives? Have they the abstract hatred of violence which is supposed to be regnant in every pacifist breast? How many are Tolstoyan anarchists who think that all force is wicked? Perhaps such people exist; the papers say that they do, but they are very hard to find. Let us summarize the real varieties of pacifists, not in the terms which and enemy would put into their mouths, but in the way they do actually think.

Exhibit A (tall, lanky, bony figure with the appearance of a farmer from somewhere in the Middle West): "You Easterners always turn your minds towards Europe. Look at America a little. No foreign nation could conquer the United States and nobody is going to try, but if we mix in with that European scrap it will mean the death of thousands of us and no good to come from it at all. Let's just keep ourselves to ourselves till things have quieted down a bit across the water."

Exhibit B (smoky red hair and a gray eye alight with the fire of battle; a palpable Irishman): "Ah, they want us to go in with that old tyrant of the seven seas that starved and slew the Irish for generation after generation. It's them Wall Street dudes that's always turning up their trousers here whenever it rains in London that wants war. If it was to fight England now—"

Exhibit C (Russian Jewish type, with a copy of The Masses under one arm and a package of no-conscription leaflets under the other): "I tell you what, my friend. The capitalists want world markets and they send us out to die to fill their money bags. When we fight let us fight against our own tyrants right in this country."

Exhibit D (student, with black ribbon on his eyeglasses and a habit of arguing with his forefinger): "Much may be said for the use of force in civil society, but modern war is quite another thing. It means not only the loss of human life—a deplorable but minor matter—but the halting of all internal reform, the wastage of the resources of civilization, the degradation of the human stock by the destruction of its best types, the suspension of civil liberties and the enthronement of military tyranny. No possible good can counterbalance so many and such manifest evils, and therefore I oppose war under all circumstances."

Exhibit E (an elderly man with the courtly bearing of a stand-pat Senator but an ardent advocate of radical causes): "Yes, it is all right to fight when you have a cause worth fighting for, but national honor or even national existence is not such a cause. Nationality is played out. What difference does it really make whether we speak English or German or Esperanto? The only important thing is the advancement of the common civilization of mankind."

These five wholly different cases are all types of the ultra-pacifists. Not one of the five has any physical or moral aversion to combat and not one of them can be answered by talk about cowardice or supine submission to the country's foe.

Percy MacKaye: "A Potential Substitute for War"

The dove as a symbol of peace most obviously reflects the biblical story of Noah, who released a dove to search for land after the great flood. The dove returned with an olive branch to show that land had been found, and so God's anger had come to an end. But the symbol itself predates the Bible, and can be found in cultures around the world. Perhaps it is the behavior of this bird that has charmed cultures throughout history. Doves mate for life and are loyal to their companions in building nests and raising young. Unlike some more aggressive species, they do not attack other birds, eat seeds, and can be trained to eat out of human hands—symbols of love, loyalty, and a peaceful spirit.

North American Review, May 1915

Of all the causes in history the cause of international peace is probably the noblest, yet—of all symbols appealing to the world's imagination—its symbol, the dove, is probably the most anemic. Some other, more compelling, must take its place before its cause can plead effectually against that of its rival. The Dove is no match for the Devil. If war is ever to be vanquished, it will be by St. George or Raphael, not be the bird of Noah. In brief, it is only Peace Militant, not Peace Dormant, that can supplant the heroic figure in War in the hearts of the nations.

But by Peace Militant I do not mean Peace panoplied upon dreadnoughts, glaring at her image in two oceans through Krupp-steel binoculars: for such is that false peace, no other than war disguised, which betrayed the world in August, 1914.

No; I mean by Peace Militant—not War disguised as a hypocritical time-server, but War self-purged and self-subdued to the functions of social service: not Peace armed with a sword, but Peace armed with the symbol of a sword—that "moral equivalent of war" of which William James has written with wise eloquence.

But the mere existence of a moral equivalent is not enough; it must be made effectual. Social service exists among all peoples, but it is not made to appeal sufficiently to popular imagination.

My object, then, in this article is to suggest that the "moral equivalent of war" can be made fascinating and effectual by utilizing (and perhaps only by utilizing) the dynamic arts of the theater to give it symbolic expression.

Thus a practical substitute for the dramatic conflict of war would be its moral equivalent expressed through the manifold forms of dramatic art.

Bertrand Russell: "War and Non-Resistance"

Bertrand Russell was one of the most important philosophers of the century and also one of its most ardent pacifists. As a University of Cambridge don he was convicted twice for his antiwar activities, imprisoned six months the second time. His idealistic argument in favor of a central force to stop war could be compared to the current United Nations peacekeeping forces, although their effectiveness has not been able to reach Russell's high hopes.

Atlantic Monthly, August 1915

All these three motives for armaments—cowardice, love of dominion, and lust for blood—are no longer ineradicable in civilized human nature. All are diminishing under the influence of modern social organization. All might be reduced to a degree which would make them almost innocuous, if early education and current moral standards were directed to that end. Passive resistance, if it were adopted deliberately by the will of a whole nation, with the same measure of courage and discipline which is now displayed in war, might achieve a far more perfect protection for what is good in national life than armies and navies can ever achieve, without demanding the carnage and waste and welter of brutality involved in modern war.

But it is hardly to be expected that progress will come in this way, because the imaginative effort required is too great. It is much more likely that it will come, like the reign of law within the state, by the establishment of a central government of the world, able and willing to secure obedience by force, because the great majority of men will recognize that obedience is better than the present international anarchy.

A central government of this kind would command assent, not as a partisan, but as the representative of the interests of the whole. Very soon resistance to it would be seen to be hopeless and wars would cease. Force directed by a neutral authority is not open to the same abuse or likely to cause the same long-drawn conflicts as force exercised by quarreling nations, each of which is the judge in its own cause. Although I firmly believe that the adoption of passive instead of active resistance would be good if a nation could be convinced of its goodness, yet it is rather to the ultimate creation of a strong central authority that I should look for the ending of war. But war will end only after a great labor has been performed in altering men's moral ideas, directing them to the good of all mankind, and not only of the separate nations into which men happen to have been born.

Frederic Lyman Wells: "The Instinctive Bases of Pacifism"

Philosophers have explained pacifism from both the duty-based and consequence-based perspectives. Those who believe pacifism is a duty argue that respect for human life must always be considered paramount. Those who argue against war's consequences argue war is clearly wrong because of the destruction it creates. Frederic Lyman Wells contends both concepts of pacifism grow as a society becomes more civilized and less patriotically bound to support the group. Selfish motives overshadow primitive drives that encourage war. This does not explain why the century's most horrible wars took place among the world's most culturally advanced states.

Atlantic Monthly, July 1916

Especially from this instinct of self-abasement grows the pacifism on the doctrinaire. The man of affairs would respond little to such a trend of thought, were it not powerfully reinforced by a better understood, but still instinctive factor. In order that a man may best enjoy his pleasures, make money, found a family, and rear children, he tends to give all his energies to the following of these personal instincts. He does not do this so well if group interests, of which strength for war is one, make their demands upon his energies. Personal and group instincts thus come into fundamental conflict. Pacifism expresses the outcome of this conflict, when personal instincts get the upper hand of group instincts. The rationalizations of pacifism do not then take on such an other-worldly character as when they spring chiefly from the trend of self-abasement. War is opposed because it dulls one's "finer" sensibilities, because it interferes with property, because it endangers the continuity of the family.

Because war does these things, it arouses, as Professor Cannon points out, hostility against itself. As with increasing civilization there is more personal pleasure to be got out of life, men conform less to conditions that may make them part with it. the anthropologist observes that the death-fear is far greater among the enlightened than among savages. Those living under the freest social conditions can get the most personal satisfaction out of life. The recent experiences of England illustrate that men so situated are less ready to make personal sacrifices for group motives.

The instinctive bases of pacifism are therefore two. First, the instinct of self-abasement, which inhibits the supreme combative efforts that war demands. This instinct of self-abasement (here conceived in harmony with the regression of Professor Ribot) opposes the instinct of self-preservation with pacifism, and it opposed the sexual instincts with prudery, and economic instincts with glorifications of poverty. Second, the various pleasure-seeking, familiar and economic instincts conflict with and block the instincts that involve self-sacrifice for the group. The continuity of tribe or nation has always demanded this sacrifice of individual motives to group motives, and the nations surviving have been those in which this sacrifice was made. With the security of the group assured, selfish motives have time to grow. Gradually they become stronger than the group motives, and this is the first cause of the decay of nations. Without discipline inside the group, there is no strength against rival groups. Such might may not make right, but it makes history.

Questions

1. Describe two arguments in favor of pacifism, as presented by World War I writers.
2. Describe two arguments against pacifism, as presented by World War I writers.
3. Does sports or entertainment serve as a substitute for war in modern society? How?

Chapter 12

Race and Language

The years surrounding World War I in the United States could easily earn the distinction of most racist of the entire twentieth century—perhaps in all of American history. President Woodrow Wilson himself set an unfortunate tone. His roots in the grotesquely racist American South grew into an entire campaign against American blacks, beginning at the pinnacle of American government.

As a candidate Wilson promised to treat all races fairly and fight against lynching. But as president, he worked to remove traces of dark skin from his sight. African American government employees, if they had to stay, were partitioned off in separate desks curtained away from whites, compelled to eat at separate cafeteria tables and use separate restrooms. People of color, as African American writers often called themselves during this period, were removed from whatever diplomatic jobs they had and were shut out of other government positions. Postmaster General Albert S. Burleson contributed by adding more formalized segregation to his vast army of federal employees. His actions were condoned by the president who brushed aside black protest by calling it "insulting." In the South lynching actually increased during the war; the federal government not only did nothing to end this outrageous trampling of American ideals, but in fact encouraged separatism by formalizing military segregation. Blacks worked mostly behind the lines because military leaders feared they could not be trusted with firearms. The only training camp for black officers, in Des Moines, was a compromise between those in the military who balked at the idea of any black officers, and African American groups such as the NAACP, which pushed for complete integration.

General Leonard Wood, a strong supporter of Theodore Roosevelt's preparedness policies requiring military service, agreed that asking men to train together would help mold the mosaic of races and nationalities into one nation, a true melting pot. Except for African Americans. The possibility of intermarriage between blacks and whites disgusted the general, who feared "a breed of mongrels." Wilson's racism may have been most obvious, but he generally reflected contemporary fears that the country's blacks could threaten "white" moral and political culture. Despite the name calling ("coons," "niggers," "darkies"), the segregation and the abuse, 370,000 black men served the United States in World War I; 200,000 were sent to France, serving mostly behind the lines. Most black newspapers supported the war, if not Wilson himself. Those editors of so-called race newspapers who dared to criticize the administration for ignoring the growing wartime lynchings (38 in 1917, 58 in 1918) risked having their publications accused of disloyalty and shut down.

In response to widening violence and deepening oppression, many African Americans searched for ways to escape. In worst straits were those who lived in the old South. One possibility was to move north, but the industries there that could offer them jobs preferred to hire immigrants who also would work long hours for meager pay. World War I, however, proved to be a turning point: the flow of immigrants from Europe slowed to a trickle while labor shortages became critical as war demanded more production but drafted the men who could do it. Robert S. Abbott's *Chicago Defender* staged an aggressive publicity campaign during the war, encouraging southern blacks to join "the great migration" to jobs and a better life in the North, particularly in Chicago. The white South reacted with fear as it faced the possibility of losing the cheap labor that had sustained their culture. Retaliation included banning newspapers such as the *Defender*, fining people who recruited blacks to move north, persuading railroads to forbid black passengers, and threatening and intimidating blacks intending to move north and anyone intending to help them. After two centuries of maltreatment, these tactics only heaped more abuse onto the country's most persecuted minority. Record numbers of southern blacks moved north; 110,000 came to Chicago alone between 1916 and 1918. Others moved to Detroit, St. Louis, Kansas City, Pittsburgh, Omaha, and other major northern cities. The power of the black press to move its readers led the circulation of the *Defender* to 100,000, but those issues were passed from reader to reader until they fell apart. True readership probably reached 500,000.

Blacks moving north may have found a better life than they had in the South, but only slightly, as the North was hardly without racial prejudice. Trade unions refused to admit blacks. In one despicable episode, protests over blacks recruited in east St. Louis to counter the growing power of unionized whites erupted into a murderous full-scale race war. Another dozen race riots swept the country in the year after the armistice, feeding the Red Scare frenzy, in which newspapers blamed socialists for inciting racial violence.

But the country's African Americans were not alone in suffering maltreatment while Wilson worked to make the world safe for democracy. About a third of the country was foreign born or first-generation Americans, 32 million, and many had emigrated from suspect nations. The most obvious physical and cultural target was the German population, as noted previously. German language usage in churches, communities, and schools stood on an American tradition dating back more than a century, but in the hysterical wartime mentality, anyone who could say *guten tag* was a suspected traitor. Schools and universities around the country dropped German-language instruction, putting longtime instructors into the unemployment line if they could not be reassigned. Those classes that did remain hobbled along with a few brave students. Lutheran churches dropped traditional German-language services, while government leaders declared that they would battle against the "traitorous language" whenever possible.

This is not to say that other suspect immigrant populations were spared. Irish Americans opposing a war alliance with England also became suspected traitors as well as Swedish Americans, who generally opposed the war. Judge John F. McGee, a member of the Minnesota Commission of Public Safety, stated that "The disloyal element of Minnesota is largely among the German-Swedish people. The nation blundered at the start of the war in not dealing severely with these vipers."[1] As for those as different as the Chinese and Japanese, no easy accommodation could be possible with immigrants who didn't at least look Caucasian. Wilson declared it impossible to blend with such a different-looking people. Concerning American Indians, their plight on the reservations was so distant it hardly even reached public consciousness. Despite that, World War I also proved to be a turning point for Native peoples: 80,000 volunteered for the military, despite a conscription process that excluded them because they were not legally American citizens. American Indians in the army were not segregated, as were blacks, and were able through their service to convince the military they could be assimilated into the general population. They were awarded legal citizenship in 1924, shortly after women were given the right to vote (Nineteenth Amendment, 1920) and after everyone lost their right to drink alcoholic beverages (Eighteenth Amendment, 1919). Rights and privileges of Americans were debated at their fundamental level during this era, producing both winners and losers.

War and Difficulties of Race

Booker T. Washington: "Inferior and Superior Races"

Booker T. Washington, an educator born a slave before the Civil War, became the most influential spokesperson for African Americans between the end of the nineteenth century and his death in 1915. In what was apparently one of his last articles, Washington emphasized his favored theme of peaceful coexistence. He did not support assertive protest and mass exodus to the North, and so clashed with the NAACP. The year of his death marked the beginning of the movement that was to bring a half million blacks—some sources say up to one million—from the South to the North.

***North American Review,* April 1915**

There is a certain advantage in belonging to a race that has to make its way peacefully through the world; a race that prospers, if it prospers at all, because it has made friends rather than enemies of the people by whom it is surrounded. There is a certain satisfaction, also, in belonging to a race whose hope of success in the world consists in making itself useful to that world, and it is not wholly a disadvantage to the Negro that, though he should fight in every war as he has in this, it is not to maintain his own superiority, but that of some other race, that he fights. . . .

What we should strive to do, to put it simply and squarely, is contribute our part toward bringing into existence a civilization in which superiority is based on service, and not contribute more than we have to maintain a civilization in which superiority is based on force. We should look forward to a civilization based on racial peace rather than one based on racial war and racial subjugation.

Such a conclusion will seem very simple-minded and quite impractical. To choose such a course would mean that the lesser peoples, in their struggle upward, must be willing to plod painfully, patiently forward, winning their way as they go, proving that in each gain they make for themselves they are at the same time enriching the world at large, that in each step upward they have lifted not merely themselves, but the whole world above them.

Editorial: "The Week"

This editorial reflects the beginning of shame for a southern (and sometimes northern) lynching culture that had grown to heinous proportions by World War I. Prominent black editors persistently pointed out the hypocrisy of a country declaring its moral high ground in the world war while at the same time treating its black population in a manner no better than the atrocities committed by German troops. The government preferred to ignore this blatant contrast. Race-related lynchings continued in America well into the 1930s, even beyond. A large photo archive of these crimes shows children as regular witnesses at lynching "parties" in which victims were burned and sometimes mutilated for souvenir body parts.

Nation, January 21, 1915

Four human beings were done to death last week without process of law. An entire family—father, son, and two daughters—were hanged, and their bodies riddled with bullets. They were not Belgian francs tireurs caught in the act. They were not East Prussian spies who met retribution at the hands of the Cossacks. They were negroes arrested for resisting an officer of the law and assaulting him, and lodged in the jail at Monticello, Ga. They were taken from the jail by a mob and "Strung up."

Barber's daughters were hanged first. The son came third and Barber last. His body was left hanging, the three other bodies being piled just beneath his feet.

Thus the passion of mob murder extends its sway over the "manhood" of the South. From punishment for the "unspeakable crime," mob murder has long passed into punishment for negro crime in general. From punishment for crime it is passing into punishment for any infraction of the law. From vengeance on supposed enemies of society it has not come to the hanging of women. Further than this it cannot go, unless it takes to stringing up negro school children. And there are people who would have our Government protest against the "atrocities" of Europe!

Editorial: "Strict Accountability"

Robert S. Abbott's Chicago-based Defender *became by far the most important "race" newspaper read by blacks throughout the country. In its great campaign to persuade blacks to migrate north, the newspaper included railroad timetables and job listings. Its success during World War I made dramatic changes to the culture of important northern cities such as St. Louis, Detroit, and Chicago.*

Chicago Defender, March 31, 1917

"He kept us out of war," made a winning campaign slogan and our President rolled up a neat majority that assured him another four years at the White House. It is the big and liberal thing to do to let bygones be bygones, bury the mistakes that cannot be remedied, again have faith, and all pull together for a common cause. But human nature isn't built that way, and especially the human nature that is wrapped up in the average American citizen. When you fool them once it is the other fellows' fault; when you fool them the second time at the same game, it is their fault.

The main issues are the protection of our citizens, and by citizens we do not mean exclusively WHITE citizens, for the black citizens need protection right here at home, the upholding of our honor, the preparation for our safety and the securing of our prosperity. "He kept us out of war," of course, is a farce. He kept us in ignorance of war, is nearer correct.

War for Benefit of Race

Anonymous: "The War: Effect on Prejudice"

African Americans responded to the extensive prejudice and segregation of the U.S. armed forces by signing up anyway. Few saw combat, as military commanders believed them unworthy and perhaps unreliable, but they worked as general laborers, particularly in shipping. This was in contrast to black men from the colonies of France and Britain, who fought and died alongside white troops without segregation. American blacks in Europe for the first time discovered what a world could be like in which they were treated as equals. Paris was particularly interested in the new music of the American black culture—jazz. It swept into the city's clubs after the war and became as popular in Europe as the United States. Perhaps more so.

Crisis, July 1915

What effect will the Great War have on color prejudice? Saint Nihal Singh, writing in the Southern Workman, says:

"The necessity that has led to the employment of colored soldiers on the continent of Europe deals a shattering blow to racial prejudices. After the war is over, the position of the dark people in the political economy of Greater Britain and Greater France will never be the same that it was before the conflict took place. The destiny of the Indian subjects of the British Empire and the Negro citizens of the French Republic is bound to be completely re-shaped as the aftermath of the war. Hints of it have already begun to appear in the British and French press, even though both the nations are engaged in a life and death struggle and have no time to think of any constructive work.

"In thus writing about the issues that have led to the employment of dark-skinned soldiers on the continent, and of their behavior on the battlefield, I have not sought to glorify war. Carnage is utterly repugnant to every humanitarian. All I have attempted to do is to show that good may come to the colored races out of this ghastly struggle in Europe. The war which has stirred up strife between white man and white man, may serve to reconcile the Caucasian to his dark-faced brother."

Editorial, W.E.B. Du Bois: "Soldiers"

W.E.B. Du Bois faced criticism for his wartime exhortation to close ranks and join the whites in a common fight against Germany. Detractors felt that such a commitment should be based on promises of better treatment and integration at home. Secretary of War Newton D. Baker, former Cleveland mayor, responded by acknowledging that needs of about 10 million black Americans in a country of fewer than 92 million should be acknowledged. Baker met with prominent blacks to consider improvements to camps and provisions for African Americans, as well as the racist nature of local draft boards.

Dr. William Edward Burghardt Du Bois was editor of Crisis, *NAACP's influential magazine, for a quarter century. While he supported the U.S. entry into the war, he remained a fierce critic of the country's increasingly racist government policies and shameful legacy of toleration for lynchings of African Americans. Courtesy of Library of Congress.*

Crisis, April 1916

We now appeal to you [federal government] to suggest that four of the new regiments about to be created be designated specifically for the enlistment of colored soldiers.

The Adjutant-General has stated that he doubted if 175,000 regulars could be recruited in the United States. There is no difficulty in recruiting colored regiments. Yet, while officers are tearing their hair to get white recruits, the sign is up, "No colored men wanted." Does it not seem a ridiculous program of preparedness which deliberately excludes the best material we've got?

That is no idle boast. When the Fifty-Fourth Massachusetts stormed for Wagner in '63 it established for all time the fact that the colored soldier could fight and fight well. The history of the Ninth and Tenth Cavalry in the Indian fights between 1868 and 1890 piled up evidence of their courage and loyalty.

There have been notably fewer desertions from the colored regiments than from the white. The Ninth Cavalry once astonished the army by reporting not a single desertion in twelve months, an unheard of and undreamed of record.

Their service during the Spanish War and since has shown our colored troops to be infinitely better fitted for service in our tropical dependences than white troops.

Editorial, W.E.B. Du Bois: "Germany"

Competition for colonies among Britain, France, and Germany deserve a share of blame for World War I. Germany's four African colonies comprised three on the west and one on the east: Togoland, Cameroons, German Southwest Africa (Damaraland, now part of Namibia), and German East Africa. In response to a 1904 revolt, German troops killed up to 65,000 native Herero people in Namibia. But colonial brutality was not exclusive to Germany.

Crisis, February 1916

Someone writes to ask what the effect on the Negro will be if Germany should triumph in the present war. We do not for a moment pretend that the German people are ogres and the Allies saints, but we confess that based on unchallenged records there can be no doubt that Germany's attitude toward colored races is indefensible.

Lewis R. Freeman says in the World's Work: "In Damaraland between the years 1904 and 1907 as the consequence of the killing of a single child the Germans wantonly did to death 30,000 Hereros, a simple pastoral tribe of scant fighting capacity. Never since Nero and Attila had there been a parallel to Von Trotha's infamous order of extermination.

"'Within German borders' read the proclamation of this Teutonic barbarian 'every Herero with or without rifle, with or without cattle will be shot. I will take no more women or children. I will drive them back or have them fired on.'

"For several years Germany seemed actually to be trying to make Damaraland a 'white man's country' by killing the blacks. It has reaped in failure the logical harvest of this sowing of brutality."

German Language: Benefit to America

James B. Dudley, Greensboro, North Carolina, Letter to the Editor: "The Teaching of German"

Scattered voices urged moderation in the frenzy of hate directed against anything even vaguely related to the German language. U.S. Commissioner of Education Philander P. Claxton joined several prominent university presidents in urging Americans to reject wholesale censorship and destruction of German books and language courses. Claxton, who had studied in Germany and had held a number of educational supervisory positions in the South, could not rise above the noise of state and local people such as the Illinois superintendent of education, who declared that the more hatred against anything German, the better.

North American Review, September 1918

My impressions from the constant and regular reading of your editorials did not prepare me to receive from you an endorsement of the movement that is now so general to condemn the teaching of German in our schools. I have taught quite a number of young men who are now in France. I shall soon have others who may soon be in France. It seems to me that the value of these men would be increased by their studying French in order that they may be better prepared to cooperate with our Allies. It seems also to me that it would be increasing the usefulness of these men to have them study the enemies whom they are to fight, and among other things to study the German language. I am sure that if I should attempt to teach German here there would be considerable objection, based upon the same reasons that are set forth in your editorials. I am not quite sure, but it seems to me that the teaching of German and the study of German need not at all be detrimental to the best interests of our cause; in fact, it seems to me that it could be used for the advancement of our cause.

Editorial: "Intellectual Preparedness"

The "Hymn of Hate" that allied propaganda contended played throughout Germany was composed by Ernst Lissauer in 1914. It did reflect German outrage that Britain would join the war against them. The lyrics conclude:

French and Russian they matter not;
A blow for blow, and a shot for a shot;
We love them not, we hate them not. . . .

We will never forgo our hate,
We have all but a single hate,
We love as one, we hate as one
We have one foe, and one alone—England.

Independent, September 21, 1918

Americans who formerly held the funny notion that they were doing a favor to a people they liked by learning its language, now think that they can spite a people they dislike by refusing to learn its language. They imagine that they can "cut" a country as they would an offending acquaintance by declining to speak as they pass by. In fourteen of the United States German is excluded from the schools, in some cases even from the universities, and the movement is spreading rapidly, altho it is opposed by the administration. Dr. Claxton, United States Commissioner of Education, says: "For practical, industrial and commercial purposes we shall need a knowledge of the German language more than we have needed it in the past." In this policy he is in agreement with the European belligerents. The Germans are not fond of the English, as the Hymn of Hate shows, yet they are studying English harder than ever. The University of Edinburgh, in spite of the war strain upon its finances, has appropriated $62,500 for a professorship of German language and literature. The committee appointed by the Prime Minister in 1916 to consider the deficiencies of the educational system of Great Britain has recently reported a radical program of reforms. . . .

What we need to know is the modern world, how it came about, and what it is to become of it. We must try to understand our allies and our enemies, not merely their language but more their mentality.

German Language: Destructive to America

Editorial: "Enemy Speech Must Go"

In 1910 waves of immigration had brought the United States population born abroad up to 15 percent of nearly 92 million. Of those conscripted to serve in the military, eight percent could not speak or understand English. Large ethnic groups supported important foreign language newspapers while many immigrants learned English poorly, if at all. German-language newspapers were the most important and powerful of the foreign-language press before the war—Joseph Pulitzer actually learned journalism by working on the St. Louis German-language press. But few could survive the censorship and bullying of 1917–1918.

North American Review, June 1918

Some of the foremost German newspapers in the country have voluntarily suspended publication or gone out of existence altogether—if we may call that voluntary which is done under overwhelming moral compulsion or in prudent anticipation of legal constraint. In many places, including some of the largest cities, news dealers will no longer handle German papers, and in some places there have been issued municipal ordinances or administrative decrees forbidding under penalty the sale of them.

This movement is being much discussed, pro and contra, a few prominent American papers affecting to consider it intolerant and short-sighted; though apparently on altogether mistaken grounds. The notion seems to prevail with them that the purpose of the suppression of the German press is to prevent German propaganda, which is quite erroneous, and which, if it were true, would stamp the movement as futile. Of course, German propaganda should be suppressed and prevented, by any means which may be found necessary. But it would probably be not at all necessary to abolish the German press for that purpose, since it is of quite insignificant importance as a propagandist. Its utterances can be watched just as carefully and just as thoroughly as those of the English-printed press, and can be dealt with in the same way. Moreover, German papers are read only by Germans, and it is not so much to them that Germany aims to present her propaganda as to Americans. Thus one line of propaganda in an English-printed paper would be more effective for Hunnish purposes than a column in a German sheet.

It is therefore not for that reason that the German press is denounced and is to be abolished, but rather because its existence is at all times inimical to American national unity. It retards the growth of Americanism among a numerous class of immigrants and their descendants. It prevents or delays the political assimilation of naturalized citizens, and makes for the perpetuation of an alien element in the state. Such things are great evils. It is obviously desirable for all immigrants to become not merely legally naturalized but also mentally and spiritually acclimated and assimilated, so that they will think American thoughts and get into practical and controlling sympathy with American institutions and with the spirit of American democracy.

Clyde William Park: "The German Language Press"

Carl Schurz was one of nineteenth-century America's most famous German-Americans. He served under Lincoln as a general during the Civil War, and after the war became a senator and secretary of the interior under Rutherford B. Hayes. He also was an important journalist in both German-language and English-language newspapers, having been part owner of the influential Westliche Post *of St. Louis, and cofounder of the* New York Evening Post. *He promoted patriotism for America while claiming continued respect for his German heritage. Schurz died in 1906.*

North American Review, May 1918

A tolerant, though watchful, Government, realizing the difficulty of their position, gave them the benefit of every doubt and made it as easy as possible for them to become reconciled to the painful reality of war between America and the Fatherland.

The editors were careful, of course, to avoid technically treasonable utterances, though for a time many articles were well within the twilight zone of implied disloyalty. Occasional editorials breathed an old-fashioned Carl Schurz type of Americanism, but these welcome exceptions were rare. A potent corrective for the negative attitude of certain papers was the increasing pressure of an awakened patriotism among all Americans, including the vast majority of citizens of German ancestry. With many editors, perhaps, an even more powerful influence than public sentiment was much to blame. And yet, after having idealized Germany for years and after having defended her war measures against a preponderance of adverse American opinion, they could hardly be expected to oppose her without a reasonable period of mourning for their dead illusions. The adoption of a properly hostile attitude toward the Fatherland was doubtless made easier by the accumulation of evidence in the hands of the Untied States Government showing the brutal selfishness of Germany's rulers. At least these revelations, brazenly and cynically confirmed by the accused Government, proved the folly of attempting further to palliate Germany's crimes against humanity, or to oppose the overwhelming force of an aroused public opinion.

Editorial: "German in Public Schools"

A suspicion that German language study retarded the assimilation process and progress toward the goal of "100 percent Americanism" led dozens of American cities and state governments to ban German-language study. Three states, Connecticut, Minnesota, and California, created censorship boards to scour texts for possible German propaganda.

***San Francisco Chronicle,* May 2, 1918**

Whatever difference of opinion may exist concerning the desirability of abandoning the teaching of German in our public schools, there will be complete unanimity on the point of dispensing with the study of that language at present and permanently if textbooks cannot be provided that are not open to the suspicion that they are vehicles for the propagation of Teutonic ideas.

Under the circumstances, in view of the ingenuity displayed, it may be wise to scan with suspicion everything German. The mind of youth is easily warped, and textbooks may be made the instruments for accomplishing that purpose. If when the strained relations now existing are relaxed the disposition to teach German in our school is reawakened, the textbooks employed should be as carefully prepared and as critically examined as those used in teaching English.

Questions

1. How did African American newspapers react to Wilson's declaration of war?
2. How did African American editors argue that the war was really a "race issue"?
3. In addition to the German-language press, what groups in American society were persecuted for continuing to use the German language?

Note

1. Philip Permutter, *Legacy of Hate: A Short History of Ethnic, Religious and Racial Prejudice in America* (Armonk, N.Y.: M. E. Sharpe, 1999), 160.

Chapter 13

Socialism and Labor

Harsh treatment of some Americans at the hands of other Americans during this period did not end with the country's racial and ethnic minorities. It also extended to political minorities, that is, those who questioned the system of government, specifically Western capitalism. Socialists were most prominent of these groups.

Socialism before the war had become a significant force in Europe and a considerable one in the United States. By World War I, socialism—the concept established in the nineteenth century that capitalism and private property must be eliminated and the working folk, or "proletariat," must take control of society by revolution—had splintered; some groups believed this to be a revolutionary process, others an evolutionary one. The more evolutionary European socialist parties had become powerful forces within governments of Germany, Britain, France, and other countries. Germany's socialists were among the world's most powerful. In the United States socialism also became associated with a growing labor movement, and reflected in the development of two major associations: the American Federation of Labor (AFL) and the Industrial Workers of the World (IWW). Of the two, the IWW held the most radical socialist ideals, including revolution. It could not support what it believed was a capitalist war. The AFL under Samuel Gompers, on the other hand, did support Wilson's war declaration. That ensured its survival in an America that strongly distrusted labor unions and their so-called socialistic goals of collective bargaining, rights for workers, and, when necessary, strikes.

The beginning of war in August 1914 had shattered socialist illusions both in Europe and the United States. Central to socialism was the unity of workers bound together not by patriotic nationalism but by an international spirit of unity among the working classes regardless of national borders. Moderate socialists such as Jean Jaurès in France believed socialism could prevent war, if not politically, then directly by a general strike. War, many socialists believed, would not be possible if those most likely to fight it simply refused to show up.

The disappointing reality to international socialism was that few workers put socialist ideals ahead of an older feeling of patriotism for their homelands. Socialists could not prevent war, could not alter the course of the war, could not even meet to discuss the war, as European governments banned international socialist conferences and refused to let socialist delegates attend those that took place in neutral countries. The power of labor acting through principles of socialism seemed to have been broken by nationalism. Until February 1917.

Czarist Russia was least open to evolutionary socialism because it was most despotic in its control over government affairs. Socialists in that country, who before the war had initiated a series of terrorist attacks in an attempt to bring socialism to Russia through revolution, found a more sympathetic audience than they might have in Western democracies, or even somewhat less democratic Germany. The war's brutal trials rocked every country that participated. In Russia, a brittle incompetent government could not survive the quake. Revolution in February 1917 swept the czarist dynasty into history's dustbin in favor of capitalist democracy that pleased Wilson. Now he could accurately say the war was making the world safe for democracy—all democracies. Alas, the new Russian government decided to keep its promise to the allies by continuing its participation in the war, a promise that could not be sustained. A small number of socialists of the most extreme stripe led by a revolutionary in exile managed to wrest control of the huge nation. Revolutionary socialism had come to power in its most extreme form, communism.

Vladimir Lenin lost no time toying with the idea of continuing the war. His accommodation with Germany, the Treaty of Brest-Litovsk, gave vast tracts of Russia to Germany, but Lenin had little choice: to continue the war would be to lose the revolution. The infant communist government also expected it would remain in power by rekindling the international drive of socialism, encouraging revolution throughout the Western belligerent nations. Those countries' leaders, particularly in Germany, England, and France, were already beginning to deal with a labor class at the end of its rope. Striking workers showed that socialist revolution could mean more than a simple parlor debate about the esoteric philosophies of Karl Marx. It could destroy governments.

In the United States, socialist labor movements had already demonstrated an occasional willingness to use violence as a means to workers' rights. Authorities responded with violence of their own. On the eve of war, in 1914, one of the country's worst battles between labor and management erupted in

Colorado. Ludlow miners struck with demands for an eight-hour day, among other things. State government backed the mine owner, John D. Rockefeller, one of the country's richest tycoons. The Colorado governor chose confrontation by authorizing the National Guard to arrest the strikers. The miners fought back; four guards and a scab (strikebreaker) were killed. Authorities reacted with disproportionate force, thundering down on strikers in tents, shooting anything that moved, and torching the camp. Twenty-five people died, a dozen of them children. The United States had set a precedent it would follow during the war: socialism would be crushed, literally.

As the country moved closer to joining the allies, two distinct strands of America's labor movement grew even farther apart. The AFL under Samuel Gompers declared unstinting support for the Wilson administration. Gompers built the AFL on the platform of working for reform through the existing political system and so supported that system in its determination to defeat Germany. A few AFL members believed Gompers had established a inappropriately cozy relationship with the Wilson administration, but most detractors had long left the AFL for the more radical IWW. The Wobblies (origin of the nickname is uncertain), established in 1905, subscribed to the doctrine of strict socialism, allowing no accommodation with capitalist government. But the IWW was also fractured. The more moderate faction, represented by Eugene V. Debs, urged change through peaceful political means. The second faction, represented by William Haywood, chose the course more attractive to Lenin: general strikes and possible sabotage.

Both factions declared opposition to what they called the capitalists' war. Other socialists opposed to war but not necessarily IWW members became the strongest knot of protest in a country now reaching a dangerous delirium of hate and suspicion. Authorities, who had little tolerance for IWW members before 1917, undertook a massive campaign to crush the socialists for good. The Espionage Act gave the U.S. Justice Department the legal tool it needed to descend on every IWW office in the country—nearly 50 of them—and arrest about 200 IWW leaders. Prison sentences of up to 10 years were handed down. Haywood, out on bail, escaped to Russia. He never returned. Even Debs, five times a presidential candidate for the socialist party, saw his opposition to the war rewarded with a 10-year prison term. A pardon had to wait until 1921, after Wilson left office.

Socialists who weren't harassed by the government still feared harassment from the public and patriot groups. Two people died at the hands of mobs and, by 1920, some 6,000 supposed socialist or communist sympathizers had been arrested. The government's brutal determination to put the IWW out of business between 1918 and 1920 did indeed effectively eliminate the power of organized socialism in America. On the other hand,

Gompers, who spoke against radical socialism and in favor of Wilson, was named to represent labor at the Versailles peace conference.

Ability of Socialism to End War

Anonymous: "The Socialists in the War"

The St. Louis meeting that produced the following message was hastily assembled following Wilson's war declaration on April 6, 1917. Declaring their opposition, socialists called for antidraft demonstrations, which attracted some 20,000 Americans. Wilson responded to protests by encouraging legislation that made such opposition a crime. Scores of socialists were arrested, including prominent politician Eugene V. Debs, who actually ran for president while in jail in 1920. He received one million votes.

New York Times Current History, April–September 1917

American Socialist Party

Meeting in St. Louis on April 14, delegates of the Socialist Party of the United States addressed this open letter to "the Socialists of the Belligerent Countries":

Comrades: Now that the people of the United States have been forced by their ruling class into this world cataclysm, as you have been heretofore by your own rulers, we, the Socialists of the United States, feel it our right and duty to address you on this most momentous subject.

We wish to say at the outset that the workers of this country have no enmity toward the workers of Germany, and that we, the Socialists of the United States, feel that the great affliction now shared in common by the workers of the United States and Germany should, and we hope that it will, strengthen that consciousness of a common brotherhood between them which will ultimately bring about peace between these two countries, and a general world peace with it.

We also wish to convey to you our firm determination, and we pledge ourselves to do out duty and make the sacrifice which may be necessary, to force our masters to conclude a speedy peace, and we hope and expect that, whatever may have been the policies which some of you may have followed in the past, you will henceforth adopt rigorous measures to force your masters to the same course of action.

We therefore call upon you to join hands with us so that all of us may use all the means at our disposal in a common effort to bring about a general peace which will be just and lasting, without indemnities, and without any forcible annexations of territory by any of the belligerents, whether avowed or sought to be hidden by some less offensive term that may be invented for the purpose; so that no nation may be deprived of any part of its liberty or made in any way dependent, politically or economically, upon any other nation; and that no change of territory shall take place without the consent of its inhabitants, freely and unmistakably expressed.

Down with war! Down with misery and hunger and mass murder, must be the war cry of the proletariat. Long live peace! Long live the brotherhood of nations and the solidarity of the proletariat!

William English Walling: "The Socialists and the Great War"

The great socialist movement of the nineteenth century had achieved strong influence throughout Europe by the eve of the war—as long as socialists abjured violent overthrow and committed themselves to change through politics. But the war overturned the political stage. Revolutionary socialists found opportunity where government authority slipped away and war-weary populations became fed up. Russia fell most precipitously into socialism of the hard-line Bolshevist slant, but in Germany and Austria, too, new governments replaced centuries-old monarchies. But the people of these nations did not so easily acquiesce to the revolutionary socialist alternative. In Berlin a January 1919 attempt by Marxists Rosa Luxemburg and Karl Liebknecht, a former member of the German parliament, to lead a Communist revolution was crushed by military forces that captured, tortured, and killed dozens of socialists, including Luxemburg and Liebknecht.

Independent, August 24, 1914

Who is to pay for the vast burdens the war will entail? The classes that pay will have to submit to a lowering of an already fixed standard of living. Everybody knows how much harder people will fight against such an outcome than they will to gain an advance. And the working people will be the most formidable in this fight. In separation they will not only use the methods of sabotage, they will use every method. And even if they did not resist, the efficiency of industry requires the efficiency of the workers and minimum standards of living. If the employers of one country do not see this those of another will take away their trade.

The resistance of the workers will force the capitalists—large and small—to pay the bill. And another and even fiercer class war will break out to see which group of capitalists shall pay the bill. In this war the large capitalists are bound to be annihilated (as capitalists) and genuine democracies established both in Germany and in every country where existing governments are sufficiently humiliated and where Socialists have prepared the way. The large capitalists' functions will be assumed by the new state. Socialist governments and society will pass into the firm control of the small capitalists and skilled labor majorities.

Such will probably be the ultimate result in France and Great Britain. But in Germany, Austria and Russia it is probable that the people will find a much shorter and radical solution. The larger part of the wealthy classes of Russia and Austria and a large part of those of Germany are landlords. It is these that furnish the nobility, the army officers and higher officials; it is they who sustain militarism and religious persecution, and live on the backs of the millions of peasants, keeping them in ignorance, poverty and degradation.

Their wealth—the land—is what is most needed by the people and is most easily confiscated. But besides this there will be no other source of wealth sufficient to pay the huge costs of the war—far greater for Germany and Austria than for the other contending governments, to say nothing of the almost certain indemnities. As to impoverished Russia, she is near bankruptcy now. Six months of such a war as this will mean, first, the repudiation of the national debt—which would involve the loss of some $3,000,000,000 to France, and cause an absolute financial collapse there (which is what the French Socialists desire)—and, second, it would necessitate the expropriation of all large estates.

Samuel Gompers, President, American Federation of Labor: "European War Influences Upon American Industry and Labor"

Samuel Gompers declared himself to be a pacifist in his younger days, but the beginning of war in 1914 brought persuasive voices from all sides urging the influential labor leader to prepare his followers for war. In favoring preparedness, he had been encouraged by British prowar labor leaders, who may also have appealed to his sympathies as an immigrant (he was born and raised in London). Gompers believed that his support of the war could secure a government ear more sympathetic to labor's demands of collective bargaining, improved working conditions, and better pay. His request of labor leaders to join him in 1917 in support of Wilson's war declaration received a less than enthusiastic response, particularly from the United Mine Workers.

Annals of the American Academy of Political and Social Science, September 1915

When the wage-earners refuse to bear the consequences of deeds and policies for which they are in no way responsible then will those in authority consider more carefully, before they start into activity, forces whose evil consequences will bring hardships and suffering. The working people are more clearly conscious of the extent and the nature of their power than ever before, hence they are in a position to secure for themselves increasing recognition in determining the affairs of industry and of international relations. The wage-earners will, I am sure, make their power felt.

In addition to the industrial and commercial issues that the war has raised, the working people of the world are concerned as to what shall be determined with regard to the evil forces that are largely responsible for the war—autocracy and militarism. Through their organized economic power the wage-earners exert a tremendous power in political affairs as well as in industrial and commercial, and they propose to see to it, through their international economic organizations, that democracy shall be assured control in international affairs.

Democracy must be established and endowed with power and authority. That can be done without militarism. Militarism must fall through gradual disarmament.

Democracy will be maintained by able, free citizens alert to discern their own rights and to distinguish the right, able and willing to maintain justice for all.

When democracy shall have established justice in international relations, then shall the wage-earners of every land have greater opportunities to give their ideals reality in everyday life and dream and plan greater things for all mankind. They will no longer be unresisting pawns for war slaughter or the less spectacular slaughter of industry and commerce. In every relation of life organized labor will establish the principle of the sacredness of human life and will not only oppose the brutalities and the waste of war, but also of peace.

Failure of Socialism to Prevent War

John R. McMahon, Member of U.S. Socialist Party: "Socialism's Moral Collapse"

On the eve of war European governments presumed a socialist call to international strikes in case of a war declaration might disrupt military mobilization plans. Authorities in Paris even drew up a list, the so-called Carnet B, of people presumed to work in opposition to war and therefore subject to arrest. But the speed in which international socialism peeled away to reveal underlying patriotism in all belligerent nations surprised socialists and nonsocialists alike. Most socialists not only supported the war, but positively welcomed it, joining in the "short, just war" rhetoric with nearly everyone else. Algernon Lee had been a socialist labor organizer and editor of socialist newspapers before the war.

Independent, October 12, 1914

Socialism in Europe is guilty of a monstrous crime. It has swallowed its principles, spat upon brotherhood, betrayed the class it professes to represent, everlastingly disgraced the red banner of internationalism. It has surrendered to the enemy; it has joined with enthusiastic abandon the capitalistic and dynastic butchers who are turning Europe into a people's killing bed.

These are severe charges for a Socialist to make against Socialists. I make them, and I know that hundreds of my comrades in this country are making them in their hearts, tho they may not have yet publicly exprest them.

William English Walling, writing in The Independent of August 24, 1914, treats socialism in Europe with mild and academic tolerance. He gently blames the compromising majority of German Socialists and apparently rather approves the attitude of the parties in other lands. It will not do. Scientific apology for Judas may have its place. But this is not the time or place for apology or extenuation. Let us understand the facts, yes. But once having the facts, we are forced to give a verdict in accordance with them.

Algernon Lee, a prominent American Socialist, wrote from Amsterdam that we should suspend judgment on European socialism for three months. Why? The evidence of a foul and frightful betrayal has been mounting up for six weeks, and we could not learn more to the point if we waited for six years. We dare not delay judgment. Events are moving at railroad speed.

The cowardly surrender of this false army of peace, eight million able-bodied and "class-conscious" men, has already had terrible results and will yet spread chaos over the whole earth. The example of treachery has been set, the futility of socialism has been demonstrated. If European socialism failed, how can American socialism succeed? Our organization has a trifling strength compared to theirs.

I am not a sentimentalist. I do not utterly despair of the world. I believe the final results of the Great War will be beneficent. But the welter and loss of attaining to beneficent results are chargeable to incompetent and criminal socialism. Whatever happens in the future, whatever socialism yet accomplishes toward world peace and justice, the blot upon its record and the stain upon its banner cannot be wiped out.

Editorial: "Socialists and the War"

Socialists made up for their failure to prevent the war by their determination to recast postwar European society. Waves of strikes disrupted postwar rebuilding in England and France, while revolutionary socialists in Germany and Austria tried unsuccessfully to recreate the Bolshevik revolution of Russia. United States socialism split from the militant Communist model of Soviet Russia. Some old-guard American socialists such as Algernon Lee distanced themselves from organizations that became dominated by Communist Party members.

***Nation*, April 19, 1917**

Reaffirmation by Socialists of internationalism, and of the solidarity of workingmen everywhere, has necessarily to-day a melancholy sound. It echoes the failure of high hopes at the beginning of the war in Europe. That fraternization between peoples which the Socialists had preached for years; their threats to paralyze the war lords by strikes or refusal to do military service; above all, that propaganda of peace to which the Socialist party professed to be devoted—all this structure fell with a crash the moment war was declared. The international Socialists became in a twinkling intense nationalists. German Socialists vied with the French in voting war credits and in flocking to the colors. The dream of peace securely built on Socialist doctrines vanished like the morning mist. It is thus at once a perfunctory and a sorrowful act of the American Socialist party to hark back at this time to the frustrated expectations and the shattered plans of 1914.

Editorial: "Lessons in Socialism"

The Communist Manifesto, *published in 1848 and based on the writings of Karl Marx and Friedrich Engels, is about as fundamentally opposed to nationalism as it could be. Its call at the end to a workers' proletariat is unequivocal: "Let the ruling classes tremble at a communistic revolution. The proletarians have nothing to lose but their chains. They have a world to win. Working men of all countries, unite!"*

***North American Review*, September 1918**

As an international force to prevent war, or to compel the cessation of war, then, we must regard Socialism as practically null. The vast majority of Socialists everywhere remain loyal to the nation rather than to the class, and they are likely thus ever to remain. Indeed, they are coming to recognize and to adopt the sane and logical principle which has been propounded by their ablest leaders in this country, that nationalism is a necessary prerequisite of Internationalism, and that therefore the most efficient devotion to the international welfare of the people must be based upon unwavering patriotism. Tolstoi could denounce patriotism as the wickedest of crimes, and Henry Ford may say that he does not believe in patriotism, and that no man is patriotic, and may pervert the application of Ursa Major's epigram that "patriotism is the last refuge of a scoundrel." Socialists in general will not accept such abominable doctrines.

John Spargo: "Socialism and Internationalism"

World War I dashed the ideal of international socialism, but that was only a start of ideals that would fall to political realities. Nearly everyone living in a fighting nation, even most socialists, came to believe by 1918 that they were fighting for some of civilized humanity's noblest principles: a war against barbarism, a war for the survival of civilization, a "war to end all wars." Wilson constructed his Fourteen Points to guide the armistice on an idealistic foundation cemented with the most important hope for future peace, the League of Nations. Western society's pervasive postwar disillusion flowed from the realization that every ideal for which so many perished would prove to be a chimera.

Atlantic Monthly, September 1917

The outbreak of war revealed the fact that proletarian internationalism was a frail wand, not the sturdy staff we had believed it to be. Once again it was shown that a great movement had been inspired by a shibboleth which it had never closely scrutinized. The watchwords of internationalism have been of incalculable service to the Socialist movement. To declare one's belief in internationalism gives one a sense of exaltation, a feeling of the imminence of the Kingdom of Human Brotherhood. But when the war came, it was apparent that the shibboleths of internationalism so fervently chanted for two generations had lacked intellectual significance because they had never been precisely defined.

Amid the agony of the war and the bitter humiliation of failure the Socialists in all lands are now engaged in the task of defining the old terms. They have discovered that two may say the same words but have meanings as far apart as the poles. To the non-Socialist the controversies which have arisen within the ranks of the Socialists upon this matter of definition appear as manifestations of the ancient struggle between instinct and reason—instinct leading outward to the vision of world brotherhood, reason holding down to the national need. That there is this conflict between spiritual romanticism and the prosaic realism of life it were idle to deny. That is the experience of every great movement, as it is the experience of every sincere and thoughtful mind. How few there are among us who have missed the despair that comes from trying to keep our feet upon the mud and clay of earth the while we hitch our wagons to far-off stars!

Why Socialists Should Support War

John Spargo: "Why Socialism Is Pro-Ally"

John Spargo certainly builds a case based on socialist ideals, particularly the promise of internationalism and the defeat of imperialism. He does not, however, address the capitalistic economic systems that sustained the war in all belligerent nations. The more militant socialists maintained this was to the benefit of rich industrialists and to the detriment of working class minions. Only one former belligerent after the war seriously addressed obvious abuses of capitalist power: Russia. In other nations, reform that began during the war did not continue after the armistice.

***Independent*, July 20, 1918**

There are many very weighty reasons why American Socialists should support the war. I propose to set forth five which seem to me especially weighty:

Because the Allies are fighting for socialist internationalism.

Internationalism means the inter-relation of all nations by ties of friendship, sympathy, understanding and trust. . . .

Because Germany is the worst enemy of democratic socialism.

Notwithstanding the fact that the Socialist party in Germany was numerically strong before the war, it was really very weak in influence. . . .

Because America cannot maintain her democracy unless the Prussian military system is destroyed.

It is not a question of crushing Germany, but of crushing the military system which the German Imperial Government maintains. That can only be done by force of arms. There is no other way. . . .

Because the triumph of the Allies will give freedom to Jews, Jugoslavs, Armenians, Poles and other oppressed nationalities.

That the interest of the Jew is with the Allied Nations is beyond question. . . .

Because victory by the Allied Nations will see the people of Germany and Austria free.

It has long been a commonplace of international socialism that Germany could never realize political and industrial democracy until her great military machine was defeated.

Why Labor Should Fear the War

J. H. Thomas, M.P., and Secretary of the British Amalgamated Society of Railway Servants: "When the War Is Over"

For Britain, the final cost of World War I from 1914 to 1918 reached more than $35 billion, second only to Germany's nearly $38 billion. European rulers who declared war in 1914 could not have seen such immense financial consequences for the Old World. Europe lost its mantle as humanity's political and cultural cradle. Britain's debt to the United States topped $4 billion. London could no longer afford to defend and expand its worldwide empire. Nationalist forces fostered by the war's dislocations as well as Wilson's call for self-determination spelled doom for Europe's extensive colonial holdings. The legacy of what became of those colonies still influences the geopolitics of the twenty-first century.

***New York Times Current History*, October 1917–March 1918**

A Day of Reckoning

The working classes for a number of years before the war when agitating for old-age pensions, better housing, and other social reforms were told that to spend twenty-five or thirty millions on such things would mean bankruptcy. Now it was found that Great Britain could spend $40,000,000 a day in the destruction of humanity, apparently without any trouble. It was said there was plenty of money in the country. Was it realized that there must be a day of reckoning, and that from the beginning of the war Great Britain had only met 30 percent. of its expenditure? If the war ended tomorrow it would have to provide $1,500,000,000 interest on present commitments; on pensions, another $250,000,000; on a sinking fund on a basis of thirty years, another $250,000,000. Adding the pre-war budget of $1,000,000,000, the Chancellor of the Exchequer of the future would have to raise $3,000,000,000 a year at least. There was glib talk today about taxes on capital, and he recognized that it was a plausible thing to talk about, but it cut both ways, and anything that tended to check industrial development reacted on the working classes. Serious consideration, however, must be given to taxes on wealth, as distinct from capital. It had to be realized that, so far as workers were concerned, the pre-war standard would never be accepted again. Some people said that the taxation of German goods would bring relief, but he would not insult them by discussing that. He considered the situation in the light of facts.

Questions

1. Despite their power in Europe, why were socialists not able to prevent the outbreak of war?
2. Why did some American socialists oppose Wilson's decision to join the war?
3. How did U.S. authorities respond to socialist protests against the war?

Chapter 14

Joining the War: Arguments of Patriotism and Politics

Europeans in August 1914 required little official persuasion to join the war. In fact, the transition from countries that had known decades of peace to extreme belligerents came so fast even leaders were surprised. From shopkeepers to socialists, men threw down their tools and grabbed their weapons and a train car to the front.

Why did war come so easily to people who had never fought in one? Perhaps that was a reason itself: never having experienced modern combat, men pulling on the soldier's uniform had no idea what grotesque violence awaited them. But even if they had known, it seems unlikely they would have stayed put to protest; after all, by World War II the world, including the Germans, knew well what war meant. In 1914 people flocked to the colors apparently because they perceived that their country was threatened by imminent invasion, and believed it their duty to defend their nation. In other words, they fought based on a spirit of patriotism.

The idea that one ought to be loyal to one's country and defend that country to the death certainly exists from ancient times. To glorify one's country and military leaders is a common theme in art, literature, history, and song. But before World War I the idea of common loyalty to one's country had been attacked by the strength of socialist internationalism. Throughout the Western world the working class, it was presumed by socialist leaders, was replacing nationalism with internationalism and patriotism with the unity of comrades. Economic arguments too predicted that old-style patriotism could not overcome the force of economic ties that bound countries to peace, lest a war declaration shatter a world interdependent on trade and finance.

Those prewar forces of reason and political discourse seemed to display airtight rationalism, with a presumption that patriotism was probably dead, certainly moribund. Then the guns spoke. Emotion trumped reason.

Arguments for trade or international brotherhood shattered like brittle veneer as patriotism drove millions to their colors. The belief that patriotism could not drive society to such a fever in the modern era was based partly on the assumption that people could not be internationalists and patriots at the same time. But those who believed in the peace of internationalism and trade had not thrown away loyalty to their own countries. French radicals descended from a line of bloody protest against not only their own repressive monarchies but also the threat of invasion from enemies on all sides. Memories of the Paris Commune of 1871, and the German invasion that spawned it, still animated liberal republican politicians. In Germany an ancient tie to language and culture spoke to emotional sentiment far stronger than a staid economic argument. In Britain, calls to duty and honor swept aside the instinct for self-preservation.

Perhaps none of this would have been sufficient to rally troops to the frenzy of 1914 had there not also been the perception that every nation was under attack. Every government save Britain could easily make the argument that theirs was a fight for survival. The British government spoke for fealty to the crown and duty to protect poor Belgium. In all countries the press contributed, promising to support the war by self-censoring the horror, glorifying the sacrifice, and arguing the probability of easy victory. Even in church pulpits the wonder of patriotic virtue could persuade pastors into lofty sermons of military inspiration. It seems incongruous that war would be honored in houses of Christ, but mainline religions in Europe had so closely aligned themselves to the society and the state that they could do little but reflect the dominant view.

The United States was different. By 1917, as Woodrow Wilson prepared his administration for war, Americans had lived through 30 months of neutrality. Therefore, the question of how much military preparation a peaceful country should undertake became the basis of raging debate that sparked cabinet resignations and mass demonstrations. Moreover, nationalism did not mean in the United States quite what it did in Europe. The disposition of the States in 1914 could hardly be considered one of patriotic unity. One third of the country was immigrant, or had at least one parent who had immigrated. The largest majority came from nations such as Germany, now the enemy. Beyond that was a patchwork of races, particularly African and Native American, who had been so severely oppressed that their patriotism was in grave doubt. The strength of pacifist religion combined with that of pacifist socialism probably could not be appeased by any level of patriotic appeal. Wilson, who prided himself as a great orator, would need to draw from every persuasive cell in his body to match the challenge of those questioning his country's entry into the war.

Arguments against the United States joining the war were based on assertions of the country's cherished neutrality, as well as on suspicion in some circles that the war was fought to protect American loans to the allies, particularly Britain. A practical argument in favor of war centered around the need to defend American shipping rights—although antiwar leaders contended that shipping could be defended without declaring war. Progressive leaders such as Walter Lippmann, John Dewey, and Herbert Croly tried a more idealistic approach. They supposed that the war could bring to the country the kind of social reform they had not achieved in peacetime: better working conditions, greater equality, and stronger control over capitalism's excesses. "Superpatriots" such as Henry Cabot Lodge and Theodore Roosevelt hoped military service would heat the melting pot and increase assimilation.

In the end, rational argument was swept away by patriotic fervor. In 1917 Americans, primed by years of perceived German offense against their country along with tales of barbarism sometimes embroidered by British propagandists, rallied as quickly to the flag as had the men of Europe in 1914, squashing detractors with a steamroller of invective. Washington happily helped out with legislation that seemingly made free speech treasonable. In this war every fighting nation had one clear winner, patriotism, and one clear loser, rationalism. But, as Bertrand Russell noted, enthusiasm for war was like a love affair: exhilaration, return to normality, grumbling, and finally, perhaps, quiet despair.

Joining the War for Patriotic Ideals

William E. Borah: "Senator Borah [Idaho] on Our War Aims"

Borah emerged as one of the Senate's most influential Republicans who helped determine the country's foreign policy roles through the interwar years. His less-than-ringing support of Wilson turned into implacable opposition after the armistice as the president tried to persuade Congress to support the League of Nations. Borah's ardent speech on November 19, 1919, was credited as playing a key role in the opposition to Wilson. Borah concluded, "No, your treaty means injustice. It means slavery. It means war. And to all this you ask this Republic to become a party. You ask it to abandon the creed under which it has grown to power and accept the creed of autocracy, the creed of repression and force."

Perhaps more than any other, World War I was the war of the poster. Governments showered their countries with posters commissioned by famous artists, proposing all sorts of patriotic sacrifices necessary for good citizens to support their warring governments. Boy Scouts in particular were used in Britain and the United States to promote patriotic virtue. Courtesy of Library of Congress.

***New York Times Current History,* April–September 1917**

I voted for war to preserve and make safe our own blessed Republic, to give honor and dignity and security to this democracy of ours, and to keep it if we could as our fathers transmitted it, whole and triumphant. I felt that self-respect was the very breath of life of a democracy, that while other Governments might continue on in humiliation, and even in degradation, without self-respect a democracy could not long endure. I felt that a free Republic living alone and existing only in the affection and the devotion of the citizen could not long survive the day when that Republic should refuse to defend the rights and protect the lives of its citizens. So I voted for war because the most vital thing in our national life was and is involved, and for no other reason on earth would I have cast that vote and aided in plunging our nation into the midst of this world conflict.

As I view it, from that hour this was no longer a European war to settle and adjust European affairs, to rehabilitate European nations, but an American war, to be carried on, prolonged, or ended according to American interests, and to be adjusted upon American principles, and to settle, once and we hope for all time, that while slow to wrath we are swift to avenge those wrongs which challenge national honor and imperil the security of our own people.

Randolph S. Bourne: "Trans-National America"

After a century of separation from the world's political quarrels, the United States had grown into a mighty industrial and financial power. It had not, however, grown into a mighty military power. In fact, the country's wide division of opinion reflected a national ambivalence regarding the role and obligations of a traditionally isolationist nation faced with challenge of world upheaval. The election of 1916 reflected this, returning Wilson to office by a tiny margin. Republican Charles Evans Hughes nearly served the country during the critical years of 1917–1920. Aware of his splintered nation, Wilson wrote later, "It was necessary for me by very slow stages indeed and with the most genuine purpose to avoid war to lead the country on to a single way of thinking."

Atlantic Monthly, July 1916

The war has shown America to be unable, though isolated geographically and politically from a European world situation, to remain aloof and irresponsible. She is a wandering star in a sky dominated by two colossal constellations of states. Can she not work out some position of her own, some life of being in, yet not quite of, this seething and embroiled European world? This is her only hope and promise. A trans-nationality of all the nations, it is spiritually impossible for her to pass into the orbit of any one. It will be folly to hurry herself into a premature and sentimental nationalism, or to emulate Europe and play fast and loose with the forces that drag into war. No Americanization will fulfill this vision which does not recognize the uniqueness of this trans-nationalism of ours. The Anglo-Saxon attempt to fuse will only create enmity and distrust. The crusade against "hyphenates" will only inflame the partial patriotism of trans-nationals, and cause them to assert their European traditions in strident and unwholesome ways. But the attempt to weave a wholly novel international nation out of our chaotic America will liberate and harmonize the creative power of all these people s and give them the new spiritual citizenship, as so many individuals have already been given, of a world.

Editorial: "With Malice toward None"

While it is true that the United States had never fought a war against Germany—it had fought two against Britain—the specific issue over which Wilson declared war actually echoed a familiar American complaint. A century before it had fought the War of 1812 over British shipping interference, and British interference again angered Washington in the war years before 1917. The difference this time was that British interference did not extend to the extreme of actually sinking American ships. The German torpedoing of the Lusitania *in 1915 enraged so many that should Washington join the war, it was a conclusion obvious to all which side they would join.*

Independent, **February 12, 1917**

There is abroad in the world a malignant and menacing spirit that would not let us be. We have sought with full sincerity to hold aloof from the conflict this spirit waged against our neighbors in the world. We have tried, and tried again, to hold the balance even between the contestants in this titanic struggle. But the evil spirit that possesses the leaders of the German Empire would not suffer it to be. Driven by desperation and proud willfulness it so threatened civilization's very foundations that we had no choice but to end the friendly relations which have continued for one hundred and forty years.

If Germany wills that we shall fight, fight we must. Heavy hearted, for that we know the price that we must pay, but mighty spirited, for that we know the pricelessness of what we fight for, we shall give our hearts and our hands to this cause.

If Germany will not recant we shall endure to the end. We shall strike hands with those who for two years and a half have poured out their blood and treasure in this great cause. We shall give everything that we have and are that the right may prevail. We shall enter upon this terrible adventure with malice toward none, but with an overwhelming hatred of the ruthless and merciless spirit of evil that possesses those we are called upon to fight. God willing, we shall not hold our hand until that demoniac spirit is exorcised from the world.

Editorial: "Our Country, Right"

The "right or wrong" saying that was frequently applied to U.S. policy by patriots, and decried by protesters, apparently comes from a surprisingly little-known source: Carl Schurz, one of America's well-known nineteenth-century German-Americans. He actually said, "Our country right or wrong. When right, to be kept right; when wrong, to be put right." However, variations of the phrase had been voiced for at least a half century before that.

Independent, May 5, 1917

We have always objected to the use of that misleading phrase "Our country, right or wrong," because it implies that a nation should have no conscience and should not repent its misdeeds. But at least an equal objection to the saying is its subtle implication that we are doing something that won't bear analysis. If it is ever appropriate, now is certainly not the time when the United States is engaged in the most righteous and completely justifiable war which we have ever fought. With a good conscience we can say "Our country, right," without weakening our assertion by a superfluous explanation of what our attitude would be if it wasn't.

Theodore Roosevelt: "Standing by the President"

Roosevelt opposed Wilson in just about every possible way, from public policy to personal demeanor. His contemptuous use of Wilson's phrase "too proud to fight," part of the president's speech given after the Lusitania *sinking, nearly brought the country to war and seems to paint Roosevelt as a warmonger without concern for the fractured state of the country's public opinion on the war. Roosevelt's jingoism during this era, however, belies previous efforts to forge peaceful agreements between nations, for which he received the Nobel Peace Prize in 1906.*

New York Times Current History, October 1914–March 1915

As regards the export of munitions of war, the morality of the act depends upon the use to which the munitions are to be put. It was wrong to subjugate Belgium. It is wrong to keep her in subjugation. It is an utterly contemptible thing not to help in every possible way to undo this wrong. The manufacturers of cannon, rifles, cartridges, automobiles, or saddlery who refuse to ship them for use by the armies that are striving to restore Belgium to its own people should be put on a roll of dishonor.

Exactly the same morality should obtain internationally that obtains nationally. It is right for a private firm to furnish arms to the policeman who puts down the thug, the burglar, the white slaver, and the blackhander. It is wrong to furnish the blackhander, the burglar, and the white slaver with weapons to be used against the policeman. The analogy holds true in international life.

Germany has herself been the greatest manufacturer of munitions of war to be supplied to belligerents. She supplied munitions to England to subjugate the Boers and to the Turk to keep the Christians in subjugation. Let us furnish munitions to the men who, showing courage which we have not shown, wish to rescue Belgium from subjection and spoliation and degradation. And let us encourage munitions makers, so that we may be able to hold our own when the hours of peril comes to us in our turn, as assuredly it will come if we show ourselves too "neutral" to speak a word on behalf of the weak who are wronged and too slothful and lazy to prepare to defend ourselves against wrong. Most assuredly it will come to use if we succeed in persuading great military nations that we are too proud to fight, that we are not prepared to undertake defensive war for our own vital interest and national honor.

ENCOURAGE PATRIOTISM: CONSUME LESS

Anonymous: "Why Not Dress Alike and Save Money During War Time?"

The government did not require a national home-front uniform, as practical as the writer here might have believed it to be. But fashion did change dramatically during the war, particularly women's fashion. The highly decorative or more extravagant styles vanished, to be replaced by practical, sensible clothing for women who often were working in war industries. In France returning soldiers were sometimes annoyed to see women dressed too fashionably while men at war were living in the mud of the trenches.

Popular Science, July–December 1917

Why not a civilian uniform as a measure of economy in clothing? suggests a Canton, Ohio, man. It could be worn by everyone, man, woman and child, and thus eliminate foolish dressing, the dude, and the spending of hundreds of thousands of dollars on needless finery. It would certainly bring home to the civilian population their part in the war, and the ladies would need to apologize no longer for appearing twice in the same dress. As the result of investigation carried on by the Ohio man, a standardized suit of wool of excellent quality could be sold for less than twenty dollars.

Anonymous: "Fat People Are Unpatriotic: Give up Your Fat to the Nation"

While two thirds of American adults were considered overweight by the beginning of the twenty-first century, at the beginning of the twentieth century the problem was as often that people were too thin. Photos of World War I recruits show lines of skinny men clearly undernourished. Former president William Howard Taft, at 6 feet and 300 pounds, was rare for his girth during this period, but his size would be unremarkable a century later. The view that it was unhealthy and not natural to gain weight as one got older did not become widespread until the 1940s, with the revision of the Metropolitan Insurance Company's "ideal" height and weight tables.

Popular Science, July–December 1917

According to statistics compiled by the Life Insurance companies, there are, between the ages of thirty-five and fifty-five years, a vast number of people who are hoarding and accumulating fat enough to supply energy equivalent to that of 690,355,533 loaves of bread, enough to supply an army of 3,000,000 men for sixty days. A man who is forty pounds overweight is carrying on his body the equivalent in fuel value of 135 one-pound loaves of bread.

If the guilty ones would cease this accumulation (which they are willing enough to do) it would release much-needed fuel foods, such as wheat, corn, oats, barley and rye. There are two ways of surrendering this fat. One is by judicious exercise and the other is by substituting other foods for the fat-building kinds.

Theodore Roosevelt: "No Pigtail for Uncle Sam"

Authorities feared shortages as the government scrambled to feed not only a vast army of conscripts but also France and Britain, both allies growing in desperation as German submarines and the loss of Russia as an ally cut into food supplies. In response to possible shortfalls at home, America's leaders urged patriotic conservation. Posters and advertisements encouraged Americans to show their support for the boys with meatless days and wheatless days, and encouraged the patriotic to watch out for those who were not doing enough to conserve. This in combination with economic incentives pushed up production, and so the country suffered no shortages during this war.

Independent, May 22, 1916

I appeal to Americans everywhere to stand against the crass materialism which can show itself just as much in peace as in war. I appeal to our people to prepare in advance so that there shall be no hideous emergency which renders it necessary to submit to inordinate profit-making by the few simply because, when the emergency comes, we must improvise at whatever cost the things that for our sins we have failed to provide beforehand. We cannot afford to leave this democracy of ours inefficient.

Our national character is in the balance. Americanism is on trial. If we produce merely the self-seeking, ease-loving, duty-shirking man, whether he be a mere materialists or a mere silly sentimentalist; if we produce only the Americanism of the grafter and the mollycoddle and the safety-first, get-rich-quick, peace-at-any-price man, we will have produced an America faithful only to the spirit of the Tories of 1776 and the Copperheads of 1861, and fit only to vanish from the earth.

Encourage Patriotism: Consume More

John R. Eustis, Director of the Independent Motor Service: "The Patriot Who Owns a Car"

The Ford Model T, promoted as the first car inexpensive enough for common folk, began production in 1908. By the eve of war Henry Ford's production line had become so efficient it could turn out one car every hour and a half; more than 15 million were produced between 1908 and 1927. By World War I, Ford along with other auto manufacturers were pouring cars onto the American public. Demand was enhanced through saturation advertising campaigns and exhortations by industry promoters that suggested every true American had to own an automobile.

Independent, April 6, 1918

Despite the fact that the automobile is now an all-year vehicle and there is no longer a general laying up of cars over the winter season, yet springtime, and especially the month of April, seems to inaugurate the motoring year. Consequently now is the time that the passenger car owner is making his or her plans for the coming season, in so far as the use of an automobile is concerned.

Judging from talks I have had recently with a number of motorists it seems that there is a certain reluctance to use passenger cars as freely this season as heretofore. The reason given, of course, are those prompted by patriotism. According to their belief gasoline and rubber supplies should be conserved for military uses, and among the sacrifices that must be made to win the war are included the pleasures and much of the convenience of motor travel. It is not strange that such beliefs exist, because certain interests and individuals have been to considerable pains to influence the public along these lines, altho their real motives have been no part of their propaganda.

However, let us consider the facts in the case. . . .

It behooves us all, from official Washington to the humblest patriot, to increase business and personal efficiency as a means of winning the war. Economy of time is important in this respect and the automobile is perhaps the greatest saver of time that was ever invented. A thousand cars in a community, saving an average of an hour a day to their owners engaged in any line of manufacturing, business or in the professions, save for that community daily 125 business days. Again, intense application to business cannot be kept up without some relaxation, some change of environment, and a few breaths of good fresh air. The passenger automobile is the ideal means by which to secure a maximum of these benefits in the minimum of time. About the only recreation President Wilson gets in these trying days is his afternoon automobile ride.

Is it not then a false conception of patriotism to restrict the use of passenger automobiles? One might just as logically curtail one's telephone service or walk less for exercise in order to save shoe leather.

And if one can afford it there should be no hesitancy about buying a new car. Replacing old machinery with new and improved machinery is one of the first steps in increasing efficiency in a factory. You will help the Government just as much as tho you bought additional Liberty Bonds with the purchase price. It only means that others will be able to buy the bonds.

Discourage Patriotism: Destroys Careers

Anonymous: "Thoughts of a Teacher of German"

The bellicose American Defense Society—Theodore Roosevelt, honorary president—took as its mission the eradication of German-language teaching. One publication titled Throw Out the German Language and All Disloyal Teachers *contended, "Any language which produces a people of ruthless conquistadors such as now exists in Germany, is not a fit language to teach clean and pure American boys and girls."*[1]

Atlantic Monthly, September 1918

We do not need to turn to campus gossip for substantiating the prevalent distaste for Deutschtum. I, this year, have seen pathos and tragedy in the careers of many of my fellow teachers in other schools. Young women are devoting day and night to replacing their German by a heroic turn to French. Three men who had gained renown and honor some time ago in research on German subjects, are not floundering in a series of economic lectures of which they but recently learned. One professor I know has been sacrificing for eight years, burning more than midnight oil and energy, preparing for the publishers a book, big in both content and extent: a study of the environmental and hereditary influences that shaped the peculiar characteristics of Uhland. He has given the work up. And he is like a man lost.

Another young associate professor and his wife, as much devoted to his work as he, came to our campus three years ago brimful of enthusiasm. They were as much rapt in the contemplation of the new long-dreamed-of home that they would soon build, as we had been in materializing our Deutsches Haus for the campus home of our boys and girls. They treasured everything that would help to realize their hopes more quickly. They were too happy to realize just how they were yielding up in every form to make possible the home they longed for. Now, while they are at last in position to have their own hearth, to revel in the joy of their own inglenook, they will not build. He has given up his German teaching and will leave for work with the Red Triangle.

I am still teaching German. I have seen my department fall from the most popular to one regarded with uncertainty and even with distrust. There is no longer the zest in the Lieder or times of conversation at the meetings of Der Deutsche Bund. In reality the German Club no longer exists. We have held meetings to interpret Pangermanism, the doctrines of Hurrah and Hallelujah, the explanations of Von Jagow, Dernburg and Bethmann Hollweg. That has been largely the gist of our work this year—disclosures, divulgences, a campaign of anti-autocracy that verges now and then into a Hasz-programme—not an ideal course for college students.

Theoretically, I ceased teaching German in 1915. What I am doing now is nondescript. I should leave the whole work, I am convinced; but it is not easy for a college professor At times I feel that I would stake everything that has heretofore been my pleasure and my happiness to be able to go now into technical or scientific work. It may be that I shall soon find it impossible longer to remain in the chair of German. I have a small farm. I am learning, in an orderly, hazy sort of way, all I can get in scientific agriculture, and to this I may turn.

But the soul of me cries out against that system that has robbed me and thousands of others in my position of the joy and inspiration and the sense of a mission in teaching to aspiring college students the idealism of Licht, Liebe, Leben.

Discourage Patriotism: Destroys Creativity

Editorial: "The Week"

Owen Wister became one of the early century's most well-known authors for his archetypical western, The Virginian *(1902). He had been encouraged to write his story of cattle battles in* Old West Wyoming *by Theodore Roosevelt, another Easterner who spent time in the West. Despite their friendship, Wister apparently did not match Roosevelt's level of wartime patriotic fervor. He published a biography of Roosevelt in 1930.*

***Nation*, November 30, 1918**

Mr. Owen Wister has said a brave and timely word in regard to the banishment of German music from our concert programmes. Speaking before the Drama League of Philadelphia, Mr. Wister denounced this policy as a "mistaken patriotic sentiment." Most of the German symphonic music, he pointed out, was written by men who never knew and never shared the spirit of modern Germany. "They wrote the most beautiful music in the world. To banish it from our programmes is to make bricks without straw." Of course Mr. Wister did not fail to point out that an orchestra from Paris played a German symphony in Philadelphia last week and that England and France, "who are certainly not behind us in patriotism, have been playing German music right along." We hope these words of Mr. Wister will find a prompt echo in New York. True, the Philharmonic has already played Beethoven's Fifth Symphony without arousing anything but applause, but our conductors are still under the fear of being attacked by hysterical women and the alleged patriotic societies who do not know that, to quote Mr. Wister's words again, "Beethoven wrote no hymn of hate but a hymn of brotherhood. Wagner composed the greater part of his works while in exile because of his being a revolutionist." There is no longer any reason whatsoever why the Metropolitan Opera Company should continue its ban on Wagnerian opera.

Editorial: "Posters and Slogans"

World War I's most famous recruiting poster depicted a stern Uncle Sam pointing a forefinger and exclaiming, "I want YOU!" The poster was not original. It was based on a British illustration first published in the September 1914 issue of London Opinion, *in which Lord Horatio Kitchener, minister of war, with handlebar mustache and military hat, admonishes Britons to join the service. Designed by Punch illustrator Alfred Leete, the poster was copied with variations to fuel all kinds of propaganda campaigns on both side of the Atlantic. Its iconic power has been so enduring that a century later designers are still borrowing elements to promote everything from rock concerts to club picnics.*

Nation, June 21, 1917

Now that the Liberty Loan is safe in port, it is not giving aid and comfort to the enemy to admit that most of the pictured and verbal advertising in behalf of the bonds has been exceedingly mediocre, from the point of view of aesthetics or effectiveness. A good many citizens will not be free to confess to a vast sense of irritation aroused by the wild-eyed female who shouted from the store windows, "YOU buy a bond lest I perish!" There was more of wrath than fear in the lady's orbs. With her halo askew and the minatory finger darting out at one as a person suddenly turned the corner, the text that flashed to the mind at once was "What do you mean by coming home at this hour of the night in such a condition?" There was about her not the least impression of impending demise as an alternative to your not buying. The intimation was rather that if you failed to come to the scratch, Mrs. Liberty would step right out of the window and make use of her concealed torch or her palladium or some such national weapon. A Liberty truly in distress would have been highly appealing. It speaks well for the patriotism and self-control of the manhood of the nation that the bonds should have been sold in spite of the picture.

The truth is that there has been more "punch" than poetry in our patriotic advertising, more "pep" than persuasion. By contrast with our irate bond-selling lady one thinks of the magnificent poster which the French Government used to advertise the Victory Loan. Like the whirling wheels of flame which Ezekiel saw in his dreams, the French artist drew a huge coin rolling forward like an avenging chariot upon the shrinking figure of the German infantryman with bayonet and helmet, and from the face of the flashing wheel the Gallic cock launched itself forward, striking at the invader's eyes. It was the difference between a trumpet call and an alarm clock.

Mrs. Liberty, with the accusing finger, was the perpetuation of an advertising formula which has long lost whatever force it may have had. These many years clean-cut and strong-jawed gentlemen have been stretching peremptory fingers out of magazine covers and fence hoardings and commanding us to register with a correspondence school or buy a Jacobean dining-room set on the club plan. A close relation is the forceful gentleman who smites his clenched right fist into the palm of his left hand and insists that you investigate the merits of his real-estate "proposition." By contrast with these dynamic manual artists one thinks with gratitude of the celebrated Munyon forefinger upraised to heaven. That, at least, pays you the compliment of arguing with you. The pointing finger merely tells you. Alas, young women in excessive décolleté are no Frolickers. After that, it is only anti-climax when Uncle Sam points his finger and says he wants you for his army. The trick has been weakened and vulgarized. The prevailing texts are too often like the pictures, striving for "zip" and attaining zero. They are over-crisp, excessively laconic, and wanting in effectiveness because lacking in spontaneity. They are too evidently the product of a mind which said, "Go to, I will invent a slogan that will make 'em sit up."

Joining the War for Political Ideals

Arthur Bullard: "Our Relations with France"

As a nation France has been one of Washington's longest and most steadfast allies. As a people it has frustrated Americans for nearly as long with its seeming refusal to see things the American way. The golden age of Franco-American relations came during the World War I era, when the French impressed Americans with their sang-froid (cool-headedness) and jusqu'au boutisme (determination to persevere to the end) facing the enemy. On arriving to France, one exuberant American officer (probably not General John J. Pershing, as is sometimes claimed), demonstrated his appreciation for France's aid during the Revolutionary War by shouting "Lafayette, we are here!"

Atlantic Monthly, November 1916

There is a realpolitik argument in favor of an alliance with Republican France, which will perhaps have more weight with some than a sentimental appeal for loyalty to our ideas. History abundantly proves that the strength of coalitions lies, not in the number of soldiers, but in the similarity of desires which inspires the constituent nations. Current events point the same moral. To the mere statistician, the Powers of the Entente were always immensely stronger than the Germanic Alliance. But it is obvious that Britain and France and Russia, Belgium and Servia, Italy and Portugal—and now Rumania—have not been fighting in unison, have not been inspired by the same ideals. It has taken them two years to acquire a tardy and precarious unity. The Central Powers have been stronger in action than on paper because their desires, even if more predatory, are more uniform. The durability and strength of an alliance depends more on similarity of aspirations than on mere numbers.

In superficial ways we differ largely from the French. They are an ancient people and we very young. They are homogeneous and we so "hyphenated." The structure of their economic life is different from ours. France has been worked over so long that wealth is only acquired by industry and thrift. No Frenchman has ever discovered gold in his backyard; none hopes to. We rely overmuch on such luck. But when subtraction is made of such surface differences, the residue is strikingly similar. We have more in common with the French than with any people of the Old World.

The war has brushed away an old prejudice. No nation of degenerate pleasure-lovers, no people enslaved by vice, could have stood up with such sublime and simple heroism under this storm of war. The mass of our people to-day recognize as never before that "frog-eaters" is an inadequate epithet. It is regrettable that opportunity has not been given us to live down our bad reputation in France. Such ill-repute is always mutual. Those of our tourists who have brought us back descriptions of the French, based on experience in the night cafes of Montmartre, are those who spent much money and time in such resorts. We have too often judged the French by their stories. But just as often the French have judged us by them. The current French opinion of us is not flattering. We can only hope that, if some great misfortune, such as war, falls upon us, we may disprove their estimate of us, as they are in these days so nobly disapproving our light judgment of them. The present universal admiration of the way in which the French have borne the first shock of the war, and held the pass till their more slow-moving allies could come up, is a sound foundation for a new and more intimate relationship.

Carl Kelsey: "Forward"

The German resumption of unrestricted submarine warfare was the immediate reason the United States declared war. To uphold homefront morale, U.S. government propaganda moved toward an appeal to American ideals of freedom and democracy, a self-governing republic versus an authoritarian monarchy. This argument was easier to make after ally Russia—an authoritarian monarchy of the more extreme kind—left the war at the end of 1917. It certainly could be persuasively argued that a Germany dominated by Prussia during this period sustained a military tradition beyond that of any other Western nation.

Annals of the American Academy of Political and Social Sciences, July 1918

From many standpoints war is a conflict of ideals rather than a clash of people and of arms. It turns on our standards of life, on the things which we want, the things for which we will fight and for which we will die. It is now clear that the present conflict is primarily between democracy and oligarchy, between the people who are seeking to develop themselves as they think best and other people who are submitting to overhead control, exerted primarily in the interests of the few. Democracy is not a method, it is an ideal. England, with the forms of monarchy, has been, in many respects, more democratic than the United States.

The point of my first illustration can now be seen. Devotion to ideals must come from the common experiences of every day life; of those ordinary things which after all are most fundamental. If these common experiences cannot be had, common ideals will not arise. Even in a democracy we must recognize this and secure the substantial freedom of all individuals to develop themselves.

Editorial: "A Sad Spectacle"

Robert M. La Follette's opposition to U.S. participation in the war centered on his belief that the Wilson administration had declared a perfidious neutrality while in reality supported the allies with munitions and financial credits. The administration now was declaring war to save the rich who feared catastrophic losses should Britain lose. For this the senator suffered heaps of scorn only slightly lower than those that fell on the Kaiser himself. However, his contention that Washington's neutrality actually favored the allies was correct; Berlin had concluded that years before. That this was America's war of capitalism, however, ignored the facts of German attacks on civilian vessels, its anti-American intrigues, and its atrocities as occupiers in Belgium and northern France.

Independent, March 16, 1918

The Legislature of Wisconsin has administered a stern rebuke to Senator Robert M. La Follette for his attitude toward America's participation in the Great War. The words of the resolution adopted by the Senate by a vote of 26 to 3, and in the Assembly by a vote of 53 to 52, are scathing:

We condemn Senator La Follette and all others who have failed to see the righteousness of our nation's cause, who have failed to support our Government in matters vital to the winning of the war. We denounce any utterance of theirs which has tended to incite sedition among the people of our country and to injure Wisconsin's fair name before the free peoples of the world.

It is a deserved rebuke. But the necessity for its administering must be a source of regret to every one who realizes, and is grateful for, the splendid fight on behalf of enlightenment and progress made by Mr. La Follette in Wisconsin in the early years of the twentieth century. The La Follette of today is not the La Follette of that earlier time. He has taken the wrong turning somewhere.

It is a sad spectacle to see the man who fought so courageously and effectively for democracy in his own state and nation now taking a course which puts him on the side of those who are fighting for autocracy and imperialism in the world.

Walter Lippmann: "The World Conflict in Its Relation to American Democracy"

As a strong supporter of Wilsonian idealism, Walter Lippmann's eloquent defense of war participation showed his hope that the struggle for justice abroad could inspire a movement for justice at home. But Wilson showed less than stellar regard for oppressed peoples in his own country, particularly African Americans. As a result, World War I did little to make minority Americans free at last. It did lead to legalization of suffrage for women and citizenship for Native Americans. Both groups had shown their loyalty and devotion to duty during the war.

***Annals of the American Academy of Political and Social Sciences*, July 1917**

If it is our privilege to exert the power which turns the scale, it is our duty to see that the end justifies the means. We can win nothing from this war unless it culminates in a union of liberal peoples pledged to cooperate in the settlement of all outstanding questions, sworn to turn against the aggressor, determined to erect a larger and more modern system of international law upon a federation of the world. That is what we are fighting for, at this moment, on the ocean, in the shipyard and in the factory, later perhaps in France and Belgium, ultimately at the council of peace.

If we are strong enough and wise enough to win this victory, to reject all the poison of hatred abroad and intolerance at home, we shall have made a nation to which free men will turn with love and gratitude. For ourselves we shall stand committed as never before to the realization of democracy in America. We who have gone to war to insure democracy in the world will have raised an aspiration here that will not end with the overthrow of the

Prussian autocracy. We shall turn with fresh interests to our own tyrannies—to our Colorado mines, our autocratic steel industries, our sweatshops and our alums. We shall call that man un-American and no patriot who prates of liberty in Europe and resists it at home. A force is loose in America as well. Our own reactionaries will not assuage it with their Billy Sundays or control through lawyers and politicians of the Old Guard.

William Howard Taft: "The Health and Morale of America's Citizen Army: Personal Observations of Conditions of Our Soldier Cities by a Former Commander-in-Chief of the United States Army and Navy"

Taft, a Republican, was president before Wilson defeated him in the 1912 election. During the war he became co-chair of the National Labor Relations Board, beginning his service in April 1918. The board displayed vigorous interest in mediating concerns of labor and management to avoid disputes that could hamper war production. Its progressive mandate included recognition of trade unions. After the war Taft became chief justice of the U.S. Supreme Court. He called it his greatest honor, as he claimed he did not like politics and served recalcitrantly as president.

National Geographic, March 1918

This war differs from other wars that we have been in, in the necessity for propaganda to explain its issues and its profound importance to the people of the United States. When it came on, in August, 1914, the whole people rejoiced that we were so remote from the seat of war, separated by the Atlantic Ocean, and so barred from it by our national traditions that we would escape the vortex of destruction and suffering that was opening to the European nations.

For three years we occupied as near a judicial position as the circumstances permitted and discussed the issues between the nations with an impartial state of mind. Then we were forced into war through a violation of our rights at sea. It was difficult to arouse our people to the importance of those rights in a zone of the high seas so far away as Great Britain and Ireland.

The statements of the President properly set forth as our object in the war certain ideals of a world character and importance. Our material interest in maintaining those ideals, however, it was difficult for the people to appreciate.

The issue was not as it was in our Revolutionary War, at our doors, and had not been the subject of political discussion for half a century, as the slavery and secession issue had been before our Civil War. Prosperity and money-making, high wages and high profits, absorbed the interest of our people, and it was difficult to challenge their attention to the inevitable consequence of German victory. Hence the consciousness of the fact that we are really in war has but slowly been stealing over our people as a psychological fact.

Editorial: "We Must Kill to Save"

Of the government's concerns that American wartime morale could not be sustained was the fact that the conflict was an ocean away, and unlikely to endanger North American territory. A credible case for threatened invasion could not be made. Propaganda centered on calls to patriotism and duty to freedom and democracy. Most of the American press happily toed that line, in sometimes alarmingly violent terms. Unfortunately affected by the angry rhetoric, some Americans could not separate the "bad" Germans overseas from the German immigrants who may have lived next door to them.

North American Review, February 1918

Our duty is to kill Germans. To the killing of Germans we must bend all our energies. We must think in terms of German dead, killed by rifles in American hands, by bombs thrown by American youths, by shells fired by American gunners. The more Germans we kill, the fewer American graves there will be in France; the more Germans we kill, the less danger to our wives and daughters; the more Germans we kill, the sooner we shall welcome home our gallant lads. Nothing else now counts. There is no thought other than this, no activity apart from the duty forced upon us by Germany. The most highly civilized nations are united as they never were before, actuated by the same impulse. In England, France and Italy, among the English speaking peoples of the new world, under the southern cross and on the torrid plains, they like us see their duty clear. It is, we repeat, to kill Germans.

We have no apologies to make, no excuses to offer, no regard for having unclothed the masquerade of rhetoric and put the case in stark and naked words. Doubtless we shall offend the over nice sensibilities of those well meaning but unbalanced persons who waste their sympathies over the sufferings of the lobster as his complexion turns from dirty blue into delicate pink while they are unmoved by the knowledge of the misery and distress of the poor and unfortunate. We hope so. We are endeavoring to arouse the millions of easy going, complacent Americans, unctuously flattering themselves they are good Christians because they feel no hate, to whom the war has as yet no meaning, to a realization of what this war means, not only to them but also to their men; that it is the lives of their men against the lives of Germans.

Joining the War against German Perfidy

Sir Edward Grey, Secretary of State of Foreign Affairs for Great Britain: "Reply to the German Chancellor"

As prewar foreign secretary, Edward Grey had to accept at least partial blame for the outbreak of World War I. He had negotiated secret treaties promising that Britain would come to France's aid in case of war against Germany; when Germany marched toward France, Grey felt his country had to honor these treaty obligations, regardless of whether Belgium stood in the way. That this decision meant world war shocked Grey who, reportedly casting an eye out his office window toward the drab streets of London as the gaslights were being lit, uttered the famous phrase, "The lamps are going out all over Europe; we shall not see them lit again in our lifetime."

***Current History*, October 1914–March 1915**

In the Reichstag, too, on Aug. 4, 1914, the German Chancellor stated, in referring to the violation of the neutrality of Belgium and Luxemburg: "The wrong—I speak openly—the wrong we thereby commit we will try to make good as soon as our military aims have been attained."

The violation of Belgian neutrality was therefore deliberate, although Germany had actually guaranteed that neutrality, and surely there has been nothing more despicably mean than the attempt to justify it ex post facto by bringing against the innocent and inoffensive Belgian Government and people the totally false charge of having plotted against Germany. The German chancellor does not emphasize in his latest speech that charge, which has been spread broadcast against Belgium. Is it withdrawn? And, if so, will Germany make reparation for the cruel wrong done to Belgium?

Booth Tarkington, Popular American Novelist: "Why Americans Are Pro-Ally"

Booth Tarkington was one of the more important American novelists of the early twentieth century. His social commentary chronicling the dramatic changes of American life at the turn of the century included his most well-known novel, The Magnificent Ambersons, *published in 1918. Unlike many leaders before the country entered the war, Tarkington in this excerpt emphasized the rallying power of the American melting pot, and not the division of "hyphenated Americans." The explosion of patriotic enthusiasm following the war declaration seemed to validate his viewpoint.*

New York Times Current History, April–September 1916

Almost all of the newspapers are "pro-ally," though numbers of them pose as neutral. But you may accept it as the fact that all officials and politicians and editors who are educated Americans are actually "pro-ally." The "great mass of the "proletariat" are vaguely "pro-ally," but more definitely, as about everything, pro-nothing. They do not know that the war affects them, and they do not think about it.

The American is "pro-ally," but not because he is characteristically of English descent. Characteristically he doesn't know his descent. He sometimes guesses at it, idly, concluding, if his name be Baker or Knight, or Thompson, that his ancestors may have been English—he doesn't care. Nor does he regard England as the "Mother Country"; nor is that saying much in his mind: "Blood is thicker than water." He is not "pro-ally" out of sympathy. Who thinks he is fails to understand the American. The American is pro-Belgian out of sympathy; and he is anti-Teuton, in the Belgian matter, out of indignation; but he is "pro-ally" because history is "pro-ally."

We were the onlookers from the beginning, and we saw that Germans made the war. We saw that the German Nation went into the war with a patriotic stupidity, magnificent and horrible; that the German Nation was wholly in the grip of a herd instinct which had been used by manipulators; and that these manipulators, having made the Germans into a loyal, warlike tribe, brought on the war in the approved manner employed by all war chiefs desiring a war. Their unblemished hypocrisy was of an old, old model always employed by war chiefs—and absolutely obvious to any mind not under the sway of herd instinct.

The Germans saw what had happened here. They understood that an impartial national mind had judged them; so they naturally organized a stupendous campaign attacking our judgment. For their purpose, their propaganda accomplished precisely nothing. Now, this is the American mind; this is how the American thinks of the war: the German Nation has been revealed as a warlike tribe, wonderful in that capacity, but not to be thought civilized merely because it uses typewriters.

H. G. Wells: "America's Opportunity"

Herbert George Wells was one of the last century's most prolific writers in the English language. Born in Bromley, now part of London, he is today most well known for his science fiction, including The War of the Worlds *and* The Time Machine. *But he also wrote works of history and social commentary.*

***New York Times Current History*, April–September 1916**

So far as I can judge, the American mind is eminently free from any sentimental leaning toward the British. Americans have a traditional hatred of the Hanoverian monarchy and a democratic disbelief in autocracy. They are far more acutely aware of differences than resemblances. They suspect every Englishman of being a bit of a gentleman and a bit of a flunky. There is nothing to reciprocate the sympathy and pride that English and Irish republicans and radicals feel for the State. Few Americans realize that there are such beings as English republicans. What has linked them with the British hitherto has been very largely the common language and literature; it is only since the war began that there seems to have been any appreciable development of fraternal feeling. And that has been not so much discovery of a mutual affection as the realization of a far closer community of essential thought and purpose than has hitherto been suspected.

The Americans, after thinking the matter out with great frankness and vigor, do believe that Britain is, on the whole, fighting against aggression and not for profit; that she is honestly backing France and Belgium against an intolerable attack, and that the Hohenzollern empire is a thing that needs discrediting and, if possible, destroying, in the interest of all humanity, Germany included.

Joining the War against British Perfidy

Theobald von Bethmann Hollweg, German Imperial Chancellor: "Great Britain and Germany"

Britain's blockade of shipping to Germany resulted in thousands of civilian deaths throughout Central Europe. Berlin's desperate attempts to break the blockade with the only means it had available—stealth and the submarine—was the direct cause of U.S. entrance into the war. Britain continued its blockade even after the armistice in an attempt to force Germany to sign the peace treaty. A common sight on German streets was starving and malnourished children. That this callous action continued for a half year after the shooting ended can be considered no less a war atrocity than German action in Belgium.

New York Times Current History, October 1914–March 1915

The fable that England participated in the war only for the sake of Belgium has been abandoned in the meantime by England herself. It was not tenable. Do the smaller nations still believe that England and her allies are waging war for their protection and the protection and freedom of civilization? Neutral commerce on sea is strangled by England. As far as possible goods destined for Germany must no longer be loaded on neutral ships. Neutral ships are compelled on the high seas to take English crews aboard and to obey their orders.

England without hesitation occupies Greek islands because it suits her military operations, and with her allies she wishes to constrain neutral Greece to make cessions of territory in order to bring Bulgaria to her side. In Poland, Russia, who is fighting with the Allies for the freedom of peoples, lays waste the entire land before the retreat or her armies. Villages are burned down, cornfields trampled down, and the population—Jews and Christians—are sent to uninhabited districts. They languish in the mud of Russian roads, in windowless, sealed goods wagons. Such are the freedom and civilization for which our enemies fight. In her claims to be the protector of smaller States England counts on the world having a very bad memory.

In the Spring of 1902 the Boer republics were incorporated in the British Empire. Then their eyes were turned to Egypt. To the formal annexation of this there was opposed the British Government's solemn promise to evacuate the land. That same England that to our proposal to guarantee to her Belgium's integrity if she remained neutral proudly replied that England could not make her obligations relative to Belgian neutrality a matter for bargaining; that same England had no scruple in bartering away to France her solemn obligation, undertaken toward all Europe, by the conclusion of a treaty with France, which was to give to England Egypt, and to France Morocco. In 1907 the southern portion of Persia, by agreement with Russia, was converted into an exclusively English sphere of interest, and the northern portion was delivered over to a freedom-loving regiment of Russian Cossacks.

Not Joining the War: Political Ideals

Woodrow Wilson: "The State of the Nation"

The U.S. government in principle emphasized its neutrality by allowing American business to trade with whatever country was buying—Entente *power or Central power. In reality, the British Navy's blockade in the Atlantic and mining of the North Sea guaranteed the only trade possible would be with the allies. That was good enough to push the United States into an economic boom. Exports increased from $2 billion in 1913 to $6 billion in 1916 and, after decades of financial obligations to the Old World, the United States became a creditor nation. Americans certainly could not condone the killing but also did not want the prosperity to end.*

New York Times Current History, October 1915–March 1916

We have stood apart, studiously neutral. It was our manifest duty to do so. Not only did we have no part or interest in the policies which seem to have brought the conflict on; it was necessary, if a universal catastrophe was to be avoided, that a limit should be set to the sweep of destructive war and that some part of the great family of nations should keep the processes of peace alive, if only to prevent collective economic ruin and the breakdown throughout the world of the industries by which its populations are fed and sustained. It was manifestly the duty of the self-governed nations of this hemisphere to redress, if possible, the balance of economic loss and confusion in the other, if they could do nothing more. In the day of readjustment and recuperation we earnestly hope and believe that they can be of infinite service.

In this neutrality, to which they were bidden not only by their separate life and their habitual detachment from the politics of Europe, but also by a clear perception of international duty, the States of America have become conscious of a new and more vital community of interest and moral partnership in affairs, more clearly conscious of the many common sympathies and interests and duties which bid them stand together.

Not Joining the War: None of Our Business

Editorial: "The High Duty of the United States"

The Monroe Doctrine had been revisited only a few years before the war. American administrations took seriously the declaration that Europe must stay out of the affairs of the Western Hemisphere. In 1905 Roosevelt, as president, warned Germany against taking action in Venezuela for defaulting on its European loans. In the so-called Roosevelt Corollary, the president declared his country would "speak softly but carry a big stick." The intrigues of the Zimmermann Telegram affair in early 1917—Germany proposing a pact with Mexico against the United States—offered obvious evidence that Germany would not respect the Monroe Doctrine, and so helped persuade Americans to join the war.

Independent, 1914–1915

In the great European war the United States is seriously concerned. But it need not convulse us. Luckily we have the Atlantic between us and Europe. It is their war, not ours. We can keep cool and accept our share of the general misfortune, while rejoicing that we and the republics of the two Americas are not of the chief sufferers.

We have no concern with the European balance of power. Nor are we Servia's Big Brother. Russia is her Big Brother. We are Big Brother to our American republics, and if any European power should endeavor to take any of their territory, we should speedily protest with army and navy. We should thus keep the peace, prevent robbery, and make the most of our Monroe Doctrine. Russia has a parallel doctrine for the defense of the Slav states; and if one of these days those Slav states should choose to cast in their lot with a regenerated Russia, we could not grieve. We would not like it to have either Austria or Russia take them without their good will, just as we would not have the United States take one rod of contiguous or non-contiguous territory without the assent of its people. The larger a nation is the better, if it is only a really free, self-governing nation. Enlargement means fewer custom houses and fewer chances of war.

Baron D'Estournelles de Constant: "America's Duty"

The America of 1914 believed with Wilson that it alone could provide a moral beacon through the scheming and corruption of old Europe. The sentiment coalesced into Wilson's Fourteen Points, but moral advantage could not be pressed into persuasive reality without proof of sacrifice. The United States lost more than 126,000 young men in the war. Nearly four-and-one-half million were mobilized. For many it was the most harrowing, awesome, defining experience of their lives.

Atlantic Monthly, December 1915

When I am asked, as a Frenchman, how I regard the duty of the United States, I can only refer to what I have always said and written: I am more than ever convinced that a great and young country such as the United States can realize its destiny only through peace. In these days, a war of conquest would be folly and nonsense, for the United States more than for any other country.

For its own good and for the good of all nations, the duty of the New World is to experiment with a new policy, a policy of conciliation, and respect for the Right, in the place of the traditional antagonism and adventurousness of which we in Europe see the irreparably tragic results. The United States, which were held up to us in Europe, twenty years ago, as a danger, ought, on the contrary, to be our guides, like strong and clear-signed children who end by guiding the footsteps of their parents when the old people's eyes are dimmed by age. But they cannot play this fine part unless they have no doubt as to the course they should follow and unless they do not allow themselves to be led astray by wrong education, by yellow newspapers, by bad and interested advice, and by the bad example of Europe. My duty as a European and a true friend of the United States is to say, with the utmost possible emphasis, "Do not let yourselves be led away on the wrong path as we were. Keep your youth and strength free from the blunders we have been committing for centuries. The price always has to be paid in the long run; the sins of the fathers are visited upon their children and their children's children. If you are wise to-day, you will sow prosperity, glory, and happiness for your descendants. Your error will be their misfortune."

Questions

1. We speak of patriotism as a virtue, but America's experience in World War I showed the consequences of taking this virtue to an extreme. What were some of them?
2. How did the British blockade affect America's decision to join the war?
3. How did Progressives argue that the war could benefit Americans at home?

Note

1. Frederick C. Luebke, *Bonds of Loyalty: German Americans and World War I* (DeKalb: Northern Illinois University Press, 1974), 216.

Chapter 15

Joining the War: Arguments of Religion and Civilizing Ideals

It seems incongruous during peacetime that religion and spirituality could be tied so closely to violence and brutality. But the mind at peace cannot truly comprehend what it was like to be part of war on a global scale: The anguish, the incomprehension, the profound shock as death swirled through society like an malevolent, man-made hurricane. Victims at the front and at home could only look desperately for touchstones, some way to make sense of it all. One possibility was God.

Every country during the war evoked God as a guiding force in battle. "God with us" was translated as necessary; German soldiers even inscribed it onto belts and helmets, *Gott mit uns*. It was said that during a battle even atheists prayed, and from the indescribable horror of the fetid World War I trenches the prayers grew together no matter what the belief, or non-belief, of the soldiers who voiced them. Christians who might not have even spoken to Jews, or even Catholics to Protestants, and none of them speaking to atheists, forgot their prewar prejudice in their quest for spirituality facing a common enemy. In the German army, the ever-oppressed Jewish soldiers fared considerably better than before. They were even allowed to be officers. That 12,000 German Jews died in World War I tragically did not help them avoid becoming the postwar scapegoat of Nazi Germany. But during World War I spirituality was patriotism, and patriotism was spirituality. Both were required of soldiers who hoped to cling to sanity as the world shattered around them.

The idea that the war was a spiritual quest sustained not only the soldier in battle but also the loved ones on the home front. The deep distress of watching young sons and spouses torn away from their homes into a situation from which many, many would not return too often could turn to grief as parents received the news they so dreaded. The soldiers were young. Children are not supposed to die before their parents. It is not the natural order of things. To give meaning to the death every society during the war created a spiritual quest, an affirmation that their sons had died for values so lofty they defined civilization itself. Spirituality, perhaps tied to a religion but not necessarily, became infused with patriotic virtue and love of country. To defend the homeland, family, and values was not only a duty but also a privilege. Conservative French author Maurice Barrés noted in 1916 that "the soldiers will tell future astonished generations that they never lived their faith better and that it was never of greater support than when they were upholding the union." He spoke for the French, but could have just as easily spoke for the Americans, the Germans, or any other soldiers during this war. Some religious leaders extolled the war as an opportunity to return to purity, to basic virtues so long tainted and tarnished by the greed and secularism of modern life. War, indeed, could resemble the purifying experience of the baptismal font. "Baptism of fire" was more than a cliché.

The sweep of spiritualism sometimes beyond the boundary of particular religion posed a challenge to church leaders. On the one hand, dominant religions in the west, particularly Christianity, were not bound by national borders. Lutherans worshipped in Germany as they did in America. Catholics recognize no spiritual leader but the Roman pope. And all religious leaders preached the virtues of peace and reconciliation with one's enemies. Could Jesus the peacemaker support war? Could Jesus the savior advocate the patriotic virtue of hatred and the moral virtue of sacrifice not for one's soul but for one's government?

On the other hand, organized churches represented establishment values and sometimes political power. Even in France, which had separated religion and state only a decade before in a bitter struggle, recognized that the Catholic hierarchy still wielded moral power over its many devout churched. The responsibility of a pastor to his faith clashed with responsibility to his congregation. Believers caught up in the emotional combine of spiritualism and patriotism expected their church fathers to lead the way as they did in all important areas of their lives. Moreover, they expected their pastors to offer comfort as they grieved the loss of loved ones on the battlefields. Priests and ministers could not see how they could offer consolation without affirming that these young men had died for a cause greater than themselves, greater than a material culture, a cause no less than the saving of God's people and the civilized world.

Most did that. Sermons not only accurately reflected secular sentiment, but sometimes even went further, advocating "kill, kill, kill the enemy" in fiery pulpit style. The war became a sacred duty of the righteous against the infidel—a crusade. The call to a crusade could appeal as a medieval European symbol of Christian moral duty.

Some church leaders could not reconcile nationalist fervor with religious principle. Pope Benedict XV guided flocks in all warring nations. He was unable to choose sides, and so repeatedly pleaded for general peace and reconciliation. In August 1917 he announced his Papal Peace Proposal, seven points that urged belligerents to lay down their weapons and submit to international arbitration. No government leader even responded save Wilson, who called the proposal premature. Warring countries in return heaped scorn on Benedict for not choosing their side because, plainly, theirs was God's side.

In the United States, as previously noted, Mennonites were the most obviously pacifist. and could not accept war under any circumstances. In response, mainstream Americans moved from simply reviling them as cowards, yellow, and pro-Kaiser, to occasional abuse and even torture. Nearly all German-Lutheran churches quickly jumped to declare their patriotic support for the war, although they were not necessarily ready to abandon their German-language services and cultural habits of the Old World. The explosion of anti-Germanism that marked the reverse of patriotic ardor persuaded many that they had better abandon these traditions, at least ostensibly. When a country declares a crusade, continued neutrality becomes dangerous.

Joining the War for Religious Ideals

Horace J. Bridges: "The Duty of Hatred"

The idea that there can be a "just war" has been debated within Christianity since its inception. While the Old Testament of the Bible does defend "holy war," and actually describes God as initiating wars, Jesus Christ in the New Testament denounces war in several unambiguous instances. Early Christian scholar St. Augustine did concede that a just war could be righteous if used to protect innocent people and done to minimize destruction. It is difficult for those who did not experience the white-hot emotional hatred of World War I to find clear biblical justification for such human and material destruction.

Atlantic Monthly, October 1918

To live above the battle, in a private shrine of serenity and peace; to pray without discrimination that finely discriminating prayer of Christ for his enemies; to censure the ranging resentment of the victims of outrages that we have not suffered, and of the witnesses of atrocities that have not offended our eyes; to see haloes on "conscientious objectors" to the struggle that is saving our lives and the freedom of our land; to prate of pardoning the distant sinner against others, without confessing to ourselves how we should feel if his sins were committed against us: all this is feebleness and folly, or else mortal treason. It is immorality using the Sermon on the Mount for smoke-screen; it is spiritual cowardice wearing the airs of Christian heroism; it is surpliced impiety and sanctimonious blasphemy. "The doctrine of hatred must be preached as the counteraction of the doctrine of love when that pulls and whines." Now, if ever, is the time for every heart to vibrate to that iron string.

Forgiveness is for unwitting or repented sins; not for sins conscious, deliberate, unrepented. It is the recognition that the sinner knew not what he did, with the clearly implied condition that, had he known, he would not have done it. or it is the recognition that a professed contrition is sincere, and that an incipient amendment of life is to be lasting.

Edward T. Devine, American Red Cross, Paris: "War Relief Work in Europe"

War has for centuries been tied to religious fervor; the deep wellspring of emotion that humans find through religious belief can be extended to the emotional well of patriotism during wartime. Comrades in arms battle against the perfidious enemy in hope of cleansing the home nation of the vapid values of selfish consumption and immorality and finding purity of purpose in the selfless sacrifice of combat.

***Annals of the American Academy of Political and Social Sciences,* September 1918**

The war has its spiritual blessings. We must by all means make the most of them. America, especially, latest of the great nations to enter the war, had no alternative, if she were to save her soul alive; and right gloriously she has—even as I write—brought her sacrifice to the altar. Clear thinking and clear seeing as to the cost of the war in terms of human life and physical well-being, will not diminish but increase our appreciation of its regenerating influence on national character and its revolutionary effect on spiritual values.

The broad fact, is that wealth is daily destroyed—deliberately on our part—that civilization may live. The broad fact, is that daily young men and men in middle life, vigorous, normal, sound in mind and body, are crippled for life or disabled for weeks, months, or years, and so made into dependent hospital patients; and that others are killed outright. The broad fact, is that families are dependent for their daily bread on the state or on voluntary charity because their natural breadwinners are at the war, or have been killed or disabled. The broad fact, is that whole communities, populations which must be counted now by the millions, are dislocated, driven away from their homes to live—often unwelcome—among strangers: doubly dependent because their sons and fathers are fighting and their women and old men and their children are civil prisoners and refugees. The broad fact, is that the war has suddenly blocked or diverted into other channels a great volume of good will, experience and trained service which in every country had begun to show concrete results form organized social efforts, to reduce human misery and promote social welfare.

Max Eastman: "The Religion of Patriotism"

Eastman was editor of the most well-known socialist newspaper of World War I, The Masses. *It was harassed out of existence in 1917 by the Espionage Act as interpreted by Postmaster Albert Burleson, who revoked its mailing privileges. Eastman was twice tried unsuccessfully for treason. After the war he spent a year in the Soviet Union to study Lenin's Communism, but concluded it was not the utopia some on the political left presumed. In later years Eastman repudiated communism and actually supported conservative voices such as Wisconsin Senator Joseph McCarthy's anti-Red tirades.*

Masses, July 1917 (Transcribed by Sally Ryan for marxists.org)

When ordinary alert perception has been renounced, it is needless to say that the extreme ethical visions of Jesus must go, and that God—long suffering God—will be denounced from the pulpits that were his last refuge. I suppose the pew-holders of Henry Ward Beecher's church are satisfied with Newell Dwight Hillis, for they have stood a good deal from him besides his preaching, and here is his creed of patriotism:

> "All God's teachings about forgiveness should be rescinded for Germany. I am willing to forgive the Germans for their atrocities just as soon as they are all shot. If you would give me happiness, just give me the sight of the Kaiser, von Hindenburg and von Tirpitz hanging by the rope. If we forgive Germany after the war, I shall think the whole universe has gone wrong."

When God is thus enthusiastically ejected from the rostrum of the most famous church in the country, to make way for the patriotic emotion, I think we are justified in the fear that patriotism may become our religion.

Patriotism indulges that craving for a sense of union with a solitary herd, which is an inheritance of all gregarious animals. It is a craving which our modern sophisticated, citified, and diverse civilization leaves unfed in normal times. There is a great swing towards war on this account even among the most pacific people. They are flocking for a drink of this emotion. Men are willing to be dead, if they can only be dead in a pile.

This quite organic and almost animal craving is what makes us talk so much about the "great spiritual blessing" that war will bring to our unregenerate characters. When a desire springs so deeply from our ancient inheritance as this gregarious hunger does, we always feel it as mystic and inscrutable, we attribute a divine beneficence to the satisfaction of it. As a matter of fact, it would be better for the progress of society, in science and art and morality and happiness, if this terrible solidarity could be mitigated instead of enlarged. For it inhibits individual experiment, and it falsifies the facts of life, always pretending the nation is more socially and brotherly organized than it is. The "great spiritual blessing" is in fact a distraction of men's minds from the pursuit of truth and from realistic progress. It is the temporary indulgence of a facile emotion.

Joining the War for Civilizing Ideals

Take Jonescu, Leader of the National Democratic Party in Rumania: "Honorable Neutrality Impossible"

World War I was immediately called the Great War. People sometimes refer to it that way today, particularly in Europe. As people recognized that this was a world war, a war unlike any before in its vast reach around the globe, they concluded that their place in this terrible cataclysm must also be as important, as vast, as great. Only great human foundations—God, civilization, morality, national survival—could serve as fit beacons to guide such an enormous undertaking.

New York Times Current History, October 1916–February 1917

The entire movement can have but one explanation, namely, that we are confronted with a transformation of the human race, a transformation which expresses itself in the form of a general massacre. It is a struggle between two worlds, and we shall see which of the two shall succeed in obtaining the mastery. Were it otherwise this war would not be possible, and it would not be waged with the fury that distinguishes it from all others.

Gentlemen, the truth is that in this war, which was most certainly provoked by the Germans, we see the last attempt made by a single people to secure for itself a universal hegemony.

If the German soldier were to win today the first result would be that the same military force, which is the greatest in the world, would also be the greatest naval force, and there would be no more independence, no more liberty for any one in the world, not even for the great American democracy. If ever the day should come when one and the same State had domination not only on land but also on sea—the day on which the Roman Empire should be reconstituted in conformity with the affirmation once made by the emperor William that the time would come when all men would be happy to call themselves German, just as formerly one exclaimed joyously, "Civis Romanus sum," then the free life of each one of use would be at an end.

Oliver Lodge: "The War: A British View"

The origin of the Crusades dates to the Middle Ages. The word comes from the Christian symbol of the cross, which was worn as a cloth design on those who undertook the first invasion of Muslim-controlled Jerusalem and Palestine in 1095. Soldiers from Europe's Christian nations responded to the call by Pope Urban II to battle infidels in ancestral lands of Jesus Christ. For the next century and a half, succeeding Crusades mostly were unsuccessful, but the word became part of all Western languages to generally mean a righteous moral battle against evil forces.

***North American Review*, January 1915**

The war is a veritable crusade, waged against the powers of evil, against a policy of lies, and of engineered and intentional brutality. The agents themselves, being men and not fiends, may sometimes have failed to execute to the full all the consequences of the abominable doctrine of their leaders; but enough has been done, and more, alas! will be done, to demonstrate their evil guidance.

If that view of life predominated, if the doctrine were successful that everything and anything was justified that seemed likely to strengthen the State, or to answer its immediate purpose, without any higher power dominating and redeeming the physical, then indeed hell would have come upon earth, and humanity would go down into the pit.

Anonymous: "Criticism of the President's Plan for 'Peace without Victory'"

Wilson based his ideology on a foundation of strong Christian beliefs. Americans of this era generally were steeped in Christian theology, and even Wilson's strongest detractors, such as Theodore Roosevelt, used the Bible in an attack on the president. Here Roosevelt borrows from the Old Testament (Judg. 5:23) to suggest that Wilson neglected his duty to battle against oppressed peoples.

New York Times Current History, October 1916–February 1917

President Wilson's address called forth a violent diversity of opinion in the United States. The cleavage for the most part followed party lines. Leading Democratic newspapers pronounced the utterance epoch-making, a message to mankind, a summary of the broad principles of liberty and justice upon which alone a durable peace is possible. Republican papers for the most part condemned it as untimely, harmful, or at best an "oration on the millennium." Elihu Root declared himself in sympathy with the President's ideas, but added that our entry into a league for peace would be worthless and meaningless without ships and soldiers to do our part in enforcing its mandates. Theodore Roosevelt issued an attack on the President's proposition, concluding with this passage:

When fear of the German submarines next moves Mr. Wilson to declare for "peace without victory" between the tortured Belgians and their cruel oppressors and taskmaster, when such fear next moves him to utter the shameful untruth that each side is fighting for the same things, and to declare for neutrality between wrong and right, let him think of the prophetess Deborah, who, when Sisera mightily oppressed the children of Israel with his chariots of iron, and when the people of Meeroz stood neutral between the oppressed and the oppressor, sang of them:

> "Curse ye, Meroz, said the Angel of the Lord, curse ye bitterly the inhabitants thereof; because they came not to the help of the Lord, to the help of the Lord against the mighty."

President Wilson has earned for this nation the curse of Meroz, for he has not dared to stand on the side of the Lord against the wrongdoings of the mighty.

Not Joining the War: Greatest Evil

Roméo Houle, Canadian Soldier: "The Horrors of Trench Fighting"

We often complain in our modern-day workplaces that management doesn't listen to the people "in the trenches." The metaphor, of course, dates from World War I. No one knew what this war was really like save the men in the trenches. Historians writing about their experiences struggle to explain how the power of patriotism, duty, and loyalty could compel men to persevere under such conditions. Canada, still tied to Britain as a colony, sent more than a half million soldiers to serve in the war; 66,655 were killed, a lamentable number from a country of only eight million.

New York Times Current History, April–September 1916

If you Americans have the choice, never vote for war. You do not know what war is, who have not seen it. I did not know. I could not know. It is not like the sanguinary conflicts of the civil war—they were little fisticuff battles compared to this gigantic slaughter of heroes. Now calm science, cruel, unutterably cruel, calculating a hundred deaths with the precision of the crazed murderer, lays out the battle schemes, and goes seeking through science for new forms of death more horrible than the old. We fight underground and undersea, on the land and in the air. We fight with fire, with steel, with lead, with poisons, with gases, with burning oil. We are lower than the brutes, lower than the lowest and most degraded forms of life.

I do not know why we fought. No Archduke's little life was worth the titanic butchery of the world war. The beginning was petty and small. And I, looking back at horror, horror, horror, cannot forget the extraordinary friendships we made with the men in the enemy's trenches. We were both only human beings, after all, Fritz and I. We had no wish to kill each other. We had much rather sit at the same table, with our wives and children around us, and talk of gardens, of fair pictures, and of great books. But for our officers and the nations which they represented peace would have been declared right there in the trenches—and that by the soldiers themselves.

I am only Roméo Houle, a barber. But I have lived—God I have lived! All the slaughter of heroes by the Meuse and on the Belgian border and in Northern France has passed before my eyes. And I, Roméo Houle, am forced to write this: Man is given life to enjoy it, not to destroy it. We cannot make ourselves better or the world we live in more worth while by killing each other like beasts gone mad.

Not Joining the War: Tool of Capitalists

Carleton H. Parker: "The I.W.W."

Among the groups (small in number) that would not support Wilson's decision to join the war was the International Workers of the World (IWW), representing the radical anticapitalist labor movement. In 1916 it issued a proclamation declaring, "We condemn all wars, and for the prevention of such, we proclaim the antimilitaristic propaganda in time of peace, thus promoting class solidarity among the workers of the entire world, and, in time of war, the general strike, in all industries."[1] In return and in outrage the federal government in effect declared war on the IWW, all but destroying its leadership with arrests and harassment. Nearly eradicated, the organization did recover to survive to the twenty-first century, and had not softened in the least its anticapitalist message.

Atlantic Monthly, November 1917

It is perhaps of value to quote the language of the most influential of the I.W.W. leaders.

"You ask me why the I.W.W. is not patriotic to the United States. If you were a bum without a blanket; if you had left your wife and kids when you went West for a job, and had never located them since; if your job never kept you long enough in a place to qualify you to vote; if you slept in a lousy, sour bunk-house, and ate food just as rotten as they could give you and get by with it; if deputy sheriffs shot your cooking cans full of holes and spilled your grub on the ground; if your wages were lowered on you when the bosses thought they had you down; if there was one law for Ford and Mooney, and another for Harry Thaw; if every person who represented law and order and the nation beat you up, railroaded you to jail, and the good Christian people cheered and told them to go to it, how in hell do you expect a man to be patriotic? This war is a business man's war and we don't see why we should go out and get shot in order to save the lovely state of affairs that we now enjoy."

Editorial: "The Case of Senator La Follette"

Robert M. La Follette, one of the country's most prominent antiwar politicians, became a lightning-rod for those superpatriots who contended that any utterances against America's participation, no matter how mild, constituted a treasonable offense. The Sedition Act of 1918 specified exactly what was considered treasonable: to "incite or attempt to incite, insubordination, disloyalty, mutiny, or refusal of duty, in the military or naval forces of the United States," to "willfully utter, print, write or publish any disloyal, profane, scurrilous, or abusive language about the form of government of the United States" and to "utter, print, write, or publish any language intended to incite, provoke, or encourage resistance to the United States." The law was repealed in 1921.

Current Opinion, November 1917

This avalanche of protests was started by the Public Safety Commission of Minnesota after Senator La Follette (Wisconsin Senator Robert M.) had addressed a convention of the Non-Partisan League held in St. Paul on September 20. Some of the reports of that speech have been declared inaccurate by the Senator, but the following extracts seem to be unimpeached:

"It behooves a nation to consider well before it enters a war of that sort how much it has got at stake. If all it has got at stake is the loans the house of Morgan makes to foreign governments and the profits that the munition makers will earn in shipping their products to foreign countries, then I think it ought to be weighed, not in a common hay scale, but in an apothecary's scale . . . [ellipses in original]

"For my own part I was not in favor of beginning the war. I didn't mean to say we had not suffered grievances. We had at the hands of Germany serious grievances; we had cause for complaining; they had interfered with the right of American citizens to travel upon the high seas on ships loaded with munitions for Great Britain. We had a right, a technical right, to ship munitions, and the American citizen had a technical right to ride on those vessels . . . [ellipses in original] I didn't believe we should have gone into this war for that poor privilege. . . . [ellipses in original]

"But somebody will tell you that American rights are involved. What American rights? The right of some venturesome person to ride on a munition-laden vessel in violation of an American statute that no vessel which carries explosives shall carry passengers. Four days before the Lusitania sailed President Wilson was warned in person by Secretary of State Bryan that the Lusitania had six million rounds of ammunition on board, besides explosives, and that the passengers who proposed to sail on that vessel were sailing in violation of a statute of this country, that no passengers shall travel on a railroad train or sail upon a vessel which carries dangerous explosives. And Mr. Bryan appealed to President Wilson to stop passengers from sailing upon the Lusitania."

Mr. La Follette expressed much the same sentiments in Toledo in September, where he denied that Congress, in declaring war, had represented the will of the people, and again in his weekly, La Follette's, when he said last May: "This is no more a war of democracy than that which was forced upon the German people by the German autocrat."

The Rights of Free Speech in War Time

In response to the calls for expulsion, the Senate, just before adjournment, appointed a special committee, with Senator Pomerene, of Ohio, at its head, to investigate. Senator Pomerene construes the power of the committee as limited to matters of fact, that is to say, to ascertaining, first, just what the Senator from Wisconsin said, and, second, to the truth or falsity of his statements of fact. This seems to focus the inquiry upon the last of the extracts quoted above, and concerning this Mr. Bryan has publicly stated that he "had not known until after the sinking of the Lusitania that it carried ammunition in its cargo," and President Wilson is reported to have told the committee that no such information was conveyed to him by Mr. Bryan as stated by Mr. La Follette. Mr. Roosevelt points out what he considers another misstatement of fact in the speech, namely, the statement that we went to war for the right of Americans to ride on a munition-laden ship. "He said nothing," Mr. Roosevelt points out, "about the sinking of the hospital ship Sussex, and the 'technical right' of the doctors and Red Cross nurses who sank with her to be on board."

Not Joining the War: Religious Ideals

William Lyon Phelps: "War"

The oft-quoted biblical passage in which Jesus tells his followers to "turn the other cheek" (Matt. 5:38–41), meaning to suffer insults, perhaps was what Wilson meant when he declared the country "too proud to fight." Similar admonitions can be found in the texts of most major religions, including sayings attributed to Mohammad: "There should be neither harming nor reciprocating harm" (Forty Hadiths of Al-Nawawi 32).

North American Review, November 1914

Even now some Americans are insisting that we go in for increased armaments and a great navy; that we should take money needed for education and internal improvements and spend it on fighting-machines. Would it not be well to give Christianity a trial? The religion of Christ is as reasonable as it is noble. It is the only method of settling quarrels that combines absolute good sense with pure ethics. In time of war, for the purpose of inflecting death, mutilation, and destruction on those whom we call our brothers, every one is called upon to make heroic sacrifices. Would it not be fine in the future if the United States of America should make some actual sacrifices to prevent war? Would it not be splendid if we actually sustained insults and material damage from some other country and did not fight? A faith is no good unless one is willing to suffer for it. Peace will never come to this uncivilized planet until some nation shows, not by its professions, but by its behavior, that it believes in peace. Some nation will have to suffer in the cause of peace as so many nations have suffered in the evil cause of war. Will it not be fine if that nation should turn out to be our own?

[Response] Ernest Dimnet, Paris, Letter to the Editor: "The Other Phase"

Who was to blame for this war? This has become the central question of World War I historiography. After nearly a century, there still is no absolutely uncontested answer. Before Russia left the war every countries' peoples accepted without question their governments' arguments that they were blameless. But questions surfaced after Lenin's Soviet government made public the secret treaties that bound the allies together and, it seemed, dragged them together over the precipice like a tether of clumsy mountain climbers. By the 1920s, the popular approach was to distribute the blame widely. Recent scholarship, however, has recast primary blame on Germany.

***North American Review*, January 1915**

The effect of Mr. Phelps's pages on many minds with less training and less leisure than he has himself, and ought to use to dispel clouds, will be to convince them that everybody is equally to blame in the European war, and that this purely negative attitude is the best kind of neutrality. The reason which he gives in support of his point of view, viz., that the "good and intelligent people" in every one of the nation's at war are all equally convinced of their right, will probably strike some people as irrefutable and will leave them under the impression that it is useless to go into the details of an insoluble question.

This is what I think extraordinary in a university professor whose business it is to give the example of a virile critical spirit. Mr. Phelps can handle an historical question; he can make use of documents; he certainly knows the trend of European history in the last fifty years. Bearing this in mind and with the recent evidence at hand, how can he say that France, England, Russia and Germany are all equally responsible for this war? In fact, the same issue in which Mr. Phelps's effusion appeared contained discussions of facts which he must have thought destructive of his position, and I only wish to point out what I consider an intellectual example of the more dangerous character because it is given by an unquestionably noble and Christian character.

Editorial: "Moral Reactions of the War"

Is war an addiction? Some who have observed belligerent nations have found it a useful analogy. We go to war intoxicated with a spirit of patriotism that seems as powerful as religious passion. As the losses mount we recoil in the hangover of disillusion. Then, a new generation again chooses with vigor the path to war, renewing the endless chain of humanity's apparent fascination with death and destruction.

Independent, October 4, 1915

For many generations it has been a commonplace of popular sociology that religious feeling is quickened by war, and predictions have freely been made that a great revival of religion will bring a measure of spiritual compensation to the human race for the destruction and desolation now going on. Particularly in France and England, it has been said, faith will return. England will again become Puritan, we have been told, and France Catholic. Protestant Germany will once more be devout, and even in the United States the churches again will attract the masses.

We shall not venture to forecast the disappointment of earnest men and women who are finding comfort in these prophesyings, but as a fact of observation there is curiously little evidence, so far, that they are anything more than an assumption that the close association of war and religion in former times still holds good. It is noticeable that we hear almost none of the "improving" discourse that everybody indulged in a hundred or even fifty years ago. We are not day by day reminded that Providence is working out a mysterious design, or that God is punishing the earth for wickedness that could no longer be permitted to flourish unrebuked and unchastised. . . .

It is not unwarranted, we think, to see in these moral reactions of the war evidence that the human race really has made progress in other than material ways. It has at least learned to look upon itself as responsible for conditions, and it sets about its task of improving them in a common sense, scientific and businesslike way. It is not too much to hope that in this way, and under a sense of responsibility, it will resolutely set about the task of preventing the unspeakable calamity of war.

Editorial, W.E.B. Du Bois: "War"

While the Old Testament is ambiguous regarding war, Jesus Christ in the New Testament squarely declares his pacifism. Does the Bible teach that war is inevitable? The Book of Revelation depicts the four horsemen of the apocalypse. The second, the red horse, has been interpreted as symbolizing war, the red representing blood spilled on the battlefield: "Then another horse came out, a fiery red one. Its rider was given power to take peace from the earth and to make men slay each other. To him was given a large sword" (Rev. 6:4).

Crisis, December 1914

Some time ago we published an article on Moshesh, the great black king of the Basutos in South Africa. Recently there has come to our notice this passage in Casalis' "My Life in Basutoland":

"It was a great stumbling block to Moshesh when he learned that the nations which recognized Jesus Christ still loved war, and applied themselves to perfecting the military art. 'It was excusable in us,' said he, 'who had no other models than wild beast, but you, who profess to be the children of Him who said "Love your enemies," for you to take pleasure in fighting!' All that we could say to him about the alleviations which Christianity had introduced, as, for instance, the ease of the wounded, the absence of personal hate, etc., only increased his stupefaction. 'Then you work this evil without anger, mixing wisdom with it! I can make nothing of it, except that war must be a rod which God does not choose to break, because he will make use of it still for the chastisement of men!'"

Questions

1. Why did many people during World War I consider their participation a spiritual crusade?
2. Why did religious leaders, whose theology preached peace, find it difficult to resist the call to war?
3. Explain why some detractors considered the war a "tool of capitalism."

Note

1. See http://www.spartacus.schoolnet.co.uk/USAhaywood.htm.

Chapter 16

Virtue and War

"War! What is it good for? Absolutely nothing." The Vietnam War era rock song by Edwin Starr became antiwar anthem of a generation and a number-one selling record in 1970. But other generations of Americans have disagreed, particularly during World War I. People who thought joining the war was a good idea found a dizzy array of virtues that could be encouraged by fighting in the trenches. History was mined to produce arguments for the virtue of war, even looking back to ancient times. War could be counted on for three positive outcomes: to improve economic power, to improve society, and to improve individual character.

Those who support the economic argument point out that production in many sectors must expand rapidly to supply army operations. A government will respond by flooding the country with contracts, enriching both capital and labor as they share in the prosperity of high demand. World War I did bring boom times to the country's financial markets and industry. The nation turned overnight from a debtor to a creditor. After the war, the smoke cleared and the United States stood as the world's most powerful financial and industrial nation. Clearly, those who claimed this war would establish America's financial might were correct. As the Great Depression (beginning in 1929) tested the country's financial resilience, it actually took a second world war to again pull the country's economy back into ebullience.

That war creates economic benefit, however, has not always been the case for Americans. As the Johnson and Nixon administrations tried to finance the Vietnam War though loans and inflation, an economic malaise of the 1970s could only be checked by the Federal Reserve Board's hard fiscal conservatism. But those who claimed that war keeps the cash drawer full can find much evidence to support their opinion. Moreover, those countries most soundly beaten after World War II, Germany and Japan, have become among the world's greatest economic powers, encouraged by the United States in its foreign policy approach aimed at containing a communist threat. Did a war against a communist threat benefit South Korea? Undoubtedly some prosperous residents of Seoul would think so.

In addition to the impact of thriving private businesses in wartime societies, war is supposed to engender those esteemed virtues people at peace supposedly forget. Some consider the strict discipline of a soldier's training to be an honorable value for a society that otherwise might become dissolute with wealth, comfort, corruption, and individual selfishness. War requires cooperation, the "sacred union" of an entire society toward a common goal. It requires sacrifice and hard work, willingness to forego comforts of the moment for a larger national aim. This is the society America ought to be, argued those who favored war, and the battlefield may be the best way to achieve it. Preparedness advocates such as Theodore Roosevelt and General Leonard Wood found an even greater virtue in the teamwork expected of a society at war. The salad bowl of dissimilar immigrant cultures that posed a challenge to the early-twentieth-century American union could be brought together through military drills, a rough-and-ready inculcation of American models, and a forced binding of different kinds of people in one barrack, one mess hall, and one troop.

Those who saw war as a force for positive change in American society pointed to scientific and social advances that in peacetime might have required many years, now expedited by the verities of battle. Advances in medicine, engineering, and science would pay off far after the conflict ended. Progressives saw in war the momentum for social change they had only dreamed of before, a more egalitarian society in which workers would obtain justice and racial minorities would obtain freedom. Women hoped the war would advance the suffrage movement.

On a personal level, war advocates admired the quiet values of fortitude and courage found in the trained military man. One could break the chains of a certain future tied to the drudgery of dead-end employment and join a cause as important as life itself. The army could become a teacher and guide to those without education, could encourage habits of personal hygiene, self-esteem, and trial by fire. Men who have known war may return home feeling superior to civilians for having experienced the defining moment of their lives, the experience of battle, something no noncombatant will ever know.

It is true that some of war's virtues touted by prowar advocates flowered in postwar American society. Women did get the vote shortly after World War I. Native Americans were given citizenship, partly thanks to their exemplary military service. Wars have accelerated development of wondrous inventions such as the airplane, and great medical advancements, such as antibiotics. But wars have also accelerated development of terrible weapons, most obviously the Atomic bomb. The balance sheet still shows that war does have its virtues, but these virtues cannot be appreciated by the more than 600,000 young American soldiers in America's twentieth-century wars who did not survive service to their country.

Modern War Encourages Common Virtues

L.B.R. Briggs: "Intercollegiate Athletics and the War"

Most people are aware of the historical parallel between war and sports. Jousts were so popular in the late middle ages that the Roman Catholic church found it necessary to discourage the violent games. Today the violence of most sports is not designed to truly hurt an opponent—with the exception of boxing—but the metaphors borrowed from warriors still make the sports pages resemble stories of violent conquest. The metaphor should not be taken too far, as L.B.R. Briggs notes here. By the twentieth century, war had no sporting challenge, no heroes, no good losers, only death, anonymous and ubiquitous.

Atlantic Monthly, September 1918

When America declared war on Germany, nothing, not even our money, disappeared faster than our college athletic teams. This is a war of which students are quick to see the meaning; and while certain mechanics seize the opportunity for an increased pay that shall allow their comforts to remain undiminished and shall strengthen their hold on political power, thousands of young men, with everything that would seem to promise worldly comfort, stake instantly, and as a matter of course, their hopes and their lives at the first call of the "voice without a reply." And this they do for a war in which the part played by romance—as the word is commonly understood—seems unprecedentedly small. An athlete would be expected to accept, out of hand, the sporting challenge of old-fashioned warfare—to lead mad cavalry charges, to match himself like a knight of old with every newcomer as man against man; but outside of certain naval activities and aviation, that supreme test of sportsmanship in life and death, the call of this war is a call, first to the unrelieved monotony of the camp, and next, to the unrelieved horror of the machine-gun and the gas-bomb. These pampered boys, who insisted on special training-tables, who craved special or limited trains, who had to be kept good-natured and happy before big games by automobile rides and musical comedies, and who, if victorious, would have felt slighted without complimentary dinners; boys coached by men who scorned street cars and scarcely used their legs except on the field; boys waited on by a series of stewards called managers, and supported by second teams who required eatable and drinkable rewards of a service which they struggled for the honor of performing—these boys gave proof unmistakable that they were not spoiled, that they still were men at last; that they could leave all and follow an ideal which some of us saw in only a few of them, which probably only a few of them saw in themselves. This war has come nearer justifying our methods in intercollegiate athletics than we had thought possible.

Theodore H. Price: "Do Wars Really Cost Anything?"

The second wind that some long-distance runners feel—that late burst of energy after a period of fatigue—may be an apt metaphor for a wartime economy. But apparently it can't be explained by "unused lungs" working toward a higher capacity. Medical research today believes the body works harder than the lungs can follow, so muscles incur an "oxygen debt," feel fatigued, and the exerciser slows down. As the person catches up on the debt, he feels revived, thus the "second wind."

***World's Work*, March 1915**

The late William James, of Harvard, maintained that men only rarely worked up to the limit of their powers and he cited the pain in the groin which precedes the "second wind" in running as a corroborative of his theory. Because men do not generally breathe as deeply as they should the abdominal muscles which fully expand the lungs fall into disuse. In running, deep breathing is necessary and the consequent activity of the unused muscles is painful until they function naturally and the lungs are working to their full capacity.

So it seems to be with war. It calls for and it generally develops many qualities and resources that were latent in time of peace. In increases valor, self-reliance, and the capacity for sacrifice.

Editorial: "A Mental and Moral Housecleaning"

Throughout history, friends of warfare have been attracted to its virtue as an opportunity to start fresh—to sweep out the detritus of self-centered peaceful societies and remake a more virtuous state. The clean-slate argument is based on evidence, in that it often does destroy governments or aspects of society that could not have been moved in peacetime. World War I ended with the destruction of centuries-old monarchies in Germany, Austria, and Russia. But it is debatable whether their "clean slates" through warfare engendered positive changes to their postwar societies.

Independent, July 7, 1917

The war is clarifying ideas and stimulating the moral sincerities. These reactions are generally recognized. What is quite as important, it is disposing for good and all of a lot of useless mental baggage, a great store of hypocrisies, and a multitude of presumptions and policies which we knew or suspected were rubbish or worse, but which, in the easy years of peace, we did not bestir ourselves to do away with.

A war brings us to the right apprehension of these things, as "moving" brings us to a right appraisal of household accumulations which we are too lazy or too sentimental to assort sanely under ordinary circumstances.

With few exceptions the presumptions and humbugs that we are discarding are certain extreme claims, privileges and immunities that are related to the so-called class struggle. Great Britain has discovered that the Empire can survive a mighty curtailment of the ancient rights of landlords and peers, and an almost staggering curtailment of the profits of industry and commerce. It has discovered that laissez-faire is not the last word in economics or in politics, and that a highly organized governmental control of business may turn out to be an excellent thing for business itself. But the discoveries and innovations are not all so one-sided. The further discovery has been made that the venerable idiocies which trade unionism and industrial democracy have clung to as tenaciously as to ideas that are sound and claims that are just can be sat on and "swatted," as that they must be. The intolerable folly of opposing inventions and improvements, of making work by waste, of protecting dishonest and incompetent workmen, and of penalizing superior ability, has been endured as long as the world can stand it. . . .

Organized society after this war will be a more intelligent affair and a much more sincere affair, as well as a far more effective machine for promoting human well-being, than it has been hitherto. Privilege will have to go. Excess profits will have to go. Individualism that disregards the rights and interests of fellow-men will have to go. Slacking, wasting and obstructing will have to go. Anarchism and a systematic protection of malefactors will have to go. The world will be neither nationalistic only nor internationalistic only. It will be neither socialistic only nor individualistic only. It will be a practical, relatively sincere and relatively intelligent world, pretty carefully scrutinizing every proposition and trying out plans on their merits.

Franklin K. Lane, Secretary of the Interior: "What Is It to Be an American?"

Franklin K. Lane was secretary of the interior from 1913 to 1920. He oversaw the creation of the National Park Service. Before joining government service, he spent several years working on newspapers in California and Washington State. Lane's comments reflected the widespread hope that the war would homogenize American culture. In specifically referring to peoples of the "civilized world," his remarks might be construed to exclude African Americans and Native Americans, the two most oppressed minorities of the era. Native Americans were not considered American citizens, while during this era African Americans suffered the worst persecution since the days of slavery.

National Geographic, April 1918

There is no such thing as an American race, excepting the Indian. We are doing the unprecedented thing in saying that Slav, Teuton, Celt, and the other races that make up the civilized world are capable of being blended here, and we say this upon the theory that blood alone does not control the destiny of man; that out of his environment, his education, the food that he eats, the neighbors that he has, the work that he does, there can be a formed and realized spirit, an ideal which will master his blood. In this sense we are all internationalists. . . .

America has never sought to be a world power. She does not now. But America has nothing to live for if Germany becomes the one dominant power of the world. And against that possible day your boys and my boy must give their lives, their ambitions, their dreams, if need be.

And we who are not permitted to fight, what shall be our part? Let it be our resolution that when our sons return they shall find a new spirit in America, a deeper insight into the problems of a striving people, a stronger, firmer, more positive and purposeful sense of nationality. We shall make America better worth while to Americans and of higher service to the world.

Editorial: "The Unity of America"

It was French president Raymond Poincaré who on the eve of war coined the term union sacrée, the sacred union of a nation at war, telling parliament through a speech by his Prime Minister, René Viviani, on August 4 that "nothing will shatter, facing the enemy, the union sacrée." Every warring nation during World War I declared a similar sentiment. It might be better called a truce than a union, because differing groups merely agreed to postpone, not forget, their disagreements. A similar feeling of unity during war swept the United States in 1917, but with a difference: unlike Europe, the United States faced little possibility of actual invasion or ruin. The union represented an ideal as illuminated by Wilson's call for a war of democratic principles.

Nation, March 21, 1918

The war has brought much talk of the achievement of American unity. It would be far nearer the truth to say that it has revealed American unity. During the trying days of neutrality, many patriotic citizens were profoundly agitated over our differences of opinion and feeling, and were for starting all sorts of "Americanization" movements—to make their fellow-Americans think and feel as they did themselves. They were confident that our recent immigrants do not understand America—in some case their own American ancestors could be traced as far back as 1870—and therefore they were for instituting universal military service, for jailing dissentients, for doing anything and everything to compel us all to be alike. Because we were not all alike, they were confident that the country was on the high road to destruction. Incompetent for peace, we were to show ourselves impotent for war.

To-day these voices are largely silenced. We have seen the nation carried into the war by its intellectual and political leaders. We have seen the great mass of the people quietly accepting the judgment of those leaders as to the necessity of the struggle, and soberly taking the measures and making the sacrifices called for by the responsible authorities. . . . Not unnaturally we are called on to admire the unity that is being created by the war.

The war, however, has not created a really new unity; it has only revealed a profound underlying unity that existed before. When the war is over, if we mistake not, Americans will disagree no less heartily concerning policies, will dispute no less warmly concerning methods, will struggle no less vigorously concerning ideas, than was the case before the sounding of the trumpet summoned them to the common task of making war. the sinking of such differences, though necessary for the time being, is not permanent or even desirable, except in so far as it is a purging of selfishness. For the America we know and love is an America, not of uniformity, but of unity, not of race purity, but of race mixture, not of conformity imposed from without, but of harmony evolved from within, not of similarity of talents, ideas, and outward circumstances, but of like aspirations and hopes and dreams.

Underneath our diversity, our struggles, our selfishness, there is a principle of unity which for a century, in a degree we cannot realize, has made America a beacon light of hope to the peoples all over the world, a principle which makes the war-torn and weary millions hang to-day on the words of an American statesman as the voice that announces the way out of the world blackness. It is that principle which has given to a hundred millions of people, coming from every country under the sun, living under every variety of geographical and climatic conditions and economic circumstances, to rich man and poor, to Maine lumberjack and Mexican cowboy—has given to them all the mysterious unity that dwells in the word American, and that the war has now again revealed—a unity not of blood or of race or of religion or of education or of language or of customs or even of government, but a unity of the spirit which is indeed the bond of peace. We speak no mystical language, nor do we imagine that the spirit can live unless it body itself forth in fitting institutions.

A British Officer: "The Paradox of War"

Some men may have found benefit in their World War I service, returning as the more disciplined, serious man the army was supposed to make him become. Not obvious to home-front writers during the war were those men who did not come home whole—mentally. The term "shell-shock" was coined in 1917 by a British medical officer, Charles Myers, but the disorder grew to encompass a variety of mental trauma brought on by war, even in some who did not actually serve in the trenches. War's brutal breakdown of any appearance of humanity sent some victims back to society hallucinating, quavering, physically ill, and unable to function. Some 80,000 British soldiers ended up in hospitals for shell-shock, which today we recognize as Post-Traumatic Stress Disorder (PTSD).

New York Times Current History, October 1915–March 1916

The following reflections on the effects of war upon character are from a letter written to his wife by a British officer at the western front:

Generally we all feel in much the same way—the British soldiers at the front. I was telling a Chaplain yesterday of a raid that had been made on the German trenches, and had added, "I suppose about sixty Germans were killed." "Is that all?" he said, with a real sorrow and disappointment in his voice. If I could have said six hundred he, a Christian priest, would have felt more content. Yet he was a gentle-hearted man.

Talking with him before, he had been exchanging with me observations going to show the great trough of tenderness, of chivalry, of dutiful generosity among the soldiers. We both could cite instance after instance, some of which brought a quaver to the voice and a dimness to the eyes. Put down side by side these two facts: (1) That in the main the British soldier at the front is a better man for his present experience, better in his thought of his family, to his mates, to the civil population around him, to the animals who serve him, to his German prisoners, and that he is also, clearly, a "softer" man; (2) that he is sternly (cruelly, if you like) set upon destroying Germans, and talks of Hun-killing as the most desirable thing in life.

There appears between the two a chasm of paradox. And I suppose it would be very hard by any process of logic to bridge the chasm. Go behind logic, however, and search in the deeper motives of instinct, and the position is plain enough. A deep, passionate instinct teaches the man in the fighting line that all that makes for the betterment of human life, chivalry, generosity, candor, fair dealing, is threatened with extinction, and he finds himself unconsciously striving to cherish and foster the gentler side of life at the same time as he sets himself with savage sternness to exterminate the forces which are working for its destruction.

William Howard Taft: "Great Britain's Bread upon the Waters; Canada and Her Other Daughters"

Many European wars before the modern era were fought primarily by elite, well-trained professionals who made the military their career. Napoleon broke that tradition by assembling large armies of patriotic citizens able to fight huge battles on several fronts. World War I became the largest war the world had ever fought, and it required enormous reserves of men far beyond what a professional army could muster. As huge conscription operations eventually became necessary in all warring nations, large propaganda campaigns also became necessary to persuade the conscripts and their loved ones that the fight was worth their sacrifice. More than 70 million men were mobilized for World War I; about nine million died.

National Geographic, March 1916

The strain of the great war now raging is a test of the character of the peoples engaging in it, and of the institutions to which they have committed themselves and in behalf of which for decades and centuries they have labored. It places their ideas of government and their philosophies of the life in a crucible under the intensest heat. It is no respecter of preconceived theories, and it lays bare weaknesses that were not suspected. The war has shown a high spirit of patriotism and self-sacrifice as the common trait of all those engaged in it. . . .

It is not true that popular government unfits a people for war, saps their unselfish patriotism, or dulls their willingness to make the sacrifice. The armies of France raised in the wars of the French Revolution refute any such notion. Our own Civil War shows that participation in government and the consequent sense of ownership in it prompt the highest spirit of sacrifice for the country.

Major John L. Todd, Board of Pension Commissioners for Canada: "The Meaning of Rehabilitation"

In 1914, Canada, a British colony, presumed that it would join the war with its mother country. Despite its geographic isolation from the battlefields, Canadians volunteered with enormous enthusiasm for service in Europe. From a standing army of barely 3,000 troops, enlistment swelled to 32,000 in just a few weeks. In total, more than 600,000 served from a country of only eight million. Nearly 11 percent of those who served perished.

Annals of the American Academy of Political and Social Sciences, November 1918

During reorganization after the war it will be unbelievably easy to achieve social ideals which before the war seemed impracticable and impossible of attainment. It will be especially easy on this continent not only because ours are young peoples, still in a stage of development where social structure is not stable, but also because the war has aroused a great spirit of mutual helpfulness, a desire to sacrifice self, a self-devotion. These factors cannot but leave an enduring mark upon national life. May our plans be so modeled that a measure of good may come from this evil of war.

In order that rehabilitation may be successful, it is essential that there should be a clear understanding in the mind of every citizen, not only of that which the community ought to do for itself and for the returning soldier, but also of that which every returning man ought to do for himself. Such a generous knowledge, secured by wide publicity, constitutes the most powerful means of securing right action. The urge to do that which we are taught to do, that which is expected of us, is the most powerful of all human impulses. It is the herd instinct: the desire to do that which is right is stronger than self-preservation—men die at their posts because it is their duty to do so: it is stronger than the wish for parenthood—monks and nuns remain childless because it is their duty to do so.

Let us learn this from the enemy; "Will conquers." That is the device always before the German wounded. Just as unquestioningly as they once believed in German might, every German now believes that a disabled man, if he wills it, can be self-supporting and that it is the duty of every returning man by his will and through the aid of his fellows to become a self-supporting unit, a man who pulls his weight in the boat and is not a passenger.

Major-General Leonard Wood: "Heat up the Melting Pot"

Leonard Wood was John J. Pershing's only serious rival in the choice to lead the American Expeditionary Force into World War I. Trained as an army doctor, Wood had seen broad service over 30 years, including famously leading the "charge up San Juan Hill" during the Spanish American war, in which Theodore Roosevelt played second in command. Before 1917, however, his outspoken campaign in favor of preparedness and his close friendship with Roosevelt tainted him as a politician as much as a military leader—and a Republican one at that. Democrat Woodrow Wilson instead appointed Pershing. In 1920 Wood became an unsuccessful candidate for Republican presidential nomination.

Independent, **July 3, 1916**

What is needed is some kind of training which will put all classes which go to make up the mass which is bubbling in the American melting pot, shoulder to shoulder, living under exactly the same conditions, wearing the same uniform and animated by a common purpose. This "something" will be found in a system of universal training like the Australian or Swiss, where all classes of men, Jew and Gentile, rich and poor, Protestant and Catholic, upper and lower social classes, work shoulder to shoulder, animated by a common purpose, that purpose being to better prepare themselves to discharge their military duties in case of trouble. With this training will come a better physique, a greater degree of self-control, habits of regularity, promptness and thoroness, respect for law and the rights of others and a sense of individual responsibility and obligation for service to the nation in war or peace, all of which will make for national solidarity, and the building up of a stronger and better people, who, while made up from many diverse elements, will be single in purpose.

The military value of this training is only one of the advantages to the nation. Another is the result in the way of increased national efficiency which will come from a greater degree of national solidarity. Men will learn to think more in terms of the nation and less in those of the individual or the small community. It will also be an insurance for peace, because in the end we shall be the strong man armed. This we can do without fear of being either unjust or aggressive. If we are to meet successfully the conditions of life, we must be prepared to oppose the forces of wrong with the strength of right.

Neither moral excellence nor an upright national life will serve to protect us against aggression. Mere philosophizing will not take the place of deeds. While cherishing peace we must have convictions backed by a spirit of sacrifice which will give all, even life itself, in the cause of truth and right.

Winston Churchill: "American Independence Day"

Churchill's roots included a close tie to the United States: his mother, Jennie Jerome, was the daughter of a New York businessman. During the war Churchill was First Lord of the Admiralty in the British war cabinet but was sacked after being blamed for the failed campaign to attack Turkey from the south. After commanding a battalion in the trenches, he returned to London in 1918 to serve as minister of munitions. He went on to become prime minister during World War II, one of the very few leaders who played a pivotal role in both world wars.

New York Times Current History, April–September 1918

Only One Solution

When all those weapons in which German militarists have put their trust have been broken in their hands, when all the preparations on which they have lavished the energy and schemes of fifty years have failed, then the German people will find themselves protected by those simple, elemental principles of right and freedom against which they will have warred so long in vain. So let us celebrate today not only the Declaration of Independence, let us proclaim a true comradeship of Britain and America, to stand together till the war is done, in all trials, in all difficulties, at all costs, where ever the war may lead us, right to the very end. No compromise on the main purpose, no peace till victory, no pact with unrepented wrong–this is the declaration of July 4, 1918, and that is a declaration which I invite you to make in common with me. to quote the words which are on every American lip today, and for which I ask the support of this declaration: "With a firm reliance on the protection of a Divine providence, we mutually pledge to each other our lives, our fortunes, and our sacred honor."

Modern War Discourages Common Virtues

Maxim Gorky: "War and Civilization"

Maxim Gorky's optimistic call for a union of Western minds serves as an ironic contrast to his own brutal existence in Russia. An abusive childhood led him to more harsh treatment as he wandered from town to town barely eating. At age 21 he tried to commit suicide, the wound troubling him for the rest of his life. He published work based on his experience with people of the streets, but while he was in favor of Russia pulling out of the war, he opposed the Bolshevik coup, and so fled to Italy. He returned in 1930 and died in 1936 under suspicious circumstances.

New York Times Current History, October 1915–March 1916

The noted Russian author wrote this pithy little article for a Stockholm paper. It was copied by a Russian journal, from which the present translation was made.

The effect of the war on the progress of civilization among the nations of the world will be strongly felt for generations to come. The development of civilization will be much less rapid after the war than heretofore.

The world is becoming more and more permeated with ill-will, hatred, and passion. The noble emotions give way to the bestial. The infernal forces are awakened and the inhuman has pridefully raised its head. I believe, however, in the common sense of the nations of Western Europe. I feel that that sense will yet conquer the world, and that the European civilization will become the civilization of all humanity.

The European nations must therefore see to it that the work of civilization is carried on by them in a friendlier and more co-operative spirit. The "must" is based on a very plain point of view: The Anglo-Saxons, Teutons and Latins, all together, constitute but a part of the world's population. And yet they are the ones that are and have been creating the spiritual treasures of all humanity. The right to the spiritual domination of the world belongs to Western Europe, as she is entitled to that right by virtue of her spiritual wealth, of her many generations of labor on the fields of science and art; she has won that right through her intellectual services to humanity.

This mad, bloody war affords the largest part of the world the opportunity of doubting the moral values of Western European progress, of denouncing her authority in matters spiritual, and of opposing her doctrines and principles. In a measure these doubts are justified. The slaughter in which the foremost European nations are now engaged will enhance barbarism on earth and will doubtless be the cause of many obstacles in the path of civilization's progress in Africa and Asia.

As soon as the European nations end their present criminal activities, a safe and solid ground for common work in behalf of the world will be found by them. The great minds of the neutral countries could even now begin the work of reorganizing European civilization, they could start a campaign against a return to barbarism. Several years ago Wilhelm Ostwald suggested a union of the great minds of the world. He pointed out the necessity for such a "world-brain," representing all nations. Such a "world-brain" would bring into the political, social, and nationalistic chaos the healthy human thought. Ostwald has proved the possibility of creating such a scientific institution in international politics, an institution composed of the master minds of the age, of scholars and men of affairs. Such a union must become the nervous system of humanity, the brain of the world.

Ellen Key: "War and the Sexes"

The French government during this period and before had been routinely concerned about the country's low birth rate, particularly in contrast to that of Germany. During World War I, French politicians encouraged pregnancies not only by giving soldiers home leaves, but through propaganda that showed men and women in suggestive poses, urging them to do their "patriotic duty."

Atlantic Monthly, June 1916

The fact that the battlefields swallow up millions of lives makes the birth-rate a national question and revolutionizes ideas of sexual morality. Everything is now looked upon in a Spartan spirit as being a matter of the State. All these facilities for military marriages are begin made because the State expects the men to propagate themselves before they die. It is to ensure a good crop of soldiers for the year 1935 that Joffre has, to the greatest possible degree, given the French soldiers four days' leave with free journeys home. It has been proposed in France to tax the unmarried and childless and to reduce the taxes of those who are married or have many children; and similar measures will probably be taken in the other warring countries.

What was formerly considered a sin—loveless marriages contracted simply for the purpose of having offspring—will perhaps, from the national point of view, come to be considered a duty hereafter. The bearing of children outside of marriage, and perhaps other deviations from the ideal of monogamy, will be practiced openly after the war to a far greater extent than was done secretly by people of Europe before the war. Twenty months of war have already dealt heavier blows to the foundations of "Holy Marriage" than all the "apostles of immorality" were able to compass. That all new forms of sex-relation will not be officially sanctioned is self-evident, but they may have the sanction of custom; and this, in some cases, means more than the approval of the State.

T. R. Powell, New York, Letter to the Editor: "A Dark World"

T. R. Powell's pithy letter summarizes some of America's problems that progressives hoped through war to improve. In most cases, postwar government policies did not match their hopes, although agencies created temporarily during the war did leave a precedent for succeeding governments to recreate them during and after World War II.

***Nation,* November 23, 1918**

Sir: Is the world really so black as the Nation paints it? I know that Mr. Burleson isn't perfect, that Mr. Creel is a bit unreliable, that Mr. Gompers isn't Mr. Henderson, that Senator Lodge is unenlightened, that Mr. Roosevelt lacks the judicial temper, that security leagues and councils of safety are often blatant and myopic, that Republicans are protectionists and protectionists not always unselfish, that Negroes are discriminated against on account of race, color, and previous condition of servitude, that judges impose excessive sentences, that conscientious objectors are subjected to indignities, that personal liberty is annoyingly curtailed, that war provokes passion, and I think with the Nation that it would be better if it were otherwise. But after all is it so bad as you make it out? What are the objections to amiability and a sense of proportion?

QUESTIONS

1. World War I propelled the United States to prosperity and set it on a road to superpower status. It lost comparatively little in lives and treasure. Was the American sacrifice of 1917–1918, therefore, worth the long-term benefits to Americans? Why or why not?
2. Progressives were disappointed that World War I did not bring about many of the changes they hoped for in American society. But what did change?
3. The strenuous training of soldiers is presumed by some to build a character that is also valuable in civilian society. What military values might also be useful to former soldiers in civilian life? What values might not be useful?

Chapter 17

Women and War

By the eve of World War I, women in America had been fighting nearly a hundred years for equal rights and recognition. Their work toward equality had blossomed in the years before 1914, after some years in remission, and the war declaration offered a new cause to the more militant feminists. In early 1915 some 3,000 pacifist women gathered in Washington to form the Women's Peace Party, chaired by Jane Addams. As a prewar women's rights advocate, Addams and other prominent American women believed pacifism was logical extension of their ideals. Before the war these women appealed to President Wilson for continued neutrality and attempts to mediate an end to the war. They ridiculed preparedness advocates as warmongers. They organized parades and demonstrations against preparedness, reminding Wilson of his commitment to neutrality, and dominated the country's pacifist movement before 1917. The country's most prominent preparedness advocate, Theodore Roosevelt, dismissed these women as hysterical and silly. Others declared that the Women's Peace Party merely was ignorant of war's imperatives, misguided, fooled, uneducated, or simply stupid.

After the sinking of the *Lusitania,* American interest in neutrality moved toward a conclusion that Germany was the enemy. Many thought that armed conflict was the only response. Some militant female pacifists, such as Addams, supported Wilson in 1916 even after the president had acquiesced to a limited preparedness program. Other sympathizers chose silence as the climate of mania building toward the war declaration of April 1917 increasingly menaced Americans' rights, freedoms, and even lives through a culture of fear and intolerance. Women who insisted on a pacifist agenda, or discouraged their husbands and sons from serving, were declared traitors, no less. Their actions could only make sissies out of men who would be denied their right to an "aggressive young manhood."

Most female pacifists responded by joining the war effort—or at least declining to speak against it. Those most prominent faced an almost impossible crossroad, for to abandon their long-standing ideology would be choosing to be a traitor to their cause, yet to continue as before would invite condemnation or jail. Addams choose not to explicitly support the war, but did not actively oppose it, discrediting herself in the eyes of those women who believed war to be morally wrong in any context. She did encourage women to adopt virtues of conservation, and even spoke at several war bond rallies.

Other prominent feminists were not easily cowed and paid a heavy price of fines and jail time. One of the most egregious examples was the case of Kate Richards O'Hare. In the course of a speech to 100 people on July 17, 1917, in tiny Bowman, North Dakota, she said that because of the war's need for men, "the women of Europe are reduced to the status of breeding animals on a stock farm." At her trial for violating the Sedition Act, prosecutors could not say definitively that she spoke against the war, but suggested her comments corrupted motherhood and interfered with conscription. She was sentenced to five years in the Missouri Penitentiary, of which she served 14 months.

Another member of the peace party, Jeannette Rankin, served no jail time but faced other retribution for her refusal to be swept away by war fervor. Rankin was serving her first term as the first women ever elected to the U.S. House of Representatives when called to cast a vote on declaring war. True to her pacifist beliefs, she voted no. In response, Wyoming Republicans refused to endorse her for a second term and she lost the 1918 election. (She was reelected in 1940 and again opposed U.S. entry into war; heaped with scorn for her steadfast pacifism, she decided not to run again. In 1968, at age 87, she led a women's protest against the Vietnam War.)

These women were outliers. As a group, women mostly joined male Americans in supporting the 1917 war declaration. Many agreed with the progressives in hopes that the war would change everything. Perhaps social injustices woven into society would finally be addressed by a war that called into question the entire web of presumption and privilege on which society was based. These women made two basic demands: the right to vote and the right to equal opportunity in the workplace. Regarding the vote, those who hoped the war would produce change saw vindication with the passing of the Nineteenth Amendment in 1920. It is an exaggeration to say women's work in the war persuaded men that women were now capable of participating in democracy. The suffrage movement had been a decades-long march of persuasion debated widely from east to west. Some states already allowed women to vote. But Wilson's 1918 support of suffrage as necessary for the war effort along with the services of women in industry and military seemed to provide the final nudge in favor of suffrage.

Equality in the workplace proved to be elusive. It was obvious in the United States as it had been in other warring nations that the more women worked in home-front and behind-the-lines jobs, the more the men could be spared for active service. The process of opening up industries previously closed to women had actually begun before the war declaration based on the same forces that encouraged African Americans to move north: business was booming while labor shortages exacerbated by a ban on immigration made employers desperate. In the case of America's female work force, however, the entire number of working women, about a million, did not change much. What did change was what the women did. The large industry of cleaners, seamstresses, launderers, and other domestic services that employed most women fell dramatically as these women found greater opportunity in industrial and office work. Some 500,000 left domestic service for more attractive work as stenographers, telephone operators, and cashiers, as well as in the traditionally male preserves of machinists, truck drivers, and street car operators. Some 100,000 women literally kept the railroads running.

These unfamiliar female faces on the shop floors were most often not greeted enthusiastically by men who feared women were after their jobs. Some unions excluded women, although others actually recruited them. As a whole, however, women were often harassed, their work sometimes sabotaged. The federal War Labor Policies Board investigated complaints of ill-treatment, but after the war ended, the government lost interest in protecting women in the workplace.

Women also were needed in war work. Most familiar were their old roles as volunteers and cheerleaders for the men: they prepared bandages and packages for soldiers, encouraged war bond sales, coordinated patriotic campaigns, and denounced antiwar "traitors." But for a few, World War I meant more. The U.S. Navy in particular was open to women serving in office duties because the huge scale of a modern war required an army of clerical staff. The army responded with less enthusiasm, but did eventually employ many thousands of women as clerks, phone operators, and nurses. While the navy did award women rank and veterans benefits, the army did not consider women to be truly part of the military. In fact, despite having been sworn in and subject to the same military discipline as the men, some of the women who served in the American Expeditionary Force in France found to their surprise after the war that they had not really been in the army after all and so were denied benefits, including care for service-related injury or illness. Trained nurses who served in the U.S. Army Nurse Corps, 21,000 in France and at home, were recruited from the Red Cross and other groups, but had no authority so were sometimes supervised by men without medical training. Of the 234 women who died in service, 100 died overseas—all of them victims of the Spanish Flu epidemic. Women never served in combat during this war, but three were injured by enemy fire. Another 1,000 trained Red Cross nurses who happened to be black were denied service. They eventually were allowed to tend wounded black soldiers in the United States.

The extensive and important service of women to the war effort did not lead to the long-term equality so many had dreamed of. After the war women were laid off from their jobs in favor of returning soldiers. Government investigations into harassment and unequal pay were abandoned as the country recast itself into a prewar isolationist mindframe. Some unions asked women to do their new patriotic duty—to leave their jobs to the men. Unions successfully persuaded some state legislatures to ban women from many "men's jobs," including even shoe shiners in Ohio. By 1920 fewer women worked than before the war, and the future for women's rights looked bleak. But one change remained: the debate over suffrage for women was over for good.

Women Should Support and Learn about the War

Anonymous: "Letter to the Editor"

Recent research seems to show that higher testosterone levels in men explains their generally more aggressive behavior and greater strength. Throughout history men have relied on this biological difference to presume that the "weaker sex" would be incapable of battle. Episodes of women fighting disguised as men in the American Revolution and U.S. Civil War show this to be untrue, but women generally were held to be unfit for combat service until very recently in the latter part of the twentieth century. Their presence as armed soldiers still is controversial in the few countries that have extended their service to this level, including the United States.

Delineator, June 1915

Getting women into this military business will not be a bad idea, because there is nothing in a woman's courage which enables her to die for a principle; she just lives for it. A man seals his devotion to a principle when he dies for it; a woman when she endures everything of pain, starvation, and want for it. If women ever prove equal to the war problem, it will be because they will lead the world into a way to get along without it. I can not see them doing it, for fighting is an instinct with men. Men fight because they want to fight. They don't need any cause, only an excuse.

Women in war councils will keep the army on a defense footing. Women war practice will be effective only in the hospital corps. But just for the sake of strengthening the nerves and muscles of girls, I should like to see them put through a good deal of just plain military drill and target practice.

Erma J. Ridgway: "Why Defenseless Homes?"

World War I marked the first time the U.S. government allowed women to be admitted into the military with some official status. After the war, however, the hope of some women to establish a professional military career came to nothing, as the military provided no postwar opportunities for service. The picture had changed dramatically only a generation later: in World War II many hundreds of thousands of women served with troops at home and around the world, often making their way through the mud and the shells in a variety of important support roles. A small number died on the battlefield, several more became POWs, and 16 received a Purple Heart.

***Delineator*, January 1915**

Why is it necessary to leave our homes defenseless? Why can not women be taught to take care of themselves just as men are? Why in the times of war should women be left in the charge of old men, or why should old men be left in charge of a lot of defenseless women? What nation in the world would be likely to start out jauntily to invade our country, knowing that every one in the country fourteen years old and over could shoot and would?

I know some very wonderful women who trap and fish and hunt as well as any man. What's the harm? What do you think of the whole idea? Would women—would you prefer to remain defenseless if you could be taught how to defend yourselves? I suppose the pioneer women all knew how to defend themselves. I never heard that it brutalized them. I wonder if it did.

I can not see how marching and maneuvering or even shooting is going to hurt our girls. In fact, I am inclined to believe they would be a whole lot healthier if they did more of this sort of thing. Stand near your schoolhouse sometime when the young folks are coming out of school. Notice how the girls walk. Then notice how those boys who are active in baseball or football walk. I am not sure but it would be a mighty fine thing for the girls to have some drills. Even if they are not taught to shoot, they might be taught Red Cross work and camp cooking and marching. You see it is a big question.

Lily Braun, Noted German Feminist Leader: "War and the Duty of Motherhood"

Lily Braun was a socialist, atheist, and feminist who contributed a number of books on women and socialism to the feminist debate. Her patriotic pronouncement here—seemingly incongruous given her socialist underpinnings—demonstrated that nations could war against each other based on the very same arguments to duty and patriotism.

***New York Times Current History*, April–September 1916**

There are women who advocate "a strike" among the mothers of the land—who declare they will bring no more children into the world to be a food for powder. But such women are lacking in true citizenship, and it is as mothers and citizens that the State will claim our co-operation with the war. Let us so fulfill this two-fold duty as to prove ourselves worthy helpmates of the heroes in the fighting lines, and we shall then be able to look back upon this critical period in the nation's history, not as the "time of our great calamity," but rather as "the great time of our calamity!"

Women Should Not Support or Learn about War

Anonymous: "Letters to the Editor"

The virtues of military training have been extolled throughout human history, from ancient Greece to the contemporary United States. It is contended that such training turns a young man into a self-disciplined, flexible, loyal, brave, and respectful individual able to operate at a superior level in battle both physical and metaphorical. It is ironic that while American leaders were praising the benefits of military service (at least for males), they were decrying the militaristic German society that it was presumed led Berlin to launch World War I.

***Delineator*, June 1915**

Our girls can get all the outdoor life they want without military training. I shudder at the thought of such a thing.

Your article was the first definite evidence that strikes so near home of the morbid effect that the awful cataclysm in Europe has on the American mind.

In their hearts women do not accept or understand the need or reason for war, and consequently for military training.

Anonymous: "Women for Peace. The Organization of the First Women's Peace Party"

Women who banded together six months following the war declaration to declare their pacifism drew sympathy from socialists and progressives, although some of the women representing the peace party came from upper class backgrounds. Notable in the declaration here is the signature of Mrs. Louis Post. Her husband, Louis Post, was U.S. Assistant Secretary of Labor. Post was serving as acting labor secretary during a Department of Justice nationwide sweep that arrested and harassed innocent immigrants and foreigners during the "Red Scare" of 1919–1920. Reflecting his belief that the federal officials had overstepped legal authority, he canceled more than two thirds of the justice department's arrests and deportation orders.

***Independent,* January 19, 1915**

On Sunday afternoon, January 10, 3000 women crowded into the Grand Ball Room of the New Willard Hotel at Washington, D.C. They formed themselves into the "Woman's Peace Party," the first in the world. They issued a manifesto, unsurpassed, we think, in power and moral fervor by anything that has been issued here or abroad since the Great War began. They adopted a platform radical, sound, statesmanlike, constructive.

Tho not a line about the conference appeared the next morning in five of the six leading New York newspapers, which found space to devote sixty-three of their valuable columns to the man-killing in Europe and the alleged reasons why the United States should increase her army and navy, we think the conference so important that we publish in full the final document issued by it, and we urge every one of our women readers to join the party.

John Ruskin said long ago that women could stop all wars if only they were determined to do so. We rejoiced that the voice of woman is to be heard against the "greatest scourge of mankind," for all wars are primarily waged on women and children.

–The Editor.

Declaration of Principles

We women of the United States, assembled in behalf of World Peace, grateful for the security of our own country, but sorrowing for the misery of all involved in the present struggle among warring nations, do hereby band ourselves together to demand that war should be abolished.

Equally with men pacifists, we understand that planned-for, legalized, wholesale, human slaughter is today the sum of all villainies. As women, we feel a peculiar moral passion of revolt against both the cruelty and the waste of war.

As women, we are especially the custodians of the life of the ages. We will not longer consent to its reckless destruction. As women, we are particularly charged with the future of childhood and with the care of the helpless and the unfortunate. We will not longer accept without protest that added burden of maimed and invalid men and poverty-stricken widows and orphans which war places upon us.

As women, we have built by the patient drudgery of the past the basic foundation of the home and of peaceful industry. We will not longer endure without protest, which must be heard and heeded by men, that hoary evil which in an hour destroys the social structure that centuries of toil have reared.

As women, we are called upon to start each generation onward toward a better humanity. We will not longer tolerate without determined opposition that denial of the sovereignty of reason and justice by which war and all that makes for war today renders impotent the idealism of the race.

Therefore, as human beings and the mother half of humanity, we demand that our right to be considered in the settlement of questions concerning not alone the life of individuals but of nations be recognized and respected.

We demand that women be given a share in deciding between war and peace in all the courts of high debate, within the home, the school, the church, the industrial order, and the State.

So protesting, and so demanding, we hereby form ourselves into a national organization to be called the Woman's Peace Party. . . .

These officers were elected: Chairman, Jane Addams, Hull House, Chicago; honorary chairman, Carrie Chapman Catt, New York City; vice-chairman, Anna Garlin Spencer, Meadville, Pennsylvania; Mrs. Henry Villard, New York City; Mrs. Louis F. Post, Washington, D.C.; Mrs. John Jay White, Washington, D.C. Headquarters, Hull House, Chicago.

Women in War Work Will Improve Society

August Winnig, National Secretary, Building Trade Union of Germany: "The War's Effects on Women's Status"

This resounding declaration of the importance of a career to a woman's status recalls the role of prewar German socialism as the world's most modern.

Trade unions in the United States generally did not support women's rights in the workplace. The American Federation of Labor (AFL) had no interest in encouraging women to become union members, but some unions did actively recruit women, including unions of machinists and textile workers. Women happily joined their unions in strikes; more than 6,000 occurred during the war.

***New York Times Current History*, April–September 1917**

The position of woman as to her public and private rights, as to her public and intellectual life, is closely bound up with her industrial position and activity. Woman's sphere of influence in the State and in society corresponds to her field of activity. Where woman's activity is limited to the home and family, where she has no direct connection with the industrial life of the nation, there her legal and intellectual position is confined within narrow boundaries. Right here is verified Marx's declaration that society does not rest upon the law, but that the law rests upon society. Law is the legal expression of the actual social condition. Of course, like everything existing, it is ruled by the tendency to stand fast, and, consequently, it generally yields but hesitatingly, and often resistingly, to changes in conditions. . . . It is beyond question that only through that direct participation by women in the economic life of the nation which is connected with economic independence is emphasis lent to the demand for broader rights, and that only then will the great mass of women take up this demand and earnestly support it. Consequently it is evident that an increasing participation by women in industrial labor will influence the legal position of woman in the sense of a broadening of her rights.

Caroline V. Kerr, Berlin Correspondent of a New York Newspaper: "German Women as War Workers"

Women world-wide who hoped the war would make their dream of suffrage come true were sometimes rewarded for wartime sacrifice, sometimes not. The vote was granted to women in Germany and Austria in 1918 and in the United States in 1920. Women in Britain had to wait until 1928. In France women had to wait until the end of World War II, 1944.

***New York Times Current History*, April–September 1917**

The German Nation will not be able to forget that the stern fight for existence behind the front was made possible only by the unremitting efforts of the women of the land, working hand in hand with the men and contributing cheerfully and intelligently to the economic upkeep of the nation. Even women who are not avowed suffragists think that universal suffrage will be one of the inevitable results of the war, for the reason that the law-givers of all the belligerent countries can no longer deny this crowning privilege to the wives and mothers who have worked so bravely, suffered so keenly, and endured so patiently through the long years of this cruel war.

Rebecca West: "Women of England"

Rebecca West became internationally known as a young and strident feminist, suffragist, and prolific writer of articles and books. She moved in high literary circles, had a well-known 10-year affair with H. G. Wells, and traveled widely as a writer and broadcaster. Perhaps her most famous quote is from the Clarion: *"I myself have never been able to find out precisely what feminism is. I only know that people call me a feminist whenever I express sentiments that differentiate me from a doormat or a prostitute."*

Atlantic Monthly, January 1917

It is the heart of our life that is devoured, the quiet, hidden places where the future is nourished; the part of the world that is the care of women. It goes unrecorded partly because they are the sex bred to inarticulateness, and partly because, when one thinks of women in wartime, the exceptional people come forward as usual to crowd out the rest of mankind. For women have done things in this war that make one glad even under the shadow of the sword.

One does not mean the women who have acquired boots and spurs and khaki on pretexts usually connected with nursing, and who dodge into the firing line as often as the General Staff will let them; for the war has sharply revised one's aspirations, and one knows now that, however well built for adventure a woman may be, if she is neither a doctor nor a nurse she has no right to be at the front. It is not reverent to suffering Europe. The woman journalist who stopped amidst the bursting shells to powder her nose proved the crystal hardness of her nerve; but it is not good to demonstrate one's attractive qualities in the death-chamber of the nations. Moreover, the independent woman at the front prejudices the position of women in the same way that an abnormally skilled workman prejudices the position of his mates by working so quickly that the factory piece-rate is lowered. The spinster, who is an abnormally free woman, has no right to accustom men to the sight of women looking after themselves in danger, since there are women who cannot look after themselves because they are burdened with children. But there are unnumbered women who in that death-chamber are thinking only of the dying, who have taken part in war and yet kept themselves clean from its passion for disorganizing and harshening the fate of all human creatures.

It is wonderful that they should have been allowed to help. Before the war Lord Kitchener delighted to maintain his reputation as the strong silent man who despised women—a reputation which he created several years ago in the Sudan by telling the War Office that if they insisted on sending him women nurses he would duck them in the Nile. The British Red Cross Society is controlled by peeresses and other powerful women of the parasite class, and by the type of fashionable doctor whose career is a personal triumph over the rich rather than the impersonal triumph of the man of science over truth; and so as a body it showed Anti-Feminist tendencies. Yet to-day the khaki ambulances with the red cross on the sides draw up at hospitals which are wholly staffed by women, and the men who are left there are not sorry. "They give a man a chance," they say. It is an inarticulate testimony that the Victorians were wrong, and that a woman is more and not less valuable as a worker because of the slight permanent glow of sympathy which accompanies her capacity for motherhood.

Winifred Brooke Irvine: "Night-Work in a Munition Factory"

Of the male employment preserves forced open to women by wartime needs, most contentious were the mechanical trades. A woman's ability to operate a lathe, a welding torch, or a drill press struck a blow to the symbolic center of masculinity, the essence of blue collar identity. Men responded in ways not always predictable. Sometimes they accepted and encouraged their new colleagues. More often they tried to intimidate women into leaving, or hid their tools to hamper their work. Supervisors, on the other hand, found themselves pulled by the need to soothe their male work force while acknowledging that newly hired females did as well, or even better, than the men. Much to the disappointment of some women, however, an implied promise to the men was fulfilled when the war ended: the women were forced to cede their places to males.

***Atlantic Monthly*, July 1918**

March 8

A very distressing accident happened to-day: one of the lathe-operators caught her hand in the machine, and it was badly cut and bruised. No one knows exactly how it could have happened, as the machine was well protected; but they think that perhaps the ragged edge of her glove got caught. She was wonderfully brave, and didn't scream or make any fuss, although she suffered terribly. She was taken at once to the hospital, and we have felt miserable all day.

Our matron is an excellent manager of "woman-power," and has chosen the workers for the different machines in a way that shows she understands, not only the physical, but the mental capabilities of the workers. She is strict, but just, and we can always get a fair hearing when any complaints are to be made.

The stolid strong women are working the heavy milling machines, the younger, more delicate girls do the drill-work, and the tall women, with a good deal of endurance, she thinks best for the lathes. As our foreman says, "There are only certain temperaments suited to the lathes"; and I think I know what he means: one must not be stolid, but it doesn't do to get nervous and worried when things go wrong.

March 9

When we got to the factory to-day, we heard that skilled mechanics had been put on our machines. The work is not being turned out fast enough by the women, and a certain contract has to be put through before the end of the month.

I was happy to find that my machine had no operator, so I went straight to work just as if nothing unusual had happened. Mr. A—and the head-foreman laughed, and asked me if I didn't want a new job. I said, "Certainly not, I can work just as well as any man." Mr. A—turned to the foreman and said, "Put Mrs. Irvine's machine in good order, and she can try and beat the men."

The work went beautifully, and the lathe worked like a charm; no fuses were spoiled, and I am entirely content with life in general, and fuse-factories in particular.

March 10

Such a day! Such fun! This morning only five of the "skilled mechanics" were operating the lathes; nobody explained their absence and at noon only three were left.

We were told this evening that they had been a bit too skilled and quick, and had spoiled hundreds of the precious fuses by not taking enough care. If the truth were known, I really believe Mr. A—and the foreman are quite pleased at this turn of events. They have always been tremendously anxious for the women to do well, and I feel sure that only the stern necessity of business made the firm put the men in our places. Still, it is a little bit of a joke, and they quite see, appreciate, and also laugh at it, which I think is very good-natured.

March 12

The women are back in their places, and contentment reigns! I had an interesting day, as I was given the defective fuses, to remedy the mistakes the men had made. It was, fortunately, possible to save a great many of them.

March 15

I want above all things to be a tool-setter, but I believe there is a rule in the union preventing the women from taking up this branch of the work. In the English munition factories they had the same rule when women first began to work; but as time went on, and the men had to leave, the women were found to be excellent tool-setters, and the rule was changed.

Rule or no rule, I set most of the tools on my own lathe, and it saves so much time, that my record is going up for the number of fuses turned out each day.

March 20

I have my munition badge: it is given to any woman who has been employed for a month in a munition factory, and at the end of six months' work in the same factory, it has a bar attached to it, and becomes the property of the worker. Any woman who has such a badge in her possession when the war ends, will be given a medal by the government.

I set a tool to-day that is the hardest one of all to adjust properly. When I told the foreman, he gave me a whack on my shoulder and said, "We'll have to put you on the Union. You're just full of mechanics."

When I recovered my balance and had caught my breath, I felt very much amused. If I was put on the Union, I might be called the "Most High Grand Llama of the Loyal and Ancient Order of the Serrating Tool." I wonder if I should be expected to march in the Labor-Day parade, and wear a blue-silk apron trimmed with gold fringe.

Women in Work May Not Benefit Society

Honoré Willsie, Editorial: "Think It Out First"

Many men found it difficult to conceive of the possibility that women could wish to make themselves useful beyond their traditional nurturing, family roles. Continued opposition to President Wilson's contention that women ought to have the vote led Congress to debate the amendment for six months.

It took another year and a half for state ratification. Most women, detractors contended, would wish to continue in their traditional roles and were not interested in voting. Additionally, they feared that a small feminist group might be able to distort the voting system.

Delineator, July 1917

How can women go about doing the most helpful thing while America is at war?

This is the question thousands of women's clubs and individual women are asking to-day.

We would suggest that first of all, women keep cool; that whatever offer they make to their country they make after mature deliberation. Why do the hysterical, the spectacular, the short-thing, when a little thought would be productive of a really good idea?

We know the mother of three children who says she has gone in for Red Cross nursing. She is gadding about all day long, trying to raise funds and enthusiasm, while her children run the neighborhood and her husband sits down to cold and belated meals.

We know another woman who has donned a fascinating khaki uniform and is driving an automobile for a trucking firm. This woman has wealth and is a splendid executive. Why does she waste herself in the cheaply spectacular?

Another woman is making patchwork quilts for the boys in the trenches. The boys in the trenches don't want patchwork quilts. There is a great need of uniforms for our soldiers. This woman is a tailor by trade.

Thousands of women are knitting for soldiers and sailors. A splendid idea. but why not also look up the families of these men and find out whether they may not need help as much as the soldiers and sailors?

Above all things, try to be wisely productive. First of all, see to it that in your own home you are sanely economical. Free your housemaid, if you can, for work in the factories, where the need of her is dire. Do your own housework, seeing to it that your husband and your children do their just share. Do your own sewing, but see to it that in freeing your dressmaker she is put in touch with the larger needs of the country.

Questions

1. After the war, millions of conscripted men returned to civilian life without jobs. Based on their wartime sacrifice, did the women who held those

jobs have a patriotic duty to give them up to the returning men? Why or why not?

2. Women in World War I peace societies sometimes argued they were compelled to oppose war because they were women. Why would they make this argument?
3. Military leaders in World War I did not consider women fit for combat service. Why would they have held this opinion? Why do military leaders today believe differently? Have women changed or has American society changed?
4. Why did men during this time oppose women joining labor unions?

Chapter 18

Free Speech During Wartime

Debate about the war in the American press far surpassed that of Europe. In 1914 the United States enjoyed the world's most progressive, wealthy, and free journalism. It emanated from a country remarkably diverse in language and culture, supporting powerful journalists writing not only in English but also in German and other languages. The country's free-press traditions reached back more than a hundred years, longer than that of any other major warring nation. Moreover, America could stand above the melee, both politically as a neutral country and practically as a continent separated by an ocean. Leisurely debates over the purpose and value of war in society could not easily be undertaken among nations scrambling to send divisions of warriors to the front. Free speech in Europe became a luxury too dangerous to indulge in, even in liberal democracies such as England and France.

It was to America that one would look for the greatest discussion during the war, but the United States was also hampered from the start by censorship and control. Philosophical debate grew from a core of actual news, reports of battles, and aftermath. That required American reporters to actually travel to the front and to submit to the control of the military leaders. These leaders were uniformly hostile to the press regardless of whether they were from neutral nations. In fact, both Britain and France forbade reporters at the front, while the supposedly more autocratic Germany and Austria made better accommodations. America's most famous celebrity reporter, Richard Harding Davis, left Europe in a huff, saying he could not cover a war so tightly restricted. Allied sympathizer Theodore Roosevelt actually had to make a scene in London, saying the allies were hurting their cause by so tightly controlling the news from the front. The British government then begrudgingly acquiesced to a few American correspondents. The scene of press freedom in World War I before 1917 places a freedom-loving United States against a control-obsessed Europe.

But this scene changed as dramatically, as the hurricane of patriotism followed Wilson's call to war on April 7, 1917. Debate about war was declared over—first unofficially, then officially. Gusts of support for war grew to a typhoon sweeping away opposition like dust in the wind, blowing through American institutions from universities to union halls. Those few who tried to remain standing—socialists, pacifists, Germanophiles, and Anglophobes—might have felt like they were standing in a true windstorm, given that attacks threatened them not only intellectually but also physically. The day Wilson declared war marked the effective end of free speech in the United States.

Wilson had not expected such a storm of support. He considered many reasons why joining a European war would be problematic. His country was a melange of antagonistic nationalities and classes. Its most influential immigrant minority came from Germany, the enemy's homeland. A second important minority, the Irish, embodied generations of scorn for their English rulers. The United States had no military tradition and, in fact, had a strong distrust of authority, which could threaten resistance to army service. These fears drove the U.S. government to aggressively control possible subversives who might undermine the war effort, no matter how minor they may have appeared. A profusion of carrots and sticks set up through agencies and legislation assured official intrusion in just about everyone's professional and personal life. Deviance by action or utterance could not be tolerated.

A first official step was to work on the carrot. America's allies by 1917 had established far-reaching propaganda and censorship operations for Washington to emulate. While censorship of every single printed word could not be feasible in the United States, as it was in France, Americans lived in one of the world's great promotional cultures. Advertising marbled through daily life in all kinds of contexts. This culture could be appropriated to support the war through speech, posters, brochures, booklets, magazines, newspapers, films, books, articles, and advertisements—a blizzard of persuasion aimed to bury any voice of detraction from the still unbowed socialist or pacifist. Former journalist George Creel, as director of the Committee on Public Information set up two weeks after the war declaration, moved with a passion that sometimes grated on American editors. But the material his agency produced tried to tell the war story with accurate fact-based articles designed to persuade. Creel was not comfortable with censorship. He believed it beyond his mandate to encourage voluntary cooperation. Other government agencies armed with strict new legislation would take care of the sterner methods of press control.

The Espionage Act of May 1917 extended broad federal power over free speech for the first time since the ill-fated Alien and Sedition Acts of 1798.

It mandated large fines and prison terms to those who revealed the particulars of military operations. That section of the law was generally acceptable to American editors. Other sections reached beyond that and worried American publishers who expressed formal concern over its restrictions to free speech and press. Section Three called for a $10,000 fine, 20 years in jail, or both, for those who "willfully cause or attempt to cause insubordination, disloyalty, mutiny, refusal of duty, in the military or naval forces of the United States, or shall willfully obstruct the recruiting or enlistment service of the United States." Authorities interpreted this clause as open season to arrest anyone who even vaguely criticized the war effort.

It was not a foregone conclusion that the Espionage Bill would be approved. But as it came up for congressional debate just as stories of a supposed secret knot of "100,000 German spies" swept the country, it passed despite concerns of the press. German immigrants as well as Americans of German ancestry were harassed and sometimes assaulted, repudiating a long acknowledgement of German-American contributions to culture. But the assaults to free speech and liberty in 1917 marked only the beginning of a paranoid frenzy not seen before or since in the world's greatest democracy. The Sedition Act, passed in May 1918 as an amendment to the Espionage Act, extended punishable speech, including punishment for any who "shall willfully utter, print, write, or publish any disloyal, profane, scurrilous, or abusive language about the form of government of the United States, or the Constitution of the United States, or the military or naval forces of the United States." Under this generously interpreted law, 2,200 people were charged and 1,055 were convicted. Yet no one served full terms in jail. Sentences were commuted after the 1919 Red Scare excesses subsided.

Unfortunately, that happened only after a fear frenzy against suspected radicals tied to a perceived communist or anarchist threat to American society ended. Bombings in spring 1919 sparked widespread movements of private surveillance and harassment groups working in obvious contempt of civil liberties protections. Authorities often acquiesced and even participated under President Wilson's indulgence. Nearly five years to the day after the beginning of the war, Attorney General A. Mitchell Palmer created a new division designed to investigate and monitor radical groups in the United States. The director of this division, J. Edgar Hoover, amassed an index of 200,000 entries covering suspicious organizations and individuals, people supposedly encouraging a huge network of Bolshevik operatives threatening the country's foundations. The Red Scare culminated in a nation-wide, coordinated 22-state raid on January 2, 1920. About 4,000 were arrested for what Palmer called the "disease of evil thinking." The "Palmer Raids" were praised at the time, but ensuing months saw Americans becoming uneasy with some of the justice department's more egregious assaults on

Attorney General A. Mitchell Palmer (right, with Woodrow Wilson) feared Bolshevik agents were planning to overthrow the U.S. government, and so hired J. Edgar Hoover to help him identify communist sympathizers. The pair worked together to arrest 10,000 communist suspects or sympathizers in 1919, and another 6,000 in 1920. Many thousands were held without trial. No evidence of conspiracy was found, however, and critics accused Palmer of having devised the "Red Scare" that led to the deportation of several hundred Americans. Courtesy of Library of Congress.

free speech and civil rights. Americans began to agree with one of the country's most outspoken agencies that grew in response to excess of the raids: the American Civil Liberties Union. But Hoover stayed and his Red Scare–inspired agency became the Federal Bureau of Investigation (FBI).

A Free Press During Wartime: Pro

Norman Angell, London, England: "Freedom of Discussion in War Time"

Arguments against a free press during war often center around two presumptions: military secrecy avoids tipping off the enemy and political censorship avoids demoralizing the home front. Evidence can be adduced for both arguments; newspapers offered helpful information to the enemy most obviously in the Franco-Prussian War of 1870, and many critics still believe a free media turned the tide of American opinion against the Vietnam War. (In both cases historical research questions these assumptions.) Angell's argument for free speech could actually be turned against him by less liberal detractors, because not only in England but also in France, press criticism played a major role in creating unstable wartime governments that eventually fell.

Annals of the American Academy of Political and Social Sciences, July 1918

Save for the limitations already indicated, freedom of press, speech and discussion should in the interest of a sane and balanced public opinion even more necessary to democracies in war than in peace, be complete and unhampered.

I am aware it seems ridiculous to urge such a degree of toleration in war time. But I shall base the claim not on any ground of the rights of minorities to certain moral or intellectual privileges. Personally I cannot understand how any claim can be made on that ground when the existence of a nation is at stake; how, in such circumstances, minorities can have any rights, as against the common need, that should be regarded—but precisely on the ground of common need, of advantage to the nation as a whole.

Public opinion in the early stages of war, in every nation, is always in favor of a "truce to discussion." We remind one another then that the time for words has passed and the time for action come. "Talk" is disparaged. We demand the union sacrée. And almost always is that rule first broken by those who at the beginning were most insistent upon its enforcement. Take the case of England. A party truce was declared at the outbreak of war and the feeling against public criticism of the government or its policy was intense. Such public men as attempted anything resembling it were indeed driven from public life for a time, mainly by the influence of the group of papers controlled by Lord Northcliffe. What happened finally was that Mr. Asquith's government was driven out and replaced by another largely as the result of the criticism of Lord Northcliffe's newspapers.

Editorial: "The People's Right to Know"

In the waning years of the war and the waxing years of the peace, Congress considered some 70 bills aimed at restricting speech and civil liberties in the United States. Not all of them passed. The Overman Bill, introduced by Senator Lee S. Overman, a North Carolina Democrat, was an attempt to suppress Bolshevik and other radical speech.

Independent, May 25, 1918

The conduct of the war is the people's business, not exclusively the Administration's business. The people have a right to know how the war is being carried on, with what efficiency, what speed, what effectiveness. They cannot know that of themselves, or find it out for themselves. They have right to look to their representatives in Congress for assurance on this vital point.

If the President is going to insist that Congress may not inquire about these things without being denominated the President's "opponent," the people are come to a pretty pass indeed.

Efficiency in administration, in business or in government, consists in giving a job to some one, granting him full authority to do it, and then holding him to rigid responsibility for doing the job thoroly and well. The President has now been given by Congress, thru the passage of the Overman bill, the utterly free hand he has asked for in executive organization.

He has unprecedented authority in the conduct of the war. He cannot complain if he is held to the most rigid responsibility.

Now, under the American Constitution, the President can be held to responsibility only by public opinion. Public opinion is worthless unless it is based upon knowledge. The public can not know how the war is being conducted. It can either swallow the conduct of the war whole with its eyes blindfolded or it can desire its representatives in Congress to investigate and make public the facts, in so far as is possible to do so without detriment to the progress of the war.

James Harvey Robinson: "The Threatened Eclipse of Free Speech"

The United States by its very establishment as a nation of immigrants ought to have held greater tolerance for diversity of opinion. Oddly, as de Tocqueville pointed out in the 1830s, free discussion and independent opinion has often been less common and more suspect in America than in many other countries. A concern for unity of mind as a basis for a stable state became a standard of the country's leaders through the violent protests over slavery, and even over colonial religious beliefs. In World War I Wilson and many others believed diversity of opinion could dangerously compromise the country's prosecution of a war thousands of miles away, for which the country was materially unprepared.

Atlantic Monthly, December 1917

It may be urged further that war is a very ancient expedient and will bring its inevitable ancient accompaniments. When we start out to kill enemies abroad on a gigantic scale, we are not likely to hesitate to gag those at home who seem directly or indirectly to sympathize with the foe. But just here we may well stop and make a couple of distinctions.

In the first place difference of opinion is not necessarily disloyalty. This name is now applied with the utmost abandon; much as "atheist" was once used to defame any one who differed from the generally accepted religious doctrines, no matter how fervently he believed in God and the Bible. Some people in the United States wish Germany to be victorious; to express this wish publicly, or to do anything with a view of hampering the efficiency of our preparations for war, or to transmit useful information to the enemy, would certainly be disloyal, not to say treasonable. Those, however, who continue to say that they wish we had not entered the war; that some other less horrible policy might have been selected; that war has never yet begotten lasting peace but only new war; that some men loathe shooting their fellow men under government auspices in the same sickening way that they would loathe private murder—such persons are in no way treasonable, and disloyal only in the sense of failing eagerly to cooperate with the majority in a crisis. To accuse them of "giving aid and comfort to the enemy" is not only to use this legal expression in just the sense that it was designed to preclude—namely, constructive treason,—but the charge might facetiously be brought against President Wilson himself, who, by distinguishing between the German people and their government, has, according to the Germans themselves, only solidified their intimate union and fortified their resolution to defend their beloved ruler to the end.

It is this confusion between real traitors on the one hand, and on the other hand those persons whose human sympathy and idealism outrun the common bounds, that fills many of us with dismay. Few readers will feel any misgivings in regard to measures, however harsh, taken against the first group. It is the second category that raises the question of freedom of speech and its proper restraint in war-times.

Editorial: "The Week"

Some of America's most famous war correspondents hastened to Europe as soon as war was declared but all were frustrated that they were kept in the dark and away from the front. Richard Harding Davis, the closest thing the United States had to a media celebrity, gave up in disgust and returned to America as did Irwin S. Cobb, a war correspondent for the Saturday Evening Post. *Yet the dire prediction presented here did not reflect subsequent coverage, or subsequent wars, for that matter. Control over correspondents eased as the war progressed and later wartime leaders generally gave war correspondents wider access to the battlefields. That decision also led to more casualties among journalists.*

Nation, August 6, 1914

"The day of the war correspondent is gone." So telegraphs a war correspondent, Dr. Dillon, from Vienna. He knows that he would not be allowed to go to the front, or to send any reports at all on military operations. Truly the day of Forbes and Burleigh, not to go back to "Bull Run" Russell, is gone. Never again will army commanders give a free run of their headquarters to "chiefs" taking notes to be incontinently printed. The change from the old times, for which the reasons are obvious, has been slow in coming, but is now almost complete. Grim soldiers like Kitchener never had any love for newspaper correspondents, though he was forced to tolerate such a man as G.W. Steevens [sic] both in the Sudan campaign and in the South African. Our own war with Spain showed a relapse from the growing practice, and seemed, as everybody remembers, to be waged by and for the newspapers. The Japanese, in their war with Russia, kept the correspondents at a safe and inglorious distance; and by the time the last Balkan war came along, the shut-down was complete. The military argument for it is convincing. In informing the public, the newspaper informs the enemy; consequently nothing must be published until long after the event, and then only in a form agreeable to the army authorities. This may seem hard on the press, and also on a news-eager public, but it is war.

Anonymous Letter to the Editor: "The United States as Battlefield"

The United States was the ripest neutral plum that all belligerent nations hoped to persuade into war. If this country on its way to world power status could be pushed off the fence, it would become the one ally able to truly make a difference in a war that had ground to a stalemate. Germany's propaganda in the United States proved less effective than Britain's; Britain also had the opportunity to capitalize on German blunders, particularly the Lusitania sinking. The German government obviously did not understand the power of propaganda in World War I. By World War II, however, Nazi propaganda minister Josef Goebbels had studied his enemies and was able to use their techniques to effectively persuade his own people.

Nation, September 10, 1914

Sir: With all the attention that international congresses have given to defining the position of neutral states during time of war, one inevitable danger has been overlooked. That is the danger which the neutral states must suffer as the diplomatic battlefield of the warring Powers.

A neutral state, to remain neutral, must adopt sooner or later a censorship of the press. This censorship may be voluntary, as that in the United States at present, or legal, as in Switzerland. It is, nevertheless, a censorship. Moreover, the inhabitants of a neutral state must be excessively guarded in every utterance concerning the international situation. Why, then, when the neutrals themselves must exercise such care, should they be subjected to the incendiary efforts of foreign diplomats?

As neutrals, we in the United States have the power to keep out the armed forces of belligerent countries. Why should we not have the power to silence the diplomatic forces of those same countries? We certainly cannot keep out these official representatives of friendly Powers; but why cannot we confine them to their official functions, instead of allowing them to do what we ourselves are forbidden to do? Some of them (fortunately not all) take almost daily occasion to instruct us in what our attitude should be, with whom we should cast our sympathies, why we should cut short our admiration for others, in brief, why we should think and act precisely as they would have us think and act.

Gilbert Murray: "Great Britain's Sea Policy"

Britain's Defence of the Realm Act (DORA), passed by Parliament without debate in August 1914, closely regulated civil liberties, not only as they related to free speech but also in a variety of activities thought detrimental to the war effort. It eventually was extended to proscribe numerous behaviors. British subjects could not fly kites, ring church bells, use binoculars, buy a drink for a friend, or light fireworks. One legacy of the DORA is summer time, implemented to give workers an extra hour to work. What Americans call Daylight Savings Time was retained after the war.

Atlantic Monthly, December 1916

Everybody knows that in war censorship is necessary; every nation employs it, Great Britain rather more leniently than the rest. It is a pure myth to suppose that in England we are kept in the dark about important sides of the war which are well known to neutrals. I have been in four different neutral countries since the war began, and have read their newspapers; so I speak with confidence. But it is just the sort of myth that Mr. [Arthur] Bullard accepts without question. As to the Defence of the Realm Act: of course the act gives the executive tremendous powers and would, if continued in normal times, be incompatible with civil liberty. But everybody knows that some such special laws are necessary in war time; there is no nation in Europe which attempts to do without such laws.

Anonymous, *L'Asino*, Rome: "Wartime Humor in Italy"

L'Asino *is Italian for ass, or donkey, undoubtedly reflecting the satirical nature of the publication.*

***New York Times Current History*, April–September 1916**

Newspaper—What is left of the news by the censor.
Scissors—A tool that cuts in order to unite public opinion.
Censor—A man who carves while holding his head in one sack and his sense in another.

A Free Press During Wartime: Con

Ellery C. Stowell, Letter to the Editor: "Rationalism vs. Sedition"

Sedition is seldom considered a crime in contemporary America, but its companion offenses against the state, treason and espionage, still snare those Americans who take action in opposition to the government. Unlike the charge of spying or treason—actually betraying a government to its enemies—sedition is mere speech that might encourage government disruption. Because it so obviously challenges free speech, it is rarely evoked in democracies except during wartime. More people were punished for sedition in the United States during World War I than during any other era. Morris Hillquit was a prominent socialist lawyer who later wrote a history of socialism in the United States.

***Nation*, November 15, 1917**

The first requisite to conduct war effectively is a vigorous government, and the man in the street becomes confused when he is treated to the spectacle of the open toleration of seditious speech. He is not yet, I fear, educated to that ideal point where he can become all the more enthusiastic for the support of a government so liberal. Magnanimity which is bound to be misunderstood as weakness to the extent that it will bring the evil consequences of actual weakness ceases to be rational.

The suppression of the seditious press does not in fact cut off the freest political discussion. Even to-day Morris Hillquit is allowed to flaunt his refusal to support his government before every eye, but prison awaits him if from a soap box he but advise others to do the same. Unless the majority of the people are ready waiting to follow the constituted authorities in this moment of crisis, any attempt to use force in suppressing sedition will recoil on the Government. That is the test. Even after open sedition is stamped out and full autocratic power delivered over to the authorities for the vigorous conduct of the war, public opinion will yet find many a way clearly to indicate what it is thinking—the failure to support successive loans, riots against conscription, or the election of anti-war candidates.

The task of conducting a great war to a successful issue seems now to require the gift to our President of autocratic power such as the world has never known, that the republic suffer no harm. Such power in the hands of one man is fraught with danger undoubtedly, but any other course is more dangerous still. The safety of the whole transcends in importance the safety of any part. Hence, in war all our ordinary constitutional rights and privileges must be suspended.

M. A. De Wolfe Howe: "The Non-Combatant's Manual of Arms"

All allied countries (except Russia), as democracies, hoped first to rely on voluntary censorship. Governments encouraged loyalty, the union sacrée, and national solidarity in the face of a dire threat to the country. In France, England, and the United States, it worked in nearly every case. Even those sworn to bring down the government—radical socialists—generally supported their government in this war. The censorship and coercive laws, therefore, were aimed at a tiny minority of socialists, pacifists, and recent immigrants from Germany who could not support the government in war, no matter what the cause. Today it might be argued that, at least in the United States, this tiny minority had no influence whatsoever on public sentiment. But in the white heat of wartime, no stray voices would be tolerated.

Atlantic Monthly, October 1918

It is the fashion to separate criticism into two varieties, constructive and destructive. The average citizen is not confronted with frequent opportunities to use either of these in matters of universal moment. There is, however, a third variety—obstructive criticism—which he can practice with palpable effect. Far too many of us are constantly employing it. The homely American adage, "Don't shoot the pianist—he is doing his best," expresses the national reprobation of the obstructively critical habit of mind. It is a habit which in time of war leaders of consequences peculiarly dangerous. It would so wreck the discipline of an army that the first symptoms of it call for the rigorous measures by which infectious diseases are stamped out. In the host of non-combatants it must be dealt with chiefly through self-discipline; and the civilian can propose no more fruitful drill for his spirit than that which will put in the place of obstructive criticism a genuine desire to give his government credit for seeking and achieving high ends, whenever it does so, and "getting behind" it in this effort at every opportunity.

Anonymous: "Mr. Creel and the Press Censorship"

George Creel, as de facto chief U.S. propagandist, protested repeatedly that his agency did not enforce censorship, and generally he was right. True censorship came more often from the post office, justice department, and military. The military's insistence on continuing censorship after the war ended on November 11, 1918, incensed American journalists. The government contended that the end of the war did not put an end to delicate matters of national security and treaty negotiations. Thus, censorship continued several months into 1919.

***Nation,* November 30, 1918**

The following statement by Mr. George Creel, chairman of the Committee on Public Information, is printed in the Official U.S. Bulletin of November 21. Although one of the most important statements regarding the censorship issued by the Government during the war, it seems largely to have escaped comment in the American press.

> With respect to my charged connection with the cables and cable censorship, there is not such connection, nor will there be any.
>
> On November 14 announcement was made by the Committee on Public Information of the discontinuance of the volunteer censorship agreement under which the press of the United States has operated with the Government.
>
> On November 15 a formal statement was issued to the effect that all press censorship in connection with cables and mails would be discontinued forthwith.
>
> There is, therefore, no press censorship of any kind existing in the Untied States to-day. No plan of resumption has been suggested or even contemplated.
>
> The whole domestic machinery of the Committee on Public Information is being dismantled and will cease operation by December 14 at the very latest. As for my work in Europe, and that of the Committee on Public Information, it will have absolutely no connection whatsoever with the control of the cables, any form of censorship, or any supervision over the press.

[Editorial response]

Unfortunately, Mr. Creel's statement, frank and unqualified as it is, comes right on the heels of the taking over of the cables by the Government and their assignment to the care of Mr. Burleson. The seizure of the cables at this late day, when the war is over, Germany beaten, and the necessity

George Creel proved to be a controversial choice as the country's first official propagandist. Named head of the Committee on Public Information, he sometimes responded dismissively and abrasively to editors' concerns over government propaganda tactics. Historical scrutiny of the committee's production, however, has shown it to have been generally truthful. Courtesy of Library of Congress.

of Government supervision no longer apparent, is only to be explained, one would think, on the assumption of so complete a breakdown of cable service under private management as to make Government interference imperative. It is true that the cable companies were temporarily swamped with business immediately following the conclusion of the armistice, and that the rival companies are charged with failure to cooperate with each other in emergencies; but if there be sufficient evidence to show conclusively that Government control was necessary, it has not been produced. Mr. Burleson's attitude toward the press has certainly been such as to lend color to the charge that the seizure of the cables at this time was intended to give the Government complete control of newspaper cable service during the peace conference; and while Mr. Creel's statement is explicit, suspicion will not down.

Albert Lundberg, Fairdale, North Dakota, Letter to the Editor: "A Rationale of Free Speech"

Lundberg was born in 1894 in rural North Dakota. In his 30s he decided to return to school, graduating from the University of North Dakota law school in 1932, and serving as Second Judicial District judge from 1951 to 1963. Lundberg's ringing endorsement of free speech during wartime reflects the strongly independent, often socialist, sentiment of rural North Dakotans during this period in opposition to outside control by large industrial interests in St. Paul and the east.

Nation, January 3, 1918

The objections of free speech are of a kind that reveals, on the part of the objectors, a disbelief in the ability of the "man in the street" to judge intelligently—a fear that, without a guardian of some kind, he will go wrong. Yet not only does a democracy assume his ability to judge wisely, but all the superiority democracy can claim over other forms of government is due to this very competence. The popular rule that distinguishes a democracy is justified only if the people are able to discern the truth more clearly and make wiser decisions than the smaller groups in other forms of government. If democracy cannot so justify itself, it is a failure, and has no right to ask for continued existence.

Just how much safer is the judgment of democracy than that of other forms of government, I shall not presume to say; but let us assume, for purposes of demonstration, that one of three instances democracy would make two wise decisions, while other forms of government would only make one. If, knowing this, one were to admit that a certain undemocratic policy might be justified one would not thereby "confess that his principles are too imperfect to serve as a practical guide"; but merely concede that while such a measure might be justified, the odds are two to one that it would be most unwise an inexpedient. The odds in favor of free speech and the popular control which it makes possible, and the odds in favor of democracy itself.

Now that we are in the midst of a great crisis, with the most momentous problems to solve, one is tempted to ask whether it is "really rational" not to permit discussion, and invite popular judgment upon the policies to be pursued. Are the defenders of democracy to be denied the protection of the system they defend?

It will be argued, of course, that "control" of speech and press will permit all proper discussion, but a moment's consideration of things as they are will prove this contention a fallacy. Control must necessarily be exercised by an individual or a department, and is open to all autocratic and bureaucratic abuses. The evils of control differ only in degree from those of complete suppression. It stifles the most valuable of opinions—that of the moderate masses—whose voice will not then be heard until the damage done by an unwise policy is all but irreparable.

Editorial: "For a Sensible Censorship"

Most American editors requested and welcomed voluntary censorship guidelines in their patriotic effort to avoid harming the war effort. In fact, many editors zealously self-censored beyond what the guidelines suggested. These editors did not as enthusiastically favor the government's efforts to mobilize public opinion at home as it mobilized troops for the front. The flood of material from the Committee on Public Information aimed to inundate the media and by the war's end 75 million pieces of published material had been produced.

Nation, May 3, 1917

No one—no newspaper, certainly—denies that in this war a censorship is needed. In our Civil War the press had too great liberties in military matters, which it too frequently abused. Our war with Spain seemed sometimes to be a perfect revel of newspaper correspondents and sensational publications. If we had not learned something since then, and also taken to heart the lessons of the European war, it would be much to our discredit. There is no real objection to a sensible censorship. Held within its proper limits, it scarcely needs a law to establish it, since all decent newspapers and news associations would heed the requests of the authorities. But in this we speak of printing news, not of expressing opinions. A censorship that attempted to prevent the latter was, as we can at present perceive, doomed in advance in the United States. When the President avows that he has no wish to be exempt from criticism, we take it that no subordinate member of the Government will venture to assume that to find fault with him is to make glad the heart of the Kaiser.

Anonymous: "A Growing Demand for the Suppression of the German-American Press"

Hermann Hagedorn, one of several authors who issued a strong call for suppression of the American German-language press, also was a loyal supporter and biographer of war advocate Theodore Roosevelt. Among the variety of proposals to strangle the supposedly seditious German press was a call to levy a license fee of 1 to 10 cents a copy. Others called for the simple blanket suppression of every paper. Neither of these proposals were implemented, but persecution both public and private shattered the vitality of this once strong voice in the country's marketplace of ideas.

Current Opinion, September 1917

In the United States there are about 450 journals printed in the German language. The dozen largest of these, it is estimated, have about one million readers. The loyalty of this press is being sharply challenged and the demand for its suppression is becoming insistent. "Why," asks the Louisville Herald, "is there a German-American press?" It proceeds to answer its own query. Such a press exists not to teach a regard for American institutions but to keep alive reverence for Germany, to foster a "sentimental separateness" by decrying the people of other nationalities, and to "solidify the Germans among us for political reasons." Most of them profess to have independent sources of information. If the Louisville paper is correct, they "get no cable news, no specials, no information by wire that is not open to all the newspaper world," and many have no news-service whatever, simply translating from the English papers what suits their purposes best. . . .

About the same conclusions are reached by Mr. Hermann Hagedorn from his study of the German-American press. He quotes from their headlines, their news columns and their editorials—eulogies of the Kaiser and Hindenburg, abuse of England and France, sneers at America's motives, etc.—and says:

"The foregoing quotations are characteristic, not only of the Arbeiter-zeitung and the Deutsch-Amerikanische Krieger-Zeitung, but os most of the other German-American newspapers, such as Amerika, the Westliche Post, the Herold des Glaubens, the Friedensbote, all of St. Louis; the New Yorker-Herold, the New-Yorker Staats-Zeitung, the Illionis Staatszeitung, the Milwaukee Vorwarts, and certain papers printed in the English language, such as Mr. Victor Berger's Milwaukee Leader and George Sylvester Viereck's egregiously misnamed American Weekly . . . [ellipses in original] The editors say they are for America. They never say, however, that they are against Germany."

Mr. Hagedorn admits that it might be difficult, "from a legal point of view," to justify the suppression of these papers, since it is their atmosphere, rather than specific statements, that constitute the menace, and "atmosphere is an illusive peg to hang an indictment upon." But from any other than a legal point of view he regards "the speedy elimination from our midst of the German-language papers" as a desirable thing.

Anonymous: "The Case of Mr. Hearst and His Newspapers"

William Randolph Hearst's newspapers strongly opposed the country's joining the war, particularly on the side of the Britain. After April 1917 they acquiesced to support the war effort itself, but still did not support the allies, and criticized harassment and punishment of the antiwar socialist press. In predictable response the newspapers were targeted for calumny; Hearst was hanged in effigy; Roosevelt, writing in the Kansas City Star, *demanded to know why Hearst's papers had not been denied mailing privileges. Some Republicans declared it was because Hearst was a Democrat.*

Current Opinion, July 1918

There is a call form various sources for the suppression of his papers. The charge of disloyal utterances has not been raised, as far as we have noted, against his magazines; but no less a personage than ex-President Roosevelt, in a letter of about 10,000 words, presented before the U.S. Senate and printed in the Congressional Record, charges the Hearst papers with disloyalty, asserts that Mr. Hearst's campaign "is primarily a campaign in favor of Germany" and declares that "just so long as Mr. Hearst's publications are permitted in the mails Mr. Burleson is without excuse for excluding any other publication from them."

Starting a Boycott in Jersey and New York Towns

In a number of places near New York City vigorous steps have been taken to prevent the circulation of Hearst's New York papers. The West Essex Security League, with a large membership in nine New Jersey towns, whose president is a member of the Advisory Committee of President Wilson's War Board, has appealed to the Postmaster General to forbid the use of the mails to the Hearst papers. The Common Council of Mount Vernon has passed an ordinance forbidding the sale or distribution of the papers in that town. An injunction has been granted by a New York City judge against carrying out this ordinance and the Council has taken an appeal to the Court of Appeals. In Rahway, N.J., the Mayor has issued a proclamation requesting all citizens to refrain from purchasing and all news dealers from selling the Hearst papers. . . .

Freedom of the Press and Suppression of the Hearst Papers

Mr. Hearst finds defenders in at least one body—the Central Federated Union of New York City. In a series of resolutions it declares that the Hearst papers "have loyally and patriotically supported the Government of the United States in its prosecution of the war" and denounces the efforts to suppress their sale as meddling with a legitimate business upon which thousands of Union employees are dependent for a livelihood: and as "an unlawful and un-American exhibition of prejudice and intolerance." The Elmira Telegram insists that there is no better patriot anywhere than Mr. Hearst, that his papers have "fought for the uplift of humanity in this and other lands" and says deprecatingly, "the prevailing delusion is seditionitis." For the most part the press of the country, while publishing the news pertaining to the campaign against the Hearst papers, has little or nothing to say about it editorially. . . .

Mr. Hearst Issues a Challenge to Mr. Roosevelt

Mr. Hearst's response to Mr. Roosevelt takes up nearly a full page in his paper. Part of it is a vigorous denunciation of Mr. Roosevelt himself for "mental and moral deterioration" and for "the childish mental processes" of "his old age" (Mr. Roosevelt is not quite sixty, five years older than Mr. Hearst); partly to a defense of the President, construing the attack which Mr. Roosevelt makes upon Postmaster Burleson for not suppressing the Hearst papers while suppressing Tom Watson's paper and others, as an "assault upon the integrity and the patriotism of the President"; and partly to a defense of his own record. He claims that he did denounce the sinking of the Lusitania over and over again, tho not considering it an adequate cause of war. He claims to have advocated incessantly the building up a large navy and army, and to have pressed for conscription, tho he does not refer to his utterances about keeping out troops and ships and munitions and food here at home.

George Creel, Chairman, Committee on Public Information, Washington, D.C.: "Public Opinion in War Time"

George Creel's journalism background in New York, Denver, and Kansas City gave him some credibility as director of the first federal agency of persuasion designed, as Creel noted in his memoirs after the war, to undertake "the world's greatest adventure in advertising." Creel certainly did not, as he said, undertake coercive censorship. Other agencies were better able to control offending publications. The committee's press releases were reprinted in the government's first daily newspaper, the Official Bulletin, *which climbed to a circulation of 118,000 by the war's end. Its dispatches showed exemplary accuracy—as far as they went. They did broadly conceal material the government believed would harm morale at home, a decision beyond the committee's supposed intention to control only matters of direct military importance.*

Annals of the American Academy of Political and Social Sciences, July 1918

Now more than at any other time in history the importance of public opinion has come to be recognized. The fight for it is a part of the military program of every country, for every belligerent nation has brought psychology to the aid of science. Not only has Germany spent millions of dollars on its propaganda, but it has been very vigorous in protecting its soldiers and civilians from counter-propaganda. We are highly honored by having both Austria and Germany establish a death penalty for every representative of the Committee on Public Information, and imprisonment and execution are visited on everyone who is found in possession of the literature that we drop from airplanes or that we shoot across the line from mortars, or that we smuggle into the countries by various means.

Any discussion of public opinion must necessarily be prefaced by some slight attempt at definition. Just what do we mean by it? A great many people think that public opinion is a state of mind, formed and changed by the events of the day or by the events of the hour; that it is sort of a combination of kaleidoscope and weathercock. I disagree with this theory entirely. I do not believe that public opinion has its rise in the emotions, or that it is tipped form one extreme to the other by every passing rumor, by every gust of passion, or by every storm of anger. I feel that public opinion has its source in the minds of people, that it has its base in reason, and that it expresses slow-formed convictions rather than any temporary excitement or any passing passion of the moment. I may be wrong, but since mine is the responsibility, mine is the decision, and it is upon that decision that every policy of the committee has been based. We have never preached any message of hate. We have never made any appeal to the emotions, but we have always by every means in our power tried to drive home to the people the causes behind this war, the great fundamental necessities that compelled a peace-loving nation to take up arms to protect free institutions and preserve our liberties. . . .

There has been nothing so distressing to me as this absurd assumption on the part of a large number of people that the Committee on Public Information is a censorship and interested in suppression rather than expression. We do not touch censorship at any point, because censorship in the United

States is a voluntary agreement managed and enforced by the press itself. The desires of the government with respect to the concealment of its plans, its policies, the movement of troops, the departure of troops, and so on, go to the press upon a simple card that bears this paragraph: "these requests go to the press without larger authority than the necessity of the war-making branches. Their enforcement is a matter for the press itself." I am very glad and very proud to be able to say that this voluntary censorship has a greater force than could ever have been obtained by any law.

Arthur W. Page, Editorial: "Public Confidence and the Censor"

Arthur W. Page, as editor of World's Work, *reflected a number of editors' concerns that Creel's background was not of sufficient caliber to assume a role of this magnitude. But Creel had been a strong supporter of Wilson, and the president returned the favor, despite the journalist's fairly obscure credentials in contrast to the many well-known journalists of the era. Most historians have concluded that despite the contemporary doubters, Creel's committee exerted a powerful influence on opinion during the war—perhaps too powerful as it contributed to the fanatic anti-German sentiment that denied democratic rights to American citizens who would not join the prowar majority.*

World's Work, July 1917

The situation boils down to something like this: Some censorship is pretty generally admitted to be necessary. The Constitution provides that the freedom of the press shall not be abridged. There is, then, no logical theoretical solution to the problem. And when that is the case it is always wise to look for a man in whom the public puts its trust and put him in charge. It needs a man of Cabinet grade to handle the situation.

It is not saying anything against Mr. Creel to say that he has not sufficient of the public's confidence to give him a good chance to succeed in so difficult a position. Until his appointment the public hardly knew him at all. Even in his own profession he could not be considered a distinguished member. Regardless of his qualities, his appointment, therefore, could not give the press or the public the needed confidence. Nor has his conduct of the office so far made up what the impression of the appointment lacked. And on the other hand there is nothing in Mr. Creel's career that gives evidence that he has the expert knowledge that would make him particularly valuable to the State, War, or Navy Departments.

In time of war it is perhaps more justifiable than at other times to suggest that a gentleman who has undertaken to serve the Government perhaps at personal sacrifice, as many have, should resign in order that he may be succeeded by some man whose past career and reputation would give him an opportunity to serve immediately on a basis that Mr. Creel could only attain by the slow growth of public confidence in him.

Post Office Censorship: Destructive Power

Max Eastman: "Some Recent Workings of the Censorship"

A wartime climate favoring suppression of political opinions repugnant to most Americans left the post office with powers so broad the postmaster sometimes hesitated to use them. Albert S. Burleson did not suppress mainstream antiadministration publications such as Hearst's newspapers. But he happily declared unmailable the small-circulation socialist periodicals for promoting "disloyal, profane, scurrilous or abuse language" specified by the 1918 Sedition Act. Max Eastman's The Masses *of New York was the most famous socialist publication to lose mailing privileges in August 1917 for publishing antiwar cartoons and a poem. An indictment against Eastman was dismissed in 1919.*

***Masses*, October 1916**

In the past six months six radical periodicals have been suppressed by the Post Office Department without the formality of a trial and without possibility of redress: Revolt, of New York; Alarm, of Chicago; The Blast, of San Francisco; Voluntad (Spanish); Volni Listy (Bohemian); and Regeneracion (English-Spanish). All of these papers, except the last one, were denied the privileges of the mails on the grounds that the Post Office Department "did not like the tone of the paper." Regeneracion, as will be remembered, was handled more crudely: the Federal Department of Justice confiscated its presses on the ground that an article which it published, advising the Mexican people not to trust the Carranza government, was "treason." And at the same time two of its editors, the Magon brothers, were beaten into insensibility by detectives, and the entire editorial board was indicted.

The Post Office examination and censorship of mail is strictly illegal. Several times the Post Office has asked Congress to grant it definite rights in this matter, and Congress has refused. Cases which have been carried up to the United States Supreme Court have been decided on the legal merits of the particular case–the Supreme Court has refused to pass on the principle of the Post Office censorship.

This method of suppressing publications without trial was begun during the administration of Theodore Roosevelt, when La Questione Soziale, of Paterson, N.J., was so forbidden to publish or circulate.

We bring these instances of lawless tyranny to the attention of our readers, to further prove that the governing class of the United States has not the slightest respect for that "law and order" which it professes to uphold against "dangerous revolutionists" like us.

Editorial: "Censorship of the Press"

Loss of mailing privileges in a pre-Internet era almost guaranteed a periodical would be forced out of business; succeeding laws made private delivery also illegal. Nearly 50 newspapers lost mailing privileges and another 30 barely retained them by promising to avoid political topics. The German-language press, also plumb target of postal control, lost half its circulation and half its titles.

***Nation*, October 4, 1917**

It is said, of course, that this sword placed in the hand of the Postmaster-General will seldom be used. He himself promises to be merciful! But any one must be ignorant of the history of the abuses of unlimited administrative discretion, especially in war times, who does not see a danger here. It is not purely a question of the liberty of the press, but of the fundamental rights of the citizen. One of them is not to be punished before he is found guilty; but under this new plan of press censorship, a man might be irretrievably ruined before the courts got round to holding him innocent. There is surely something basically wrong in this. A newspaper cannot be accused of standing up for its own selfish interest when it points out that a blow aimed primarily at the press strikes at the very foundations of justice. No one defends the printing of treasonable or lawless matter. Upon those guilty of this offense, let the law fall as heavily as you please. But let it be the law as judicially determined, not as the whim of some administrative officer may decide. And while a man is fighting for justice in the courts, let not his property be destroyed by official order.

We have tried to state impartially and calmly the substance of the case against the new press censorship. But behind the amended legislation, fraught with possibilities of injustice as it is, there lies a mistaken philosophy. Its central vice is the notion that suppression is better than freedom. Its chief blunder is in thinking that agitation can be stopped by unjust treatment of agitators. Crime can be repressed, and should be. Open defiance of the law can be put down with a hard hand. But discussion, dissent, free criticism of officials and of policies, cannot be stamped out in one quarter without creating them in intensified form in many other quarters.

Editorial: "Must We Go to Jail?"

Victor Berger, Austrian-born editor of the post office suppressed Milwaukee Leader, *was sentenced to 20 years' imprisonment for violating the Espionage Act. It did not matter that he was also a congressman, the first American socialist elected to that office. His conviction was eventually overturned by the U.S. Supreme Court, but the court upheld the mailing ban on the newspaper. Finally, mailing privileges were restored three years after the war's end, as postwar Red Scare hysteria waned and a new postmaster succeeded Burleson.*

***North American Review*, November 1917**

The Espionage Act approved by the President on June 15 provided that no publication "containing any matter advocating or urging treason, insurrection or forcible resistance to any law of the United States is hereby declared to be nonmailable." Very good! "Treason," as we reiterated last month, "must be made odious," by all available means. But now comes a supplementary provision in the Trading with the Enemy Act, approved on October 6, to the effect that "it shall be unlawful for any person, firm, corporation, or association, to transport, carry, or otherwise publish or distribute any matter which is made nonmailable" by the Espionage Act, under penalty of $500 fine or of imprisonment for a year or both.

What does this mean? Penalties can still be exacted, we suppose, only after convictions by courts of law, but it is within the province of the Postmaster General to pronounce a periodical "nonmailable" and to ruin it by stopping its publication and distribution pending appeal and trial. The World calls this "a species of lynch law, of which "the Postmaster General is judge, jury and executioner. . . ."

The solemn truth is that this legislation, interjected surreptitiously as it was, is wicked, vicious, tyrannous and ought never to have been enacted. We beg merely in conclusion, and in friendliness, to suggest to the Postmaster General that he study carefully the First Amendment to the Constitution of the United States and reflect gravely upon the fate which befell John Adams when he undertook to impose his notion of sedition upon a nation of freemen jealous of their liberties and capable of maintaining them.

Victor S. Clark, Letter to the Editor: "German Newspapers"

Most criticism of press censorship and control came from American socialists or liberal publications, the Nation *representing the latter. One of the country's oldest magazines, even by World War I, it had been established in 1865 to promote the rights of newly freed slaves. Oswald Garrison Villard assumed ownership of the newspaper in 1900 after the death of his father,*

Henry, a German immigrant. He supported liberal causes, including women's suffrage, trade union rights, and equal treatment of African Americans. He became editor of the Nation *in 1918, but the comments here were probably written by Harold de Wolf Fuller, who was editor from 1914–1918.*

Nation, June 22, 1918

The reasons for preventing the indiscriminate admission of German periodicals and newspapers are too obvious for comment. Such considerations look primarily toward military safety. Germany has imposed an embargo upon the export of technical and scientific publications likely to contain information of value to the allied countries. Adequate provision is now made for the access of American students and writers to all the sources of information concerning current German thought and sentiment which we possess, and these sources are being largely utilized."

[Editorial response]

If the export of certain publications "likely to contain information of value to the allied countries" is prohibited by Germany, what "obvious" considerations, looking "primarily towards military safety," dictate the exclusion from the United States of other German newspapers or periodicals which are not affected by the embargo, and which, presumably, contain no information which Germany is not willing to have known? And does Mr. Clark mean to imply that a reason which is "obvious" is therefore to be regarded as conclusive?

–Editor.

Addison Hogue, Lexington, Virginia, Letter to the Editor: "Assaults on the Press"

Edward L. Godkin was founder of the Nation *and editor until 1901. It was combined with the* New York Evening Post *weekend edition, and as a liberal bastion of New York, successfully crusaded against the city's corrupt Tammany Hall politicians. Godkin also edited the* Evening Post.

Nation, June 1, 1916

Sir: When we remember that one of the strongest bulwarks of our liberties is a free press, it seems passing strange that the newspapers of the country apparently take no notice of two bills now before the House, the Siegel bill (H.R. 491) and the Fitzgerald bill (H.R. 6468), both introduced by New York members. Mr. Siegel wants the Postmaster-General to have the power to forbid the use of the mails to any publication that "contains any article which tends to expose any race, creed, or religion to either hatred, contempt, ridicule, or obloquy!" Would not that worthy official have a time of it!

Mr. Fitzgerald has introduced for the second time a bill that was smothered in the committee last year. He wishes to empower the Postmaster-General to exclude from the mails "books, pamphlets . . . or other publications, matter, or thing of an indecent, immoral, scurrilous character." As we already have laws provided for such "things," laws that allow the offending publisher to employ counsel and to have his case argued before a judge and jury, there is no possible valid reason for putting such tremendous and dangerous power in the hands of a single individual. The Fatherland has been deemed by many persons in this country to be rabidly "scurrilous" against our President; but for one man to have the power to suppress it would be perfectly intolerable, if we are to have a free press as one of the cornerstones of our liberties.

Many of the Nation's readers remember the time when Mr. Godkin was arrested time and again for his onslaughts on a corrupt organization in New York City. Mr. Godkin had his counsel and his jury, and, of course, was promptly vindicated. But suppose a Tammany sympathizer had been Postmaster-General—what then, if he alone could have suppressed the Nation?

It would surely seem that the papers of the country would sprint so earnestly to the defence of their privileges as not to leave a ghost of a chance for such bills as Messrs. Siegel and Fitzgerald have introduced. Even license in the press would be preferable to such despotic power lodged in the hands of one man. Free discussion is essential to liberty. The discussion may be acrimonious, abusive, rancorous, unfair, malignant. If it is libelous, appeal to the courts, not to a Postmaster-General. Otherwise let us stand immovably by this saying of Woodrow Wilson ("The State: Government of Rome"):

> "Discussion is the greatest of all reformers. It rationalizes everything it touches. It robs principles of all false sanctity and throws them back on their reasonableness. If they have no reasonableness, it ruthlessly crushes them out of existence and sets its own conclusions in their steed."

Post Office Censorship: Necessary Power

Anonymous: "The Press under Post Office Censorship"

Burleson was first postmaster general from Texas, and is sometimes cited as the most hated of all politicians who held that position. This is most likely because his service in that position coincided with World War I, giving the conservative Democrat an opportunity to control liberal publications. He exercised that power with clear relish. Burleson also is not remembered fondly for his racial prejudice: he segregated post offices and fired many African Americans who were working in those offices. On the positive side, under Burleson's watch rural mail service improved and air mail service was inaugurated.

New York Times Current History, October 1917–March 1918

The chief opponent of press control by the Postmaster General was Senator Norris of Nebraska, who pointed out that the new provision took away from a publisher his right to fight an order in the courts under after it was useless to fight; that it vested in the Postmaster General—an administrative officer of the Government—the power to adjudge a publisher guilty in advance of trial by any judicial tribunal, and to destroy his business through a mere edict. the Postmaster General had already put out of business thirty-eight or forty publications, under the provisions of the Espionage act, and not one of these publishers had been arrested for violation of that act. Yet, Senator Norris contended, if the Postmaster General was within his right every one of these men was guilty of a crime, and should be punished by imprisonment.

Statement by Mr. Burleson

Publications need not fear suppression under the new censorship provision, Postmaster General Burleson explained in an interview on Oct. 9, unless they transgress the bounds of legitimate criticism of the President, the Administration, the army, the navy, or the conduct of the war. Mr. Burleson continued:

We shall take great care not to let criticism which is personally or politically offensive to the Administration affect our action. But if newspapers go as far as to impugn the motives of the Government, and thus encourage insubordination, they will be dealt with severely.

For instance, papers may not say that the Government is controlled by Wall Street or munition manufacturers, or any other special interests. Publication of any news calculated to urge the people to violate law would be considered grounds for drastic action. We will not tolerate campaigns against conscription, enlistments, sale of securities, or revenue collections. We will not permit the publication or circulation of anything hampering the war's prosecution or attacking improperly our allies.

Mr. Burleson explained that the policy of the foreign-language newspapers would be judged by their past utterances and not by newly announced intentions. "We have files of these papers, and whether we license them or not depends on our inspection of the files," he said. German-language newspapers would be required to publish English translations. No Socialist paper would be barred from the mails, Mr. Burleson said, unless it contained treasonable or seditious matter. "The trouble," he added, "is that most Socialist papers do contain this matter."

That Socialist newspapers did oppose the war was admitted by Morris Hillquit, when he appeared at the hearing at the Post Office Department in Washington on Oct. 15 on behalf of the New York Call, which had been summoned to show cause why it should not be deprived of its mail privileges.

President Wilson's Attitude

President Wilson's views are indicated in a letter to Max Eastman, editor of The Masses, a Socialist magazine which has been declared non-mailable. The President wrote:

I think that a time of war must be regarded as wholly exceptional, and that it is legitimate to regard things which would in ordinary circumstances be innocent as very dangerous to the public welfare, but the line is manifestly exceedingly hard to draw, and I cannot say that I have any confidence that I know how to draw it.

I can only say that a line must be drawn, and that we are trying, it may be clumsily, but genuinely, to draw it without fear or favor or prejudice.

Many Socialist and pacifist publications have already been barred from the mails and some have in consequence ceased to exist, the most important of such defunct papers being The American Socialist, published from the headquarters of the Socialist Party.

QUESTIONS

1. During World War I the U.S. government considered free speech to be a dangerous luxury. Why was it so concerned?
2. When contemplating a declaration of war against Germany, which groups worried Wilson the most, and why?
3. When a country is at war, those who speak against the war might discourage men from participating, or might discourage others from supporting the government. Should this be considered traitorous speech?
4. It was clear that communist and anarchist sympathizers advocated revolution, that is, violent overthrow of the government. Should democratic free-speech principles protect such groups?

Chapter 19

War and the Character of the Soldier

Former President Theodore Roosevelt stood as chief advocate of military virtues before and during World War I. His personal creed of action, leading his strenuous life, as he called it, moved toward outright bellicosity after the war declarations of 1914. Roosevelt said President Woodrow Wilson should immediately declare war on Germany. Much to the ex-president's chagrin, Wilson declined. A scholar and teacher, Wilson did not share Roosevelt's conviction that military service was a great virtue and war a noble quest. But millions of Americans did, and when war was finally declared, countless doughboys took with them to France the presumptions of war's benefits that blanketed so many Western nations during this age of confidence and colonialism.

Those from the more educated classes whose ideals governed society at the beginning of the twentieth century echoed arguments as old as war itself. Combat could be a moral renaissance, they declared, a purification of the battlefield, stripped of the detritus of decadent civilization. The noble service of a soldier for his country could give him a cause larger than anything he would find in a life of peacetime endeavors. And if that service should end in the ultimate sacrifice, he would have perished knowing that his was a life given as a noble sacrifice for his country.

War as self-purification was a particularly compelling argument among conservative politicians in all the war's belligerent nations. Not only did such a view encourage some soldiers to enlist, it quelled the angst of loved ones at home, and offered solace to those left should their man not return. No argument that their loved one had enlisted in a foolhardy quest for adventure and glory, or that their government had foolishly warred in a bellicose drive for evanescent chimeras, could sully the survivors' determination to believe that their loved ones had not died in vain. Who could blame them? To face war as it really is brings rage, despair, and lasting pain that nobody wants to shoulder for a lifetime.

But if these arguments so widely believed in World War I sometimes seem less convincing nearly a century later, it does not mean society has abandoned the conviction that military service is a good thing for a man, or a woman. The U.S. Army itself still promotes its seven core values: loyalty, duty, respect, selfless service, honor, integrity, and personal courage. Anyone in civilian life would consider these no less virtuous, and many have presumed the army could take a raw young recruit from a disadvantaged background and turn him into a person of character. Self-confidence, self-control, and understanding; these could be built from scratch by tearing down the selfish ego in boot camp and building up the team player ready to submit to just authority—military now, civilian later.

Roosevelt agreed with Major General Leonard Wood that the experience of boot camp could turn a polycultural America into one like-minded nation. War work could build a real American, physically fit and mentally tough.

Enlistees didn't always care about that. They joined, or acquiesced enthusiastically to conscription, because they wanted to do their bit, not build their character. Some merely wanted the relative prosperity of finally having enough food to eat and decent clothes to wear. World War I African American recruits sang, "Joining the army to get free clothes; what we're fighting 'bout nobody knows." Some more affluent hoped for other benefits. Young men have often looked to soldiering for adventure, and have often hoped for glory, joining up as late adolescents whose concept of death is something vague and hypothetical. The terror of their first combat experience during World War I shocked most into a new appreciation of life's frailty, but by then it was too late. It was in the actual mud of the trenches that the supposed virtues of combat were put to the test. Some men there found them wanting.

"Shell shock" was first widely acknowledged during this war as a mental and possibly physical breakdown following battle. We study it today as Post-Traumatic Stress Disorder (PTSD), a condition familiar to war veterans from all of America's wars right up to the second war with Iraq. Shell shock during World War I affected large numbers of soldiers to some extent, both during the conflict and long after. Symptoms included fear and shaking, problems sleeping, nightmares, and actual physiological changes detectable in urinalysis. Some doctors presumed it might be blamed on the concussive effect of exploding shells. The longer the soldier survived on the line, the more likely he was to suffer at least some symptoms, and although the high command did not always appreciate these supposed "slackers," the soldiers themselves could easily identify those suffering. Men whose symptoms were severe enough could not fight. They were shipped behind the lines, sometimes to psychiatric hospitals back home, for rest, in hope they would bounce back enough to return to duty. Some did. Many didn't. In Britain, 80,000 soldiers left the lines suffering symptoms of shell shock. Those with less severe symptoms were returned to the line as "malingerers," and of those some deserted, refused to fight, or suicided. Recovery was uncertain, and years after the war veterans still showed impairments that could be traced to military service. How many suffered? No one knows, in this war, or in subsequent wars.

The irony of shell shock was described most effectively in *Catch-22*, Joseph Heller's iconic novel of World War II. The main character, John Yossarian, became disillusioned and refused to fly more dangerous missions. But if he declared he was insane and therefore could not fly further missions, then he must be sane, because no sane person would actually want to fly more missions. Thus the conundrum of the shell-shocked soldier is the origin of the phrase "catch-22."

Soldiers who leave the military mentally broken cannot be said to have benefited from their time as a warrior. Soldiers who left World War I physically broken, with disabilities ranging from slight to hideous, also did not benefit. But many who returned home whole and sane did claim that military service was the most interesting years of their lives. These men saw value in the opportunity to get away from their tiny world view, a familiar upbringing in isolated rural America in sheltered homes. Soldiers had become cosmopolitan from their service in France; they had "seen Paree." They also had tasted the freedom of becoming a "real man," which might include persistent profanity and frequent visits to prostitutes. Every American boy had heard of the reputation of Paris, after all. And, if by chance they should catch something, so they surmised, the army medics could cure them.

Research to trace the benefits of army service on men and on their society produces complex and sometimes contradictory results. American black and Hispanic veterans with comparable education actually made more money than similar minority men who did not serve. Researchers guessed the army gave them more skills, a more cosmopolitan point of view, and greater understanding of a white man's system in which they had to operate both in and after military service. On the other hand, studies show an increase in juvenile delinquency, marital discord, and divorce rates in wartime, perhaps blamed on an absent father. A man may return after service as an unhappy veteran haunted by his memories and trying to relate to a spouse also changed, forced by circumstances to become more independent. Some critics of military service also point to evidence that vets commit more crimes. Research does not show that to be necessarily true. In many cases those former soldiers who return to cause trouble in society showed similar characteristics before they joined the service.

In any case, Roosevelt—whose detractors called a warmonger—discovered as did many parents the sad certainty that war does nothing to mold the character of those who do not survive it. His youngest son, an aviator, died in a dogfight in 1918. Quentin Roosevelt was 20. Roosevelt's grief over the loss of his favorite son could only have been compounded by the knowledge that the former president had himself encouraged the brave but reckless youth to enlist.

The Beneficial Effects of War on Soldiers

Newton D. Baker, Secretary of War: "America's War Effort"

American draftees in 1917 reflected a smug presumption common in World War I America, that the Old World was tired, overly cautious, and spent, while the New World, with its spirit and enthusiasm, could take its place and win the war. In truth, Europe's soldiers in 1914 had joined in the same spirit of adventure and glory that American soldiers felt in 1917. But as new recruits in all wars discover, after the first bombardment, the first harrowing battle, strength to persevere stems from virtues the go beyond dash and verve.

***New York Times Current History,* April–September 1918**

The Commission on Classification of Personnel reports that a surprisingly large proportion of recruits ask to be placed in the most hazardous branches of the military service. If a reply is needed to those who say that the men in the National Army are in camp because they have to be, it is this—that those same men are going over the top because they want to go.

The desire among men in the military service to get to France and to the front is universal. The Secretary of War stated before the Senate Military Affairs Committee that he had seen grizzled men of the army turn away from their desks to hide their tears when they were asked to do organization work in America rather than go to France, where the glory of their profession lies. When the Secretary of War started for Europe and was on the ocean he was approached in a number of instances, by seamen, requesting transfer to the army in order that they might see service which seemed more active and closer to the front.

In France it was necessary to change the name of the zone behind the armies from the Service of the Rear to Service of Supply, because of the difficulty in getting men to serve in a region having the shell-proof connotation of the word "rear." Even at the actual front there is something of a tradition against the use old the term No Man's Land. Our men prefer to call it—and to make it—Yankee Land.

Maurice Barrés: "Young Soldiers of France"

Maurice Barrés was at the time one of France's most well-known novelists and essayists, and also one of its most conservative. His ferocious antisemitism and nationalism coalesced during the war into his columns published in the conservative L'Echo de Paris. *There he glorified the purity of war and the spirit of patriotism in ways that some historians contend presage the postwar appeal of fascism—despite his implacable hatred of Germany. He died in 1923, before the growth of fascism throughout Europe bore its bitter fruit of Nazism.*

Atlantic Monthly, July 1917

To-day the noble-hearted American nation is asking on its own account the question which, for nearly three years now, the French nation has been asking itself: "What will be the outcome of this war, which is modifying our national soul? What manner of men will come back to us from the trenches when victory has been won?"

For two years and a half, our young soldiers have been learning the lessons of war; shoulder to shoulder they have been winning their manhood, their croix de guerre, their promotions. They are being formed on the same model; they are being initiated into the rules of discipline and system; they are amassing a treasure of sober thoughts, and friendships which will suffice for the whole duration of their lives. By virtue of their profound impressions, their first tremendous experiences, every man of them belongs now and for all time to the world of the trenches. Such an education means a France unified and purified. On these young men is taking place a resurrection of our most glorious days. Some great thing is about to come into being.

I should like to show you the eyes of these radiant boys, turned toward the future, full of life, full of love of nature, of their parents, of their country, and consenting so readily to die; but how can I make you see the unforgettable purity of their gaze as they scan the horizon, seeking, not their own destiny, but the destiny of their country. Better far to call some of them in person from the ranks—youths chosen at random from the length and breadth of France; they shall speak to us themselves, and let us see with no barrier between us, the boundless goodwill shining from their faces. Let us listen to these soldier-boys, beloved of their comrades, unknown to their commanders, lost in the rank and file, as they open their hearts to their families.

We shall see that the task they have set themselves is the glorification of their country at the cost of their blood. It is their will that from this slaughter France, and, through her, all mankind, shall flower anew.

Young Alfred Eugene Cazalis, a pastor's son—student at the Theological Seminary of Montauban, and a private in the 11th Regiment of Infantry, who died for France at nineteen, writes to his parents,

"More and more, in the face of all those who have struggled and fallen, in the presence of the mighty effort which has been made, my thoughts turn to the France of to-morrow—to the divine France which is bound to be. I could not fight on, if I did not hope for the birth of that France, so richly deserving that men should kill one another and die for her sake."

Jean Rival, a Grenoble boy, son of a college professor, who died for France in his twentieth year, writes to his younger brother,

"My greatest comfort in the difficult moments which I must endure here is to think that you, my little brothers and sisters, are all doing your duty as I am. My task is to fight like a brave soldier; yours, to work just as courageously. Small and unimportant as you may seem to be in this great France of ours, you owe it to yourself to do your utmost to make yourself bigger, richer, nobler. After the war France will sorely need intelligent minds and strong arms; and you, the boys of to-day, will be the young manhood of to-morrow. You will be called on then to take the place of a soldier who has died for our country."

Leo Latil, the son of a doctor of Aix-en-Provence, sergeant in the 67th Infantry, died for France at twenty-four. He writes to his family,

"Our sacrifices will be sweet if we win a great and glorious victory, if there shall be more light for the souls of men; if truth shall come forth more radiant, better beloved. We must not forget for a moment that we are fighting for great things—for the very greatest things. In every sense, this victory of ours will be a victory of the forces of idealism."

A British Captain: "A Winter's War"

Propaganda offices preferred to promote articles written by the more urban and educated elite who professed the positive values of war over the supposedly less salubrious civilian toil of the working classes. This author's suggestion that losses of hundreds of thousands of human lives can balance the evils of shopkeeper boredom might have made good inspiration for Josef Stalin's famous comment: "A single death is a tragedy. A million deaths is a statistic." More than 900,000 British soldiers died in World War I.

Atlantic Monthly, November 1915

I go back to France as an officer of one of the new armies. I have read much of late of the horror and sacrifice of war, yet the men I see round me prove that there are compensations. We may have lost a couple of hundred thousand men and we may lose half a million more, but against this must be balanced those three million new men who twelve months ago were living the life of cities and the rural life of selfish idleness or ill-paid toil. Some were clerks, others were shopmen, others were rustics not far removed from serfs. For close on a year, they have lived a man's life in the open, and anybody seeing them would recognize at a glance that they are twice the men to-day that they were at this time last year.

Striking a balance, it seems to me that with all our losses, past or to be, we British are something to the good, and that in losing we have gained immeasurably, and that out of these present sorrows we may emerge stronger, saner, and healthier than we have ever been before.

Arthur Hunt Chute: "How Sleep the Brave"

United States casualties—killed and wounded—totaled eight percent of those who served. This percentage was far below any other European belligerent nation, but it still represents 364,800 soldiers, of whom one third died. Of that one third, about half died in battle. Most of the rest died of the influenza epidemic that in 1918–1919 ravaged the battlefield as "Flanders Fever," and the rest of the world as the Spanish Flu.

North American Review, February 1918

As the long lists of inevitable American casualties appear in the newspapers, we must not get into a panic of the soul, we must not pity the men who have fallen. They need no pity, and could they speak they would repudiate such maudlin sentiment. If the fallen Brave could talk to us, we know that it would be to tell us to envy them, and not to pity them, because their lives have found so glorious an ending.

Idealism wanes in prosperity and waxes in adversity. England has become a new England out of the adversities of this war, and in the same struggle a new America will be born.

Anonymous: "A Boy's Last Letter to His Mother: Story of an 18-Year-Old Hero from Perugia"

Italy, sometimes the forgotten ally of World War I, lost 650,000 soldiers after it decided to abrogate its treaty that promised support to the Central

Powers, and in 1915 join the allies. It was a disastrous decision. The country was unprepared for war on this scale, won few battles, and had to be propped up by the allies. Allied promises of territory in return for participation in the war led to little during the peace settlement. Protest and unrest paved the way for Mussolini's fascist takeover seven years later.

New York Times Current History, October 1917–March 1918

Soon after Italy's declaration of war, in May, 1915, Enzo Valentini, a boy of 18 in the Perugia high school, son of the Mayor of that city, wrote to his mother this noble letter, containing his last will and testament:

"Little mother, in a few days I am going to leave for the font. For your dear sake I am writing this farewell, which you will read only if I die. Let it also be my adieu to papa, to my brothers, to all those who loved me in this world. Because in life my heart, in its love and gratitude to you, has always given you its best thoughts, it is to you also that I desire to make known my last wishes. . . .

"Try, if you can, not to weep for me too much. Think that, even though I do not return, I am not dead. My body, the less important part of me, suffers, wears out, and dies; but not myself—I the soul, cannot die, because I come from God and must return to God. I was created for happiness and through the joy that underlies all suffering I must return to the happiness eternal. If I have been a little time the prisoner of my body, I am none the less eternal. My death is a liberation, the beginning of the true life, the return to the Infinite.

"So do not weep for me. If you think of the immortal beauty of the ideas to which my soul has willingly sacrificed my body, you will not weep. But if your mother heart weeps, let the tears flow: a mother's tears will always be sacred. May God keep account of them: they will be the stars of his crown.

"Be strong, little mother. From the beyond your son says good-bye to you, to papa, to the brothers, to all those who loved him—your son who has given his body to fight those who wished to extinguish the light of the world."

Anonymous: "To N.S., Who Died in Battle"

World War I produced an enormous outpouring of poetry, particularly in Germany, Britain, France, and the United States. The war established the genre of the war poet, the most famous of whom wrote in English. Many of these poets died in battle, including perhaps the most enduring, Wilfred Owen, who wrote while he was hospitalized for shell shock. Determined to return to the front, Owen died in action just a week before the armistice.

Atlantic Monthly, February 1918

I knew you glad to go; I envied you.
To pour the glory of your young life forth
In on libation—what more happy lot?

Be spared the slow, sad drip of dreams and hopes,
Of loves and memories, that leaves us dry
And bitter, seared and bleared with creeping age—
Who would not die in battle? Life cut short?
Nay, blossomed in a moment, rich with fruit,
Blossom and fruit together, which the years
Might never ripen, uneventful years
Of nursery-gardening, one small, precious self,
Which seeds and dies and none knows why it was.

I knew you glad to go; you knew not why—
The sting of high adventure in your blood,
The salt of danger savoring nights and days;
And in your heart the wave of some unknown
Deep feeling shared with comrades, that bore you on
The tideways that the coward never knows,
Nor he who hoards his life for his own ends.

O happy boy, you have not lost your years!
You lived them through and through in those brief days
When you stood facing death. They are not lost:
They rushed together as the waters rush
From many sources; you had all in one.

You filled your little cup with all experience,
And drank the golden foam, and left the dregs,
And tossed the cup away. Why should we mourn
Your happiness? You burned clear flame, while he
Who treads the endless march of dusty years
Grows blind and choked with dust before he dies,
And dying goes back to the primal dust,
And has not lived so long in those long years
As you in your few, vibrant golden months
When like a spendthrift you gave all you were.

The Destructive Effects of War on Soldiers

Harriet Fox Whicher, New York, Letter to the Editor, Reply to Alan Seeger: "As a Soldier Thinks"

Alan Seeger was one of many young soldier-poets whose work became well known after their deaths on the Western Front. Seeger, who graduated from Harvard University in the same class as T. S. Eliot, joined the French Foreign Legion in 1915, before the United States declared war. His poetry was not published until after his death in 1916. But his book Poems *did not sell well after the war, as people turned away from the idealistic fervor that carried soldier-intellectuals like Seeger into the war.*

***New Republic,* May 22, 1915**

It may seem to a man on the battlefield that wars are the "birth pangs of new eras." But the metaphor is nothing more than an empty phrase. New eras are the result not of war, but of slow, careful and painful effort in time of peace. It is hard to see what can be ushered in by war except the transfer of territorial or commercial advantages.

Robert L. Hale, New York, letter to the editor, reply to Alan Seeger: "Mr. Seeger's Philosophy."

The first is the puritanical idea that suffering is a good thing. The pains of childbirth are accepted as inevitable and desirable for women; the pains of war should be so accepted for men. He does not mention the suffering war brings to women, but that is doubtless an added advantage.

The second thought in Mr. Seeger's philosophy is that true civilization consists in increasing the range of emotional vibrations and enthusiasms. War accomplishes this in two ways—it is accompanied by intense enthusiasm (as is the lynching of a negro), and it causes intense sorrow which tries the heart "with that kind of affliction that alone can unfold the profundities of the human spirit." Our advance in civilization since savage times doubtless consists in the greater extent of the afflictions caused by our improved methods of warfare.

Harold Begbie: "Can Man Abolish War?"

Heinrich von Treitschke, German historian and professor who died in 1896, is not as well known today as he was during World War I. Reprints of his work during the war led allied writers to contend that as a nationalist and Anglophobe he and his disciples promulgated a philosophy that encouraged war. Friedrich Nietzsche, on the other hand, has become a household name today for his criticism of Christianity, famously declaring "God is dead." He is blamed, perhaps undeservedly, for being a proto-Nazi.

***North American Review,* May 1917**

All those social virtues, all those noble qualities of human character, which manifest themselves in a nation under the scourge of war, are not the fruits of war. They are the witnesses to an immediate and natural reaction of the human spirit against war. The fruits of war are massacre and murder, wounding and death, destruction and ruin, mourning and lamentation, rapine and rape, desolation and despair, hatred and the legacies of hate.

Those things which quicken the beatings of our hearts, which pulse through the national life in waves of strengthening enthusiasm, namely, the valor of the soldier, the devotion of the doctor and nurse, the self-sacrifice of the whole people, and the stoic silence of the mourner, these things are but the manifestation of a spiritual reaction against war. War is Satan let loose upon the earth. All the splendor that we associate with war is humanity's instinctive reaction against Satanism.

If there be any man left in Europe who still cherishes the tradition of Treitschke, or who still finds a more wholesome manhood in Nietzsche than in Christ, let us be sure of this: that he is far from "the bath of blood"—and far beyond the utmost range of the guns. To those who make War, whose bodies are shaken by the shuddering thunder of the shells, whose bayonets are red with human blood, whose eyes have seen the blanching terror of a crouching enemy, whose days are spent in earth burrows, whose nostrils are filled with foulness, and whose hearts are heavy with home longings, war is hell. And to those millions who mourn, to these also war is hell.

W. R. Houston, A.M., M.D., Professor of Clinical Medicine in the University of Georgia: "Amazing Effects of Shell Shock on Soldiers' Nerves"

Doctors during World War I had to cope with the effects of heavy artillery. These shells produced wounds more extensive and complicated than those of previous wars, challenging medics beyond what they had learned from their elders. "Shell shock" during this period came to mean a psychological illness, but doctors during this time still investigated a possible physiological cause produced by shell bursts. On the positive side, medical advances meant the infections and diseases that killed so many in previous wars could be more effectively controlled during this modern war.

***New York Times Current History*, April–September 1917**

In the accounts of the great bombardments we have all read of men who were found dead in the trenches, unwounded. Death had resulted from the air concussion in the zone contiguous to the exploding shell. The concussion is more intense and the danger greater if the shell explodes in a closed space, as in the deep chambered trenches of the western front.

Countless Internal Wounds

Most of our commotion cases were injured in the trenches. Often they were hurled some distance, dashed against a wall, and buried alive. If an examination is made of the bodies of these dead, or of those who have survived a few days before death, it is found that there has taken place an intimate tearing of the finer structures throughout the body. the lungs are torn; there are abundant hemorrhages in the pleura and stomach. The blood vessels in the brain are ruptured, and minute hemorrhages are found throughout.

Many are killed outright, but most survive. Even these survivors bleed in many cases from the ears, the lungs, the stomach, the bladder, and bowels. There are sometimes hemorrhages into the retina and under the conjunctivae. The normally clear cerebro-spinal fluid is found blood tinged. Even after blood is no longer found the fluid is often discovered to be under high pressure, the white cells and globulins that indicate damage to the meninges continue to be found in it for months.

The patients seldom regain memory of the beginning of their accidents. At most they recall the whistling sound that preceded the arrival of a shell. In certain cases there will be found only a more or less transient clouding of consciousness, or a very painful sensation of having been beaten on the head. Usually the patient is unable to walk, and as he is carried on the stretcher every movement is painful. The limbs are inert, the head drops on the shoulder. Even when sitting he collapses if not supported. Any movements made are maladroit and imprecise. the sphincters are relaxed; almost all arrive at the aid stations soiled with excrements. Later they may have retention, but in the beginning the contrary is the rule.

The facial expression is typical—comparable to that seen in the cerebral type of infantile paralysis—the corners of the mouth droop, the tongue is paretic, the lids droop, and the eyeballs are without motion. The pupils are dilated, almost always unequal.

Major-General William P. Duvall, United States Army, Introduction by Editor Honoré Willsie: "The Ideals They Teach Your Boy in the Army"

Duvall's stirring admonishments address problems common among those who served in the army, particularly the understandable inability to forget what they had experienced. A familiar soldier song reflected disappointment that men were expected to simply deny their terrifying ordeal: "No one knows/No one cares, if I'm weary./ Oh, how soon they forgot Chateau-Thierry."

Delineator, April 1918

This war is not a war merely of peoples. It is a war of ideals. The splendid ideals which our military leaders are impressing on the young men of our new army are set forth in the address General Duvall made, in presenting commissions to two thousand new army officers at Fort Oglethorpe. He said:

"In the supreme test of war the profession of arms will demand that you bring to it all that is best in you. There is no talent or intellect too brilliant, no gift of character too noble for sacrifice on the altars of patriotism, and there will be need and service for every one of the qualities you possess. Do not follow the modern fashion of dragging the horrors of the battle trench into the firelight of the hearth. Steel yourself and your men by discipline and sheer courage to do the thing it is given you to do, and then bury it on the field with the dead.

"Fight as your fathers did when they met on this hard-fought battleground, when to the limit of human endurance they suffered and struggled and killed and died, which is all that nay men can do in any warfare. When you return, leave behind, as they did, the savage deeds and blazing ferocities which are sacred on the field of valor but loathsome on the tongue of the boaster. Let only the great invigorating and exalting influences of war impress your souls; and strive to mirror back upon our people only war's glorious aspects; for in the officers who lead its armies to battle a nation beholds its flower, and in your image the young of America will shape her coming manhood."

Anonymous, Alan Seeger: "Voices of Living Poets"

T. S. Eliot, in a 1917 review of Seeger's work, wrote, "It is high-flown, heavily decorated and solemn, but its solemnity is thorough going, not a mere literary formality."

Current Opinion, May 1917

Alan Seeger's one unforgettable poem is the one entitled: "I Have a Rendezvous With Death." Since his death, July 4, 1916, incurred while charging with his comrades of the Foreign Legion on the German trenches at the village Belloy-en-Santerre, this poem has achieved wide fame. His work as a whole, as it appears in this volume (published by Scribner), is uneven; but at its lowest it is full of promise, and at its highest, in the war-poems, it is excelled by only two or three poems produced by the war. He was but twenty-eight when he died and, as William Archer says in a long and adequate introduction, "of all the poets who have died young, none has died so happily." He was born in New York City, of New England stock, educated at Harvard, and the great war found him vainly trying to publish his volume of earlier poems in London. Before the war was three weeks old he had enlisted in the Foreign Legion.

I Have a Rendezvous with Death
By Alan Seeger

I have a rendezvous with Death
At some disputed barricade,
When Spring comes back with rustling shade
And apple-blossoms fill the air—
I have a rendezvous with Death
When Spring brings back blue days and fair.

It may be he shall take my hand
And lead me into his dark land
And close my eyes and quench my breath—
It may be I shall pass him still.
I have a rendezvous with Death
On some scarred slope of battered hill,
When Spring comes round again this year
And the first meadow-flowers appear.

God knows 'twere better to be deep
Pillowed in silk and scented down,
Where love throbs out in blessful sleep,
Pulse night to pulse, and breath to breath,
Where hushed awakenings are dear. . . .
But I've a rendezvous with Death
At midnight in some flaming town,
When Spring trips north again this year,
And I to my pledged word am true.
I shall not fail that rendezvous.

Anonymous: "The Point of View: Fatalism"

Fatalism, the idea that human beings are powerless to control the outcome of events, has not been as popular among Western cultures as it has been in Islamic societies. But World War I soldiers found they were unable to control their vulnerability to long-range shelling: death from above, killing comrades seemingly at random. An enemy seen might be an enemy dealt with, but the majority of casualties during this war came from unseen enemies. Furthermore, soldiers in previous wars were less likely to be locked into trenches, unable to flee even for a short respite. Fatalism, then, was not so much a philosophy as a fact of a soldier's life.

Scribner's, May 1918

Another reason that will help in bringing a touch of fatalism in the heart of the fighter is that all levels of human activity seem to be shattered, not to work in the usual way. Before the war a man with money in his pocket was a powerful man; now his banknotes are often not available any more, and even with his money he will often not be able to buy food. I remember in the early period of the open warfare money was useless to buy food. Lately, during the Verdun battle, I would have paid any price to get some water; for during five days my whole regiment could get only eighty-six litres of water; so terrible was the shelling that nobody could cross this zone of death.

Thus the man sees that on the battlefield it is useless to run away—for the bullets will always catch him; that it is useless to hide in deep dugouts, for he has seen many of his comrades buried in overthrown dugouts while others who fought bravely, facing death every moment, came out of the fray unhurt. On the other hand, all his habits, his ordinary mode of living, have been changed; everything to which he has been accustomed from his childhood on is different, even the very landscape which has taken such a strange and abnormal appearance that he is obliged to compare it to a moon landscape. It seems but natural, therefore, that he should be resigned to his fate; hence the feeling of fatalism.

Roméo Houle, Canadian Soldier: "The Horrors of Trench Fighting"

War is eternally horrible, but each war is its own fresh hell. Battles before World War I lasted days, not months. After the battle the dead were dragged away and buried, usually still in one piece. But World War I soldiers lived on a line of more than 400 miles. It moved little over four years, fought over again and again, leaving remains of perhaps one million human beings—more if you count each piece—rotting among the men still alive. Soldiers dined with the dead, slogged through mud mixed with their blood, appropriated their gear, and joked grimly about their constant companions.

New York Times Current History, April 1916

Rats? What did you ever read of the rats in the trenches? Next to gas, they still slide on their fat bellies through my dreams. Poe could have got new inspiration from their dirty hordes. Rats, rats, rats—I see them still slinking from new meals on corpses, from Belgium to the Swiss Alps. Rats, rats, rats, tens of thousands of rats, crunching between battle lines while the rapid-firing guns mow the trench edge—crunching their hellish feasts. Full fed, slipping and sliding down into the wet trenches they swarm at night—and more than one poor wretch has had his face eaten off by them while he slept.

Stench? Did you ever breathe air foul with the gases arising form a thousand rotting corpses? Dirt? Have you ever fought half madly through days

War correspondents during World War I were tightly controlled and seldom allowed to join or embed themselves with troops in the trenches. Late in the war they were often escorted to the front in controlled groups. Many of the remarkable action photos of the war were actually taken by soldiers themselves using small Kodak cameras, even though the military discouraged the practice. This photo was taken from the stereo view cards that flooded the market during this era. Courtesy of Library of Congress.

and nights and weeks unwashed, with feverish rests between long hours of agony, while the guns boom their awful symphony of death, and the bullets zip-zip-zip ceaselessly along the trench edge that is your skyline—and your deathline, too, if you stretch and stand upright? . . .

At Richebourg we entered trenches of our own. There Charles Lapointe of Montreal, the first of our company to die, looked over the edge of the trench. That is death. Machine guns all day sweep the trench edges. If you raise your hand, your fingers will be cut off as by a knife. And once I saw a poor wretch, weary almost to death of the trench, raise his right arm at full length. He was sent home, maimed and in agony, as he had wished. And who can say that his act was cowardly? He who has lived in the trenches for weeks and months knows. The soldier had courage to raise his hand. Perhaps some who clung to the mud at the trench bottom were greater cowards than he.

Charles H. A. Wager: "The Hope of the World"

More than 4.3 million American men served in World War I. A fraction saw combat; the rest served in a wide variety of capacities and returned home with a wide variety of experiences. Generalization is therefore impossible. But research has shown that many of those who actually saw action returned with a variety of disorders based on what they saw and traits they brought with them when they joined the army. The presumption that former soldiers respond more violently to civilian concerns has been supported by research, but only modestly, evidenced by the more violent responses veterans gave to tests using hypotheticals.

North American Review, September 1918

Day by day, under the severities of discipline, a new man was forming silently and unconsciously in our young soldier; his soul was becoming "simple, unified, elemental." The narrative ends with these words: "To be the slave of one's idea is not given to everybody. The servitude of the army exists, as the servitude of the priest exists and the servitude of the thinker. But in all the world, only these slaves are free."

There is the point. Like the priest and the thinker, the young soldier is, consciously or unconsciously, the slave of an idea. First from observation and then from experience, he learns that "the invisible leads the world." He is fighting for a cause. He undergoes these incredible dangers and hardships for an idea. Will he be quite so ready, when he comes back to us, to fall in with our practical materialism? Having offered his life daily for an intangibility, is he likely to devote the remainder of it wholly to "the god of things as they are?" Even the so-called fatalism of the soldier, his carelessness about death, which figures so largely in our matter-bounded thoughts, what does it mean except that he places something higher than physical good, though it be but a manly sense of honor, or even the fear of fear?

Winifred Kirkland: "The New Death"

Survivors react to death on an individual level with a variety of responses, depending on the situation of the person who died, and the personality of the survivor. In World War I death was not only an individual tragedy, however; the immense toll of fallen young people forced entire societies to consider ways to mourn and to remember. No one who joined the war in August 1914 was prepared for the immense slaughter that was to come: about 10 million, some 6,370 a day. Grief during the time often was private; society encouraged stoic suffering in silence. But as a culture, from city to village, death was commemorated through memorials and rituals. Armistice Day became Veteran's Day after World War II, but its official date, November 11, marked the armistice of World War I.

Atlantic Monthly, May 1918

This new spiritual valuation of daily existence is still vague, but struggling toward clearness, toward continuity, toward community effort. We long to dignify our daily work by devotion to some cause; we long to know ourselves in line with them, our dead. Always in healthy revulsion at the wastage of their lives, we keep searching, searching for those ultimate standards that shall harmonize their apparent loss with their actual usefulness. We, the obscure, sorrowing fathers and mothers, sisters and brothers of young soldiers killed, we, the mourners all over the world, want to feel that our lives are moving in tune with theirs. And this need for better ordering of our everyday life intensifies our scrutiny of their dying. What is the force so mysterious, so coercive, which commanded them to die? What is the force so mysterious, so coercive, which commands us to live as they would have us live? The New Death is asking with an intensity and a universality never known before. Where are our dead? Is there a God? The need of direction for our energy, and of a standard of valuation, profoundly affects the two most important characteristics of the New Death, its essentially practical acceptance of immortality, its essentially practical approach to God. . . .

Conviction of immortality as shown in the soldier-records is in the main profoundly intuitive, but so powerful and so common that one cannot believe that so many men, and these alert in every fiber, could be altogether deluded. It seems more scientific to query whether perhaps they possess truer illumination than mere intellect, unsupplemented by the subtler capacities of soul evoked by their tragic situation, could ever attain.

In so far as their marvelous inner security has for themselves any basis in reason, it rests partly on the immortal renewal which they observe in nature. Sunrise and recurrent star and the pushing up of the indomitable flowers are arguments for human persistence, since man, too, is a part of the great earth force. Apart from the reasoned argument of nature's exhaustless vitality, many a soldier reveals a consciousness of an indestructible immortal something within him. He would still feel this inner confidence even if all communication with external nature were denied him, if he could hear no bird-songs, see no stars. Page after page of Lettres d'un Soldat testify to the sense of eternity which is the core of his courage and his calm.

Frances Fenwick Williams: "Before Verdun"

The 10-month battle of Verdun began February 21, 1916, Germany's attempt to "bleed the French army white." Its terrifying stories of struggle and heroism became among the war's most famous legends thanks to a French army decision to employ mobilized journalists whose sole duty was to cover the battle for the French propaganda service. Frances Fenwick Williams is not among familiar war poets, and apparently was female, but she did publish occasional short magazine fiction in other publications at this time.

***New York Times Current History*, October 1916–February 1917**

No prayer can help, no agony atone,
As I came into life I go—alone!

Another man is lying by my side,
Another, caught in death's fast-brimming tide.

Mine was the hand that struck his life away,
And his the hand that laid me low today.

Yet now, as nearer draws the dreadful end,
He seems to me a brother and a friend.

What is he thinking as his life ebbs fast?
(How lonely each poor soul is at the last!)

If I could hear him speak before he dies
I should not feel so desolate—but he lies,

Silent and spent. His lips grow slowly white—
I hate to look upon the piteous sight!

I have some water here. If I could crawl
Close to his death-place he should have it all.

Ah, I have reached him—but he shrinks. Poor friend!
My wish is but to share your bitter end.

He smiles—he drinks! Ah, me, how eagerly
He laps the water and leans back to die.

Oh, while the death-guns shriek, the madmen fight,
Speak to me, brother! Darker grows the night,

And I am friendless, and my life ebbs fast—
(How lonely each poor soul is at the last!)

He smiles. He speaks. Oh, brother, louder pray!
I'm growing deaf (That means death's near, they say.)

"No war where we are going?" Friend, your hand!
Together let us seek that longed-for land.

"No war!"—how white he is, how cold a thing!
But his dead face has robbed death of her sting.

Questions

1. In what ways did war supporters believe military service would benefit soldiers?
2. In what ways did supporters believe military service would benefit American society?
3. In what ways did war opponents believe military service would harm individuals and society?

Chapter 20

War and Technology

The Great War offered a canvas to display the triumphs of the machine age. The great innovations of this industrial era could serve in so many ways to bring new developments of science to the ancient techniques of warfare. War means slaughter. Science brings efficiency. The result: efficient slaughter.

The icon of the machine age was the machine gun. In short bursts it could sweep away advancing troops at a rate of 400–600 rounds a minute. This gave it the firepower of at least 80 men with rifles. Nested together as defensive weapons, the guns could make any assault so murderous that hardly a man was left to actually reach the defenders. But the deadly efficiency of this "weapon of mass destruction," as it was called during this war, was not easily appreciated in the general headquarters of the high commands. World War I generals throughout the Western world were slow to see the incompatibility between machine-age advances in ordnance and traditional battlefield tactics. Leaders carried into this war the values of a previous era. The *élan* of the troops in an enthusiastic offensive would overcome the determination of an enemy in dogged defense. France in particular followed this offensive strategy to enormous losses during the first battles of fall 1914. At least 300,000 French soldiers died. Napoleon had said that spirit of his men would trump their inferior numbers, but his men did not face bullets like a cloud of locusts. Noted one shocked British observer of World War I's battlefields, the French attackers were "knocked over like rabbits."

The trenches developed spontaneously to the efficiency of World War I weapons. No one expected this frenzied digging would lead to a stalemate almost impossible to overcome. In fact, subsequent munitions development generally was aimed at one goal, to break the stalemate that smothered Europe in a four-year bloody blanket. Technical developments most significant to modern war almost all saw their beginning in World War I: automatic weapons, heavy artillery, submarines, torpedoes, chemicals, tanks, and air power. Missiles were not part of this war, but the German army's greatest field piece, the railroad-mounded "Paris Gun," presaged the nature of the missile. The Paris Gun fired projectiles 24 miles high, nearly into outer space, and at civilian targets, namely Paris, from 75 miles away. After the initial shock, Parisians took their periodic shelling into account and refused to cower. More than 300 were killed. The weapon showed how war could reach civilians from far away.

Officers who most often carried small arms more and more relied on automatic weapons, invented a few years before by John Browning, an American. The German Luger is the most famous automatic pistol from this era, but the American Colt Model 1911 worked so well that it continued to be favored throughout most of the century. The semiautomatic action—a shot chambered each time you pulled the trigger—saw quick advances into the fully automatic action that has become standard to today's battlefield assault weapons.

Other World War I innovations, the submarine and its torpedo, have come to represent one of the great symbols of the nuclear age. Germany jumped into the lead, building U-Boats that dramatically changed naval defense strategy and proved particularly costly to Britain, the world's greatest surface sea power. Germany initially cross-haired only military targets. Its move to hit civilian vessels came with hesitation, as did its decision to abandon the old rules of warfare that required ship captains to warn passengers and crew before firing on a ship. Warning a civilian ship in the age of radio—another new invention used in this war—could give a captain time to call in military reinforcements with depth charges. It was Germany's response to this conundrum that so infuriated the United States and immediate reason for Wilson's war declaration. Germany gambled that its unrestricted submarines could knock Britain out of the war. By April 1917 it seemed that subs just might prove to be the key to victory, as 866,000 tons of shipping went to the bottom of the Atlantic. But it proved to be another German illusion. A convoy system helped to protect British shipping and turn the menace back on the U-Boats.

This war of human versus machine took an even more sinister twist when industrial chemists produced an array of gases designed to, in odious ways, cripple first and kill later. Chlorine gas first rolled out from the German lines in 1915 soon gave way to even more lethal clouds, phosgene and mustard. The first two are still important to modern industry. Chlorine is a disinfectant and bleach. Phosgene is an important industrial chemical, used in pesticides, fertilizers, and the manufacture of polyurethane. Mustard gas is important only for war. The manufactured product has nothing to do with the mustard plant, but supposedly smells vaguely of mustard or horseradish. Several hours after exposure it produces grotesque blisters on skin and lungs and causes blindness and often death. This weapon of World War I has been used in warfare throughout the century, although napalm is a more modern equivalent.

In the desperate search to find ways to break through the lines, military engineers devised two new weapons that would come to dominate modern warfare: airplanes and tanks. Tanks began as a British response to the murderous machine gun fire that made attack so hazardous. The armored vehicle shielded against small arms fire and artillery flak, while moving slowly (originally at three miles per hour) over difficult terrain on caterpillar tracks. The first efforts of 1917 saw limited success, as the lumbering machines usually broke down or got stuck, but by 1918 tanks were playing a significant role in shattering the stalemate. German high command did not see the benefits until it was too late for their armament manufacturers to turn out tanks in number. Americans loved them, an innovation that has played central roles in subsequent U.S. actions world-wide.

Aircraft, on the other hand, did not initially interest U.S. military leaders. While the airplane was invented in the United States by the Wright Brothers, before the war military aviation budgets reached $7.4 million in France, $5 million in Germany and Russia, $3 million in Britain, $2.1 million in Italy, and $125,000 in the United States. France built 1,400 planes a year from 1911 to 1914; the United States 43 in 1913. The United States has since caught up to fly the world's mightiest air force, but during this war American fliers piloted mostly French planes.

The commitment of European belligerents to airplanes might seem to indicate that commanders held high hopes for their impact on warfare. They did not, and in this case, their hunch was correct. Air power in World War I consisted of pilots scattering a few bombs over a vast trench network. Occasional reports of aviators targeting civilians have been made, but generally airplanes posed little threat to human populations on the ground. They were useful for reconnaissance, eclipsing the need of commanders to find a hill from which to survey their armies. Pilots determined to prevent reconnaissance set out to battle their adversaries, and the result, the dogfight, became the most enduring "romantic" legend in an otherwise ignoble war. Despite the sideshow of aviation, 50,000 pilots died in World War I, and 10,000 planes were deployed. Their real importance was in the future, in tactics and experiments that grew to become the single most decisive power in twentieth-century warfare.

Technological innovation during wartime leads to improved capabilities in subsequent wars. This war's machine-age developments amply demonstrate that. Whether such innovations reap benefits beyond the battlefield is less certain. The most obvious example worth considering is aircraft. World War I aircraft grew in power and multitude, but that power did not come with greater efficiency of design. Military contracts supplied builders with their first mass market, and they responded by building what the military wanted. What they did not do was tackle the needs of a civilian airline industry looking for more efficient, more robust planes capable of flying loads of people and goods. Wartime aviation innovations included little attention to aerodynamics. Technological advancements in 1914–1918 were based on battlefield needs and unquestionably produced ordnance for future battles. Whether those war innovations benefited civilian needs is less certain.

The Promises of Technology and War

Eustace L. Adams: "Destroyers of the Air"

Even a decade after the first flight at Kitty Hawk, North Carolina, the airplane remained more of a curiosity than a practical machine. Loops and rides for brave passengers might entertain crowds at the county fair, but no manufacturer either in the United States or abroad relied solely on aviation for its livelihood. Those who believed airplanes could be more than novelties had to approach the military as possible large-scale contractors to make their manufacture profitable. The military responded, modestly. While the war did not see technological development useful to civilian aviation, it did seem to persuade people that airplanes could be more than toys. The United States inaugurated air mail service with its first air mail stamp, depicting the Curtiss JN-4 "Jenny," in May 1918. A printing mistake that sneaked into one of the sheets depicted the plane flying upside down, the most famous stamp error in American history.

Popular Science, January–June 1916

Until very lately, the aviation motors made in this country have been manufactured by companies which had little or no previous experience in motor designing. The Packard Company has designed a promising twelve-cylinder aviation motor, and the Simplex Automobile Company is equipping the rejuvenated Wright Aeroplane with a well-designed and carefully built motor, which in its first tests has justified the hopes placed in it by its designers.

When automobile manufacturers cooperate with aeroplane builders and succeed in developing an aeronautical motor which is as dependable as the automobile motor of to-day, the most formidable obstacle in the path of aviation will have been overcome.

If the war has accomplished no other useful end, it has advanced the progress of aviation many years. In the United States, without the spur of military and naval aeronautics, aviation was regarded as a profession from circus performers, whose main duty was to "loop the loop," and provide thrills for the crowds. Now, with aircraft manufacturers turning out aeroplanes at the rate of sixteen a day, the public is beginning to realize that it is a remarkably healthy infant industry, closely rivaling the unprecedented growth of the automobile industry in its early stages. One of the foremost aeronautical experts in the country recently said to the writer:

"Within one year after signing of peace between the European powers, the first aeroplane will make a successful flight across the Atlantic Ocean. Very soon aeroplanes will be carrying our mails to inaccessible spots. Shortly after this will come the carrying of passengers on a schedule as regular as that of our Twentieth Century Limited. Many of us will live to see the aerial expresses with many planes, multiple engines, and an enormous carrying capacity, which will take us to San Francisco or even to London and Paris as easily as we can now ride to Kansas City."

Joseph S. Ames: "Science at the Front"

While planes were indeed much more powerful by 1918 than they had been in 1914, some aeronautical researchers of the period were not persuaded they had significantly improved. Speeds had not increased greatly from the 130 miles per hour before the war. Only in Germany were engineers trying the more efficient monoplane design; bi-planes remained the standard elsewhere. Passenger service in the United States was still nearly nonexistent in 1921.

Atlantic Monthly, January 1918

As to air-planes, where can one begin, and having begun, how can one stop? The time has gone by when the village blacksmith can make one, and when the inventor, who is tired of trying to persuade a banker to become interested in perpetual motion, turns his hand to an air-plane "on an entirely new principle." The air-plane of to-day is the very last word of the physicist, the engineer, and the manufacturer. The physicist has designed the planes of the machine and the shape of the body; the engineer has used the utmost of his skill in calculating the structural strength of its parts, and in furnishing an engine of unheard-of power in proportion to its weight; the manufacturer uses the same refinements in his work that he would in making a piano for an exhibition. The finished product is a real work of art. The workmanship to-day is nearly perfect. A great French manufacturer, whose factory turns out its thousands of machines each month, told me with pride that since the beginning of the war not one of his machines had broken in the air. And the engines. No one who is not an expert, and I am not, can appreciate the progress made within three years; progress in lightness, in power, in durability.

Charles Lincoln Freeston: "The Motor in Warfare. Power and Speed in the Great European Conflict"

The immense armies of World War I could not have been moved or victualed without the automobile engine, and the wide variety of vehicles on which they ran. In September 1914, with Paris threatened, General Joseph Gallieni found a modern way to rush 6,000 French reinforcements to the front—by commandeering 1,200 Paris taxis. In 1916 France's immense army of defense at Verdun was supplied by a single small road from Bar-le-Duc, 38 miles south. The voie sacrée (sacred road) fed a stream of 3,000 trucks a day, a motorized lifeline without which Verdun certainly would have fallen.

Scribner's, February 1915

"This is not a war of men. It is a war of machines." Such was the dictum of a distinguished officer when the great European war had been eight weeks in progress and it had become evident that the quick-firer and the machine-gun were the most potent weapons of offence on either side.

Bu the war is also one of "machines" in a totally different sense; and whereas quick-firers and Maxims, though more liberally employed than in any previous campaign, are no new things of themselves, the feature which is new and paramount alike is the use of the "petrol" motor in its every shape and form. Without it, indeed, history might conceivably have had to record another Thirty Years' War. With millions of men drawn up in battle array at one and the same time, to handle them effectively by old-time methods would have been impossible. Even before the opposing fronts were extended to their fullest degree in France alone, they were officially declared to have attained a length of three hundred miles, and one of two hundred and seventy miles in the east—figures which not only convey some indication of the stupendous size of the engaging forces, but even more emphatically suggest the tremendous responsibilities of the commanders-in-chief.

Nevertheless, although they have to deal with millions instead of tens of thousands, the commanders concerned have never had their forces so completely under control; in every phase of the warfare, whether of transport, attack, defence, or supply, the keynote of the operations passim has been effectiveness of the completest kind. The motor, in short, has "speeded up" the war in a way that could never have been dreamed of by former generations.

Never have the movements of troops been so rapid; for, instead of men having to wait for ammunition and food-supplies, these have been conveyed by motor-wagons which can travel, if need be, much faster than the armies themselves. Never, too, have the firing-lines been kept so continuously in action, for motor-lorries have brought up ammunition in constant relays; they have been driven right up to the very front, and shells and cartridges have been served out as fast as they were required.

William J. Robinson: "The Machines"

The modern gasoline-powered automobile was a German invention, dating from 1889. France and the United States saw auto manufacturing beginning at about the turn of the century. Car manufacturers prospered from large contracts to produce designs and engines for trucks, airplanes, tanks, ambulances, and motorcycles. By the end of the war the American Expeditionary Force in France employed one motor vehicle for every 30 men, 60,000 total.

Atlantic Monthly, May 1916

When the British blockade was tightening its coils about Germany, a sigh of relief went up from the Entente powers, and their press proclaimed that with gasoline and rubber cut off from the enemy the war would soon come automatically to an end. I am not concerned with the failure of these prophesies to reckon with German chemical ingenuity; they merely throw light on the interesting fact that modern warfare, with its demand for swift-striking movement in every branch of the complicated military organism, could not exist without the motor-vehicle in its various forms.

Through the illustrated weeklies and the moving pictures, Americans have become familiar with the Skoda howitzers, taken to pieces for travel, rumbling along behind great Mercedes traction-motors. they have seen the London motor-busses, loaded to bursting with grinning Tommies on their way to the front, flaunting Bovril and Nestle's Food signs against an unfamiliar background of canals and serried poplar trees. They cannot realize, however, because they have not witnessed with their own eyes, the vast orderly ferment of wheeled traffic that fills the roads on both sides of that blackened, blasted battle-line between the armies of Western Europe. Where once the task of fulfillment fell to straining horse-flesh, the burden is now laid on by wheels winged by gasoline. From the flashing wire spokes of the dispatch-rider's motor-cycle to the clanking, crushing "feet" of the caterpillar tractor that pulls the big guns into action, the incredibly complicated machinery of war is now dependent on an element which, at the time of the Spanish-American War, was unknown to military use.

Anonymous: "Phonographs on the Firing Line"

Recording sound was old technology by World War I; Thomas A. Edison invented the phonograph in 1877. His invention actually made patterns of scratches on a cylinder, which corresponded to sounds. The scratches were picked up by a needle and amplified. This recording method endured until about 1985, when digital technology replaced analog. By World War I Edison's cylinders were being replaced by flat records and interest in popular music was on the rise. The era's iconic march and an inspiration to the troops, "Over There," was written by George M. Cohan and recorded by several well-known vocalists, including opera singer Enrico Caruso:

Over There (chorus):
Over there, over there,
Send the word, send the word over there.
That the Yanks are coming,
The Yanks are coming,
The drums rum-tumming
Ev'rywhere.
So prepare, say a pray'r,
Send the word, send the word to beware.
We'll be over, we're coming over,
And we won't come back till it's over
Over there.

Also recorded in 1918 was the first sound of war, a gas shell bombardment.

Independent, October 26, 1918

Talking machines have penetrated even into the trenches, and if the various seagoing and warfaring "Maggies" could tell their tales, they would often be of heroic stuff. For in trench, dugout and shell-hole, they have found a place to perch and grind out the rags, the stirring patriotic songs and the old-home tunes which they boys love—and which they actually need, as acutely almost as they need sleep, food, shelter.

Lieutenant Colonel Thomas Stanyan of the Salvation Army on his return from a special mission abroad reported that he had found Commandant Hughes of the Salvation Army in a dugout, playing a talking machine to six men who comprised the gun crew. The artillery opened fire, and the signal came to shell the enemy lines. As the men rushed out, several shouted back to Hughes to bring along the machine, as he followed after them, with it held tightly in his arms. While the men served, pointed and fired the gun, Hughes skirmished about till he found a tree stump with a fairly level top, where he placed the machine and proceeded to grind out popular airs in the midst of din and smoke. A gas shell broke up the concert and the gun crew's activity, but the doughty little phonograph was rescued and is still grinding out tunes behind the lines.

Dr. Louis Rocher, Professor, University of Bordeaux: "Removing Projectiles from the Brain by Electromagnet"

By the eve of World War I, medical techniques had been so revolutionized that surgery moved from being a desperate, often fatal, last-ditch effort to a reasonably reliable and safe procedure. World War I soldiers, unlike their hapless predecessors, could benefit from anesthetics to control pain, antiseptics to control infection, and new procedures to speed recovery. Unfortunately, penicillin and other broad antibiotics were not discovered before World War II.

New York Times Current History, October 1916–February 1917

Up to the present time it has been conceded as a general rule that one should not remove balls lodged in the brain (uncertainty and danger of operative procedures, risk of false routes, and of augmenting the injuries to the brain). To us it now seems that with the method of extraction by the electromagnet, the technique is simplified to the point of presenting the maximum of safety, being, as it is, more sure and less destructive than the methods hitherto employed.

Consequently, it seems as if the extraction of balls from within the brain were restricted only by the progress of operative technique.

Knowing the service rendered to ophthalmologists by the large electromagnet as a means of removing metallic bodies from the eye, we conceived the idea of adopting this method for removing foreign bodies from the brain, after having located them by means of the X-ray. In fact, a splinter of shell the size of a twenty-centime piece and two millimeters thick was so removed in June, 1915, from the front of a soldier's brain, and that without anesthesia, and with recovery.

Anonymous: "The Contributors' Club: Tanks"

The tank was a completely new weapon. It was made possible by the invention of the gasoline-powered engine, and made necessary by the development of entrenched soldiers defended by machine guns. The British invention was developed under supervision of the navy, under the rationale that it was a "land ship." Its code-name, "tank," came from its resemblance to storage tanks. British tanks were slow to show their value, as the original ones deployed in 1916 mostly stalled, but by 1918 they played important roles in the allies' final advances over German positions. During this war it was almost exclusively an allied weapon; British and French produced more than 6,000, Germany, 20. The United States, relying mostly on French machines, had produced 84 by the war's end.

Atlantic Monthly, July 1918

But most of them are outside in the fields, some sheeted and some bare, monstrous and prehistoric in their rows. They really are terrifying things, oppressively evil and ominous. They daunt one's imagination to such an extent that I should always have the instinct to run away if I saw a tank advancing down upon me, even if I knew quite well that it was a perfectly friendly tank, which was bringing me tea. And I think I realize why it is they are so dreadful.

Humanity has an old ancestral horror of everything that moves otherwise than on feet or wheels. That is the only choice for all respectable decent movables; we hate slugs and snakes and snails, for instance, and everything that goes uncannily on its belly (women, being the older half of us, have that hatred even stronger than men). And it is for the very same reason that one's primitive instinct loathes the tanks. They break the law of foot-or-wheel; it makes them unrighteous and frightening merely in themselves, without a thought of their guns and terrors. In fact, it is obvious to compare them to slugs: neither has anything apparent to move with, yet they do move.

E pur si muove: it is this that makes them so malign.

I do not feel that they waddle, as John Buchan says; their footless advance is ponderous, even, and smooth—exactly like the unctuous, inexorable advance of the great bulks that develop upon you in nightmare. As one climbs inside, however, one has no such comparisons, but rather feels as if one were prosaically getting into a 'bus. A 'bus not built for passengers, though: one crouches, and clutches, and braces one's feet, and clings passionately to any projection that comes handy (usually it is a boiling-water pipe), as off the thing goes lumbering. Over the ground it monumentally grinds; it is filled with clangor and roar, and emits eldritch screeches as it goes: the pandemonium is deafening, and as it turns it has a sleek, horrible effect of skidding. Anyhow, it is not from inside that you best appreciate the marvelousness of a tank: there you are merely deafened, dithered, and "churned to a pummy."

But imagine some music-hall on Olympus, and the time come for a tank to do its "turn." Before it there is a deep trench, or pit, more than thirty feet across, and as many deep. The rounded rhomboidal mass of Behemoth sits leadenly on the far side, lifting his blunted nose. then, with a jangling roar, the monster starts. "Without the smallest plunge or caper," he advanced implacably toward the trench; his nose hangs over, his four-quarters, half his body—more. Behemoth's centre of gravity must lie incredibly far back: for it seems a long age, and a monstrous miracle of magic, as he hangs out across the trench. One shivers in endless anticipation of the critical instant when the inevitable happens, and Behemoth nose-dives into the depths with a cataclysmal crash. And then, slowly, agonizingly, he roots up again on the near side, horribly like a gigantic, footless beast in agony, entrapped, nuzzling and nosing his way up, and up, and up, until he staggers, half-erect, against the brink; and so, higher and yet higher, till at last once more the centre of gravity is passed, and with a shattering crash, Behemoth falls forward on his belly again, and, after a few wild rockings fro and back, blandly proceeds toward his next trial.

Alfred Rosenblatt, Professor, University of Cracow: "The Civilizing Influences of War"

The supposed benefits of war throughout history is ever an open debate, but it does seem true that technology has often flowed through military invention. Even Leonardo Da Vinci, the great Renaissance genius, sold himself first as an engineer—and the main role of engineers during his lifetime was in the military.

New York Times Current History, October 1916–February 1917

We have to thank war for the founding and the development of cities and for their growth and strength. War forced the inhabitants of scattered districts to unite, to build fortified towns, and to organize places for defense against the dangers of war. The Princes' need of money, induced by the wars that they carried on, was often the cause of progress in their matter of public institutions and rights; that is to say, the sovereigns engaged in war needed money for the war and the cities furnished them with it in return for rights and privileges which made possible and also promoted the prosperity of the cities.

The greatest human blessings, religion and ethics, science and art, owe much more to war—as Professor Dargun points out—than would be believed without an investigation of the question. Through wars religion and ethics have found their way to all parts of the world.

Many branches of science receive their greatest advancement through wars.

In the first line comes geography. It is not necessary to prove that war requires a thorough and detailed study of the hostile country, thus promotes geographical and ethnical science, and contributes to the spread of this knowledge.

The great progress of modern technique stands in close connection with military technique. The mighty advance in the technique of fortification and the manufacture of arms promoted by war's needs has reacted in an animating manner upon all other branches of technical work and has aided invention. The mastery of the air by human beings and the unexpected development of the art of flying may certainly be traced indirectly to war. The extension of lines of communication, especially in the form of great and far-flung networks of railroads, is the result of the necessities of war.

The Problems of Technology and War

Anonymous: "The War and Aviation"

Growing revulsion during the nineteenth century over the brutality of war led governments to negotiate limits on what a warring power could do, even in battle. The 1907 Hague Convention did not specifically address the actions of airplanes, then in their infancy, but did address naval bombardment of civilian areas. It declared: "The bombardment by naval forces of undefended ports, towns, villages, dwellings, or buildings is forbidden." Unfortunately, warriors on both sides sometimes ignored this, although critics continued to question the morality of bombing civilians. It seems that World War I was the last time warring powers concerned themselves with such ethical debates. During World War II, bombing of civilian targets killed hundreds of thousands and flattened large cities. It has since become an accepted tactic of warfare.

***Nation*, November 12, 1914**

No one can have followed day by day the accounts of the war in the foreign press without being convinced of the value of this new instrument of warfare. But not as a destructive agent. The net result of all the bomb-dropping on both sides has been of the slightest, so far as concerns actual injuries or killings, or the destruction of property of value to the enemy. [U.S.] Gen. [George P.] Scriven is so impressed with this that he believes that bomb-dropping on land will be stopped by the consent of all civilized peoples. Humanity stands for almost every atrocity in war, but the killing of women and children by aviators, however unintentionally, seems beyond the pale. The fact that the British have not imitated the German tactics, in their flying over Bruges, will accentuate the demand that this form of warfare be placed alongside the poisoning of wells.

It has been but seldom that a discharge from aeroplane or dirigible has done substantial damage. At the outbreak of the war the French, whose achievements in aviation and possession of Clement-Bayard dirigibles had led to the belief that they would be the masters of the air, let loose a whole swarm of aviators. They not only crossed the German frontiers and bombarded some Rhine cities, but one even reached Nurnberg and dropped useless missiles upon that city—a fact which Germans are constantly citing in reply to the criticisms of those who denounce them for similar acts. This French air raid was a total failure.

Gilbert Grosvenor, Editor: "The War and Ocean Geography"

Of the war's new weapons, the submarine, played an important strategic and diplomatic role in the war's evolution. Submarines had been tried before, most famously in the U.S. Civil War, but the British development of a diesel-powered craft more reliable, more powerful, and more safe than previous subs made it the choice of Germany, which did not have power to command the sea from the surface. Its enthusiastic deployment of U-Boats (Unterseebootes) culminated in the single event that most turned American opinion against Berlin. On May 7, 1915, a German submarine torpedoed the Lusitania, *a British passenger ship, sending one of the Cunard Line's most elegant liners to the bottom. In total, 1,201 passengers perished and another 761 were rescued.*

National Geographic, September 1918

With more ships afloat than there were before the heartless Hun ran amuck with the submarine, there will be a greater demand for minute surveys of all shallow water in coastal territory—thousands of square miles will need even the intensive method of the wire drag, which does not trust to soundings to reveal pinnacle rocks, but touches every square inch of water at the appointed depth, and thus makes sure that nowhere is there an obstruction reaching above it.

It is probable that the submarine, an American invention prostituted to foul use by the Hun, will be rescued from its ignoble use and made to serve humanity where now it outrages civilization. Able now to descend to the bottom hundreds of feet below the surface, it is not improbable that before many years have passed submarine expeditions will take the place of polar expeditions and many mysteries of the sea will be solved.

One of the pressing problems of the after-the-war period will be that of the derelict. Among the millions of tons of shipping destroyed by the submarine, it is too much to hope that every ship torpedoed beyond the redemption of the salvage forces now lies harmless at the bottom of the ocean. That some of them are drifting derelicts, adding their menace to navigation, is certain.

S. Reinach, Paris, Letter to the Editor: "What about the Other Devices?"

Talk of limiting the destructiveness of armaments can be traced to ancient Greece. Efforts began in earnest as the industrial age gave real definition to the concept of weapons of mass destruction (WMD). Conferences at The Hague, Netherlands, at century's turn attracted leaders from 26 nations to address the issue. After the war the League of Nations tried to contain growing destructive power, but nations in World War II disregarded their guidelines. Nuclear weapons raised the stakes even higher. In the late 1960s the Soviet Union and United States met to consider arms control, with some success. A 1993 treaty sought to ban the most ghastly innovation from the trenches, chemical weapons.

Nation, August 2, 1917

The world must interfere and prohibit submarine warfare. But what about the bomb-throwing, baby-killing aeroplanes and Zeppelins? What about the huge shrapnel-shells and poison-spreading bombs? What about the use of gas and of liquid fire? Are those new methods of warfare less monstrous and less inhuman than the submarine? Do they not disregard to the same extent the difference between belligerents and non-belligerents? Are they not a shame as well as a scourge to the twentieth century? Are they not a return to the most primitive savagery, through the highway of perverted science?

I venture to believe that even the rabid Pan-Germanist now realizes that the time has come when all such fiendish devices must be suppressed, just as torture, slavery, and the like. But in order to make their return impossible after the present war—nay, to prevent that worse horrors should disgrace the future—there are no two methods available, but only one. This I had the honor of submitting to the readers of the Nation (June 15, 1916), and later on to those of the Journal de Genève (August 14); an enlarged version of the same article has been printed as a pamphlet ("Paix précaire ou paix durable") and, though not for sale, can be sent to any address for the asking. As an appendix to my paper, I collected and classified various expressions of opinion, which go far to show that many statesmen and thinkers are prepared to agree with this proposal—the international prohibition of any weapon or device intended for wholesale murder, or capable of being used to such an end. A few objections to my scheme have been raised and may be briefly dismissed as follows:

(1.) In spite of international prohibition and inspection, some sort of cheating might be resorted to by an ambitious Power, planning an unexpected attack. No cheating would be possible if a very large premium (from ten to twenty thousand dollars) were awarded to any workman or foreman revealing to the permanent Committee of Peace the doings of a secret factory. The guilty Power or individual would have to pay a heavy fine, larger than the premium, so as to prevent any tempting collusion between the informer and his employers.

(2.) Even if weapons for wholesale murder were prohibited, pugnacious nations could wage war with carbines or cudgels. Nonsense! No cudgels nor carbines can overcome a fence of barbed wire, and every frontier would henceforth be thus protected against a raid.

Arthur E. Holder, Legislative Representative, American Federation of Labor: "Growth of Industrial Democracy: Machinists as Peacemakers"

Machinists manufacture precision parts, and so played a critical role in World War I arms production. Some socialists encouraged unions of machinists to stage a general strike in response to a "bourgeois" war declaration, but none did. During the war their ranks swelled as new operators were recruited to match huge production goals. Women in particular could be trained in the role of providing precision parts using lathes and milling machines.

Annals of the American Academy of Political and Social Sciences, July 1917

I am a working man, a machinist. I must apologize for the lack of forethought and foresight of my trade. We are the ones who are really responsible for this war—our trade, the machinists—throughout the world. If we had been blessed with foresight, if we had possessed sufficient intelligence to have seen what was coming, if we had cooperated and united our forces with those of our fellow machinists in Germany, Great Britain, Italy, France and Russia, we could have said to kaisers, emperors, kings, princes and potentates, "If you want to fight, you make your own weapons; we machinists will not do it."

If I live, I am going to devote the balance of my life to seeing that, when this awful struggle is over and the butchery is ended, there will be a delegation of trade unionists representing the machinists of the United States, who will visit their fellow machinists in the several European countries and say to them,

Let us unite on behalf of peace and brotherhood. In the skill of our hands lies the destiny of the world. We can control it for peace and happiness, or for death and destruction. Let us put an end to machine butchery. Let us refuse to make weapons of war. We can if we will and for humanity's sake we will be, we must be, the great peacemakers in the future, so that the world shall never again be torn apart in the awful way that it has been during the three years, 1914 to 1917.

Editorial: "'Real War' and War As It Is"

World War I closely followed technical advancements that made photography easy enough for amateurs and flexible enough for professionals working in difficult conditions. Roll film and Kodak cameras were cheap enough for everyone to carry, including soldiers. They insisted on photographing their experiences, usually in spite of it being officially forbidden. Professionals shot miles of film, both as stills and newsreels, and publishing technologies perfected a dozen years earlier allowed those photos to appear directly in publications. Many newspapers offered special World War I photo sections or photo books. Still to come, however, was the portable 35 mm cameras, developed in the 1930s, and the flexibility of military censors who allowed photojournalists to record the brutal realities of death on the battlefield.

***Independent,* April 5, 1915**

At exhibitions of the motion or still pictures which are coming from Europe one often hears expressions of disappointment that there are no photographs of "real war." These soldiers entrenching—they might as well be Italians laying sewer pipes. This gun going off—where's the enemy? These sick and wounded, doctors and nurses—they might be in any hospital. This train of supplies—it is as dull as the loading of a ferry-boat. These refugees—why, they can't be real, for, see, the children are laughing, not crying, and the women have on their best clothes.

The popular disappointment is natural, but it arises from the fact that we are now getting for the first time real pictures of real war. This is actually what war is, nine-tenths of it, ninety-nine hundredths of it, mere ditch-digging, and firing at an invisible target and convalescing in the hospital and carting and being cheerful in adversity. What the painters have palmed off upon us before the rise of photography is not real war, or at most, only a small part of it. There are still occasionally hand-to-hand fights with the bayonet and cavalry charges, but one who gets his idea of warfare from Meissonier, De Neuville or Détaille will find it a very different thing when he enlists. Thanks to the silver film war is now being stripped of the glamour with which artists and poets have conspired to invest it and now stands revealed in all its dreary nakedness.

Editorial: "Lessons of the War"

The United States grew to rely on air support as its primary war weapon, and armor as its most formidable threat on the ground. But experience in Vietnam seemed to show that even these advanced versions of World War I inventions usually need to be supported by traditional infantry.

World's Work, April 1915

The threat of submarine operations has added tremendously to strategic and patrol problems in naval warfare, but it has not taken from the dreadnaught its place of primary importance.

Nor has the aeroplane become a deciding factor in war. It has fastened that honor more securely than before upon the guns. It has given eyes to the artillery so that supremacy in the air means chiefly better service of the guns and better intelligence of the enemies' movements. Attacks by aeroplanes and Zeppelins have had little or no direct military effect. The airship, like the submarine, has complicated warfare and added to its destructive powers. Neither has developed into a decisive method of attack itself.

The automobile also has increased the speed of troops and increased the commissariat facilities so that larger bodies of men can be maintained at the front than would otherwise be possible. In a few instances armored motor-cars have served in direct attack. But like the aeroplane, the motor-car has chiefly been useful in its auxiliary services to the men and guns at the front.

Questions

1. What technological innovations from World War I have grown to play a major role in subsequent wars?
2. How can wartime innovations benefit peacetime society?
3. Some critics contended that poison gas should be outlawed in warfare. Why is it considered worse than bullets or shells?
4. How did the automobile engine make possible war on the vast scale of World War I?

Chapter 21

Searching for Peace

The outbreak of a general war in 1914 did not physically affect most Americans. But ideologically it profoundly troubled many. They had long watched with unease as aggressive European rivalry, both in the Old Country and though an extensive network of global colonies, seemed to offer ample opportunity for well-armed governments to try politics by other means.

The same fears were growing in Europe itself, even as governments postured and threatened. Great Western philosophers throughout history had sought a means to avoid war in this traditionally bellicose subcontinent. Desiderius Erasmus, the Renaissance humanist, decried war's evils, while Hugo Grotius a century later tried to lay down rules for a just war. On the dark side, Nicolo Machiavelli's *The Prince*, written shortly after Erasmus's work, offers robust justification for European war. Thus thinkers through centuries of European history have wrestled with the lure of war versus the lust for peace.

The industrial age upped the stakes of choosing war, however, and the benefits of keeping peace. So much so that in 1898 Russian Czar Nicholas II asserted to the world of aggressive nation-states that something had to be done before Europe strangled itself. Coming from a notoriously conservative Russian monarchy, such a proposal surprised government leaders and peace philosophers. But its attractions led 26 nations to a peace conference at The Hague in an attempt to rekindle interest in establishing laws of war and limitation of arms. But if everyone agreed modern war would be horrible, no one was ready to denounce war as a tool of sovereign states. British naval dominance and German determination to build itself into a powerful competitor left two of the world's greatest powers skeptical of any pact that smacked of pacifism. Could there be a substitute for war as a valid political tool? The powers represented at the conferences of 1899 and 1907 could not agree. They did, however, agree to forge limits to the more brutal tactics of modern warfare—limits subsequently found unenforceable.

If no real progress had been made in the early twentieth century toward blunting the human tendency toward warmongering, thinkers continued to ponder and publish various ideas through articles and books. Most famous during this period was Norman Angell's *Europe's Optical Illusion*. Angell wrote his argument against war in 1909, following the First Moroccan Crisis, which nearly led Europe to blows. Disagreements between France, planning to chop Morocco into colonial spheres with Spain under Britain's encouragement, and Germany's objections, built to a diplomatic impasse. German Kaiser Wilhelm II sailed to Tangiers to demand an international conference in hopes France would be politically isolated. But the 1906 conference in Algeciras not only sustained colonial influence over Morocco, but bolstered the France-Britain entente.

War fears barely abated as Angell's pacifist contention that war could wreck the economies of both victor and vanquished led to discussion groups and classes that examined peace and economic advantage. Angell had worked on American and British newspapers, but resigned as editor of the *Daily Mail* Paris edition to advocate peace. Meanwhile, as Angell's expanded argument became his most famous work, *The Great Illusion*, Europe's diplomats again slipped toward the brink. The 1911 Agadir Crisis again pitted Germany against France and Britain over Morocco. Contending the Entente powers had not upheld their part of the 1906 bargain, Germany sent a threatening vessel, the *Panther*, to dramatize its concern. This "gunboat diplomacy," as the British called it, confronted Britain's control over Gibraltar and France's influence in Morocco. War seemed likely, but negotiations ended after Germany backed down in return for French concessions in the Congo. Still, the agreement did little to disperse the clouds of war cast over Europe, and talk of avoiding war intensified as fears of cataclysm daunted those who knew what modern weapons could do. In 1913 Angell founded *War and Peace*, a pacifist journal that included contributions from some of Britain's well-known peace theorists.

The flurry of interest in peace theory obviously failed to prevent the war. But talk didn't end in August 1914. While censorship settled most discussion in Europe, a debate continued in the United States. In December 1914 the Carnegie Endowment for International Peace began its study on the political and economic impact of war, while the media buzzed with arguments on how the conflict started, first, and more importantly, how it could be stopped. But those who joined the debate proposed arguments for peace so drastically different that consensus seemed impossible. This implacable debate actually mirrored similarly unbridgeable viewpoints between actual warring governments. Why did this war, immeasurably destructive to all involved, not end in common-sense peace talks? President Woodrow Wilson, as a credible neutral, tried to bring aggressors to the table. Toward the end of 1916 the Central Powers made a public overture to the allies offering to discuss peace. Terms of such a peace were not specified, however, so the offer was rebuffed. Wilson tried again, acting as an independent mediator. He suggested no warring power need announce its terms beyond one simple dictum: "peace without victory."

No power was willing to do this. In fact, had Berlin actually met with London and Paris at the same table, their demands would have been as incompatible as their languages. Opponents sought territorial gains and rights unacceptable to their rivals. Despite the frightful carnage, no one was ready to give up war aims that more and more took on a cloak of sacrosanct minimums. The growing number of war casualties could not be allowed to have died in vain.

Individual politicians tried to work around official channels for peace, treading perilously close to the shoals of treason. Joseph Caillaux, French premier during the Agadir Crisis, proposed peace negotiations and actually was charged with treason (but acquitted). The socialists—some of which were mortified that their rank and file had so enthusiastically joined the colors in 1914—tried to bring the faithful together in Zimmerwald, Switzerland, in 1915. Only 38 delegates attended. Subsequent attempts to remake the socialist international political force foundered as governments refused delegates visas to leave the country. By spring 1917, when the United States joined the war, talk of negotiated peace clearly was going nowhere. After Wilson declared war, debate over the road to peace dwindled to mostly a single viewpoint: peace through victory. Such became the actual slogan of the Carnegie Endowment for International Peace. In France Georges Clemenceau became a near-dictator whose famous response to any suggestion of peace without victory was those three little words militarists longed to hear: "I make war."

Searching for Peace by Conciliation and Religion

Fannie Fern Andrews, Member, Central Organization for a Durable Peace: "Central Organization for a Durable Peace"

No one in 1914 apparently even considered using the Hague Court of Arbitration, established in 1907, as a means to avoid war. A World Court formed along with the League of Nations after the war did no better in preventing an even worse carnage, World War II. After 1945 the World Court was resurrected as part of the United Nations. It still serves to arbitrate between conflicting states, although how successful it has been is open to debate.

Annals of the American Academy of Political and Social Science, July 1916

It is necessary to organize peace if it is to be durable. The program proposes, in addition to the Hague Court of Arbitration, a Court of Justice, a Council of Investigation and Conciliation, and the permanent organization of the Hague Conference. Thus no entirely new institution is included in the plan. the Hague Court of Arbitration presents a successful record since its organization in 1902. The Second Hague Conference voted by a large majority the project of an International Court of Justice, although, as is well known, if failed to realize on account of the difficulties incident to the problem of its composition. The idea of a Council of Investigation and Conciliation for dealing with non-justiciable questions, those indeed which are most likely to lead to war, has developed from the Commission of Inquiry established by the First Hague Conference. Finally, to look forward to the development of the Hague Conference into an international assembly, meeting periodically to formulate and codify rules of international law, coincides with the spirit of the Second Hague Conference in providing for the calling of the Third.

Besides urging the consideration of those principles of durable peace which should govern the Peace-settlement Congress, and the plan for international organization, the Central Organization for a Durable Peace states that the stability of peace will never be maintained by measures of international order alone. In speaking of the limitations of international law, Mr. Root said: "Law cannot control national policy, and it is through the working of long continued and persistent national policies that the present war has come. Against such policies all attempts at conciliation and good understanding and good-will among the nations of Europe have been powerless." the Program mentions two measures in this domain which are especially indispensable: (1) the guarantee to the national minorities of civil equality, religious liberty and the free use of their native languages; (2) the parliamentary control of foreign policies with interdiction of all secret treaties.

James Bryce: "War and Human Progress"

In his most well-known work, Politics, *German historian Heinrich von Treitschke wrote, "The grandeur of war lies in the utter annihilation of puny man in the great conception of the state, and it brings out the full magnificence of the sacrifice of fellow countrymen for one another. In war the chaff is winnowed from the wheat."*

Atlantic Monthly, **September 1916**

The great creative epochs have been those in which one people of natural vigor received an intellectual impulse from the ideas of another, as happened when Greek culture began to penetrate Italy, and, thirteen centuries later, when the literature of the ancients began to work on the nations of the medieval world.

Such contact, with the process of learning which follows from it, may happen in or through war, but it happens far oftener in peace; and it is in peace that men have the time and the taste to profit fully by it. A study of history will show that we may, with an easy conscience, dismiss the theory of Treitschke—that war is a health-giving tonic which Providence must be expected constantly to offer to the human race for its own good. Apart altogether from the hopes we entertain for the victory in this war of a cause which we believe to be just, we may desire in the interests of all mankind that its issue should discredit by defeat a theory which is noxious as well as baseless. The future progress of mankind is to be sought, not through the strifes and hatreds of the nations, but rather by their friendly cooperation in the healing and enlightening works of peace and in the growth of a spirit of friendship and mutual confidence which may remove the causes of war.

Harold de Wolf Fuller, Editor: "To the Readers of the Nation"

Peace delegates after the armistice searched for ways to reflect needs of peoples who feared great European power blocs, but still longed for self-determination. Hope that the former belligerent nations could accept renewed friendship and so act toward their neighbors with charity and patience proved to be far fetched after four years of slaughter. In fact, the delineations of territory designed to protect the rights of small nations from the wishes of larger failed as democracies fell to rapacious dictatorships in the 1920s and 1930s.

Nation, **December 28, 1916**

The promotion of democracy has been one of the few blessings of the war. Over and above the hates which have been engendered is the significant fact that the countries of Europe are becoming known to one another. The highly composite personnel of the Entente is even more important. Already the interplay of nationalities in this large group must have done much to level differences and thus to promote the idea of human brotherhood. England, as we know, is cultivating an admiration for Russian ideas; France's respect for England is now touched with the warmth of friendship, and all three of these powerful lands have inevitably gained in their sensitiveness to the claims of small nations. For the moment Europe is divided into two hostile camps, yet the exercise of sympathy which negotiations for peace will involve ought to furnish a basis for common understandings and by so much advance the cause of the peoples concerned—the cause of democracy.

Pope Benedict XV: "A Just and Durable Peace? The Pope's Appeal to the Belligerent Nations"

The Pope tried where Wilson had failed, to be a neutral mediator hoping to end the war. He sent messages offering himself in that role to all belligerents. In response, many Catholics chastised him for not supporting their country, which was obviously God's chosen belligerent.

***Independent,* August 25, 1917**

Toward the end of the first year of the war we addressed to the nations in conflict most lively exhortations, and more, we indicated the part to be followed to arrive at a stable and honorable peace for all. Unfortunately, our appeal was not heard and the war continued desperately for another two years with all its horrors. It became even more cruel and extended over the earth, over the sea and in the air, and one saw desolation and death descend upon the cities without defense, upon peaceful villages and on their innocent population, and now no one can imagine how the sufferings of all would be increased and aggravated if other months or, worse still, other years are about to be added to this sanguinary triennium.

Is this civilized world to be nothing more than a field of death? And Europe, so glorious and so flourishing—is it going as if stricken by a universal madness to run the abyss and lend its hand to its own suicide?

In such a terrible situation and in the presence of a menace so serious we, who have no particular political aim, who do not listen to suggestions or to the interests of any of the belligerent parties, but are solely compelled by a sentiment of our supreme duty as the common father of the faithful, by the solicitation of our children who implore our intervention and our pacifying word, thru the voice, even of humanity and of reason, we once more emit the cry of peace and we renew a pressing appeal to those who hold in their hands the destinies of nations.

Searching for Peace by Making War

Edgar Stanton Maclay: "The Horrors of Peace: This Article Was Written before There Was Any Indication of the Present European Outbreaks"

The argument that the globe can support a finite number of human beings has been advanced since Thomas Malthus first published his essay on population development in 1798. Still popular more than a century later, it did not take into account the "Green Revolution" of the late twentieth century, which increased food production many times over.

North American Review, **September 1914**

We must not close our eyes to the fact that there are fewer than thirty million square miles of land suitable for the support of mankind on this globe. Centuries of experience show that this land will not support more than an average of 100 persons per square mile; so the world's population would seem to be limited to three thousand millions. Already the earth's population exceeds half this limit. If all nations are to cease preparations for war and concentrate their energies in the pursuit of peace and happiness, the world's population will be more than three thousand millions in a single generation.

Obviously, if the world's population is not kept down by war, it must be restricted by other means. It is for the advocates of disarmament and universal peace to decide whether or not war is more horrible than the practice of infanticide, the burial alive of widows with the deceased husbands (now modified by the prohibition of widows marrying again), the periodical extermination of millions of men, women, and children by ruthless foreign invaders or by famine, pestilence, and floods, or by the wholesale prevention of children before they have had a chance to demonstrate their fitness to survive.

Aristide Briand, Premier of France: "Peace Through Victory Alone"

Briand served the French in a variety of government ministries during the first third of the twentieth century, including multiple times as prime minister. Despite serving in that capacity for 18 months during the war, Briand's longest struggle both in government and out (as a journalist for several newspapers) aimed at abolishing war as a tool of government policy. Toward that end he negotiated in 1928 the Pact of Paris with U.S. Secretary of State Frank B. Kellogg, a declaration renouncing war.

His efforts earned him a Nobel Peace Prize, although they failed to stop a second world war.

***New York Times Current History*, April–September 1916**

Peace will come out of the victory of the Allies; it can come only out of our victory. Peace must not be an empty formula; it must be based upon international law, guaranteed by sanctions, against which no country will be able to take its stand. That peace will shine on humanity and bring security to the peoples who will be able to work and evolve according to their genius. Blood will no longer be upon them.

It is this ideal which gives our task its greatness. It is in the name of this ideal that our soldiers are fighting and exposing themselves so lightheartedly to death; it is in the name of this idea that mothers, wives, daughters, and sisters in mourning are keeping back their tears, knowing that the sacrifice of a son, husband, father, or brother will not have been useless to their native land and to humanity. That is the only peace for which we must strive. It is by that peace that our countries will grow nobler and finer. We shall obtain the victory of our arms, which will assure us this peace, by united action and by a ceaselessly active and increasingly intimate fraternization. We owe this victory to humanity—and it is coming.

Lord Cromer, Former British Ruler of Egypt: "Wilson's Mediation Not Acceptable"

Evelyn Baring, the first Lord Cromer, is remembered as a colonial overlord steeped in the values of imperial British rule. The work here reflects distrust of the Wilson administration's peace efforts felt generally in London. The British somewhat resented Wilson's determination to act unilaterally to find a way to peace. Wilson also did not consult British allies before presenting his famous Fourteen Points for peace in early 1918, although they were similar to proposals already made by British statesmen.

***New York Times Current History*, April–September 1916**

As note has succeeded note and speech followed speech, the conviction has been steadily gaining ground that President Wilson has wholly failed to grasp the view entertained by the vast majority of Englishmen on the cause for which we and our allies are fighting. this opinion will certainly be confirmed by the amazing statement that America is not concerned with the causes and objects of the war.

Confidence in President Wilson's statesmanship has been rudely shaken. Neither for the moment does it appear likely to be restored to the extent of acquiescence in the proposal that he should be in any way vested with the power of exercising any decisive influence on the terms of peace, upon which the future destinies of this country and of the civilized world will greatly depend.

Dr. von Bethmann Hollweg, Imperial Chancellor: "Attitude of the German Government"

Theobald von Bethmann Hollweg shouldered the imposing burden of mediating between liberals and conservatives during the war in a country influenced by the Prussian values of military dominance. His response to his role as the public face of the German government put him into paradoxical positions. On the one hand, he tried to avoid dragging his country into war. On the other hand, he famously called Britain's promise to defend Belgium from invasion a "scrap of paper." He tried to stay the German High Command from implementing the Schlieffen Plan against France. But he gave Austria-Hungary the "blank check" of support in their bellicose demands to Serbia that pushed the first domino that tumbled Europe into war.

***New York Times Current History*, April–September 1916**

One day when history will weigh the guilt of having started this most monstrous of all wars and of protracting it, the appalling mischief will be realized which ignorance and hypocrisy have caused. As long as the statesmen in power in the enemy countries combine guilt and ignorance, and their views sway the hostile nations, any offer of peace on our part would be folly, and would protract rather than shorten the war. The masks must be dropped first. A war of annihilation is still being waged against us. We have to reckon with that fact. We cannot make any headway or reach our goal with theories and expressions of peace. If our enemies come with proposals of peace which are compatible with the dignity and safety of Germany we are at all times ready to discuss them. In the full consciousness of the military successes which we have achieved we do not hold ourselves responsible for the continuation of the misery which afflicts Europe and the world. Nobody shall be able to say that we wished to protract the war needlessly because we wanted to conquer other dead pledges.

Dr. von Bethmann Hollweg, German Imperial Chancellor: "Peace on a Basis of the Real Facts"

After war dragged on into 1916, Bethmann Hollweg publicly indicated his support for a negotiated peace, asking Wilson to serve a mediator. The allies rejected his call. Even if they had accepted, by this time Germany was becoming in effect a military dictatorship. The high command wanted no part of a negotiated peace. Bethmann Hollweg finally resigned in July 1917, attacked by conservatives and liberals in the German Reichstag.

***New York Times Current History,* April–September 1916**

But, as I have already said to you, a general press polemic and public speeches will only tend still more to intensify the hatred among peoples. And that is not a way that leads to the ideal conditions of Sir Edward Grey, when free peoples and nations, with equality of rights and privileges, will limit their armaments and solve their differences and disputes through arbitration's decisions instead of war.

I have twice publicly stated that Germany has been and is prepared to discuss the termination of the war upon a basis that offers guarantee against further attack from a coalition of her enemies and insures peace to Europe. You have read President Poincaré's answer to that.

One thing I do know—only when statesmen of the warring nations come down to a basis of real facts, when they take the war situation as every war map shows it to be, when, with honest and sincere will they are prepared to terminate this terrible bloodshed and are ready to discuss the war and peace problems with one another in a practical manner, only then will we be nearing peace.

Whoever is not prepared to do that has the responsibility for it if Europe continues to bleed and tear itself to pieces. I cast that responsibility far from myself.

Woodrow Wilson: "Let the German People Speak! President Wilson's Answer to the Pope's Plan for Peace"

One reason the allies never seriously considered a negotiated peace can be blamed on the Schlieffen Plan. German Chief of Staff Alfred von Schlieffen had devised a secret plan based on a fast, powerful offensive to knock out France before Russia had a chance to mobilize and squeeze a vise on Germany from two sides. The operative word was fast: opposition by Belgium, or feet-dragging by civilian leaders, had to be neutralized as quickly as possible. In the eyes of the rest of the world, however, this plan made Germany appear to be the aggressor—particularly in its invasion of neutral Belgium, and alleged atrocities its soldiers committed there.

***Independent,* September 8, 1917**

His Holiness in substance proposes that we return to the status quo antibellum and that then there be a general condonation, disarmament and a concert of nations based upon an acceptance of the principle of arbitration; that by a similar concert freedom of the seas be established; and that the territorial claims of France and Italy, the perplexing problems of the Balkan States, and the restitution of Poland be left to such conciliatory adjustments as may be possible in the new temper of such a peace, due regard being paid to the aspirations of the peoples whose political fortunes and affiliations will be involved.

It is manifest that no part of this program can be successfully carried out unless the restitution of the status quo ante furnishes a firm and satisfactory basis for it. The object of this war is to deliver the free peoples of the world from the menace and the actual power of a vast military establishment, controlled by an irresponsible Government, which, having secretly planned to dominate the world, proceeded to carry the plan out without regard either to the sacred obligations of treaty or the long-established practices and long-cherished principles of international action and honor; which chose its own time for the war; delivered its blow fiercely and suddenly; stopped at no barrier, either of law or of mercy; swept a whole continent within the tide of blood—not the blood of soldiers only, but the blood of innocent women and children also and of the helpless poor; and now stands balked, but not defeated, the enemy of four-fifths of the world.

This power is not the German people. It is the ruthless master of the German people. It is no business of ours how that great people came under its control or submitted with temporary zest to the domination of its purpose; but it is our business to see to it that the history of the rest of the world is no longer left to its handling.

Editorial: "The Way of Peace"

Hope of a negotiated peace to end the war dwindled by the close of 1917. In France, Georges Clemenceau had been named prime minister. "The Tiger's" fierce response to any suggestion of peace without victory was: "I make war." In Germany, Bethmann Hollweg, having failed to persuade the military that resuming unrestricted submarine warfare would lead to his country's defeat, resigned. Russia was out of the war, but the United States was in. And after America jumped off the fence, talk of negotiation became treason. Although belligerents postured a fight to the finish, the war did end in an armistice. The losing side's military remained intact, and the allies did not march into Berlin.

Nation, October 26, 1918

It is a curious fact that the United States, having gone to war to abolish militarism and the rule of force, and with solemn declaration of its purpose to make the world safe, not for armies, but for democracy, should now be urged by Republican leaders to spurn all offers of peace in advance, overrun Germany with its armies, and dictate the terms of settlement at Berlin. This is Junkerism and militarism of the most approved German sort. However its particular object may be camouflaged by talk about freeing Europe from oppression, its spirit and method are essentially at one with those of the Kaiser and his supporters. With such a programme, discussion is of course quite out of the question; the peace for which the world yearns, the political freedom which Americans have believed was somehow the birthright of all mankind, is to be achieved only by smashing through to Berlin.

Searching for Peace as Prelude to War

Sydney Brooks: "Side-Issues of the War"

Of Wilson's Fourteen Points, nine touched on the right of self-determination in Europe, including Turkey. After the war the Treaty of Versailles addressed boundary changes in a wide variety of countries and colonies around the world. Wilson hoped ethnic self-determination would help to avoid the tensions that contributed to war, but his ideals were undercut by other allied victors who had long before the end of the war concluded secret agreements to reward those who participated in the war on allied side.

Atlantic Monthly, September 1915

But all forecasts, all possibilities, are subject to the issue of the struggle and the nature of the peace. The world is at war to-day very largely because the Congress of Vienna one hundred years ago redrew the map of Europe on the artificial and transient lines of dynastic claims and antiquated technicalities, and ignored the rights and sentiments and individuality of the people it was dealing with. Since then democracy and nationality have made themselves felt as the most potent of all forces in the politics of to-day. If the settlement is guided by them, a new and saner dispensation may be created such as Europe has not seen since the peace of the Antonines was broken. For by far the most crucial question propounded by the war is not its effect upon this country or upon that, but whether it is to end merely to be renewed later on, or whether "the greatest of all wars" is to be also the last.

Ellen Key, Noted Swedish Champion of Woman's Rights: "War, Peace, and the Future"

Many writers before World War I predicted a general European conflagration; the term "great war" had long been coined before the Great War began. After the Great War, many prognosticators were no longer optimistic. The disappointing Treaty of Versailles seemed to show that no one could put Europe together again, that despite the lofty idealism of the soldiers and the propagandists, the war had solved nothing. The 1920s began in a world shattered and disillusioned.

***New York Times Current History*, April–September 1916**

That many generations may yet have to succeed each other before this light can rise for the nations of western Europe there can be little doubt. I am far from believing, as many do, that the present war will increase the possibility of peace in the future. It may be that greater political activity on the part of European women and the working classes will influence the existing understanding of what constitutes national power, honor, and glory. But notwithstanding all this, it may take hundreds of years before the insanity of the world war will see itself conquered by the common sense policy of world organization through reason.

Searching for Peace by Abolishing War

Andrew Carnegie: "A League of Peace—Not 'Preparation for War'"

Steel magnate Andrew Carnegie retired in 1901 as one of the world's richest businessmen. He spent the rest of his life building libraries and establishing philanthropic foundations, including in 1910 one devoted to peace, the Endowment for International Peace. His mission, "to hasten the abolition of international war, the foulest blot upon our civilization," was not successful, although the endowment still exists in hope that someday his vision will be realized.

***Independent*, October 19, 1914**

We have seen that "preparation for war" by one nation begats similar preparation by those nations which feel themselves endangered. The remedy for this is evidently one world-wide organization of as many peaceful powers as possible to prevent war and insist that differences between nations shall be peacefully adjusted by the Hague Conference, or other tribunal satisfactory to the contendents. In the last resort, if necessary, the World Peace Court could deliver judgment by a majority vote, which would be binding upon the powers.

Without separate armies and navies there could be no war, the world would be at peace. This fact cannot be gainsaid. It is therefore in this direction that men of peace should labor. . . .

War, as the guardian of international peace, after twenty centuries of trial, has proved a traitor thereto, waging as it is today, the greatest of all wars that ever devastated the earth and sacrificing thousands of men weekly to death in this, the Twentieth Century of Christianity.

I submit that we have tried this enemy of the Peaceful Brotherhood of Men too long. Now the hosts of blest World-Peace should be summoned to perform their stern duty, which shall cease only when the prophecy is fulfilled, "Men shall beat their swords into ploughshares and their spears into pruning hooks; nation shall not lift up sword against nation, neither shall they learn war any more."

Any platform short of this fails to bridge the chasm between Peace and War. We must span the roaring torrent from side to side—and never rest until the day of blest peace returns.

We have abolished slavery from civilized nations, the owning of man by man. The next great step that the advanced powers of the civilized world should take is to abolish war, the killing of man by man. God speed that day!

George Bernard Shaw: "The Falling Market in War Aims"

The Irish playwright George Bernard Shaw, like many socialists, opposed Britain's entry into World War I. Unlike many socialists, Shaw also was one of the era's most famous writers. He spared little of his famous wit unmasking the folly of the war and the ineptitude of its protagonists. His collected writings on the war include Common Sense about the War, *published in 1914.*

New York Times Current History, October 1917–March 1918

When everything that can be said for war has been said a thousand times; when to the wretched plea that the distribution of our wealth was so bad, the condition of our people so poor, and our public sloth and carelessness so disastrous that an iron scourge was needed to drive us to do better, we add the less disgraceful claim that pride, honor, courage, and defiance of death flame up in war into a refiner's fire, yet nothing can conceal the blasting folly, the abominable wickedness, the cruelty and slavery with which war wreaks life's vengeance on those who will respond to no gentler or holier stimulus. In the midst of our stale paraphrases of the heroics of Henry V our eye lights on some name of youthful promise in the roll of honor, and sees suddenly through the splendid mask of victory to the grinning skull beneath.

E. A. Smith, Los Altos, California, Letter to the Editor: "Roosevelt and Wilson"

Theodore Roosevelt set the standard as an American man of action in the early twentieth century. The world's most famous politician was also its most famous adventurer, leading, as the title of his inspirational 1904 book asserted, The Strenuous Life. *The book begins, "I wish to preach, not the doctrine of the ignoble ease, but the doctrine of the strenuous life, the life of toil and effort, of labor and strife; to preach the highest form of success which comes, not to the man who desires mere easy peace, but to the man who does not shrink from danger, from hardship, or from bitter toil, and who out of these wins the splendid ultimate triumph."*

North American Review, April 1918

Roosevelt, with almost or quite German fervor, has lauded war as war. Years ago he said: "We must play a great part in the world, and especially perform those deeds of blood, of valor, which above everything else bring national renown. * * * By war alone can we acquire these virile qualities necessary to win in the stern strife of actual life." (The Strenuous Life.) To-day, in spite of the incredible sufferings of the war-worn, overtaxed world, he reiterates that his hope for future peace lies in our building up an army after the war which shall be "the most efficient in the world." To the President's statement that: "In every discussion of the peace that must end this war it is taken for granted that that peace must be given by some definite concert of power, which will make it virtually impossible that any such catastrophe should ever overwhelm it again," he scornfully replied that "war might end when the millennium had come and human nature had changed."

It takes vision of a noble sort to be a leader in the changing of that same human nature, which now, as never before, is prepared for the change by universal suffering: to see that not even how long the war lasts is so vital as that it should end war. The tragic pity of it is that such a forceful natural leader as Roosevelt has not that vision; will not cast his great influence on the side of the world's desperate need—on the side of progress.

Searching for Peace by Changing Mental Attitude

Anonymous: "War Madness"

Throughout the centuries, enthusiasm at the commencement of hostilities has become an expected public response to war. In World War I, every country's leaders saw jubilant multitudes swarm the streets on its war declaration—including the Untied States on April 6, 1917. By 1917 it cannot be said that Americans did not know how murderous this war had become. They still celebrated. Celebrated what? Wartime enthusiasm was an act of patriotism, the true patriot maintaining that the individual should put loyalty and sacrifice above personal self-interest. The power of patriotic fervor could induce citizens to sublimate even the natural instinct toward self-preservation, an instinct that in normal circumstances would lead rational human beings to flee combat. The strength of patriotism does tend to disintegrate as a war lengthens. In World War I it reached a point where one government, Russia, could not continue.

Nation, July 30, 1914

Bishop Butler once speculated on the possibility of a whole nation going suddenly insane. If he were alive to-day, he could extend his query and ask if a half-dozen nations at once might not become crazy. In Vienna, in Paris, In Berlin, in St. Petersburg, he would see signs of acute mania afflicting large bodies of people. Mob psychology often shows itself in discouraging and alarming forms, but is never so repulsive and appalling as when it is seen in great crowds shouting for war. Lest we forget, indeed! About nothing does the mob forget so quickly as about war. The Parisian crowd is crying out to-day "à Berlin!" just as if the same madness had not filled the streets of Paris in 1870, with what ravage and humiliation to follow, others have not forgotten even if the French mob has. And the way in which the war-fever has seized upon Berlin seems equally to call for the services not of a physician, but of an alienist. If one looked only at these surface manifestations, one would be tempted to conclude that Europe was about to become a gigantic madhouse.

John Bassett Moore: "The Peace Problem"

John Bassett Moore, an American authority on international law, served on the Hague Tribunal and World Court, the first American to act as a jurist for that assembly. He spoke against the tangling alliances that he believed led to World War I and advocated neutrality as a way to avoid future wars. He wrote several standard works on international law.

North American Review, July 1916

For the preservation of peace all devices, such as international conferences, arbitration, mediation and good offices, are or may be useful, according to the circumstances of the case; but back of all this we must in the last analysis rely upon the cultivation of a mental attitude which will lead men to think first of amicable processes rather than of war when differences arise. To this end it will be necessary to rid the mind of exaggerated but old and generally prevalent notions as to the functions of the State, of superstitions as to "trial by battle," of the conceptions that underlie the law of conquest, and of the delusion that one's own motives are always higher, purer and more disinterested than those of other persons, to say nothing of the passion for uniformity that denies the right to be different.

Bertrand Russell: "War As an Institution"

Russell's remarkable 97-year lifespan included a tremendous output of writings on logic and philosophy, and consistent antiwar agitation from World War I through the 1950s. His antiwar activities cost him his Trinity College Cambridge lectureship in 1916, although he returned there in 1944. In 1918 he spent six months in jail on a second conviction for his war protests.

Atlantic Monthly, May 1916

The impulse to quarrelling and self-assertion, the pleasure of getting one's own way in spite of opposition, is native to most men. It is this impulse, rather than any motive of calculated self-interest, which produces war, and makes the difficulty of bringing about a world-state. And this impulse is not confined to one nation; it exists, in varying degrees, in all the vigorous nations of the world.

But although this impulse is strong, there is no reason why it should be allowed to lead to war. It was exactly the same impulse which led to dueling; yet now civilized men conduct their private quarrels without bloodshed. If political contest within a world-state were substituted for war, men's imaginations would soon accustom themselves to the new situation, as they have accustomed themselves to absence of dueling. Through the influences of institutions and habits, without any fundamental change in human nature, men would learn to look back upon war as we look upon the burning of heretics or upon human sacrifice to heathen deities. If I were to buy a revolver costing several pounds, in order to shoot my friend with a view to stealing sixpence out of his pocket, I should be thought neither very wise nor very virtuous. But if I can get sixty-five million accomplices to join me in this criminal absurdity, I become one of a great and glorious nation, nobly sacrificing the cost of my revolver, perhaps even my life, in order to secure the sixpence for the honor of my country. Historians, who are almost invariably sycophants, will praise me and my accomplices if we are successful, and say that we are worthy successors of the heroes who overthrew the might of Rome. But if my opponents are victorious, if their sixpences are defended at the cost of many pounds each and the lives of a large proportion of the population, then historians will call me a brigand (as I am), and praise the spirit and self-sacrifice of those who have resisted me.

Searching for Peace through Human Rights and International Justice

Philip Marshall Brown, Princeton University: "Elements of a Just and Durable Peace"

How is peace to be defined? This question was central to the plethora of writings and societies on peace that sprung up after the war. The simple definition, an absence of war, was to many too negative. Peace must be defined in a positive way, they believed. Defining it as a freedom—freedom from war—emphasizes its attractions as part of human rights cherished in Western democracies. But freedom from war does not always mean total freedom. A brutish dictator might keep his country at peace, but is that more valuable than a people's revolution, and perhaps a better peace in the future? The question of peace has been examined more methodically in recent years with the establishment of academic departments and institutes for peace studies. But they have been controversial; detractors contend such programs merely provide a cover for liberal activism.

Annals of the American Academy of Political and Social Sciences, July 1917

First of all, we should recognize that peace is not the supreme aim of society. Like pleasure, contentment, character and virtue, peace is only a by-product. It is a result. It comes to the individual and the community alike when men live honestly and justly; when they have fought with the beasts at Ephesus, and conquered the forces of evil. Peace comes through warfare with vice and injustice. The supreme aim of society is not peace itself, but the triumph of justice. And men often know peace only when they are actually engaged in the fight for justice.

Nothing could have been more infellicious than the choice of the name of "The League to Enforce Peace." The enforcement of peace would be as abhorrent as it would be futile. The idea is as offensive as the so-called "pacification" of peoples by the armies of tyrants or conquerors. There can be no enforcement of peace, no true pacification where wrongs remain unavenged, and justice does not prevail. The true aim of all who desire peace should be, not the enforcement of peace, but the enforcement of justice.

Justice, then, being the final goal of society, how is it to be attained? In any association of men for mutual benefit, the first aim is to determine their interests and rights. They then seek to find the most effective way to protect their rights.

In order to determine rights, it is essential that men should share common conceptions of rights and obligations. They must think fundamentally alike. In order to protect their rights, they must have a direct control over the making of law, its interpretation and enforcement. Men are unwilling to abdicate entirely their rights into the hands of any absolute, final authority. The sentiment of justice is, indeed, a primitive instinct. Though torrents of blood must flow, men will never cravenly surrender the cause of justice for the cause of peace.

L. Simons: "Neutrals and Permanent Peace"

World War I ended with an armistice, that is, a truce. It did not end with a decisive allied victory. The German army was on retreat, but still a fighting force, and still occupying parts of France and Belgium. Allied troops were nowhere near Berlin and never got there. Obvious by fall 1918, when the German high command asked for peace, was that the allies were winning, and that Germany itself was threatened by revolution. But their decision to quit while still in the fight handed an opportunity to the country's postwar critics who contended that Germany lost the war not because it lost on the battlefield, but because it was sabotaged from within by internal enemies—such as the Jews. Would Hitler have had the ideological ammunition he needed to grow Nazism had the allies rejected the armistice and drove all the way to Berlin?

Atlantic Monthly, August 1917

War is nothing but a disease in the body politic, like fever in the human body. If we want to know how to prevent it, we must first study the causes which lead to it, and the hygienic measures which are most likely to remove those causes. The question of medical or surgical treatment comes in only when hygiene has proved unsuccessful in its preventative working. As regards the present war and its effect on future peace or strife, my article on "Neutral Europe and the War" is as clearly outspoken as any one could desire, my aim having been to prove beyond doubt that, if this war were to end with a decisive victory of either side and the consequent crushing of the vanquished beneath the conqueror's feet, the world would be ripe for a fresh period of unrest, ending in a more terrible war; just as the peace of Frankfort, in 1871 had as its sequel the nursing of French revanche and the present war. When President Wilson in December addressed the belligerent powers, he gave weight and prestige to the same point of view.

If the world is to be given a chance for anything like a permanent settlement at the conclusion of this war, it will have to adopt the basic principles of no annexations, no economic leagues of one group against the other. the watchword of the future will have to be international cooperation, certainly not international economic strife assisted by protection and elimination.

George W. Kirchwey, PhD, Professor of Law, Columbia University: "How America May Contribute to the Permanent Peace of the World"

At the war's beginning in 1914, the United States declared itself neutral and pacific. Whether it was economically neutral is debatable, as it was shipping goods and making loans to the allies. But it was relatively pacific; the U.S. Army in 1914 consisted of a 128,000-man contingent designed for domestic defense, with modest stocks of armaments. To turn America into a nation capable of conducting battles on the scale of World War I required immense effort. But the United States, as the world's greatest economic power, proved to be up to the task, producing an army of five million by war's end. After the war the country's deep isolationist tradition reasserted itself, but once America fell into World War II, it never returned to its neutral roots. Its huge arms buildup during the second half of the century, and its participation in numerous wars, has led some historians to conclude the United States clearly has embraced values of militarism.

Annals of the American Academy of Political and Social Science, July 1915

The point that I wish to insist upon is this: that we must not be driven by panic into adopting an attitude of militarism towards the rest of the world, as the nations of Europe were driven by panic into the militarism which finally resulted in this war. In that way destruction lies, and nothing but destruction. We are, then, to maintain our position as a pacific, peace-loving people.

And in the second place, we are, by virtue of our position in the world, the great neutral, as well as the great pacific, power. As such we owe to all other neutral peoples a duty—the duty of leading them in the ways of peace—of cooperating with them in the great work of making the world a world in which a nation shall be free to lead a peaceful life without undue interference from nations that are still dominated by the war spirit. And it seems to me that this duty cannot be property discharged by use if we continue to work alone and for the protection solely of our own national interests; it requires us to get into close working relations with all other neutral peoples, to enter inter conference with them with a view to common, concerted action for the protection of neutral rights and interest.

In the third place, we are, in a peculiar sense, trustees of one of the chief goods of civilization, the international law of the world, that body of rules and principles which represents what Gladstone called "the public right" of Europe and the civilized world—perhaps the greatest achievement of the international mind, during the last hundred years. This public right has no sanction, in the strict legal sense. No military force, no international politic stands behind it, to give it power. It rests solely upon the public opinion of the civilized world—and the public opinion of half the world is paralyzed by war, and that of the other half is benumbed by fear or by indifference. It is for us, I believe, to come out into the daylight, to take our place in the sun, and to stand for these violated principles of international law, to the end that public right shall not perish from the earth.

John J. MacCracken, PhD, LL.D., President, Lafayette College: "The Basis of a Durable Peace"

Despite isolationists advising the president to avoid involvement in peace terms, by 1917 President Wilson decided that only a strong neutral nation could lead Europe out of the quagmire. His efforts to find a "peace without victory" grew into the Fourteen Points, unveiled in January 1918. The ideas contained in the points had been long debated in progressive circles favored by Wilson. But in the end, the president fashioned his points without seeking input from colleagues or allies. Not allowing France and England to "buy in" before announcing the points perhaps weakened their utility during peace negotiations. On the other hand, collaboration with allies who disagreed on peace terms might have delayed the points indefinitely.

Annals of the American Academy of Political and Social Science, July 1916

Discussions of peace terms are premature. The war is not yet over. For Americans to assume that they will have much to say about the terms of peace, except in so far as those terms affect the rights of neutrals, would be justly resented by those who are bearing the burden of the war. If Washington's maxim, "avoid entangling foreign alliances" prevents us from lifting a finger to stay a cataclysm, certainly it should prevent us taking any part in the distribution of the plums. I take it, therefore, that in discussing the basis of a durable peace it is not intended that we should discuss the terms of peace which may conclude the present war; whether Germany should keep Belgium or Alsace Lorraine, whether Poland should be independent, whether Servia should be annexed to Austria-Hungary, whether Germany's colonies should remain in the hands of France or England, returned to Germany, or made independent. Whether the peace to be concluded in 1917 or 1918 will endure until 2017 or 2018, will depend largely on what the terms of that peace are. Nevertheless, they are not our business.

We may, however, as political philosophers, subscribe to certain general propositions:

(1) A peace may be durable because protected by overpowering force.
(2) A peace may be durable because held in equilibrium by nicely calculated adjustments of the balance of political power.
(3) A peace may be durable because it rests upon justice and because the conditions which it creates or inherently reasonable. . . .

Nor can we say that the only condition of a durable peace is the decisive defeat of one side or the other. If Germany is victorious a durable peace may come, backed by an invincible army and economic vassalage. If the allies win, a durable peace may come backed by nice balances of power and the limitations placed upon militarism. A drawn conflict might conceivably be followed by a century of peace, through a new alignment of the allies. Stranger things have happened in history than that Russia and Japan, England and Germany should make common cause. As President Tupper has recently said: "The cessation from war may be prolonged for a century through causes not one of which may be to the honor of peace." No, it is unprofitable to be drawn into European family troubles, and to be made a divider of family estates between brothers.

Searching for Peace by Morality in Materialism

L. P. Jacks: "War and the Wealth of Nations"

Economics had become a topic of serious study as early as the 1500s. But it was not until before World War I that economists began to establish a scientific and statistical approach to production, consumption, and transfer of wealth. The economic theories of Karl Marx inspired ideals of American socialism during one of its most influential periods. Prevalent among explanations for war was the conviction that wars result from economic dislocations poorly managed by national leaders.

Atlantic Monthly, September 1915

What is the cause of the terrible calamities which are now falling on the civilized world? Surely it lies in the fact that the economic development of mankind has outstripped the moral development. The nations of the world have grown richer without becoming wiser and juster in a corresponding degree. We all know that the possession of great riches is a dangerous thing—dangerous for the possessor and dangerous for his neighbors. We all know what the dangers are; we know further that they can be averted only if the moral development of the man's character keeps pace with the economic development of his wealth. I suppose that few of us would object to a man's increasing his possessions tenfold, provided that the sense of justice and his wisdom were increased to correspond. But if his wisdom and sense of justice lagged behind, while his fortune when ahead, we should be justly alarmed for the consequences both to the man and to his neighbors. This holds good of nations as well as of individuals. And the fact is that during the past fifty years the wealth of the world has gone ahead by leaps and bounds, while the morality of the world has moved only at a snail's pace.

Indeed, there are pessimists who maintain that morality has not improved, but rather deteriorated. That I do not believe; at all events it is a disputable proposition. It may be true of certain countries—I believe it is true of Germany—but it is not true of the civilized world taken as a whole. At the same time it is indisputable that morality, by which I mean justice and wisdom, has not advanced, anywhere, in the degree that is needed to deal justly and wisely with the enormous accession of riches which has suddenly fallen to the lot of the human race. Material prosperity has taken the world unawares; morally the nations were unprepared for it; some of them made ready for war, but none of them made ready for the greater dangers of peace. The nations have acquired all this wealth, but in the deepest sense they don't know what to do with it; they don't know how it ought to be handled; they don't know how to make it a blessing, or even how to prevent it from being a curse. This disparity between the moral and the economic development is the prime cause of our present trouble.

QUESTIONS

1. One reason why World War I countries at war could not accept a negotiated peace centered around the belief that many thousands of soldiers who had died could not die in vain, that only victory would make their sacrifice worth while. Is this a reasonable argument? Why or why not?
2. Why would President Wilson be seen as a credible mediator for peace among European nations?
3. Is there a point in holding a conference to agree on limits to war, as in 1899 and 1907, if those limits are not practically enforceable?

Chapter 22

The League of Nations

An association of nations had been the dream of political philosophers and activists in the years before the 1918 armistice. The principle of nationalism that coalesced into powerful new countries, particularly Germany in 1871, drove major powers to protect their influence through secret treaties. This system of nations maneuvering through rivalries, confrontations, and large standing armies, detractors believed, dragged the world into a war no one wanted. The answer to avoiding a similar mistake could be found by establishing a supra-national association that could make redundant treaties between nations, arbitrate disagreements, and enforce decisions that would make war costly and pointless. The proliferation of books and articles debating such an association attracted British Foreign Secretary Edward Grey, who championed the liberals in proposing a society of nations. Grey's credibility was marred by his partisan role as foreign affairs minister for one of the war's principal belligerent powers. His proposal fell with little effect. It is probable, however, that it influenced President Wilson. The president certainly read commentaries of the progressives in the United States who also promoted the idea. On January 8, 1918, Wilson proposed his Fourteen Points in a speech to Congress, a platform on which he believed a durable peace could be built. His faith that these idealistic precepts could work relied on the influence of an association of nations, a League of Nations. In announcing point fourteen, Wilson told Congress, "A general association of nations must be formed under specific covenants for the purpose of affording mutual guarantees of political independence and territorial integrity to great and small states alike."

The League of Nations was designed to work by mutual agreement of all member states, in particular the most powerful. These would examine claims and enforce decisions. How would they be enforced? Economic sanctions, certainly. Possibly military sanctions as well, a multinational armed force that could make large national armies unnecessary for security. French Prime Minister Georges Clemenceau, among many skeptical about the utility of a League, was one who promoted a common army. Wilson and British Prime Minister David Lloyd George opposed Clemenceau. In fact, the French leader's view of humanity was cynical at the core, skeptical at the outset. Wilson's idealistic promotion of the League only provoked Clemenceau to scoff, "we shall see," and to propose instead a traditional defensive military alliance against a Germany, a country that had invaded his twice in his lifetime.

The League's first purpose, as Wilson envisioned it, was to stop the kind of war that had horrified the world and left almost 10 million dead. Nations would be invited to join a general assembly, whose purpose would be to evaluate nations applying for admission, manage League finances, amend the League covenant, and discuss issues of war and peace. To take action against warring nations required a unanimous vote of the League council.

The council could avert war in three ways. Its first approach, mediating between disputants at League headquarters in neutral Geneva, Switzerland, might lead to a warning against offending belligerents. If this were not heeded, a second approach, economic boycott by all member nations, could force compliance by bankrupting an offending power. Should this also not be effective, military force could be used. The League covenant provided for no military force of its own, however, and could not require members to provide troops to conduct League actions. This proved to be a serious weakness. The only council members effectively strong enough to lend troops to the League—France and Britain—had been drained by the recent war and so were loathe to undertake costly operations for the League.

This weakness became all the more glaring as the world's most powerful emerging states did not originally join the council. Membership was to include the world's most influential countries. Britain, France, Italy, and Japan originally were invited to join. Germany and Russia were not. Because Germany was declared responsible for World War I, according to the War Guilt clause of the Treaty of Versailles, it was not considered a member of the international community. Because Russia was a new Communist state, it was considered a dangerous rogue government also not fit to become part of the international community. Actually, the allies were surreptitiously supporting Lenin's enemies in the Russian civil war of 1919–1920.

The United States declined to join. A conservative Congress pulled by the attractions of American isolationism questioned the entanglements required by the League covenant. Particularly Article Ten: "The Members of the League undertake to respect and preserve as against external aggression the territorial integrity and existing political independence of all members of the League." Republican congressional leaders in particular feared this suggested the United States must supply troops to the League. The article actually was a watered-down version of Clemenceau's request for an international army to counter aggression, but many in Congress worried the League could weaken American autonomy.

Wilson argued furiously for his League, but his credibility with Republicans had been weakened, as the strongly partisan Democrat had not included a single representative from the rival party on his Paris peace negotiations team. Furthermore, the president could accept no compromise that might have salvaged the League in Congress. In the end he advised his own party to vote against the Treaty of Versailles as amended in Congress. Finally in 1921 Congress voted to accept the Paris peace treaties, but not the League.

Failure of the United States to join the organization proposed by its own leader probably more than any other single factor doomed the League. America had become the world's most powerful nation. It was expected to play the role of world leader. It declined that crown, preferring instead to reject the invitation to foreign entanglement. As Washington rejected the League, the moral power of the council could not include the force of three world powers.

Eventually, in 1926 Germany was allowed to join the league. But in 1933 it withdrew in protest of a League refusal to change treaty terms limiting its military strength. Russia, now the Soviet Union, feared Hitler's warlike posturing, and so joined in 1934, but was expelled in 1939 for attacking Finland. Fascist Italy withdrew in 1937 to join an alliance with Germany and Japan.

The League obviously failed to stop World War II, but it did have limited success in several smaller conflicts. Its mandate to manage the mosaic of nations created by the Versailles Treaty also left it with an almost impossible mission, as Paris negotiators had created new nations and borders fraught with tension between ethnic and political demands. On the other hand, the League's social programs included worldwide programs to eliminate smallpox, leprosy, and child slave labor, to improve the status of women and to eliminate drug smuggling and addiction. These have continued to grow under its successor, the United Nations.

Promises of a World League

Emily Greene Balch, Emergency Peace Federation, New York: "The War in Its Relation to Democracy and World Order"

Wilson hoped that negotiating a new world based on his Fourteen Points would include the principle of self-determination, that is, the right of ethnic groups to decide for themselves which country they would like to join. As an ideal this seemed fair and democratic. In practice it was hindered by complexities of rival ethnicity. One obvious example was Danzig, a German city in the newly created Polish Corridor designed to give Poland a seaport. Self-determination would dictate it should be German. The solution was to make Danzig a "free city" under League supervision. It governed itself, but allowed Poland to use the port. In 1939 Germany demanded that Poland cede Danzig to Germany. When it refused, Berlin invaded. World War II had begun. Danzig (Gdansk in Polish) became part of Poland after the war.

Annals of the American Academy of Political and Social Sciences, July 1917

Too often we conceive of an end of all war, of a world order, in a merely negative sense. We conceive of it primarily, too often, as a coercive league to prevent any of the partners breaking out into the use of violence for the achievement of an individual national end. Surely this is a most deformed and inadequate conception of the goal. Surely what we want is a free society of nations, with active, deliberate and interested cooperation for the great common ends. I do not desire so greatly a world in which we shall all, somehow or another, checkmate one another's desires to make war as I desire a world in which we stand shoulder to shoulder, all peoples working for those great ends which interest all people alike, and to which the native differences of different peoples are the greatest possible contribution, and which would lose by the stagnation of uniformity. We want the harmony of a symphony employing every conceivable type of instrument, not the dullness of similarity.

Editorial Response to Letter to the Editor: "Problems of a Peace League"

An enormous sense of hope for change swept through America at the end of World War I, the "war to end all wars," to "make the world safe for democracy," as President Wilson put it. Those groups that had been disappointed by slow progress for social change hoped war could bring all Americans to a new starting line, that everyone truly would be equal. That proved to be an illusion, although progressive policies engendered by the war did offer a precedent to eventual government policies supporting more rights to minorities, women, and labor unions.

North American Review, March 1917

Whatever objection may reasonably be urged against the projected World-League for Peace, the objection that it is "the dream of an idealist" is not, as our correspondent seems to think, a crushing one. Every great liberalizing movement that has in the past lifted humanity a little higher above the brutes has had its origin in "the dream of an idealist." Lincoln dreamed an idealist's dream. Those who insisted that the abolition of slavery was a fantastic impossibility were "practical men." And what nation today is, par excellence, the nation of "efficiency," of practical men? We leave the inevitable answer, with its implications, to be brooded upon by our valued correspondent.

—Editor.

Oliver Lodge: "A League of Nations"

Wilson planned the League with a sole purpose, to avoid war. In this it failed. Yet the legacy of the broken League reconstituted as the United Nations can trace considerable success in making the world a better place. An obvious example is the World Health Organization, a UN agency that renewed a pledge of the old League to eradicate world disease. In 1967 it declared its intention to wipe out smallpox. By 1984 there was not a single case of smallpox world-wide.

North American Review, November 1918

So long as a league of nations thinks only of coercion and suppression it will encounter difficulties; those who think of this side alone regard the ideal as impossible. But what it must chiefly exercise its energies on are the corporate works of peace. Let it turn its chief attention to these, let its police agency be tacit and understood, not flaunted, but let it take all world-wide enterprises under its protective and helpful jurisdiction. The scientific world has already shown the way to an intelligent internationalism in science. In the arts there are no national boundaries. This must spread to commerce also, and then to politics; until gradually we approach the ideal—the Parliament of Man, the Federation of the World.

A. Lawrence Lowell: "A League to Enforce Peace"

The immense national effort that put more than four million Americans in uniform within 18 months found its postwar sequel in an apparent turn away from the international stage. Newly inaugurated President Warren G. Harding, speaking in May 1920, set the theme, saying, "America's present need is not heroics, but healing; not nostrums, but normalcy; not revolution, but restoration; not agitation, but adjustment; not surgery, but serenity; not the dramatic, but the dispassionate; not experiment, but equipoise; not submergence in internationality, but sustainment in triumphant nationality."

Atlantic Monthly, September 1915

Except by colossal self-deception we cannot believe that the convulsions of Europe do not affect us profoundly, that wars there need not disturb us, that we are not in danger of being drawn into them; or even that we may not some day find ourselves in the direct path of the storm. If our interest in the maintenance of peace is not quite so strong as that of some other nations, it is certainly strong enough to warrant our taking steps to preserve it, even to the point of joining a league to enforce it. The cost of the insurance is well worth the security to use.

If mere material self-interest would indicate such a course, there are other reasons to confirm it. Civilization is to some extent a common heritage which it is worth while for all nations to defend, and war is a scourge which all peoples should use every rational means to reduce. If the family of nations can by standing together make wars less frequent, it is clearly their duty to do so, and in such a body we do not want the place of our own country to be vacant.

To join such a league would mean, no doubt, a larger force of men trained for arms in this country, more munitions of war on hand, and better means of producing them rapidly; for although it may be assumed that the members of the league would never be actually called upon to carry out their promise to fight, they ought to have a potential force for the purpose. But in any case this country ought not to be so little prepared for an emergency as it is today; and it would require to be less fully armed if it joined a league pledged to protect its members against attack, than if it stood alone and unprotected. In fact the tendency of such a league, by procuring at least delay before the outbreak of hostilities, would be to lessen the need of preparation for immediate war, and thus it would have a more potent effect in reducing armaments than any formal treaties could have, whether made voluntarily or under compulsion.

Theodore Marburg, M.A., LL.D., Baltimore, MD: "The League to Enforce Peace—A Reply to Critics"

Wilson's League of Nations included the requirement that squabbling members meet in Geneva to present their case for consideration by the assembly. This could influence outcome only insofar as those nations on the assembly could carry the power and prestige to enforce its opinions. Loss of the United States to League membership, and initial denial of membership to Germany and Russia, dramatically crimped the credibility of the League as mediator.

Annals of the American Academy of Political and Social Science, July 1916

Our critics, pointing out that conciliation is a voluntary process, assert that to force conciliation is a contradiction in terms. They set up their own straw man and then proceed to knock him down. The League does not force conciliation. It simply forces a hearing, leaving the parties free to accept or reject the finding. Under the League, nations are prevented from going to war to get what they suppose to be their rights until, by means of a hearing, not only the outside world but—that which is of high importance—their own people have the facts of the dispute spread before them. They are not prevented from indulging in that costly pastime if, after a hearing, they still hold to the opinion that they are being wronged.

In the meantime, pending the hearing, each disputant is enjoined by the League, under penalty of war, from continuing the objectionable practice of proceeding with the objectionable project.

Problems of a World League

H. M. Chittenden: "Questions for Pacifists"

Nationalism, the feeling that a group sharing common language and culture should belong together in a political division, has dominated history of the last century. By world history standards, however, it is fairly new. Before the middle ages people felt a loyalty to their tribe or town. Europe's first nation-states included England, France, and Spain. Germany and Italy did not unify until 1870 and 1871. People who band together as nations often feel an enhanced patriotic pride and willingness to sacrifice for their country. But disadvantages of nationalism became obvious during World War I: antagonism between nations, call to glorification of military virtues, and patriotic zealotry.

Atlantic Monthly, August 1915

The distinctive characteristic of the state is its sovereignty. It recognizes no higher authority than itself. Some states have greater power than others, and are able, by its arbitrary exercise to impose their will upon weaker states; but there is no such acknowledged right. Now to bring into existence any form of world-organization, or to recognize an international police force, is to surrender pro tanto this sovereignty. It would be in itself a complete revolution in human affairs. It is difficult to estimate what this means, particularly to strong and vigorous states, proud of their nationality, intent on working out their separate destiny, biding their time, and watching their opportunity for greater development. Nothing is more repugnant to such a state than the thought of surrendering any of its prerogatives. It has been one of the most difficult things to accomplish, even on a relatively small scale. Our own country is an example. To-day we can scarcely appreciate the reluctance, the dread and suspicion with which our little original states gave up a part of their sovereignty to form a union, and their unwillingness to subject themselves to the possibility of compulsion; and how for two generations, until quenched in a mighty war, the claim of the right to assert this sovereignty persisted. The history of the long process of merging the many German states into a single empire is full of examples of this unwillingness to give up any portion of independence. How much stronger must this feeling be where states are so much more unrelated than in the examples cited—often of different races, languages, systems of religion and government, and estranged by historic antagonisms and prejudices! One cannot expect such a consummation among such states except as a result of slow evolution. It may come—it would seem that ultimately it must come in some form—but it will not be to-day or to-morrow or at the close of the present war.

Oscar T. Crosby, Warrenton, Virginia: "An Armed International Tribunal: The Sole Peace-Keeping Mechanism"

French Prime Minister Georges Clemenceau, age 77 when the war ended, had seen his country invaded twice, had participated in the hideous Paris Commune civil war that killed 20,000, and had been both prime minister of France and an important journalist for 50 years. His Old World realism, bordering on cynicism, was a dramatic counterpoint to Wilson's New World idealism. Clemenceau believed Germany would rise again to threaten France, and that without military guarantees of defense from the allies, France would not be able to stop another assault. He acquiesced to the League, saying, "I like the League. But I do not believe in it."

Annals of the American Academy of Political and Social Science, July 1916

Let us briefly consider some of the compromises now much mooted. There is, first, limitation of armaments by mutual agreement. Small armaments—or even disarmament—cannot guarantee peace. It only diminishes the peace-time cost of war. We may fight with less expensive weapons than dreadnaughts. But we shall find no way of controlling war-preparation by rules which smack of the Sermon on the Mount. Strength will not write itself down to the level of weakness, while physical violence remains as the ultimate determinant of international disputes. And if such folly were put into words, the inventor would bring them to naught. He will sleeplessly defeat any attempt to fix exact ratios between ready-to-use capacity for destruction.

Next, we have various forms of "cooling off" devices—agreements to delay war after failure of diplomatic agencies—by submission of disputes to various forms of forceless courts.

The vice of all these methods lies in this—that very frequently the issue will be resolved in favor of one or the other contestant, during any period of delay beginning after failure of all formal and informal methods that have always been open to states. To delay will mean to yield. We may always do that without treaties and toothless courts. And meanwhile, what suspicions, what hates, will be engendered as we learn—or fancy we learn—of our rival's preparation for the ultimate shock of arms!

Next we have the proposal of the League to Enforce Peace. Again forceless courts. Again final resort to arms. But something else beside. We must see the miracle of unanimity among all on-looking nations who are to judge when a supposed recalcitrant shall have committed an "act of hostility" before going to a court. But we have cut each other's throats for ten thousand years expressing differences of view as to what constitutes an "act of hostility!" Why should we agree in the future? And if the League program be modified to provide for a central organism of judging and enforcing, then we reach the Armed International Tribunal—sole peace-keeping mechanism.

To attain it, we must amend our Constitution. A proposal to that effect is now pending before the United States Senate. it may produce the great desideratum—Simultaneous Discussion in Responsible Parliaments of Identical Propositions for an International Tribunal.

C. W. Dustin, New York City, Letter to the Editor: "Problems of a Peace League"

The value of formal arbitration as a means to settle conflict was recognized at the beginning of the nineteenth century. Peace conferences held at The Hague, Netherlands, in 1899 and 1907 set up machinery for a Permanent Court of Arbitration, with the enthusiastic participation of U.S. Secretary of State Elihu Root. In 1913 it moved into a Peace Palace built by donations from American steel tycoon Andrew Carnegie. After the war it became the Permanent Court of International Justice, offering advice to the League of Nations. It was not, however, part of the League. It was rebuilt as the International Court of Justice ("World Court") in 1945 under United Nations jurisdiction.

***North American Review,* March 1917**

Sir—Perhaps I have overlooked it, but I have not happened to see a detailed development of the idea of a "League for Peace," or of an "International

Court of Arbitration League," to determine questions that may arise hereafter between the nations, or some of the nations, of the earth. . . . The whole scheme, therefore, it seems to me, is based upon the plan of representation, which presents a maze of difficulties.

The establishment of a World Court seems to me like the dream of an idealist; but, being open to a contrary conviction, I have written this with the purpose of bringing out the views of others, not as to its desirability, but its possibility.

Roland Hugins, Ithaca, NY, Letter to the Editor: "The False Dawn in Europe"

Benjamin Disraeli, twice Conservative Party British prime minister during the nineteenth century, was a strong supporter of Britain's colonial ambitions, and one of those whose goal was to make London capital of the world's most powerful nation. He succeeded in doing so, until World War I marked the beginning of England's demise as an empire.

***Nation,* July 1, 1915**

A permanent peace in Europe cannot be wrought by the sword. So long as the Allies seek, as at present, to extort as much from their enemies and cajole as much from each other as possible, all talk of a concert or a League is merest moonshine. National self-interest is not a strong enough cement to bind together Russia, England, and France for long. And a Concert of Europe which left an armed Germany and Austria outside its pale would be a farce. There can be no happy family if two big brothers are outlawed.

It is difficult, moreover, to see how Germany could be brought into an entente with her opponents. We know clearly enough on what conditions she would insist. Even though in the dust she would demand two assurances: an effective guarantee that she would not be attacked by Russia, and an effective guarantee from England that the seas be neutralized and capture of private property at sea forever abolished. Public opinion in Germany sounds no ambiguous note. To the accomplishment of these two objects the Teutons have consecrated themselves almost to the last unit. However much more they may desire, they never will be satisfied with less. . . .

Any one nation, or indeed each of them, may experience a literary renaissance or a political liberalization after the war. But it does not follow that each national culture will not be embittered or that Europe will not be riven by new hatreds.

World politics distinctly has retrograded. "War," said Disraeli, "is never a solution. It is an aggravation." Only strife is bred from strife. Peace can be prepared for only in times of peace.

Editorial: "Critics of the League to Enforce Peace"

It is true the United States declined to join the League, but it is not necessarily true that American foreign policy turned its focus inward to the exclusion of interest in European affairs. While President Harding argued for a return to normalcy that might be construed to mean prewar isolationism, the country did use financial incentives to encourage solutions for European disputes involving reparations and security. Washington did not, however, move to oppose Hitler's blatant disregard of Germany's treaty obligations, and remained on the sidelines of World War II for more than two years.

Nation, January 4, 1917

The League to Enforce Peace is not finding its path unobstructed. Primarily, it has encountered the opposition of those radical lovers of peace who believe that the reliance upon force of any kind is a mistake. But attacks have come from other sources. Thus Dr. Felix Adler feels that the emphasis is being put in the wrong place; that what we should be talking about is a parliament of parliaments. He feels that the weakness of the League's position is that there cannot be a small body to police the world until there is disarmament, and disarmament he fears is further off now than before. As to this there are certainly two opinions. But he is assuredly correct in believing that if less stress were put by the League upon the use of force, it would be, pace Mr. Roosevelt, in a far stronger position.

Dr. Samuel T. Dutton, so long a student of and worker in the peace cause, joins ex-Secretary Garrison in his dislike of our entering any league of nations which would make the disputes of small and large nations those of the Untied States. He is certain that the people of this country "will never permit the Government at Washington to enmesh this country in the shifting, uncertain, explosive affairs of the Old World," or to be placed in the position of having to go to war, by order of a coalition, against some country with which it has not quarrel.

H. C. Nutting, Berkeley, California, Letter to the Editor: "The Argument for Peace"

Clemenceau argued that only allied defense treaties and arms control could temper German aggression. He did not get the kind of defense guarantees he hoped for, but peace negotiators did deal severely to blunt German military prowess. Berlin was limited to a small force of 100,000 soldiers, was not allowed conscription, war academies, or a military air force. It was allowed six small war ships but no submarines. Hitler disregarded these limits, but in the 1930s no former ally was willing to risk another war by forcing compliance to the treaty.

***Nation,* December 29, 1915**

It is interesting to note that even some rather uncompromising advocates of peace—though still demanding, somewhat illogically, immediate disarmament—are beginning to incline to the view that war cannot be eliminated finally except by a process of education that will uproot aggressive national and racial ambitions, establish the principle that right is might, and make every one content to submit to an award of arbitration, even though it is a disappointment. It is hard to understand, however, how even the most ardent advocate of peace can hope for a consummation of this kind in the near future; and, on the other hand, when one views the present turmoil in Europe, the plans of the League to Enforce Peace do not seem to offer any prospect of immediate relief. It certainly would require a large and effective world police force to cope with a situation like the present.

Albert Thomas: "The League of Nations"

World War I produced two significant politicians named Albert Thomas. The first, French, was a former editor for the socialist daily L'Humanité, *who as munitions minister managed the stupendous industrial expansion necessary for France to conduct a war of such magnitude. The second, Texan, served as second lieutenant during World War I. In 1936 he was elected to Congress, and later became chairman of the House Defense Appropriations Committee. The American Thomas would have been only 20 at this time, however, and it seems unlikely he would have been writing for a national magazine.*

***Atlantic Monthly,* November 1918**

The fulfillment of this dream is the only clearly defined object which the proposed supra-national organization will set before itself at the beginning. Its first duty will be to eliminate, or at all events to reduce as far as possible, the chances of another war. It will succeed in that object by creating a system of rights between nations like that which the State, among civilized peoples, creates between individuals.

It is a difficult task. To progress from the anarchical condition of the world before the war to a complete organization deserving the name of a League of Nations in the fullest sense of the word—that will unquestionably be a long, long road; but we can clearly make out the first stage, which we can traverse during the war.

A court of arbitration must be set up—that is to say, a method of procedure for settling controversies between nations, analogous to that which has already been resorted to in a certain number of cases. But to avoid the repetition of an experiment which was tried in the last decades of the nineteenth century, and of which the acid test of this war has demonstrated the inadequacy, we must invest the tribunal with the function of drawing up the rules to be applied, and reinforce it with the power to execute them.

In reply to President Wilson's eloquent appeal in favor of compulsory arbitration, we saw last year the Central Empires, and even the Sultan of Turkey himself, give in a solemn adhesion to the principle. There was just one small restriction: the principle of arbitration was accepted by the representatives of our adversaries only with reservation of the "vital interests" of either of the three empires concerned. We know to-day, by the example of Brest-Litovsk, what those Empires mean by their "vital interests," and how far they carry their contempt of the most legitimate interests of other nationalities.

Of course, nations more considerate of the rights of others might refrain from such excesses; but we must recognize none the less that an attitude of distrust with respect to any given system of unconditional arbitration is altogether justifiable, even for states honestly well disposed to the principle.

William J. Roe: "Europe's Dynastic Slaughter House"

The "scrap of paper" refers to perhaps the most famous bit of British World War I propaganda. Supposedly German Chancellor Theobald von Bethmann Hollweg, in a last meeting with British ambassador Edward Goschen, said "just for a scrap of paper Great Britain was going to make war on a kindred nation who desired nothing better than to be friends with her." The three words galvanized the reputation of Germany as warmongers in the eyes of both the British and Americans. Of course, treaty obligations have throughout history shown themselves to be only as good as a scrap of paper is honored by those who have signed it.

***Popular Science,* January–June 1915**

Much has been written, and with very great ability and high sense of the obligation of "ethical values," concerning the establishment hereafter of an international "posse comitatus," to the end of enforcing peaceful relations, and of compelling acquiescence in the decrees of an international court of arbitration. The weakness of such an arrangement—most admirable if it could be assured in perpetuity—lies in this: that its permanence would depend not solely upon mutuality, but largely upon comity, upon a "scrap of paper," a contract voidable at any moment by one or the other of the "high contracting powers."

Questions

1. Which three major countries initially did not join the League of Nations? Why?
2. Some historians found Woodrow Wilson partly to blame for World War II. Why could he be held responsible?
3. What program originally established by the League has been particularly successful?

Selected Bibliography

Angell, Norman. *The Great Illusion.* New York: G.P. Putnam's Sons, [1910] 1933.

Audoin-Rouzeau, Stéphane, and Annette Becker. *14–18: Understanding the Great War.* New York: Hill and Wang, 2000.

Bourke, Joanna. "Shell Shock During World War One." Wars and Conflict: World War I. Available at: http://www.bbc.co.uk/history/war/wwone/shellshock_01.shtml.

Carnegie Endowment for International Peace. *Perspectives on Peace 1910–1960.* London: Steven and Sons, 1960.

Carnegie Endowment for International Peace. Available at: http://www.carnegieendowment.org/about/index.cfm?fa=history.

Cary, Francine Curro. *The Influence of War on Walter Lippmann 1914–1944.* Madison: State Historical Society of Wisconsin, 1967.

"The Chicago Defender. Newspapers." PBS Features. Available at: http://www.pbs.org/blackpress/news_bios/defender.html.

Collins, Ross F. "World War I." In *The Greenwood Library of American War Reporting,* vol. 5, ed. David A. Copeland. Westport, Conn.: Greenwood Press, 2005.

Creel, George. *How We Advertised America.* New York: Harper and Row, 1920.

Creel, George. *Rebel at Large. Recollections of Fifty Crowded Years.* New York: G.P. Putnam's Sons, 1947.

Crozier, Emmet. *American Reporters on the Western Front 1914–1919.* New York: Oxford University Press, 1959.

Devlin, Patrick. *Too Proud to Fight. Woodrow Wilson's Neutrality.* New York: Oxford University Press, 1975.

Dudley, William, ed. *World War I: Opposing Viewpoints.* San Diego: Greenhaven Press, 1998.

Encyclopedia of the First World War. Available at: http://www.spartacus.schoolnet.co.uk/FWW.htm.

First World War.com: The War to End All Wars. Available at: http://firstworldwar.com.

Gibbs, Philip. *Now it Can Be Told.* New York: Harper and Brothers, 1920.

Gilbert, Charles. *American Financing of World War I.* Westport, Conn.: Greenwood Press, 1970.

Gilbert, Martin. *The First World War. A Complete History.* New York: Henry Holt, 1994.

Greene, Laurence. *America Goes to Press: The News of Yesterday: The History of the United States As Reported in the Newspapers of the Day.* Freeport, N.Y.: Books for Libraries Press, 1970.

"Indian Citizenship Act, 1924." Nebraska Studies.org. Available at: http://www.nebraskastudies.org/0700/frameset_reset.html? http://www.nebraskastudies.org/0700/stories/0701_0146.html.

Industrial Workers of the World. A Union for All Workers. Available at: http://www.iww.org.

International Court of Justice. Available at: http://www.icj-cij.org/.

Johnsen, Julia E., ed. *Selected Articles on War—Cause and Cure.* New York: H.W. Wilson, 1926.

Karsten, Peter. *Soldiers and Society. The Effects of Military Service and War on American Life.* Westport, Conn.: Greenwood Press, 1978.

Keegan, John. *The First World War.* New York: Knopf, 1999.

Kennedy, David M. *Over Here. The First World War and American Society.* Oxford: Oxford University Press, 1980.

Knightley, Phillip. *The First Casualty. From the Crimea to Vietnam, The War Correspondent as Hero, Propagandists, and Myth Maker.* London: Pan Books, 1975 [1989].

"The Laws of War (1907 Hague Convention text)." The Avalon Project at Yale Law School. Available at: http://www.yale.edu/lawweb/avalon/lawofwar/hague05.htm.

Luebke, Frederick C. *Bonds of Loyalty. German Americans and World War I.* DeKalb: Northern Illinois University Press, 1974.

Lyons, Michael J. *World War I. A Short History,* 2nd ed. Upper Saddle River, N.J.: Prentice Hall, 2000.

Macmillan, Margaret. *Paris 1919: Six Months That Changed the World.* New York: Random House, 2001.

Miller, Ronald, and David Sawers. *The Technical Development of Modern Aviation.* New York: Praeger, 1970.

Mock, James R., and Cedric Larson. *Words that Won the War.* Princeton, N.J.: Princeton University Press, 1939.

Perlmutter, Philip. *Legacy of Hate: A Short History of Ethnic, Religious, and Racial Prejudice in America.* Armonk, N.Y.: M.E. Sharpe, 1999.

Peterson, H. C. *Propaganda for War: The Campaign Against American Neutrality, 1914–1917.* Port Washington, N.Y.: Kennikat Press, 1968.

Ponsonby, Arthur. *Falsehood in War-Time.* New York: E.P. Dutton, 1928.

"President Wilson's Fourteen Points." The Avalon Project at Yale Law School. Available at: http://www.yale.edu/lawweb/avalon/wilson14.htm.

Roosevelt, Theodore. "A Strenuous Life (1902)." Excerpts available at: http://www.barnard.columbia.edu/amstud/resources/strenuous/strenlife.htm.

Straubing, Harold Elk, ed. *The Last Magnificent War: Rare Journalistic and Eyewitness Accounts of World War I.* New York: Paragon House, 1989.

Vaughn, Stephen. *Holding Fast the Inner Lines: Democracy, Nationalism, and the Committee on Public Information.* Chapel Hill: University of North Carolina Press, 1980.

Williams, Ian, ed. *Newspapers of the First World War.* Newton Abbot, David and Charles, 1970.

Winter, J. M. *The Experience of World War I.* Oxford, England: Equinox, 1988.

Winter, Jay, Geoffrey Parker, and Mary R. Habeck, eds. *The Great War and the Twentieth Century.* New Haven, Conn.: Yale University Press, 2000.

The World War I Document Archive. Available at: http://www.lib.byu.edu/~rdh/wwi/.

Zieger, Robert H. *America's Great War: World War I and the American Experience.* Lanham, Md.: Rowman and Littlefield, 2000.

Index

About the Author

ROSS F. COLLINS is Associate Professor of Communication at North Dakota State University, Fargo. He edited *The Greenwood Library of American War Reporting, Volume 5: World War I* (Greenwood Press, 2005), and has published numerous scholarly articles on aspects of World War I, French journalism, and American frontier journalism. A former journalist and photographer, Collins has contributed more than 800 articles and photographs to a wide variety of non-academic publications. He has a Ph.D. in journalism history from the University of Cambridge and is treasurer of the American Journalism Historians Association.